Pluralism
Comes
of
Age

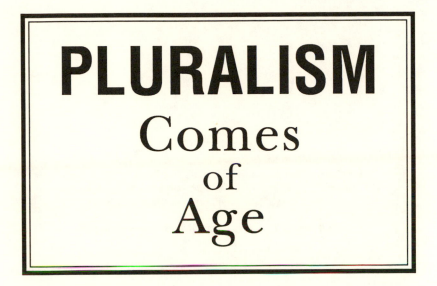

PLURALISM
Comes
of
Age

AMERICAN RELIGIOUS CULTURE
in the
TWENTIETH CENTURY

CHARLES H. LIPPY

M.E.Sharpe
Armonk, New York
London, England

*Hillsborough Community
College LRC*

Library of Congress Cataloging-in-Publication Data

Lippy, Charles H.
  Pluralism comes of age : American religious culture in the twentieth century / Charles
H. Lippy.
     p. cm.
  Includes bibliographical references and index.
  ISBN 0-7656-0150-8 (hardcover)
     1. Religious pluralism—United States—History of doctrines—20th century.
2. United States—Religion—20th century. I. Title.

BL2525.L567 2000
291.1′72′093—dc21

                                                                            99-088431

Printed in the United States of America

BM (c)   10   9   8   7   6   5   4   3   2   1

For John F. Wilson
in gratitude for three decades
of quiet inspiration

Table of Contents

Preface

Centuries and even millennia are artificial constructs to historians and analysts of culture. Rarely do movements begin in years ending in "01" and end conveniently 99 years later. So to some extent, this book's focus on the twentieth century is a bit misleading. The surge in immigration, the continuing rapid urbanization, and the boom in industrial growth—and the religious changes accompanying them—that marked the first decade of the century were part of trends that began two or three decades earlier. Hence the "twentieth century" for our purposes here really stretches back to the postbellum period. Likewise, it became increasingly clear to me that World War II marked a watershed in American religious life in ways that I had not fully appreciated as one born during the war and growing up in the 1940s and 1950s. For analytical purposes, it marks the "end" perhaps not of a century but of many of the ways of thinking and operating in the religious sphere that had been a matter of course since the end of the Civil War.

Nevertheless, when one looks at the twentieth century as encompassing the period from 1901 through 2000, one has a helpful lens through which to examine changes and trends, even if there are some abrupt shifts along the way. When I surveyed American religious life through that lens, what stood out first was the incredible pluralism that seemed to invade every facet of the story. American religious culture at the close of the twentieth century is more diverse and considerably more complex than it was at the dawn of the century—and all the richer as a result. It is that story that I set out to tell in the pages that follow. Some might argue that what I present is really simply a portrait of increasing diversity; I hope that I am able to show that the shifts in the century when taken together are more than that. Together they mean that pluralism, an experiment in religious culture with roots in the colonial past, has come of age.

Work on this book received support from many sources. A summer research stipend from the Louisville Institute in 1998 allowed me to devote three months to preparing the initial drafts of Chapters four and six. Comments and discussion at the Louisville Institute's Winter 1999 Forum stimulated much reflection and revision. I am grateful to my department head, Herbert Burhenn, and then-dean Timothy Summerlin for approving a reduction in my teaching responsibilities in the

Spring of 1999 that permitted me to complete the first draft of the whole. Paul Schadewald at Macalester College and David Roebuck, director of the Dixon Pentecostal Research Center and Archive, painstakingly read the complete manuscript and offered more sage advice than I took. I am most appreciative of their willingness to share their wisdom and expertise. It has also been a joy to work with Peter Coveney and the staff at M.E. Sharpe.

Charles H. Lippy
University of Tennessee at Chattanooga

Pluralism
Comes
of
Age

CHAPTER 1

Planting Pluralism in the United States

In his now famous endeavor to explain the American experience to a European audience in the 1840s, the Frenchman Alexis de Tocqueville noted that the Christians of America were divided into a "multitude of sects."[1] In this way, de Tocqueville highlighted what has since become a commonplace: In the United States religious pluralism prevails. When de Tocqueville wrote, that pluralism usually referred to the multiplicity of Christian groups that flourished on American soil. At the dawn of the twenty-first century, religious pluralism still prevails in the United States, but it is a different sort of pluralism than one marking a "multitude of [Christian] sects." In the twentieth century, religious pluralism came of age, for now pluralism encompasses not merely a host of groups clustered under the Christian umbrella. Changes within denominations increased pluralism as well. A range of worship styles may exist within different congregations of the same Christian group; for example, Methodists whose worship music comes from guitar, keyboard, tambourine, and drums augmented by the latest high-tech amplification system are part of the same denomination as Methodists who still look to the majestic organ to guide congregational singing. Among Christians, both Protestant and Catholic, Pentecostal and charismatic expressions became accepted from the 1960s on outside of the historic Pentecostal denominations.

Pluralism points also to the way different ethnic heritages may bring a variety of styles to a given religious tradition. African-American Protestant groups are different from other Protestant religious families in part because of the African ethnic component. Hispanic Catholicism looks and feels different from Irish or Italian Catholicism, even though all are part of the same Christian body in the United States.

Today pluralism embraces not only Christian groups, but an increasing number of non-Christian traditions, including but not limited to Judaism, Islam, Buddhism, and the Hindu religious tradition. In addition, pluralism provides a lens through which to view distinctive approaches to individual spirituality that gained currency during the twentieth century. One obvious example is the mushrooming of approaches to personal spirituality that emerged from women's experience, rang-

3

ing from a recovery of pre-Christian pagan elements to a recasting of traditional Christian belief in feminist terms.

Pluralism provides the context for movements and trends that move across the boundaries of those many groups that intrigued de Tocqueville more than a century and a half ago. Pointing to this expanding scope of religious pluralism in twentieth century United States, however, merely suggests the richness that marks American religious life; the full story is more finely nuanced.

Creating the Environment for Religious Pluralism

If we are to discern how pluralism came of age in the twentieth century, how it moved from referring to the host of Protestant communions to take in so much more, we must first understand how that earlier pluralism came to be and how social and cultural forces in place by the close of the Victorian age laid the groundwork for the new pluralism that now characterizes American religious life. We must return briefly to the religious patterns that developed in those English colonies that declared their independence from Great Britain in 1776, to why the Bill of Rights in the Constitution prohibited formal or legal establishment of a single religion and extended a measure of freedom to all, and to the Protestant consensus that emerged, even if expressed through a "multitude of sects." Then we will be prepared to understand how the massive immigration, urbanization, and industrialization of the later nineteenth century, changes in domestic culture that accompanied them, and the emergence of countless new religions (or at least religions that were new to the American experience) around the turn of the previous century significantly transformed religious pluralism in the twentieth century.

Decades ago Sidney Mead argued that space and time were fundamental to understanding how American religious patterns developed.[2] The Europeans who came to the New World left time behind in the sense that the past, including religious history, became consigned to the Old World. In North America, something new was happening without the shackles of time or tradition determining its shape. Of course, the Europeans were cavalier at best about the different sense of time and history propelling the Native American tribal cultures they so readily displaced. But the absence of the constraints of time created an openness to experimenting with new ways, with fresh approaches to structuring religion, with different understandings even of the basics of belief.

All this was possible, Mead argued, because of the space or distance separating these new Americans from Europe. The 3,000 miles of Atlantic Ocean made it difficult for colonial powers to control the settlements as closely as they desired. Yet space was not just a geographic phenomenon measured in miles. It was a psychological one, for Americans developed new collective identities out of their relationship with the space or context around them.

The seemingly limitless land stretching before those who came to North America made space important in another way.[3] For those who disagreed with others, whether on matters of religion or politics, one option was always simply to move away, to go to another space and nourish a culture molded after one's own ideas. One widely known example of how space worked in this sense is the case of Roger Williams.[4] The Puritans of the Massachusetts Bay Colony were intent on using the space that separated them from England to create a commonwealth based on their own ideals; in this sense, they sought religious freedom. But they were hardly tolerant of those who differed with them; admitting persons of diverse beliefs into a holy common-wealth would pollute its purity and ultimately bring its demise. When Roger Williams diverged from Puritan orthodoxy, the political authorities banished him from the colony. In Europe, he might have faced imprisonment or death. Banishment simply meant he took advantage of space; he moved elsewhere and began the enterprise that became the core of the Rhode Island colony, where religious seekers were welcomed so long as good order was maintained.

Space and time were not the only elements in the colonial experience conducive to the development of some forms of religious pluralism. Several of the colonies began as joint stock companies from which investors hoped to reap a profit; some were proprietary ventures from which individuals expected to see financial gain. For both, assuring the success of the colonial endeavor was paramount, and success required a critical mass of colonists. Two examples, each of which in different ways set the stage for developing pluralism, must suffice.

One is Maryland, a proprietary venture of the Calvert family, prominent English Catholic converts.[5] When Maryland was opened for colonization, overt Catholic practice in England was theoretically illegal, although particularly among some aristocrats, like the Calverts, it endured. Public Catholic practice could bring legal recrimination; Catholics by law were prohibited from voting, holding elected office, or attending such universities as Oxford and Cambridge. The Calverts intended Maryland to be a place where their coreligionists could practice their faith openly and without fear. But the pragmatics of drawing enough settlers to assure Maryland's success meant that early on, non-Catholics were welcomed and soon became a majority of the non-native population. An Act of Toleration in 1649 guaranteed a modicum of liberty for Christians, although Catholics were urged not to be blatant in public manifestations of their belief. Even though that Act of Toleration was revoked five years later when Puritans dominated the colonial legislative assembly, by recognizing multiple Christian groups and giving them all some legal sanction, Maryland buttressed an emerging pluralism.

More indicative of later developments was Pennsylvania, the proprietary enterprise of English Quaker William Penn.[6] Regarded as radical extremists, not the quietist devout plain folk of a later age, Quakers were also subject to legal recrimination in seventeenth-century England. Penn knew there were too few Quakers in England and even fewer who would come to the New World to make his colony a success. From the start, he advertised for others, particularly German Protestants who were also on the fringes of the religious establishment there, to come. So long as they promoted peace and good order, all who acknowledged belief in God were welcome. Although Quakers dominated Pennsylvania political and economic life for generations, they were soon a minority of the population. Ironically, Pennsylvania, not Maryland, boasted the largest Catholic population in the colonies at the time of independence. In Pennsylvania, too, in the early eighteenth century colonial Presbyterians first organized a structure to link their churches together.

What Penn called his "holy experiment" demonstrated that religious pluralism could prevail without shattering political stability. In European life from the time of the Reformation and the numerous wars and armed conflicts following the Reformation, a conviction prevailed that religious uniformity was essential to political stability. Because religious beliefs cut to the heart of personal identity here and in the hereafter, they could divide people, cause conflict, and generate constant political unrest unless everyone adhered to the same belief system. Pennsylvania demonstrated that such was not the case. To a lesser degree, as the Puritan strongholds in New England were forced by Britain to tolerate others, they too began to become models for an early modern pluralism.

Yet another major ingredient creating a religiously pluralistic environment in the United States is the ethnic diversity marking colonial life. The numerous German clusters in Pennsylvania represent only one part of the story. What the English called New York owed its colonial founding to the Dutch, who naturally brought their Reformed religious perspective influenced by the Calvinist heritage.[7] In areas nearby, including what later became New Jersey, Scandinavians planted churches that reflected the Lutheran tradition, but because churches usually conducted services in the native language of the congregation, there were Finnish, Swedish, Norwegian, and other churches that flourished. The Presbyterian approach linked to Scotland gained increasing prominence throughout the colonies in the eighteenth century, when Scots-Irish immigrants became the numerically largest group coming to the English New World. The same factors of time and space that paved the way for other forms of pluralism to develop also helped imprint ethnic diversity on colonial America. Different ethnic groups found there was sufficient land for each of them to carve out areas of settlement, although by the later colonial period, strict isolation of one from the others was virtually impossible.

Add to this mix clusters of Jews, concentrated primarily in coastal port cities, with Charleston, South Carolina, having the largest Jewish population at the time of American independence.[8] Although small in number, the various Jewish communities served as reminders that pluralism even in the colonial period was not restricted exclusively to Christian groups. Then, too, there was a strong African religious presence, thanks to the thousands of immigrants forced to come to the colonies as slaves. Although the Christianity of the slave owners should have nudged them to seek Christian converts among the slaves, the prevalent racism meant there were few sustained endeavors to do so until the age of the Great Awakening. Even then the religious style that held sway among the slaves represented a rich blend of African and Christian elements, making it distinctive from any other Christian expression and thus another dimension of colonial religious pluralism. Omit-

ted from most discussions of American religious pluralism are the many manifestations of tribal religious expression that gave meaning to Native American Indian
life. Although not usually subject to the same racist prejudice as African slaves,
Native American Indians were nonetheless relegated to the periphery, and their
tribal patterns dismissed as forms of paganism. All these, however, made colonial
religious life extraordinarily diverse and pluralistic for the times.

That pluralism was here to stay becomes obvious in examining some of the
religious considerations that went into the writing of the Constitution and Bill of
Rights. In the Constitution proper, mention of religion is conspicuous by its absence; the only direct reference is the prohibition of any religious test for federal
office. The Constitution's framers made a powerful statement by their silence, a
statement receiving scant clarification when the First Amendment stated that "Congress shall make no law respecting an establishment of religion, or prohibiting the
free exercise thereof." This famous sentence provides the basis for "separation of
church and state," although that term appears nowhere in the text. By establishment, the First Amendment referred to arrangements common in Europe, where
one religious body in a nation received formal recognition and concomitant ad-
vantages, such as financial support through tax monies. Others had to fend for
themselves, exist underground as dissenting movements, or in some cases be regarded as illegal. For Americans in the later eighteenth century, the most familiar
example of an established religion was the Church of England.

Two considerations regarding the First Amendment's "religious freedom" clause
are central to nurturing an ethos where religious pluralism of many varieties could
flourish. One is pragmatic: the framers of the Constitution could not have selected
one religious group for legal establishment since no single group held the allegiance of a majority of the population. To be sure, Christianity broadly construed
could claim a majority, but already so many different Christian groups were developing into denominations—Congregationalists, Methodists, Baptists, Episcopalians, several ethnic varieties of Lutherans, Presbyterians, Quakers, and more—that
none dominated nationally. Having a legal establishment was a practical impossi-
bility. A pluralism denoting the coexistence of a multiplicity of Christian bodies
was the order of the day. The other consideration regards "free exercise." If no one
religious communion was legally sanctioned, then all must be on an equal footing,
at least in the eyes of the law and the government. Hence, individuals must have
freedom to believe as they wished and engage in religious practices that stemmed
from their beliefs—or freedom not to believe—so long as they did not undercut
the primary aim of government proclaimed in the preamble to the Constitution,
promoting the general welfare.

All this represented a fundamentally new approach to how religion and the
state were properly connected. Likewise, the development of the denomination as
the standard religious institution stands as a distinctive American innovation and
contribution to the story of religion in human culture. Absence of legal constraints
meant, too, that the United States would be a place where thousands of new reli-

gions and religious movements would emerge or gain followings over the centuries, sometimes attracting just a few and often disappearing after a generation or so. Many would also mature in the American context. The Church of Jesus Christ of Latter-day Saints (the Mormons), Jehovah's Witnesses, the Churches of Christ, Christian Science, the Assemblies of God, the Christadelphians, several groups calling themselves the Church of God, and the Pentecostal Holiness Church are only a few of those that had their genesis on American soil; all of these had some relationship to the Christian tradition. There have been hundreds with roots outside the Christian orbit.[9]

The First Amendment did not mean that government had no interest in things religious or that individual states could not give formal support to particular religious groups. In New England in the early years of the Republic, some states did offer forms of financial support from tax monies to certain religious groups. Massachusetts was the last to end the practice in 1833, and the subsequent passage of the Fourteenth Amendment to the Constitution in 1868 ended even that possibility. On a federal level, what mattered about religion was its fostering morality and responsible behavior on the part of citizens. Those of the founding generation, such as Benjamin Franklin and George Washington, who were inclined toward Deism and its accompanying rationalism, believed that as long as a religion stimulated moral behavior and not fanaticism, it made a positive contribution to society.[10]

At the same time, however, Protestant notions of Christianity pretty much shaped the pluralism prevailing in the early decades of the Republic. To be sure, most U.S. citizens were not formal members of any religious group. Indeed, most estimates suggest that not more than 10 percent of the population held formal church membership at the time of the first federal census in 1790.[11] Yet that seemingly low rate of religious affiliation did not signal a corresponding lack of religious influence in society. Thousands who were not church members would have identified themselves as Protestant Christians of one sort or another. So as the various Protestant bodies organized as American institutions (some because structural ties with parent bodies in Britain were severed by the War for Independence), not only did the Protestant denomination emerge as the basic component of pluralism, but Protestant beliefs and assumptions gained widespread influence.[12] Alongside were non-Protestants, primarily Roman Catholics, Jews, and a few who were part of small ethno-religious communities. On the margins were Native American Indians and African-American slaves. The developing Protestant pluralistic culture did not heartily welcome all of them.

What planted Protestant denominational pluralism more firmly on the American religious landscape was the gradual movement of Euro-Americans westward beginning shortly after national independence was won. On the frontier in Kentucky, Ohio, Tennessee, and other areas that now seem far from being frontier regions, women and men took advantage of the seemingly endless space available for settlement, hoping to create a secure life for themselves and their progeny.

At the dawn of the twenty-first century, it challenges the imagination to envision how widely dispersed the frontier population was and how difficult it was to fashion social and cultural institutions, such as churches and schools. Denominations that sent preachers, like the Methodist circuit riders on horseback, and that explored new ways, like the camp meeting, to attract people and draw them into the circle of faith became the most prominent. Numerically largest were the Methodists, Baptists, and Presbyterians. What they shared, albeit with rather different theological supports securing it, was an emphasis on some kind of personal religious experience. To this extent all are properly labeled evangelical denominations. Their combined influence so dominated American religious life in the nineteenth century that some label the epoch the "evangelical century" in American history; others argue that evangelical Protestantism, although divided into different denominations, functioned as a kind of cultural religion, cementing the people of the nation together with a kind of religious glue.[13]

But the intoxicating freedom of endless space and the lack of a national religious establishment encouraged others to have a hand at starting their own religions. Just before the War for Independence, Ann Lee and a nucleus of her followers came to North America and soon organized the first Shaker community, giving concrete form to one of dozens of religions enterprises inspired by utopian visions of creating heaven on earth and a perfect people. Oneida, New Harmony, Amana, Brook Farm, Ephrata—the list is lengthy. Most were still under the larger umbrella of Protestant Christianity when it came to general belief and practice. Others used Protestant Christianity as a springboard to develop distinct alternatives to traditional belief and practice. The Spiritualists who flourished in the 1840s and those caught up in the Adventist fervor of the time that later branched into several smaller denominational clusters are but two examples. Some moved, often unwittingly, to form new denominations, convinced that accepted Protestant ways were imperfect or somehow misdirected. Efforts to restore primitive Christianity included those who first coalesced into the denomination known as the Disciples of Christ and then as well into the Churches of Christ, although Alexander Campbell, who guided much early restorationist activity, thought denominations themselves were a sign of a corrupt Christianity. Unique among antebellum alternative religions with a Protestant backdrop are the Mormons, or the Church of Jesus Christ of Latter-day Saints. Highly controversial from the time of their emergence in the 1830s, the Mormons illustrate afresh the importance of space in understanding the contours of religious pluralism. As they encountered opposition in New York, Ohio, and then Missouri, the Mormons simply continued to move further from the reaches of a hostile civilization until they reached the deserts of Utah (at the time part of Mexico). Many of these groups were short-lived; others became denominations alongside other denominations. Because all had some connection to the world of Protestant Christianity, they illustrate the way in which pluralism in the nineteenth century came primarily to denote a multiplicity of Protestant denominations.

Those on the periphery, although technically not liable to legal recrimination on the part of the state, often confronted a hostile religious culture because of the evangelical Protestant hegemony, no matter how diverse its component parts.[14]

Roman Catholics received the most overt opposition in the antebellum period, largely because evangelical Protestants misunderstood what Catholicism was all about. Many consigned Catholic belief to the realm of superstition and regarded recognition of the Pope as the final religious authority as tantamount to treason, since the Pope was then also the political ruler of the Papal States on the Italian peninsula. Later history singles out two related events to call attention to the difficulties presented by a Protestant pluralism to those who were "other." In 1834, suspicious Protestants forced their way into the Ursuline Convent in Charlestown, Massachusetts. Rumor had it that corpses of babies born through illicit sexual liaisons between priests and nuns lay buried beneath the cellar floor. Finding no such graves, the angry mob burned the convent to the ground. The mob got its ideas from the second event, publication of Maria Monk's lurid (but fictional) *Awful Disclosures of the Hotel Dieu Nunnery of Montreal*, which described a convent there in such terms. Monk's book became an American bestseller.[15] Not all anti-Catholicism was so blatant, but the increase in Irish Catholic immigrants coming through Boston that mushroomed in the 1840s and 1850s was already underway, further shattering illusions of keeping a Protestant culture.

There were also occasional spurts of anti-Semitism, but the small numbers of Jews, combined with their dispersion primarily among the nation's larger cities, made them more difficult to single out. Native American Indians suffered greater abuse, symbolized most prominently in the forced movement from ancestral territorial lands along what became known as the "Trail of Tears" to reservations in Oklahoma. The nation's Protestants simply could not understand—or chose not to understand—the religious meaning attached to ancestral land in most tribal world views.

The religious life of African Americans, slaves or free, extended the boundaries of pluralism more widely. By the opening years of the nineteenth century, free African Americans in northern centers like Philadelphia and New York were already moving away from biracial worship in white-dominated and white-controlled churches, starting separate congregations. Some of these churches were independent, some formed the nucleus for new African-American denominations, and some affiliated with white evangelical denominations. Among slaves, the "invisible institution" fused elements of evangelical Protestantism with practices, beliefs, and folk traditions from Africa to create a singular religious expression. That unique blend flourished despite white efforts to monitor African-American religious gatherings ever more closely as debates over slavery became pitched at increasingly higher levels. That, too, is part of antebellum pluralism, although sometimes overshadowed by the pluralism that celebrated almost exclusively a white evangelical Protestant spirit.

Seeds for a New Pluralism in Victorian America

Although all these currents contributed to the many faces pluralism assumed in the twentieth century, changes that came to religious pluralism grew more directly from seeds planted in the last third of the nineteenth century. In the Victorian era that matured following the War Between the States, immigration soared to numerical heights never again equaled, rapid industrialization moved the nation further from its agrarian roots, and urbanization proceeded at such a pace that by the 1920 census, the United States had become a nonrural nation. These large-scale movements had consequences altering American religious life.

Once the War Between the States ended, immigration to the United States picked up at such a rate that numbers more than made up for the low immigration during the war years. Immigration in the 1880s was nearly double what it had been in the 1870s, and in the first decade of the twentieth century, total immigration was nearly double that of the previous two decades combined.[16] Altogether, between 1870 and 1910, nearly 26 million immigrants entered the country. Equally striking is the shift in the ethnic and religious complexion of this massive wave of immigration. In the 1880s, for example, two out of three immigrants still came from areas of Europe that had long been primary sources of "new" Americans: Germany, England, Ireland, and Scandinavia. In the twentieth century's opening decade, two out of three came from Italy, the Austro-Hungarian Empire, and Russia. Immigrants from Mexico in 1910 exceeded the number coming from Ireland; as the century progressed, the Hispanic-Latino presence exerted ever greater influence.

The shift in nations of origin away from northern and northwestern Europe to southern, central, and eastern Europe brought a cultural diversity to American life, particularly to the cities where immigrants clustered. A century later, that heritage endures where there are echoes of a "Little Italy" or a Ukrainian or a Czech neighborhood, often with an enclave of restaurants serving cuisine indigenous to those areas. Growth of immigration, along with industrialization, helped transform the nation from a land of farms and rural communities to one of cities. As well, the bulk of immigrants coming to American shores between the close of the Civil War and the outbreak of World War I were Roman Catholic, Eastern Orthodox, or Jewish. Despite the dramatic influx of Irish Catholics from 1830 to 1850 and a significant presence of German Catholics, the overwhelming majority of immigrants prior to this epoch were Protestant. The religious identities of these immigrants of the late Victorian age altered the contours of religious pluralism significantly. No longer did pluralism simply denote the multiplicity of Protestant groups, relegating others to the periphery. It also had to acknowledge the multiplicity of non-Protestant religious traditions that found a home on American soil.

For those who perpetuated a vision of the United States as an evangelical Protestant culture, the consequences were both challenging and frightening.[17] Representative is Josiah Strong, for many years executive secretary of the Evangelical Alliance. In the mid-1880s, Strong published a provocative book entitled *Our Country*, in which with sociological and statistical precision he documented the changes resulting from immigration, urbanization, and industrialization.[18] He summoned Protestant churches to work together to Americanize and also to Christianize these new immigrants. Strong's not too subtle suspicion of Catholicism resounds throughout the pages of *Our Country*, since Catholics were not regarded as Christians but as potential converts to (Protestant) Christianity. For Strong, Protestantizing the immigrants was nearly synonymous with Americanizing them, for only by adopting moral values and a cultural style inculcated by the evangelical denominations would immigrants cease to be a threat. Strong documented differences, for example, in Sunday observance and use of alcoholic beverages, along with contrasts in clothing styles and first languages, to argue that the United States was in danger of losing its distinctiveness as an Anglo-Saxon Protestant culture—the "our country" of his title—if the Protestant churches did not act. What Strong did not realize, however, was that by the time he wrote, the diversity and pluralism that he feared had become an avalanche that could not be halted. Nor would Strong have found comfort in the realization that decades earlier (by 1850) Roman Catholicism had become the largest single religious group in the United States, albeit not as large as the combined total of all Protestant groups.

Later nineteenth-century immigration had other consequences that were primarily internal to religious families. For example, the presence of millions of Roman Catholic immigrants from Italy and Slovak cultures gave Catholic practice a different flavor than prevailed among parishes accustomed to Irish Catholic, German Catholic, or even French Catholic ways.[19] Late Victorian immigration endowed American Catholicism with an ethnic pluralism it had not previously known. The same holds true for American Judaism.[20] The Jewish population of the nation increased tenfold; more than two million Jewish immigrants came from Russia alone following pogroms attacking Jews there after 1880. The Jews of German stock who had dominated American Jewish life, striven to assimilate into the larger culture, and embraced Reform Judaism quickly became a minority, often embarrassed at the cultural divide between them and their eastern European coreligionists. The pluralism internal to American Judaism would gel into the three main strands of Orthodox, Conservative, and Reform, but in reality the picture was more complex.

On the West Coast, immigration from China and Japan brought similar concern for maintaining the purity of an Anglo-Saxon Protestant culture, even though the religious complexion of California, for example, already demonstrated a pluralism undercutting an evangelical Protestant hegemony manifested in a multiplicity of denominations.[21] Often subject to sharp racist discrimination, Chinese and Japanese immigrants nevertheless attempted to plant their own religious heritages on American soil, giving pluralism yet another dimension that would become more significant in the twentieth century as the number of Asian Americans increased.

Symbolic of the changing character of pluralism is the World's Parliament of Religions, held in 1893 in conjunction with the Columbian Exposition in Chicago to mark the four hundredth anniversary of Columbus's "discovery" of the Americas.[22] To honor the global character of this world's fair, invited representatives of various religions made presentations outlining the central beliefs of their particular traditions. A later age would see the World's Parliament as an early form of interreligious dialogue. Yet the Parliament was also a catalyst for bringing new features of pluralism to bear, ones bearing fruit in the twentieth century. For one, when authentic voices spoke, somehow the traditions they represented seemed less dangerous; listeners from other religions heard the same classical problems of the human condition addressed and the same concerns for linking faith and action. Another result came from the presence of spokespersons from religions to which Americans had little exposure who remained for a time in the United States. One example is the Hindu tradition from India. At the World's Parliament, one voice of that tradition was Swami Vivekananda, who embarked on a speaking tour that took him to major cities across the country once his work at the Parliament was completed. From the audiences at his lectures emerged the Vedanta Society, one of the first offshoots of an Asian religion to attract a western audience in the United States. Perhaps the most significant aspect of the Parliament is the simple fact that it occurred, for its very organization signaled that a multitradition pluralism had come to the United States.

The thousands of native-born citizens who poured into the cities seeking employment in the burgeoning factories and new businesses likewise planted seeds for a changing pluralism. Many well-established Protestant denominations sought new ways to minister to the spiritual and social needs of young women and young men who flocked to the cities. The YMCA and YWCA illustrate two cooperative efforts to provide low-cost housing and religious nurture in a "safe" evangelical Protestant environment for such workers.[23] The "institutional church," forerunner of the late twentieth-century "megachurch," augmented traditional church programs with a full schedule of athletic events, special interest groups, and religious education classes, often adding gymnasia and other meeting facilities to their building complexes. Some provided low-cost housing as well. Many reached out not just to their own natural constituency, but to immigrants arriving in the cities.[24] The migration of African Americans to northern cities from the rural South that escalated rapidly around the time of World War I began at least by the early 1890s. With this migration, yet another face of pluralism comes into focus, for in the fusion of rural Southern religious ways with northern urban cultural styles, a distinctive religious expression was born and new religions emerged.[25] One cultural offshoot was the rise of the musical genre called the blues.

Industrialization and the conditions workers faced in the factories reveal yet another form of pluralism coming to mark American life. Immigration and industrialization combined in many cases to provide a surplus of labor, meaning that employers were able to pay low wages and demand long hours of work. The ensuing conflict between labor and management sparked not only the formation of labor unions, but also another facet of pluralism as Americans developed a range of sometimes complementary and sometimes contrasting approaches in linking religion to social problems. This pluralism comes to light in differing responses to a fundamental question: can religion reform the basic structures of society to bring them into greater conformity with ethical principles or can religion only rescue individuals from a basically evil social order, convinced that a just society can arise only when all its members are righteous?[26] In other words, religion's variant blueprints for the ideal society added new contours to pluralism.

The later Victorian era also brought significant change to American domestic life and to gender roles, with consequences for the more complex pluralism taking root. Ann Douglas and others have argued for the increasing feminization of both the home and much institutional religion in the nineteenth century, trends under way even before the Civil War disrupted national life, though in some areas there were attempts to reinforce a masculine character to religion.[27] In the later nineteenth century, the shifts became more pronounced. In a preindustrial context, the family had been an economic unit; if tasks differed by gender, each was essential to providing for the family. Work, as we use that term today, was likewise centered in the home. With the escalation of the factory system, work outside the home for men changed the understanding of the family and domestic sphere. The family was no longer a single working unit; work inside the home became the domain of women, as did what went on in the home itself. The external world, the world of the factory and all the associations that went with it, became the domain of men.

At the same time, patterns long fixed in organized religion continued, but with a new twist. For as long as records exist, women have outnumbered men as formal members of religious institutions in the United States by a margin of approximately two to one. From the 1830s on, alongside the professionalization of the clergy came tacit arrangements whereby men retained control of religious bureaucracies, although women had responsibility for the daily tasks that kept those institutions viable. Organized religion was thus technically under the control of men, but practically part of the province of women. As the home likewise became the province of women, it became the locus not of formal religion, but of personal religiosity. Historian Colleen McDannell has carefully demonstrated how the Victorian home became the space where religious expression was nurtured and sustained in both evangelical Protestant and American Catholic circles, albeit in somewhat different ways.[28]

Two consequences of this cultural metamorphosis paved the way for dimensions of the variegated pluralism coming to fruition in the twentieth century. One was what sociologists call the privatization of religion.[29] Authentic religious expression became more a personal and, therefore, private matter. The home was private space, and religious nurture and experience occurring in the home were likewise private. Evangelical Protestantism, with its denominational pluralism, had long regarded personal religious experience as fundamental to the Christian life; conversion was at heart a personal experience. With the domestic sphere taking on some characteristics of religious space, that personal experience became ever more private. One way to document this transformation is through the increase of materials published for personal use in the home. Some were designed for private devotional use. Too, the number of religious magazines, another medium intended for domestic use, spiraled.[30] Many contained pages targeting children, as did a host of books. Popular fiction addressed religious issues of the time; because novels and the like were read in the privacy of the home, how people interpreted them and what they took from them and incorporated into their own personal religious world views was very much a private matter.[31] In the twentieth century, in keeping with sociological expectations about the place of religion in a highly complex society, that privatization continued and gave a multitude of new dimensions to religious pluralism.

The other consequence concerns male religiosity. If the home and thus religion became the province of women, where would male spirituality find an expression? Mark Carnes and others have demonstrated that parallel with the feminization of the home and the location of work outside the home came a significant rise in the fraternal movement.[32] To be sure, the Masons had a venerable, if controversial, history. Between the Civil War and the Great Depression, the number of men participating in various lodges and fraternal orders like the Masons skyrocketed. With elaborate rituals akin to sacred ceremonies, the fraternal groups became a male sphere and in some ways the functional equivalent of a religious community for many members; one contemporary commentator feared that some communities had more lodges than churches.[33] Curiously, much of the language in the lodge rituals was highly feminine and overtly religious. Roman Catholic leaders, suspicious of the Protestant character of most of the fraternal movements, urged Catholics not to join, but lent support to a cognate organization for Catholics, the Knights of Columbus. Lodges never supplanted the churches, but they did symbolize ongoing gender differences in seeking spiritual fulfillment that took many new directions in the pluralism of the twentieth century.

The years spanning the turn of the twentieth century saw seeds planted for yet another facet of pluralism that came into sharp relief decades later. As the old evangelical denominations became the churches of the emerging urban middle and upper classes, worship itself underwent transformation. The exuberance of frontier camp meeting worship and even the fervent preaching that was part of much antebellum Protestant worship became muted. With a better educated and more sophisticated clientele, denominations such as the Methodists, the Presbyterians, and, in many cases, the Baptists all placed greater emphasis on decorum in worship, giving Sunday services an air of refined gentility.[34] That trend continued well into the second half of the twentieth century. But there were alternatives that moved into the mainstream of American religious pluralism by the last third of the twentieth century. One more exuberant strand was simply consistent with its heritage; African-American Protestants by and large retained a livelier esprit in worship than white Protestants, even when African-American worship echoed the same trend towards gentility and refinement. The emergence of Pentecostalism in the early years of the twentieth century, characterized by ecstatic religious experience often manifested in glossolalia (speaking in tongues) and in the gift of healing, assured that an exuberant style of worship remained an undercurrent in American religious life. Coming to national attention following the famed Azusa Street revivals of 1906 in Los Angeles, Pentecostalism quickly became diffuse, spawning several new denominations and religious communities. The more established Protestant groups often regarded these newer bodies with suspicion, thinking them exotic, bizarre, or evidence of the work of Satan. However, one face of the pluralism that typified American Protestant worship in the last years of the twentieth century was a diversity in worship styles in which some Pentecostal presence or at least some exuberant expression invaded virtually all the denominations and a host of new independent congregations.

Towards the Twentieth Century

In 1955 sociologist Will Herberg published an analysis of religion's role in American culture that quickly became a classic. Entitled *Protestant, Catholic, Jew*, Herberg's study argued that by the middle of the twentieth century, American religious pluralism encompassed at least the three large faith communities identified in his title.[35] While there was variety within those larger traditions, especially within Protestantism, these three traditions were in Herberg's estimation all functionally equivalent in providing socially acceptable religious identities. By mid-century, most overt religious discrimination had ended, although occasional incidents cropped up throughout the rest of the century. In Herberg's understanding, having a religious label mattered more than what the particular label was. Buttressing the whole was a culture based on conspicuous consumption and nationalism. Herberg called it the "American way of life," an unofficial religious establishment, although lacking the institutional trappings of organized religion.

Herberg's critique of this culture religion or civil religion need not concern us. More to the point is his understanding of how ingrained a three-pronged pluralism had become. If pluralism had originally highlighted the way numerous Protestant denominations and groups had made a home for themselves in America, by mid-century it accented two families of Christians and one of non-Christians that coexisted in general harmony. Pluralism had already been transformed. Yet Herberg's appraisal overlooked a number of other features of American religious life that were transforming that tripartite pluralism, the roots of which are found in the Victorian era. African Americans and Native American Indians, neither of whom figured in Herberg's study, were continuing to enrich religious pluralism. The immigrants coming from central, southern, and eastern Europe brought a pluralism especially to Roman Catholicism and Judaism, while securing Eastern Orthodox forms of Christianity in the United States. Challenges raised by the ethnic diversity within these bodies brought an internal pluralism on a scale previously unknown. In the twentieth century, mushrooming immigration from Latin America and Asia nudged pluralism in other directions. In some areas, Roman Catholicism took on a decided Hispanic cast. More importantly, the new immigration in the second half of the twentieth century brought a rapid increase in non-Christian religious bodies in the United States, sustained by persons for whom these were birth religions, not ones to which they had converted. The number of Muslims in the United States, for example, was statistically insignificant in 1900; by 2000, there were probably as many Muslims as Jews in the United States, perhaps more.

The increasing numbers of non-Christians among the American people raised more questions about the meaning of "separation of church and state" and the proper links between government and religion in a pluralistic society. The pluralism prompting those questions was quite different from what prevailed when the Bill of Rights helped create the setting where pluralism could flourish by prohibiting an establishment of religion and guaranteeing the free exercise of religion to all citizens.

Industrialization and urbanization were catalysts for creating a more mobile society. In the twentieth century, the need to bring vast numbers of military personnel back into the labor force following two world wars and other military conflicts stimulated that mobility. In turn, mobility fostered another facet of pluralism, for as Protestant Americans especially moved from place to place with greater frequency, they abandoned loyalty to the denominations to which they had belonged. Denominational switching became the order of the day; many of the oldline groups experienced severe losses, as new groups or groups once on the periphery stepped in to offer a mobile generation alternative means to spiritual fulfillment. Some of those alternatives centered on approaches to worship, bringing to center stage the style sustained primarily in Pentecostal circles. Shifting gender roles rooted in the later nineteenth century issued in rather different concerns for women's spirituality that sometimes included a return to the goddess or a syncretistic blend of pre-Christian paganism and historic traditions in order to reflect the unique experience of women. By the last decade of the twentieth century there emerged a concomitant concern for male spirituality. Gender gave pluralism many new faces.

Pluralism at the dawn of the twenty-first century encompasses much more than the multiplicity of Protestant denominations. Here its new features have been sketched. Let us look at the many faces of pluralism more closely.

CHAPTER 2

The Shifting Public Presence
of Mainline Protestantism

Mainstream Protestantism, as it became called, entered the twentieth century assured and confident. It was to be, according to Disciples of Christ leader Charles Clayton Morrison, "the Christian century."[1] The optimism of nineteenth-century evangelicals remained: If Protestants went about their business, they could create and sustain "a Christian America."[2] Princes of the pulpit such as Henry Ward Beecher at Brooklyn's Plymouth (Congregational) Church or Phillips Brooks at Boston's Trinity (Episcopal) Church preached to packed congregations. Estimates hold that in 1880, roughly 11.5 percent of all Americans were members of Methodist, Presbyterian, Congregationalist, Lutheran, or Episcopal churches.[3] To be sure, massive immigration from southern, eastern, and central Europe swelled the ranks of Roman Catholicism, Judaism, and Orthodoxy between 1880 and the outbreak of World War I, and immigrants from China and Japan brought new diversity to the growing population of the western states. But mainstream Protestants remained certain that they could fix a Protestant stamp on the culture if they Americanized immigrants by converting them to Protestant ways. After all, as Evangelical Alliance secretary Josiah Strong proclaimed, it was *Our Country*.[4]

A century later, mainstream Protestants found themselves in apparent decline. By 1990, just 8.5 percent of Americans held membership in Methodist, Presbyterian, Congregationalist, Lutheran, and Episcopal congregations.[5] To be sure, some (primarily Episcopalians and Presbyterians) exerted influence greater than numbers would warrant through their long prominence in business, finance, and government, giving credence to what Digby Baltzell long before dubbed the "Protestant Establishment."[6] By the closing years of the twentieth century, mainline leaders nearly all bemoaned the erosion of their denominations' power and numerical strength, fearing that rampant secularism would eclipse them permanently. It mattered little that polls conducted by the Gallup organization and others still showed that roughly the same proportion of Americans identified with religious institutions at the close of the century as fifty years earlier; the pews of the mainline seemed increasingly empty.[7]

Those trumpeting mainline Protestantism's demise, whether to mourn or to celebrate, misunderstood both the dynamics of American religious life and the seeds of change maturing over the twentieth century.[8] As the twenty-first century dawned, Protestant churches and denominations were undergoing reconfiguration on a scale unparalleled since the planting of denominations in the colonial era and days of the early republic. Reconfiguration meant redistributing strength, so that forms of Protestant expression and groups once on the periphery started to overshadow those used to privilege and power. A fresh pluralism had come of age within American Protestantism.

The success of mainline denominations in etching a broad, evangelical Protestant style on the religious culture of the nation during the nineteenth century in its own way became a catalyst for new challenges. Simply put, success kindled complacency and a vested interest in prevailing social structures. Methodists and Baptists provide good examples. In the nineteenth century, both were associated with the social and cultural ferment accompanying westward expansion. Both were popularly identified with the raw life of the frontier, drawing adherents from the less well-educated and, to some, less "civilized" folk exemplifying the democratic, self-reliant stereotype romanticized by later ages.[9] But as Baptists and Methodists added thousands to their ranks, change occurred. When frontier gave way to burgeoning settlement and the accoutrements of civilization took root, both became denominations of an emerging middle class. Both had looked to the frontier camp meeting, with its unchecked enthusiasm and emotion-charged conversions, to bring in new believers. By the later nineteenth century, camp meetings seemed more subdued as programs to nurture the converted and preaching designed more to edify the faithful than to convict sinners became standard.[10] Worship in local congregations became less emotional, taking on an air of respectability.[11] In a nutshell, those once on the cutting edge of American religious life had moved to the center. What had been "other" became the norm.[12]

Yet harbingers of change were at work even in the opening decades of the twentieth century. Some came from within American Protestantism, some from without. By the time the Great Depression gripped the nation, alternative religious styles, shifting theological currents, and new immigration patterns were all undermining the dominance of mainstream Protestantism, although their full effects became obvious only decades later. The religions posing the major challenge to the hegemony of the mainstream had roots in the Pentecostal surge of the opening years of the century. Theological currents that challenged mainstream Protestant emerged from the fundamentalism that took shape between the Civil War and World War I. Changing immigration patterns, combined with complex though somewhat fluid links between mainstream Protestant communities and social class structures, brought fresh vitality to non-Protestant religious communities, rather than augmenting the ranks of Protestant denominations. All set the stage for a new pluralism to take hold within American Protestantism. Each deserves scrutiny.

The Emergence of Modern Pentecostalism

Historians usually point to the Azusa Street revivals in Los Angeles in 1906 as marking the beginning of the modern Pentecostal movement,[13] but there is evidence of Pentecostal stirrings in North Carolina among African Americans and also among the fire-baptized who later became part of the Church of God as early as the 1880s.[14] At the center of the Azusa Street revivals, widely covered in the nation's newspapers, was the African-American Holiness preacher William J. Seymour, who counted Charles Fox Parham among his tutors.[15] Parham, from a Methodist Holiness background, ministered first in Topeka, Kansas, and then in Houston, Texas. He opened a school in Topeka and later in Houston to train lay workers for churches and candidates for ordination, but an unexpected phenomenon occurred when some students, while studying New Testament accounts of Pentecost, rejected the conventional understanding that charismatic gifts like glossolalia and healing were limited to the time of the first apostles. They concluded that the biblical testimony promised spiritual gifts to all who were holy, not just to the apostolic generation. Baptism of the Holy Spirit, usually manifested by speaking in tongues, was thus a present possibility.

Under Seymour's dynamic preaching in Los Angeles, hundreds reported receiving the gift of tongues. Equally important, those who flocked to Azusa Street or who carried its message across the land came from varied denominational backgrounds. Propelled by a zealous missionary imperative and an eschatological message that many found compelling, Pentecostalism had a broad appeal. Racial barriers also collapsed, for whites, African Americans, and Asian Americans were all welcomed at Azusa Street.

That inclusivity did not last long. Not warmly received in the mainline denominations, persons of Pentecostal inclination clustered in their own congregations, from which several new denominations gradually emerged. Race then became a factor, and the churches tended to be overwhelmingly white or overwhelmingly African-American. Among the most prominent of those predominantly white are the Assemblies of God and the Church of God (Cleveland, Tennessee); among African Americans, one leading Pentecostal denomination has been the Church of God in Christ. Some Pentecostal groups gravitated to churches influenced by the earlier Holiness movement; many coalesced into the Pentecostal Holiness Church.[16]

The formation of Pentecostal denominations made it easy for mainstream bodies to ignore the Pentecostal presence or consign it to the Protestant periphery. Popular perception held that those attracted to the Pentecostal style came from the less well-educated, lower socioeconomic groupings within society. H. Richard Niebuhr cemented that perception when he classified Pentecostal sects among "religions of the disinherited" in his classic *The Social Sources of Denominationalism*.[17] Niebuhr was only partially correct in his appraisal; looking back, it is clear that Pentecostalism was always more diverse. It is also clear that Pentecostals for decades knew the mainstream regarded their religiosity as an aberration; they were therefore inclined to remain aloof. As well, World War I allowed the mainline to ignore Pentecostalism's incipient power as religious interests concentrated on supporting the war effort.

The Fundamentalist Phenomenon

When mainline Protestantism paused to take stock after the war, fundamentalism captured its eye, not Pentecostalism. The Scopes "monkey trial" in Dayton, Tennessee, in 1925 remains the symbol for the public confrontation between fundamentalists and those they called modernists, although the story is more complex.[18] In Dayton, high school biology teacher John Scopes was found guilty of violating Tennessee law by teaching the theory of evolution. At the trial, crackerjack lawyer Clarence Darrow led the defense, while orator and statesman William Jennings Bryan became the prosecution's most well-known voice.

However, in the media, thanks largely to the Baltimore *Sun*'s acerbic H.L. Mencken, Bryan and the fundamentalists became anachronisms, relics of a bygone age when religion was synonymous with superstition. Because fundamentalists insisted on the literal inspiration of the scriptures, the virgin birth of Christ, the divinity of Christ as evidenced through miracles, the physical resurrection of Jesus after his death by crucifixion, and his eventual physical return or "Second Coming," it was easy for Mencken and other critics to see fundamentalism in conflict with the rational, scientific world view coming to permeate American religious culture.

Although mistaken, regarding fundamentalists as a vanishing breed allowed mainstream Protestantism to consign this style of religious expression to the margins. It also obscured how deftly fundamentalists regrouped and networked through Bible schools to train church workers, publishing firms to print and distribute literature, independent missionary and other auxiliary enterprises, and a host of other endeavors.[19] As fundamentalist congregations emerged, like Pentecostals some gradually coalesced into denominations outside the mainstream, but many remained independent of denominational affiliation, linked more by a loose association with one or more of the Bible schools and colleges that trained leaders of like mind. At the same time, even within the mainstream, there were always local churches of a fundamentalist bent, often isolated from denominational affairs.

This marginalization gained strength when fundamentalists generally lost out on bids to gain control of denominational machinery. As is well known, the most conspicuous confrontations between fundamentalists and so-called modernists to dominate denominations erupted among northern Baptists and northern Presbyterians.[20] For most of the 1920s, conventions and general assemblies of these groups revealed how vicious church politics could become; fundamentalists and nonfundamentalists engaged in name-calling, efforts to pack the staffs of denominational agencies, and sometimes even schism.

A convenient symbol is Harry Emerson Fosdick, a Baptist pastoring New York

City's First Presbyterian Church when the fundamentalist-modernist controversy peaked.[21] Of distinctly modernist sympathies, Fosdick aroused the ire of northern Presbyterian fundamentalists with his now famous sermon, "Shall the Fundamentalists Win?"[22] By answering his rhetorical question in terms akin to a battle cry, Fosdick intensified the sense of panic felt by both sides. At first, fundamentalists seemed victorious, for Fosdick was forced from his pulpit. But his powerful allies, especially the wealthy Rockefeller family, financed the construction of New York City's Riverside Church so Fosdick could have a pulpit. Not entirely by accident, Riverside was located adjacent to the Union Theological Seminary, which had severed its Presbyterian ties decades before when one of its professors was accused of heresy in the early days of fundamentalist furor. In the long run, because Fosdick still had a pulpit and because his sermon rallied forces hostile to fundamentalism, those inclined either to modernism or theological neutrality asserted themselves and retained control of denominational structures.

The Impact of Ecumenism

Mainstream Protestantism's confidence also received a boost from the burgeoning ecumenical movement. To some extent the roots of early twentieth-century ecumenism lie in the calls of those like Josiah Strong of the Evangelical Alliance[23] for cooperative activity to convert immigrants to Protestant ways and make the nation's cities bastions of evangelical truth. The more liberal social gospel coming to the fore about the same time also summoned the churches to cooperative ventures, particularly in locales where labor unrest and urban squalor were most rife. Symbolic of how ecumenism buttressed mainline optimism is the 1908 founding of the Federal Council of Churches (FCC) in Philadelphia.[24] Supported initially by twenty-eight denominations, the FCC held greater promise of broadening Protestant influence (one of the council's stated purposes) than earlier endeavors like the short-lived American Congress of Churches organized in New Haven in 1885. As a coordinating body, the FCC became the logical outfit to which to turn when a "normative" religious viewpoint was sought on virtually any issue. Although supported by some conservative denominations, the council at its first meeting adopted a social creed, largely taken over from the Methodists, that demanded vigorous engagement in social issues and problems. This commitment to social responsibility later caused fundamentalists to recoil at working with the FCC and in some cases its member denominations. To fundamentalists, such ecumenism brought compromise with the ways of the world and contaminated the pure truth essential to salvation. While the council and its denominations remained prominent images of American Protestantism, fundamentalists were often forgotten.

The early days of religious radio illuminate further how ecumenism and the mainline dominance obscured other expressions of Protestantism. When commercial radio stations began to develop religious programming, aired without charge, they turned to the Federal Council and its member denominations as representative of all Protestantism.[25] NBC, for example, pretty much gave the council free hand in selecting preachers for its "National Radio Pulpit." Similar free programming was extended to the other large families popularly thought to comprise religious America. NBC thus looked to the National Council of Catholic Men to plan "The Catholic Hour" and the faculty of the Jewish Theological Seminary of America, a Conservative institution, to guide "The Eternal Light." Other networks operated in similar fashion. When those outside the mainstream sought access to the airwaves, they were required to pay for air time or, like Aimee Semple McPherson, start their own stations. Cries of discrimination went unheeded.

However, by the 1940s, one of the most popular of all radio programs, religious or nonreligious, was "The Old Fashioned Revival Hour" that featured Charles E. Fuller, whose training at the Bible Institute of Los Angeles steeped him in the premillennial dispensationalism so influential in shaping fundamentalism.[26] Rebuffed by commercial networks and stations when he sought free programming, but knowing that the religious perspective he represented did not receive a fair hearing on programs like the "National Radio Pulpit" or even the wildly popular "Lutheran Hour" (where Walter A. Maier held forth from 1930 to 1950), Fuller committed himself to raising funds to sustain a radio ministry. But with their own free programs and their ready entree to network officials, mainstream Protestant leaders and denominations could dismiss Fuller and those who broadcast only on local or regional stations. What they did not realize was that those on the margins made better use of this new communications medium to disseminate their strands of Protestant belief and to create a sense of shared identity among their audience, an identity that did not require acceptance by a self-possessed mainstream. Moody Bible Institute even launched its own radio station, providing yet other links among those inclined towards fundamentalism.

Unwittingly, radio and, in time, television helped undermine denominational loyalty. Many who were part of mainstream denominations tuned in to religious radio broadcasts, unaware of the denominational affiliation of the preacher or others to whom they listened. If they were aware, the denominational label made little difference to most. Listeners absorbed what they heard and combined it with whatever beliefs and practices they acquired through their own church or denomination. While this individual amalgamation of belief contributed to the privatization of religiosity in American life, it also blurred denominational boundaries among ordinary people and encouraged a process of homogenization among the denominations.[27] Radio preachers knew that their audience came from a variety of religious orientations; in many cases they downplayed what was denominationally distinctive about their own perspective in order not to alienate listeners.

Interaction with African-American Protestants

Also easy for mainstream white Protestants to overlook were African Americans. Demographers can document the beginnings of African-American migration from the rural South to the more urban North as early as the 1890s. That migration accelerated in the early twentieth century, reaching a peak in 1916–1918, with the mushrooming of the automobile industry and the jobs it generated, along with employment opportunities created as northern industries increased their workforces to meet the demands of a wartime economy.[28] Although many made their way into historically African-American denominations, thousands sought to transplant the African-American southern rural religious ethos to the northern metropolis. Among the results were countless small independent congregations and numerous sectarian groups that together made the "storefront church" a fixture of urban America.[29] Often centered around a dynamic preacher, Christian storefronts often had a Pentecostal flavor, and in time Pentecostal communions open to African-American participation and those predominantly African-American added some congregations to their ranks.

Within mainstream denominations, congregations overwhelmingly African-American in composition were planting a pluralistic style, although the white leadership often ignored it. African-American pastors in the mainstream brought the intonation and cadence that are hallmarks of black preaching to their congregations, in contrast to the more staid style of their white counterparts.[30] The rich heritage of African-American sacred song, epitomized in the popular mind by the spiritual, punctuated black worship, but few made their way into the hymnals of the mainline denominations—even those with thousands of African-American members—until the last two decades of the century. In the wake of the civil rights movement of the 1960s, however, many mainline groups published hymnal supplements to highlight the African-American musical heritage.[31] The African-American presence, like that of Pentecostals and fundamentalists, was slowly, but steadily, augmenting the pluralism growing within Protestantism. By century's end, millions of Asian Americans and Hispanic Americans brought fresh challenges to the Eurocentric character of mainstream groups.

The Consequences of the Great Depression and World War II

Immigration, in-migration, urbanization, industrialization, the Great War—all these social currents left as enduring an influence on Protestant life as on society at large. The same holds for the Great Depression of the 1930s. Historian Robert Handy offered ample documentation for an "American religious depression" that paralleled the economic depression.[32] He called attention to declines in Sunday School and church attendance among mainline Protestants between 1925 and 1935, along with a decrease in financial support for congregational and denominational activities, such as missions.[33] While the mainline denominations survived the Depression and World War II, on paper experiencing unprecedented resurgence in the so-called "religious revival" of the 1950s, Protestantism itself, in Handy's estimation, never recovered its position of cultural privilege. Scientism, secular humanism (not yet the shibboleth that it became to conservative Protestants in the

1970s and 1980s), and behavioral psychology, Handy recognized, all offered comprehensive world views ultimately at odds with the theological world view undergirding mainline Protestantism, and all were on the ascendancy.[34] In essence, the Depression era ended any facile identification of mainline Protestantism with American culture as a whole.

Historians still debate whether the economic reforms symbolized by the New Deal, the economic stimulus provided by World War II, or some combination thereof nudged the nation out of the Depression. There is no question, however, that World War II altered the social and religious landscape of the nation permanently, furthering the decline of the mainline denominations and fueling numerous currents bringing greater pluralism within Protestantism and American religious life. World War II is a convenient focal point to mark the rise of six interrelated social movements with enormous consequences for religious life: increased social mobility, the surge of suburban development, changing patterns of marriage and divorce, the dramatic increase in the number of Americans going to college, the increase in the proportion of women in the labor force, and the rapid rise in the birth rate that gave the nation the "baby boomer" generation.

As millions of Americans made their way back into civilian life, employment opportunities frequently entailed relocation. The longstanding model of Americans growing up, maturing, and dying in or at least near the communities where they were born quickly disappeared. Relocation for many entailed finding another church with which to affiliate, often chosen for reasons other than its denominational label. If the denomination of one's birth had no congregation nearby, it was a simple matter to affiliate with another one. The suburban sprawl that accompanied the rise in mobility contributed as well. Mainline denominations raced to build new churches in rapidly growing suburban communities, often abandoning churches in downtown areas. Those who charted church growth knew that families were likely to identify with a church nearby, regardless of denomination, particularly if it had a program oriented towards young families. Denominational switching became the norm.[35]

That switching had vital consequences for the stability of the mainline and the place of the denominations themselves as the center of the nation's religious life. Denominations could no longer take for granted that those raised within the fold would retain a lifelong identification with a particular tradition and find meaning in life through its historically distinctive doctrinal and theological understanding.[36] Individuals lost a sense of deep linkage to a particular heritage, identifying only with the specific local congregation where they worshiped or held membership. Those not steeped in a certain tradition could hardly be expected to rear their own children with a firm bond to that heritage.

The rush to the nation's colleges and universities in the immediate postwar years, facilitated by the provisions of the famous "G.I. Bill" for veterans, in a different way undermined enduring denominational loyalty. For some, the collegiate environment brought the first introduction to a range of denominations and ways of being religious, although military service had done this for millions of veterans. It was not, as some feared, that the colleges intentionally sought to destroy religious faith and church membership.[37] Rather, those with sustained exposure to persons of other faiths or even from other Protestant denominations lost much of the apprehension of alternative religions embedded in American culture. As a result, they began to see the various faith communities as functionally equivalent, with none having an exclusive claim to ultimate truth. One denomination was just as good as another, for they all appeared to work pretty much the same in the lives of adherents. Of course, some Protestants demurred, particularly those of a fundamentalist cast who believed this sort of exposure dangerous, for it led to compromise with falsehood and contamination of authentic faith.

Increased mobility, service in the military, and collegiate experience were all in differing ways catalysts for the sharp increase in interreligious marriage as the nation moved into the Cold War era. While marriage across denominational lines had long been a part of Protestant life, it generally remained within the larger orbit of Protestantism. More remarkable in terms of implications was the dramatic increase in marriages between Protestants and Roman Catholics and between Protestants and Jews, for the boundaries separating these larger faith traditions were far more unyielding than those between denominations within the Protestant family.[38] Then, too, hundreds of Protestant Americans who served in the Pacific during the war brought home spouses from various Asian or Pacific cultures, who, like other immigrants, often sought to retain some sense of religious identity with their cultures of origin.

As individual families sought to carve out a religious identity of their own, confusion inevitably resulted. Some compromised by identifying with yet another religious community; sometimes husbands and wives went their separate ways in terms of religious affiliation, with children exposed to both or often just to one. Others quietly dropped out of organized religion altogether. However families resolved multiple religious heritages within a single household, new dimensions of pluralism were taking on increasing importance in the daily lives of the millions for whom pluralism was a family affair.

Add to this the steady increase of women, especially mothers with school-aged children, who made their way into the workforce following World War II. Here, too, the war years were critical. As men were drafted into the military, women were needed in industry and kindred endeavors. Although there were efforts to promote the return of women to the home after the war, once women joined the workforce in large numbers, a pattern was set that continues at century's end. For the churches, this shift in the nature of American home life had tremendous implications. Women had long constituted the bulk of volunteers whose work sustained religious organizations. Employment reduced the time available for such efforts. As well, families with both parents working had different expectations for what religious organizations might provide their children than had earlier generations.

A Nation of Three Religious Traditions

Some observers recognized that a broader cultural acceptance of all religious identities and a concomitant conviction that what mattered was having a religious label, not which label it was, were byproducts of the shifting religious currents. This awareness provided the context for one study previously mentioned, for sociologist Will Herberg published his classic *Protestant, Catholic, Jew* in 1955 to call attention to how the vast majority of the American people regarded the many forms of Protestantism, Roman Catholicism, and Judaism as equally valid in molding adherents into responsible citizens. For Herberg, the downside was the emergence of a culture religion, what he called the "religion of the American Way of Life," that emphasized materialism and conspicuous consumption in place of the commitment and discipleship permeating biblical faith.[39] That unconscious push to a common ground that minimized denominational particularities and even distinctions among faith traditions is echoed in the well-known statement attributed to President Dwight Eisenhower, that the government of the United States "makes no sense unless it is founded on a deeply felt religious faith—and I don't care what it is."[40]

Eisenhower also took part in ceremonies dedicating the Interchurch Center in New York City, a monument to the ecumenical movement. Ecumenism endowed mainline Protestantism with a triumphant spirit; the reorganization of the Federal Council of Churches into the National Council of Churches in 1950 betokened an optimistic spirit of cooperation in the postwar years, while the formation of the Consultation on Church Union in 1962 ignited visions of ending denominational separation and the union of most of the mainline groups into one Protestant church body. The excitement ecumenism engendered among church bureaucrats obscured the way cooperative endeavors, mergers of denominations even within the same religious family, and talks of church union created the impression that all Protestant bodies were pretty much alike, that denominations per se made no difference and had no abiding distinctive ways of thinking about what Christian faith was all about. If labels made no difference, then a passionate loyalty to a particular denomination also made no difference. In promoting unity among Protestants, the ecumenical movement thus unwittingly propelled the erosion of denominational loyalty.[41]

The homogenizing forces whittling away at denominational loyalty and identity seldom captured the attention of most observers or even Protestant leaders.[42] For most, the decade or two after World War II seemed instead to be strengthening the denominations. All one need do was look at numbers, not only of church members but of dollars spent on building new churches or expanding existing facilities.[43] Polls showed attendance at Protestant worship services increasing overall, returning to and sometimes exceeding prewar levels proportionately. Much apparent growth came in new suburban churches. Those in downtown areas in most of the nation's cities had already started a slow but steady decline. In the midst of growth elsewhere, that drop was easy to overlook.

The emergence of evangelist Billy Graham on the national and then international religious scene augmented the sense of optimism that swept through mainstream Protestantism through the 1950s.[44] For example, audiences packed New York's Madison Square Garden night after night from May 15 through September 2 in 1957, listening to Graham urge the nation to turn to Christ to avert the encroachment of atheistic communism or the mounting threat of juvenile delinquency. Thousands made a "decision for Christ," though analysts understood that most converts had prior religious identification and few long remained active in organized religious bodies despite their renewed commitment.[45] But the ongoing public interest in things religious created a facade of religious renewal. Reaching for some sense of meaning in life was natural for a generation that lived through economic depression and global war and now faced an ongoing Communist menace.

Facets of popular culture gave added impetus to this apparent fascination with religion. Norman Vincent Peale's *The Power of Positive Thinking* led the nation's bestseller list for two years in the 1950s, joined by Graham's *Peace with God*.[46] Cognate books by Jewish Rabbi Joshua Liebman and Roman Catholic Bishop Fulton J. Sheen likewise reached a vast audience, adding to the perception that virtually all Americans were drawn to religion. Television, becoming commonplace in the decade after the war, replaced radio as the leading medium for home entertainment. While Sheen remains the only religious personality to receive an Emmy award for his program, Graham and other prominent Protestants (including the Pentecostal Oral Roberts) explored how to use television to enhance religious life.[47] The mainline denominations also turned to print media, particularly popularly styled magazines, to buttress interest in religion. Most were oriented toward nuclear families, helping cement the mythical image of the suburban wage-earning husband and father, the homemaker wife and mother, and their children. Among them were *Presbyterian Life*, *Together* (Methodist), *United Church Herald* (UCC), *A.D.* (UCC and Disciples of Christ), and *American Baptist*, some of which were updated successors of previous denominational publication, and several of which were destined to be short-lived.

In ways denominational magazine editors and the popular Billy Graham never intended, much of what they did helped undermine the long-established denominations. While many knew that Graham was a Southern Baptist by formal affiliation, persons from all denominations flocked to his rallies. Graham's crusades had an interdenominational character; planning committees sought broadly based local support. On opening night at most rallies, that support found symbolic expression as representative Methodists, Presbyterians, Episcopalians, an occasional Roman Catholic priest, and others graced the platform. Only the most astute recognized that this ecumenical presence sent subtle signals to the masses that all these groups were at heart pretty much the same, that they were functionally equivalent, that it made no difference with which one affiliated. Graham's call for a personal decision reconfirmed the idea that religion was at base a private, highly individual matter. The growth of religious television and the spate of religious periodicals intended for reading in the home gave added credence to that conviction. Yet as religion became increasingly domestic and individualized, denominational loyalty waned. Real religion was what one felt and believed, not what the churches trumpeted.

Civil Rights and Beyond

Broader social currents at work by the mid-1950s in retrospect also reveal how much of the religious frenzy of the first decades after the war was little more than a veneer. The fear of communism, promoted by the frantic investigations led by Sen. Joseph McCarthy, loomed large. McCarthy convinced millions that Communists had infiltrated the U.S. military and the highest levels of the federal government. Communists replaced Nazis as the favorite national enemy, and because the most popular symbol of the Communist menace, the Soviet Union, was officially atheistic, the power of religious institutions in American life made the United States an epitome of virtue and righteousness. The Protestant churches by and large embraced the anti-Communist message, frequently peppering their proclamation of the gospel with a thinly disguised patriotism.[48] Good Protestants, regardless of denomination, would be good citizens of a capitalist democracy, never advocates of a society informed by Marxist socialism. How many Americans were drawn to Protestant churches in the 1950s because they represented stability and security in the face of Communist threats cannot be accurately determined. But for some, religious identity with a Protestant denomination—any denomination—was more a badge of good citizenship, of being among those opposed to communism, than a signal of abiding religious commitment.

Another of those currents was the civil rights movement, the effects of which echoed in American religious life for decades. The 1954 Supreme Court decision in *Brown v. Board of Education* that declared the principle of "separate but equal" unconstitutional and the Montgomery, Alabama, bus boycott of 1957–58 that brought Martin Luther King, Jr., to national prominence provide symbolic markers for the start of the modern civil rights movement. But the march on Washington in 1963 the summer before President John F. Kennedy's assassination and the many pieces of civil rights legislation that came in 1964 and 1965 mark its peak. Surrounding the movement was much violence, some reaching into the churches as bombings and burnings became nearly commonplace in parts of the South. Mainline leaders gradually came to support the movement, nudging their bureaucracies along with them. Some joined King and other African Americans as outspoken advocates. Yet most mainline congregations were divided along racial lines.

The Methodist Church illustrates the pattern replicated with some variation among most predominantly white mainline groups. Methodists placed black churches into separate organizational units, maintaining internal racial separatism until the Methodist General Conference of 1964 voted to disband the all-black Central Jurisdiction and bring the black congregations and their clergy into the previously all-white geographical units.[49] While the denomination lost relatively few active members as a result of trying to become more racially inclusive, the internal controversy revealed a division common to other mainline groups as well. Clergy, particularly among the top leadership, were more inclined to social activism than the rank and file in the pews, who were more prone to draw a sharp line between the truly religious and the secular. The civil rights movement blurred that line, allowing sociologists to predict that a storm was brewing in the mainline that would ultimately involve mass defections among those who believed that the churches should stick to calls for salvation and spiritual nurture, leaving political and social concerns to public officials.[50]

On the heels of the civil rights movement came the women's movement, with its calls for the ordination of women and the use of inclusive language in the churches. The women's movement struck more directly at the patriarchal dominance in the mainline than had the civil rights movement. Methodists, for example, began to ordain women to professional ministry as early as 1956, but two decades later debate still raged among mainline groups over the role and status of women. Among Episcopalians, for example, some bishops and more than a handful of priests who believed Christ demanded an exclusively male priesthood (because the biblical texts mention only men among the twelve disciples of Jesus) threatened to form their own dioceses to preserve what they thought was the pure faith once women were ordained.[51]

By the late 1970s and early 1980s, however, most of the mainline accepted women as professional clergy, with some beginning to name women to positions of leadership, such as the office of bishop for groups with episcopal polity, and many congregations using the lectionary prepared by the National Council of Churches that offered an edition with gender-inclusive language.[52] In some ways, the language issue was more explosive than ordination, for abandoning exclusively male references to Deity demolished the patriarchal foundations of the theological tradition. For many, it threatened to destroy faith itself. Those convinced that the soul of Protestant Christianity itself was at stake, much like the fundamentalists of an earlier day, often dropped out of the mainline churches, forming new congregations or finding their way to evangelical and fundamentalist churches where old traditions were hallowed.[53]

At century's end, however, it was not civil rights or feminism that provoked the greatest debates within the mainline. The hot issue was homosexuality. Like the larger culture, most mainline churches ignored the presence of gay men, lesbians, and bisexuals in their membership. But after patrons and passersby protested a raid on a gay bar in New York City's Greenwich Village in 1969, a gay rights movement mushroomed. The first direct challenge to mainstream Protestantism came a few months earlier when a former Pentecostal gay pastor, Troy Perry, organized a church in his home in Los Angeles ministering primarily to the gay, lesbian, bisexual, and transgendered communities. By the end of the century, that single congregation had blossomed into a denomination, the Universal Fellowship of Metropolitan Community Churches, with more than 30,000 members and many more thousands of regular participants.[54]

In 1972, however, the United Methodist Church, still the largest of the old mainline, adopted a statement of social principles claiming that homosexual practice was incompatible with Christian teaching. Throughout the mainline denominations came denunciations of the full acceptance of homosexuals into the life of the churches, especially into the ranks of the clergy, and prohibitions on rites blessing the relational commitment of persons of the same gender. If Christian segregationists decades earlier wanted to deny blacks equality in church and society on biblical grounds, those opposed to welcoming homosexuals into the churches sought biblical support in the story of Sodom and Gomorrah, the legal codes of Leviticus, and the writings of St. Paul; others launched ministries to "convert" homosexuals to heterosexual identities.[55] In the mid-1990s, disgruntled Episcopalians sought to bring heresy charges against a bishop of the denomination who had ordained a gay male, though church tribunals finally ruled that no specific church law had been violated.[56] Methodists, who generally mirrored the religious and social attitudes of the culture at large, conducted the church trial of an ordained minister in 1998, after Jimmy Creech, heterosexual pastor of a church in Nebraska, was accused of disobeying mandates of the denomination's rule-making General Conference by blessing the commitment of two lesbian members to each other.[57] By the same token, within all the mainline were groups of gays and their supporters, like Integrity within the Episcopal Church, who called for not only the full participation of homosexuals in all spheres of church life, but their ordination to the professional ministry as well.

Across the mainline, leaders feared that the dissension over homosexuality was so profound and so intertwined with basic theological convictions about sin, the authority of scripture, and the interpretation of biblical testimony that no accommodation between opposing camps was possible. Some denominational leaders in the last years of the century called for a moratorium on debate over homosexuality at church legislative gatherings, aware that the debates had the potential to generate schism. But even without overt schism, thousands left the mainline, some insisting that the obsession with social issues of sexuality prompted their departure.

Baby Boomers Come to Maturity

In the midst of this turmoil in church and culture, the baby boom generation came to maturity. The social-religious context of the decades when boomers were born more than suggested that boomers would ultimately feel little stake in supporting mainline denominations.[58] Some thought institutions of mainline Protestantism were morally bankrupt, having buttressed a racist culture that fostered segregation and a nationalist culture that intruded in the internal affairs of other nations (like Vietnam). Many who saw military duty in Vietnam had a firsthand exposure to Asian cultures different from that of the World War II generation. Linked not with defeat but with resistance and power, the deeply personal and individual religious style associated with Asian traditions had its own appeal. Thousands blended some religious expression absorbed from the mainline with meditation techniques presumed Asian to create an eclectic, but individual, customized piety. Sociologists noted that boomers separated religion from spirituality, shunning identification with churches (religion) but regarding themselves as spiritual.[59] Robert Bellah and his associates found that the boomers resisted commitment to all traditional institutions of American culture, including mainline Protestant churches, in part because they remained suspicious of all institutions and the authority they represented.[60]

A more subtle shift in the larger culture also undermined mainline Protestantism. At the start of the century, when the hegemony of the mainline seemed assured, the United States was predominantly rural. The Sunday of evangelical Protestantism represented a welcome break in the rhythm of agricultural life, with 11:00 A.M. picked for worship to come between daily chores. Even as the nation became more industrial and urban, the norm was a twelve-hour day and a six-day work week.[61] For a time the Sunday of mainline Protestantism remained nearly the only interruption. When the eight-hour day and five-day work week became common, Sunday remained a day set apart, thanks in large degree to "blue laws" that restricted Sunday business and commercial activity.[62] But the emergence of the "weekend" had an enduring effect. Slowly those who promoted leisure activity recognized that there were two days—the weekend—when Americans sought relief from the work week. Entertainment media, first radio and film and then television, were accessible seven days a week; radio and television even brought entertainment into the home. Sunday began to lose its sanctity as a day set apart, even among Christians.

Changes in the labor force, attributable in part to women who entered the workforce during World War II, also altered cultural attitudes towards Sunday. Many women did not return to domestic activity in the years after the war, but remained in the labor force. By century's end, the norm had become for wives and mothers to be employed outside the home. The weekend provided virtually the only time for families to shop and engage in many domestic activities that at one time would have been done primarily by women while husbands were "at work." Slowly blue laws began to crumble, and the churches found themselves competing not only with leisure pursuits but with shopping malls and other businesses. Add to this the growing societal appreciation for those outside the Christian orbit for whom Sunday was never a sacred time. Cultural support for the traditional Sunday of mainline Protestantism simply had evaporated.[63]

As well, increasing numbers of Americans with roots in mainline Protestant denominations simply did not want to dress up and spend even an hour Sunday mornings in an institution divorced from the realities of daily life. Membership rolls and numbers attending worship at mainline Protestant churches declined slowly but steadily in the last four decades of the twentieth century, with a slight upturn in attendance, not membership, recorded by some only in the last three or four years of the century. The boomers and their children, those dubbed "Generation X," sought spiritual fulfillment elsewhere.

To be sure, new congregations emerged to appeal specifically to the disaffected; many successful ones became megachurches. Some, such as the Willow Creek Community Church in South Barrington, Illinois, regularly attracted 10,000–15,000 to weekend services designed for religious "seekers."[64] Sometimes held late afternoon or early evening Saturdays, the worship services that drew thousands bore little resemblance to dignified mainline worship. Rock music combos replaced the pipe organ, drama sketches took the place of anthems and prayer, talks on practical matters like balancing budgets or seeking a spouse were more common than sermons on sin and salvation, and worshippers were more likely to be attired in T-shirts and blue jeans than three-piece suits and dresses.

Churches inclined towards fundamentalism also experienced a resurgence. Their worship style had long been more informal, and churches more Pentecostal in orientation were by nature more open to the exuberance of "contemporary Christian worship."[65] Many megachurches and congregations in the fundamentalist-Pentecostal orbit eschewed denominational affiliation, while remaining committed to strict doctrinal guidelines. They appealed to a different audience. Not all who found the old mainline alien territory were content with a highly personalized spirituality or the practical psychology proffered by megachurches. Some found fulfillment and a sense of security in the certainty promoted by resurgent fundamentalism. For decades, the larger culture had been at sea, rocked by the ambiguity of the civil rights movement, the sexual revolution, the women's movement, and calls for gay rights. For millions, the mainline churches caught in this ambiguity forfeited their responsibility to offer adherents clear-cut guidelines for belief and behavior. Neoevangelicalism and neofundamentalism did just that, standing apart from the cultural morass rather than embedded in it.[66]

In sum, by century's end, American Protestantism was undergoing a reconfiguration unparalleled since the emergence of the denomination as the basic organizational unit centuries earlier. Generations that came to maturity suspicious of all authority were less likely to commit themselves to religious organizations, like denominations, that they could not control. Increasingly inclined to look inward for spiritual fulfillment rather than to the long-established churches, Americans affiliating with Protestant churches did so on the basis of what a particular local congregation offered them, not on the basis of its theological heritage or history. The steadily increasing mobility of the population meant not only movement from one geographic location to another, but often movement from one religious community to another or to none at all, depending on personal needs and inclinations at the moment. While polls showed that more American accepted the "Protestant" label than alternatives, the mainline denominations that dominated public religious life at the dawn of the twentieth century struggled to maintain influence at its close.

CHAPTER 3

Pluralism's Promise and Perils: American Catholicism in the Twentieth Century

Roman Catholicism in the United States entered the twentieth century on the fringes of national religious life. For centuries in Europe and then in North America, Protestantism nurtured a virulent anti-Catholicism. Misunderstanding Catholic doctrine and piety, many Protestants regarded the tradition as a dangerous superstition. Catholics and Protestants both wondered how the American ethos of liberty would affect Catholicism. Protestants feared that religious allegiance to the Pope, who until Italian unification enjoyed considerable political clout in Europe, meant Catholics could never be trustworthy citizens. Protestant heirs of those who suspected Catholic plots to overthrow the government in Elizabethan England centuries later saw Catholic conspiracies afoot in the United States. On the other hand, the Catholic leadership in Rome looked askance at the First Amendment's separation of church and state that allowed for religious pluralism and toleration; according to their view, only a Catholic state could promote proper religious truth.

At the dawn of the twentieth century, one hallmark of Catholicism was the conviction that its teaching and practice alone preserved Christian truth. In the celebration of the Mass and the sacramental life of the church, all Catholics were united in one faith. The use of Latin in the Mass overcame language barriers that separated nations and people, maintaining the facade that there was but one true church, everywhere and always the same. For American Catholics, keeping that unity and sense of oneness was vital to survival until well into the twentieth century, but careful observers could discern a pluralism beneath the surface. As the twentieth century progressed, American Catholicism became increasingly pluralistic, struggling to maintain a solidarity and common identity long abandoned by Protestants apart from ecumenical ventures. Looking back, the harbingers of that increasing pluralism within American Catholicism, as with mainline Protestantism, are evident. But until mid-century, other challenges were paramount to establishing a viable institutional life in America: enabling a rapidly growing immigrant constituency to adjust to American ways, combating anti-Catholic assaults, and dealing with a Vatican bureaucracy as prone to misunderstand the American church as were Protestants. Little wonder that church leaders so strongly emphasized the unity theoretically prevailing within Catholicism, for unless the church were united, any of these forces could shatter its well-being.

The Third Plenary Council Paves the Way

The third plenary council of American bishops, meeting in Baltimore from November 9 through December 7, 1884, illuminated the challenges facing American Catholicism at the close of the nineteenth century and also set the stage for most developments in the twentieth.[1] Towering over the council was Archbishop James Gibbons, who received his cardinal's biretta two years later.[2] Of Irish stock, Gibbons signals the Irish dominance of American Catholic institutional life that was not seriously threatened until the last years of the twentieth century. Prior to the third plenary, most American Catholics were of Irish, German, or French (Canadian) stock; Catholics of English descent had long been a minority. Soon immigrants from southern, central, and eastern Europe overwhelmed them all, but those of Irish ancestry held most high offices.

Under Gibbons's leadership, the council made several decisive moves to strengthen American Catholicism internally. One example was the call to establish church schools within every parish to educate Catholic children.[3] The push for parochial schools recognized the distinctively Protestant character of much public school education and the evangelical tone present in many teaching materials. As well, public schools were unable to educate most immigrant children effectively until they understood English. Parochial schools were better poised to help immigrant children adjust to American ways in part because they could bridge the gap between immigrants' cultures of origin and the world around them by nurturing their faith and religious practices. Hence parishes and their schools began to take on a decided ethnic cast, thanks largely to the way immigrants clustered in neighborhoods in the larger cities. At the same time, the schools taught the fundamentals of Catholic belief and practice. If all Catholic children, regardless of ethnic heritage, received the same religious instruction, they would implicitly and explicitly understand that the church was one, the same everywhere. Informally, Catholics knew which church ministered primarily to an Italian constituency, which to a Polish constituency, and so on. Thus the parish system, and particularly the parochial schools, maintained the facade of a united church while preserving ethnic pluralism.

The third plenary recognized that many fears of church officials in Rome, especially those relating to labor issues, were misplaced. Catholic immigrants entered the industrial labor force by the thousands and often found that emerging labor unions were the strongest advocates of better working conditions, higher wages, and other improvements in labor's lot.[4] Church teaching, however, regarded all unions as vehicles for attacking the church's position of privilege as they were in

Europe, and forbade Catholics to join such "secret" societies. Gibbons and other church leaders knew American Catholics would align with unions out of self-interest, regardless of church teaching. They did not want to force Catholics to choose between church and union. Catholics could be loyal to both. In the twentieth century, priest and social theorist John Ryan became one of the nation's most articulate champions of labor's cause.[5]

Leaders like Gibbons also knew that Catholicism in the United States held no privileged position that organized labor could undermine. That, too, concerned the church hierarchy in America and in Rome, but for different reasons. In Europe from the French Revolution on, the church had gradually lost much of its political leverage. The hierarchy, from the Pope down, equated loss of political power with loss of spiritual influence. It also remained suspicious of American democracy and its theoretical "separation of church and state." Since the U.S. government refused to grant official sanction to one religion, it appeared to affirm dimensions of truth in all. More comfortable historically with situations where monarchical governments granted legal standing only to Catholicism, church leaders in Rome were certain that the American ethos would undermine the church and that the presence of religious alternatives would lure the faithful into falsehood.[6] After the third plenary, Gibbons devoted inordinate energy to communicating with Rome regarding the health of the American church, the loyalty of American Catholics—including immigrants who found faith affirmed in parochial schools, not lost in public schools—the need for the church to support labor, and the like.

In the long run, sheer numbers gave credibility to the claims made by Gibbons and those like him. After all, Roman Catholicism had been the largest single religious body in the nation as early as 1850; its spectacular growth in the late nineteenth century and early twentieth confirmed that a strong church could flourish in the American democratic ethos. The work of Gibbons and others in interpreting the American Catholic experience to Rome and acclimating the church to its setting was rewarded in 1908 when the American church lost its status as a missionary enterprise and its bishops received responsibility for a mature national church within parameters set by Rome.[7]

The coming of World War I put the brakes on American Catholicism's extraordinary growth; immigration slowed to a trickle. The war years also allowed the church to dislodge some residual Protestant fear that Catholics could never be loyal citizens because of their devotion to the Pope. In August 1917 delegates from sixty-eight dioceses formed the National Catholic War Council (NCWC) to coordinate support for the war effort.[8] The NCWC not only provided assistance for Catholic military chaplains, but it also worked with non-Catholic groups like the Salvation Army to provide financial support for various domestic endeavors bolstering patriotic activity. By mobilizing Catholic backing for the American cause, the NCWC whittled away at anti-Catholic prejudice. Military service also broke down some Protestant bias since training and fighting on the front brought thousands of Protestants for the first time into sustained, often intimate contact with

Catholics. The shared experience of the warfront trench diminished much intolerance by fostering a sense of common humanity.

After the war, the NCWC reorganized as the National Catholic Welfare Council to advance social justice and political action programs set forth by the American bishops. Fr. John Ryan directed the social action department of the council from its inception in 1920 until his death in 1945. Again Rome looked askance, fearing that such a council could usurp prerogatives reserved to the church hierarchy. The NCWC averted the possibility that Vatican officials would order it disbanded by changing its name to the National Catholic Welfare Conference. Under that designation it promoted a Catholic perspective on many political and social issues, primarily through lobbying activity, until its demise in 1966 in the church reorganization following Vatican II.[9]

The Persistence of Anti-Catholic Sentiment

The highly touted "return to normalcy" after the Great War revealed that anti-Catholicism still coursed through American culture. The same exclusionary policies among schools and various clubs that betrayed the depth of anti-Semitism in the United States helped keep anti-Catholicism alive. With parochial schools as the centerpiece, the American church developed a subculture that paralleled a Protestant-dominated society. Periodicals such as *Ave Maria* brought a devotional presence into Catholic homes. Agencies promulgated lists of books that leaders saw as dangerous to the faith, attempting to prohibit Catholics from reading them. The flip side came in the Catholic Book Club that offered "safe" materials to Catholic families. When film almost overnight became a popular medium for entertainment, the Legion of Decency moved quickly to identify commercial movies the devout should avoid. Those inclined to anti-Catholic sentiment criticized such endeavors as fostering exclusiveness. But so long as overt bias towards Catholics remained, the subculture helped promote a sense of solidarity, probably reaching a peak in the 1950s but crumbling quickly in the wake of Vatican II.

Yet even in the 1920s Catholics were clearly not all cut from a single mold, ethnic differences aside. Catholic attitudes toward the national experiment with Prohibition illustrate that dimension of pluralism.[10] Historians still debate the extent to which religious prejudice motivated Prohibition advocates; popular thinking linked heavy use of alcoholic beverages with immigrants and therefore with Catholics. Hence many Catholics, from church leaders to ordinary lay folk, worked for Prohibition through groups like the Catholic Total Abstinence Union of America and the Catholic Prohibition League, since they believed anti-Catholic sentiment would abate once Catholics were no longer identified with an objectionable social practice. Others adamantly opposed Prohibition, in part because they knew the xenophobia driving efforts to ban the manufacture and sale of alcoholic beverages would not disappear even if Prohibition succeeded and in part because they refused to condemn social practices integral to many Catholics' ethnic heritage.

Many of these fears coalesced in the 1928 presidential campaign when New

York Governor Al Smith, a practicing Catholic who called for repeal of Prohibition, became the Democratic party nominee. In some sections of the country, particularly parts of the South where few Catholics lived, a virulent anti-Catholic component marked the presidential campaign.[11] Both Smith and the Democratic Party got portrayed as embracing a pluralism dangerous to the integrity of American culture. Although much of that reflected continuing apprehension over the effects of the massive immigration just before World War I, quotas put in effect in the early 1920s heavily restricted immigration from southern, central, and eastern Europe. Yet much of the South, where anti-Catholic rhetoric was shrillest, voted heavily for Smith; he lost almost as heavily in some industrial states with the highest concentration of Catholics. If Catholic voters had supported Smith as uniformly as critics claimed they would, Smith would have defeated Hoover. Catholics simply were not of a single mind politically.

That pluralism in Catholic political postures comes into sharp focus with the New Deal associated with Franklin Roosevelt in the 1930s. On the one hand, John Ryan of the NCWC, who long advocated labor's cause, became so enamored with the New Deal that he picked up the sobriquet of "the Right Reverend New Dealer." Ryan was convinced that the policies of the New Deal were not only consonant with Catholic moral teaching, but also destined to improve the lot of the working class, where the bulk of American Catholics fell.[12] Ryan's work was known primarily in intellectual and religious circles, not among the mass of the American population. More adept at reaching the masses was one whose views became the polar opposite of Ryan's, though both were Catholic priests. Canadian-born Charles Coughlin launched a radio ministry from his post in Royal Oak, Michigan, in 1926.[13] His initial aim was to educate hearers about Catholic belief and practice after the Ku Klux Klan burned a cross in the churchyard of the parish Coughlin served. He became such a popular radio figure that the CBS radio network gave him his own program. Like Ryan, Coughlin was taken by Franklin Roosevelt and the New Deal, but unlike Ryan, he quickly became disillusioned. He began trumpeting views attacking New Deal programs. He also became increasingly anti-Semitic, anti-Communist, and finally pro-Nazi. Over the airwaves, Coughlin reached millions who resonated to his message; his Shrine of the Little Flower became a symbolic center for causes he espoused. Coughlin's radicalism in time embarrassed the church, particularly when he opposed U.S. entry into World War II while the church was mobilizing support for the Allied cause. In 1942 church officials ordered him to abandon his radio broadcast and publication of the magazine he had started to promote his views. This contrast between Ryan and Coughlin provides ample evidence of pluralism within Catholic political thought at a crucial time in American life.

Catholics Enter the Religious Mainstream

Following World War II, Catholics joined much of the rest of the population in opposing communism. When rumors surfaced that Communists had infiltrated the

American military and even the federal government bureaucracy, a Catholic senator, Joseph McCarthy, spearheaded investigations in order to track down and eliminate this menace to the commonweal.[14] McCarthy pursued his assault against Communists with such zeal that he became an embarrassment to his fellow senators and his church. But the fear of and hostility to communism among the Catholic masses suggested that Catholics were moving from the margins to the center of American life.

In other ways, the 1950s showed a Catholicism more and more mirroring the demographics and views of the larger American culture. Catholics joined in the move to suburban communities, and they benefited especially from the educational opportunities opened to veterans through the G.I. Bill after World War II. The 1950 census figures show that areas with a heavy concentration of Catholics had fewer persons in professional and managerial occupational categories and fewer with education beyond high school. Like the immigrant generation, most were still in the industrial working class. But the 1950s brought significant social mobility and upward movement economically, although even by 1980 Catholics would be underrepresented at the highest management levels.[15] At mid-century, Catholics remained on the periphery of social and economic power, thriving in their own subculture, but moving rapidly toward the center. The shift meant that increasing numbers of Catholics would espouse social and political views contrary to church teaching though consonant with prevailing attitudes. One form of pluralism was brewing. As the demographic profile of American Catholics came to resemble that of the overall population, anti-Catholic prejudice became harder to sustain. Recall sociologist Will Herberg's claim in 1955 that a Catholic identity was functionally as legitimate as a Protestant identity in marking one as a good citizen.[16] For many, the election of John Fitzgerald Kennedy as U.S. president in 1960 signaled Catholicism's acceptability in American life.[17] Kennedy deftly defused religious apprehension, as in his well-known address to a Houston, Texas, ministerial association, shattering the image of Catholics being beholden to the church hierarchy when it came to political positions. This shifting perception also suggests a greater pluralism prevailed among rank-and-file Catholics than many non-Catholics allowed. Catholics, like other Americans, were not necessarily of one mind in political or even moral debates. In time that pluralism brought consternation to Catholic officials bemoaning the loss of a united front in presenting Catholic perspectives in the public arena.

In the long run, more significant to American Catholic developments than Kennedy's election was the elevation of John XXIII to the papacy in 1958 and his subsequent calling of the first church council, Vatican II, in nearly a century.[18] Vatican II transformed Catholicism globally, not just in the United States. The word John XXIII used to describe the intent of the Council was *aggiornamento* or "updating," and a familiar image became that of a church opening windows onto the changing world around it. Bishops and official council observers struggled with many weighty issues of doctrine and practice. From an intellectual perspec-

tive, the council's willingness to abandon a Thomistic standard in theological inquiry looms as its most significant achievement. For most Catholic laity, other
shifts became far more important.

Symbolically and practically, replacing Latin with the vernacular as the language of the Mass was the most vital. Liturgically, the change spurred exciting
experimentation and renewal that spilled over into mainline Protestantism. Folk
masses with music provided by guitarists joined more traditional approaches to
the celebration of the Mass, bringing a pluralism to Catholic worship hitherto unknown. Once those in the pew heard the words intoned in the language they used
daily by a priest who was now facing congregants who could see every action,
much mystery surrounding the Mass disappeared.

By extension, much of the mystique and power extended to the priest as cel-
ebrant evaporated. Stripping the spiritual authority and perceptions of superiority
of those in religious vocations came more visually as nuns abandoned habits harkening back to medieval times for ordinary street clothes. Could those who looked
like ordinary folk be any other than ordinary? As mandated parish reorganization
drew lay councils into planning church programs and establishing goals and pri-
orities for ministry, the aura of authority surrounding parish priests also dissipated.
Something as simple as dropping the ban on eating meat on Fridays, except as a
Lenten discipline, removed a culturally distinctive dimension of Catholic identity.

Yet the most profound change in the way Catholics looked at their church is
something intangible. In the popular mind, the council bred a sense that everything Catholic was under review and subject to updating, from insisting on an all-
male priesthood to the traditional ban on artificial means of birth control. When
windows like those were opened, a far greater pluralism prevailed within American Catholicism than many thought possible.

The Impact of Social Currents: After Vatican II

Vatican II opened on October 11, 1962; its final session closed on December 8,
1965. During those three years, the social currents bringing new dimensions of
pluralism to mainline Protestantism—civil rights, concern over Vietnam, the
women's movement—were also transforming American Catholicism. The American church thus wrestled with changes resulting from Vatican II in the midst of
tremendous social turmoil. Those social forces likewise revealed a depth of pluralism within a religious communion long touted as being one church wherever and
whenever it existed. One aspect of that pluralism comes into focus by contrasting
the ministry of Francis Joseph Spellman, cardinal archbishop of New York from
1939 until his death in 1967, with that of the brothers Daniel and Philip Berrigan,
both priests when they came into public attention.

During World War II, Spellman added to his responsibilities those of the military vicar or bishop for the U.S. army and navy.[19] As such, he developed an extraordinary network of political contacts. He also became committed to a patriotism

that never questioned government policy and included an anti-communism as strident as that of any mainline Protestant figure or even Sen. McCarthy. Some observers believe Spellman's nationalism contributed to the increasing public acceptance of Catholics as part of the American mainstream in the 1950s. Spellman's unwavering support for government policy carried over into the Vietnam era; he sharply criticized protesters against American involvement in Southeast Asia and, as military vicar, reinforced his support for the war effort by visiting troops in Asia. Spellman resolutely endorsed historic Catholic teaching on moral issues such as birth control.

Although Vatican II came in the closing years of Spellman's life, the cardinal took an active role in the proceedings, using his influence within the church hierarchy to gain a hearing for the much more theologically moderate Jesuit theologian John Courtney Murray, whom *Time* had featured on its cover December 12, 1960.[20] Murray's thought largely informed the council's Declaration on Religious Freedom, vigorously supported by Spellman, that seemed to acknowledge Catholicism as one expression of Christianity among many because it called for a broader religious toleration than Rome had previously endorsed. Spellman was thus both a bulwark of traditional Catholicism and a bridge to the larger culture. At century's close, the archbishop of New York, John Cardinal O'Connor, while willing to criticize government social policy, followed in Spellman's footsteps by insisting on the validity of traditional church teaching on matters such as birth control and abortion.[21]

By contrast, the Berrigan brothers embraced much not usually associated with the public persona of Catholic priests as they, too, sought to engage their church with American culture.[22] Daniel and Philip Berrigan became household names because of their roles in dramatic antiwar protests, such as their pouring blood on files maintained by a Selective Service System (military draft) office. Both had cut their activist teeth in civil rights marches and related endeavors before the antiwar movement eclipsed the civil rights movement in public consciousness; both built on a tradition of Catholic radicalism nurtured by persons like Dorothy Day and the Catholic Worker movement.[23] Joined in their protest efforts by nuns or former nuns, the Berrigans demolished images of the Catholic religious as isolated from the real world in cloistered chapels.

Catholics familiar with the violent anti-Catholicism once permeating American culture were aghast at the sight of priests and nuns leading protest demonstrations; they feared Protestants would make such the rationale for new repression. At the same time, many Catholic laypeople, like their Protestant counterparts, questioned whether this sort of activity was appropriate for those whose primary vocation was sacramental and ministerial. The Berrigans and their associates helped stir the same storm in Catholic circles that was brewing in the Protestant churches. Philip Berrigan took another step unthinkable to Catholics a generation earlier when he abandoned his priestly vocation and married Elizabeth McAlister, a former nun. Daniel Berrigan destroyed yet another aspect of the mystique surrounding the priesthood when, to avoid arrest, trial, and almost certain imprisonment, he chose to go underground and become a fugitive. Daniel was later found, having been assisted in his efforts to elude legal authorities by a devout Episcopal layman.

The Berrigans and Cardinal Spellman seem diametrically opposite. Yet they all were, at least for a time, priests in the same American Catholic church, and all three insisted they were simply living out in society the dictates of their Catholic consciences. In other words, all three saw themselves as faithful Catholics. Taken together, however, they shatter the image of a united church in which one viewpoint prevails not just on matters of faith, but also on social issues. Pluralism was as central to American Catholic experience in these arenas as it was to mainline Protestantism.

A similar pluralism came to mark lay Catholic life, even if not expressed as dramatically as a protest led by one of the Berrigans. The encyclical issued on July 25, 1968, by Pope Paul VI, *Humanae Vitae*, provides a convenient barometer for measuring that pluralism.[24] Vatican II prompted considerable discussion of Catholic teaching regarding marriage and sexual relations between husband and wife. The *Pastoral Constitution on the Church in the Modern World* containing the council's final statements on marriage acknowledged that intercourse between a wife and husband existed for their fulfillment as well as for generating new life.[25] But it did not directly treat issues like birth control and abortion because, prior to the end of the council, Pope Paul VI appointed a special commission to make recommendations directly to him on these matters of tremendous controversy. Given the tenor of Vatican II, however, millions expected the commission to recommend sanctioning some methods of artificial contraception and Paul VI in turn to endorse those recommendations.

The commission, as expected, rejected absolutely the idea of arbitrary contraception or sanctioning use of something like the birth control pill if such granted license to casual sexual intercourse, particularly outside marriage. However, the commission suggested that church moral teaching allowed married couples latitude in using artificial means of contraception in exercising responsibility as Christian parents. Catholics in America, who used the pill and other means of contraception in roughly the same proportion as others,[26] rejoiced at the recommendations. Their exultation died when Paul VI repudiated the commission's recommendations. *Humanae Vitae* reasserted the church's condemnation of artificial means of contraception, insisting that the possibility of forming new life was fundamental to every act of sexual intercourse. When the encyclical appeared, the movement to legalize abortion in the United States was mounting, although the U.S. Supreme Court did not issue its landmark *Roe v. Wade* ruling until 1973. *Humanae Vitae* went on to condemn any interruption in the procreative process once it was underway, thus also reaffirming the longstanding Catholic opposition to abortion.

More than any changes emerging from Vatican II, *Humanae Vitae* polarized American Catholics. A century earlier, open defiance of church teaching would have been unthinkable. At the least, those totally opposed to church teaching would not have regarded themselves as faithful Catholics. But the developing pluralism within the church in the United States meant that thousands of Catholics retained a Catholic identity even though they jettisoned church teaching on contraception and, to a lesser degree, on abortion. If the church had once defined who could be Catholic, now individuals were doing so for themselves. Of course, millions accepted church teaching, and no member of the hierarchy openly expressed opposition (though some did privately). Parish priests became particularly torn; more than other leaders, they declined to criticize those of their flock whose consciences, informed by Christian principles, led to decisions counter to the church's position.[27] Persons claiming a Catholic identity aligned with every position along the spectrum as contraception and abortion debates confounded the larger culture.

The willingness of Catholics to defy the church and thus shatter the illusion that all Catholics are of a common mind in adhering on matters of belief and ethics continued the authority crisis precipitated by Vatican II. But that should have come as no surprise. As the profile of American Catholics began to mirror the profile of the American population as a whole, as Catholicism shed its immigrant status and moved into the mainstream, individual Catholics were bound to share views and attitudes cascading through the society around them. Even before the strife engendered by *Humanae Vitae*, Catholics began to ignore church teaching on divorce and remarriage. Like other Americans, in the decades following World War II, Catholics began to seek civil divorce in greater numbers; following Vatican II the number rose dramatically.[28] The church officially refused to recognize civil divorce, though so long as neither party remarried there were few if any effective sanctions that the church could impose. It theoretically regarded divorced persons who remarried as guilty of adultery and barred them from receiving communion. But theory and practice had long diverged. Divorced and remarried Catholics in increasing numbers refused to absent themselves from receiving the sacrament; few priests would have turned them away in any case. Even more, when prominent Catholic politicians and entertainers divorced and remarried several times and participated in the sacramental life of the church without reaping denunciation from church officials, the rank and file could hardly be expected to cast aside a Catholic identity when they did the same.

Church and Priesthood Amid Stress and Strain

Other issues coming to the fore in the decades following Vatican II revealed additional dimensions of pluralism within American Catholicism. Polls for years suggested that American Catholics attended weekly Mass at a higher rate than mainline Protestanta went to worship.[29] Vatican II started a steady decline in Catholic Mass attendance until the figure reached the level of Protestant attendance. Sociologists debate whether such figures are always inflated; that matters not.[30] What is significant is the decline in attendance among Catholics, even if earlier and current figures are both inflated. More and more Catholics simply did not regard regular attendance at Mass as integral to their identity as Catholics; no longer did the sacramental cycle define Catholic life. Some of the drop in attendance is attributable to Catholics' moving to the center of American life and reflecting the behavior of those with similar socioeconomic standing, educational levels, and so on.

More revealing of changing attitudes within the Catholic ranks is another numerical decline accelerating after Vatican II. Fewer men entered seminaries to prepare for the priesthood, while at least through the mid-1970s the number of ordained priests voluntarily leaving the priesthood skyrocketed. In 1971, for example, nearly as many resigned the priesthood as were ordained.[31] Parallel was the exodus of women from religious orders and a monumental drop in the number of women taking vows.[32] In both cases, the Catholic lexicon speaks of a decline in religious vocations. Some predicted that the shortage of priests would lead to closing of churches. By the late 1970s the drop in the number of women religious added to the crisis facing parochial schools that already confronted dwindling numbers of students in many cases; nuns had long staffed schools at low cost because teaching was a religious calling.[33] The mystique attached to religious vocation and the sense that those so called held elevated spiritual status quickly evaporated.

Some argued that allowing married men to enter the priesthood would help.[34] Historians knew that clerical celibacy became entrenched in western Christendom only centuries after the time of Jesus and that even then it was often honored more in the breach than in practice. Many voices claimed that celibacy was an aberration, less a higher calling than an unnatural restriction of forces fundamental to being human. But the windows opened by Vatican II remained shut when it came to changing official teaching about clerical celibacy. Paul VI and John Paul II repeatedly reaffirmed traditional teaching. Those who favored having married priests sometimes concluded that only an acute shortage of priests that actually did result in large numbers of church closings would spur the hierarchy to modify its stance out of necessity, not out of theological conviction. By the 1980s and 1990s, when reports of priests having sexual affairs with women in their parishes or coercing adolescent boys into homosexual activity became common and many dioceses faced huge legal costs when such priests came to trial, critics of celibacy wondered anew whether ending a practice of enforced sexual repression might not be in order.[35]

In the midst of this turmoil are signs of a new pluralism in Catholic attitudes. At the beginning of the century there was little concern whether enough Catholic sons and daughters would take religious vows; the much higher Catholic birth rate then was a positive factor. Even more, a society just beginning to support scientific inquiry into human sexuality was hardly poised to question the wisdom of priestly celibacy. In a culture where ideas of sexual harassment had yet to take shape and an untouchable authority surrounded priests and nuns, accusations of misconduct would have issued in ridicule, not criminal trials. By century's end, however, individuals who espoused diametrically opposed positions on all of these issues insisted that their views were authentically Catholic. Pluralism prevailed.

The women's movement and its push for gender equality had a profound effect on the self-understanding of the thousands of women who left the cloistered life, and Catholic women began producing feminist-based theologies.[36] For centuries, entering a convent or taking the veil had been a noble calling, a venue for ministry and service in a church where only celibate men were priests. Until the mid-twentieth century, most Christian groups accepting women as clergy were those, like some Pentecostal bodies or independent Holiness congregations, that even mainline Protestants consigned to the periphery. As more Protestant bodies ordained women and as women assumed positions of professional leadership in society, more and more Catholic women—and not a few Catholic men—came to believe the church should end its ban on women priests. In some rural areas and small towns, with parishes too small to support a priest, nuns already served virtually as *de facto* pastors, performing most ministerial functions except for consecrating the bread and wine used in the Mass.[37] When other Christian bodies claiming a priesthood in direct historic apostolic succession, particularly the Episcopal Church in the United States and then the Church of England, authorized ordination of women, pressures on the Catholic church mounted. The popes serving the church in the last third of the century, however, were adamant about restricting the priesthood to men, although John Paul II attempted to assuage his severest critics by speaking glowingly on the contribution of women to the church and endorsing conferences on the role of women, but trying to assure they would not deviate from official church positions.

In the colonial period, New England Puritans responded to rapid change and perceived decline by producing the jeremiad, a genre of literature hailing past glory and lamenting present deterioration in a call for repentance and renewal. After Vatican II, American Catholics produced a large body of literature akin to the jeremiad. Much of it came from those who had severely criticized the church when it seemed trapped in anachronistic ways, but who were even more dismayed at the ethos that disappeared when old ways were jettisoned. Garry Wills, writer of popular history, published his *Bare, Ruined Choirs* in 1972, ostensibly to explore the agony within a church adjusting to shifts authorized by Vatican II, to condemn some changes, and to call for more radical reform in selected areas.[38] In retrospect, however, Wills's extended essay is a period piece as much as a careful analysis of the church, a lament for a church that always echoes the culture around it and is thus never completely free to be a pure community of faith. In a similar vein, best-selling author Mary McCarthy, known to ridicule some of the mores and style of pre–Vatican II Catholicism, penned the autobiographical *Memories of a Catholic Girlhood* that also appeared in 1972.[39] McCarthy remained acerbic in her assaults on ways she believed Catholic practice deleteriously affected her during her formative years. Yet she betrays more than a touch of nostalgia in looking back on a world that had vanished, a world where certainty, not the ambiguity of pluralism, surrounded the church.

In the swirl of controversy surrounding Vatican II came a separate movement endowing American Catholicism with yet another form of pluralism. In 1967, a charismatic renewal erupted at Duquesne University, spreading among Catholics elsewhere as they, too, received gifts of the Holy Spirit.[40] Like Protestant charismatics, Catholic Pentecostals usually experienced glossolalia or speaking in tongues as the primary spiritual gift, though some also experienced healing powers. But unlike most Protestant charismatics, Catholics filled with Pentecostal power retained a focus on the church's sacramental life. While Protestant and Catholic charismatics had more in common with each other than with noncharismatics, Catholic charismatics did not leave the church in large numbers to start Pentecostal parishes or joint Protestant charismatic groups. Rather, they often remained within their parishes in small groups as a leaven, much like other prayer and Bible study groups. Catholic charismatic conferences provided opportunities for networking; in time, the Catholic University of Steubenville (Ohio) became a clearinghouse center for Catholic charismatics around the nation.

A New Ethnic Pluralism

Not all the pluralism within American Catholic life at the end of the twentieth century resulted from Vatican II or social currents at work in the larger society. We have already noted an ethnic pluralism prevalent in the early part of the century. Parishes in those decades often catered to a membership drawn primarily from one ethnic cluster. As the Catholic population became more geographically dispersed and as Catholics joined other Americans in flocking to the suburbs after World War II, the ethnic neighborhoods sustaining those parishes dwindled in population, just as urban and inner-city neighborhoods that once sustained mainline Protestant congregations decreased in population or became home to persons of different religious persuasions. Catholics might return to former neighborhoods and parishes to celebrate festivals that reaffirmed ties not only to the church but to one's ancestral lands. Robert Orsi captured this ethos for what was Italian Harlem in his *The Madonna of 115th Street*.[41]

By the time of Vatican II, many of these ethnic parishes no longer had the financial base to support ministry to an ever-declining membership. On paper, it seemed easy to merge parishes in order to retain a viable Catholic presence in downtown areas no longer residential in nature. Repeatedly when such efforts were proposed, fierce opposition arose, often rooted in old ethnic differences and rivalries. The Catholic church might in theory be one church, but there was simply no way, for example, to merge a congregation once serving an Italian immigrant community with one that had served a Polish immigrant community without a struggle. Americanization had not eradicated ethnicity, particularly in an age when recovery of ethnic heritage became a cultural value as it did in the wake of the civil rights movement.

Disputes over old ethnic parishes for a time obscured a new ethnic pluralism that by the end of the twentieth century had the potential to change the face not only of American Catholicism but of the Roman Catholic Church globally. By century's end the Hispanic presence within American Catholicism could not be ignored. Millions of Mexican Americans had brought different ways of being Catholic to much of the Southwest, from Texas through New Mexico to southern California. Cuban immigrants had for nearly half a century been reshaping Catholicism in much of Florida and other areas. Puerto Ricans had given Catholicism a distinctive ethos not only in Spanish Harlem (which overlapped with some of the old Italian Harlem), but in cities across the nation. By the late 1990s, few cities lacked at least one parish that offered services, including celebration of the Mass, in Spanish, the vernacular of the people it served.

The Catholicism nurtured in Central and South America, which analysts predicted would be home to more than half of the world's Catholics by the end of the first quarter of the twenty-first century, had an eclectic dimension and an exuberant style that often left church leaders ill at ease. If Italian immigrants in the later nineteenth century fused much popular lore and practice, such as belief in the "evil eye," with popular Catholic practice, much of that remained in the arena of personal devotion and daily life; it was not necessarily brought into formal ritual celebrations of the church. The Catholicism cultivated among the peasants of Latin America did just that, often to the chagrin of bishops and other officials, who saw elements of magic, folklore, paganism, witchcraft, and other pre-Christian or non-Christian elements infecting authentic Catholic life. Yet that hodge-podge was authentic Catholic practice for millions of Hispanic Americans. Thomas Tweed has shown, for example, how the Cuban immigrant community in Miami, Florida, transplanted an idiosyncratic style of Catholic practice that enabled it to sustain a viable identity in the midst of an alien church and culture.[42] A new ethnic pluralism thus left its mark on American Catholicism, an ethnic pluralism destined to swell in importance as immigration, legal and illegal, from Latin America grew.

While some of that ethnic pluralism was reflected in personal piety, another dimension of personal devotion promoted a different kind of pluralism as the twentieth century proceeded. Much modern Catholic devotional practice, particularly that oriented to the Virgin Mary, took shape in the middle of the nineteenth century as Romanticism intertwined with popular Catholic practice. Some also stemmed from devotion to particular saints, often patrons of European lands of origin. Since much personal devotion took place in homes or as individuals sat in churches in quiet contemplation, it eluded control by church officials, even parish priests. Pluralism comes into play here in the highly idiosyncratic character of much personal devotion. Traditional exercises, such as saying the Rosary, lighting votive candles while praying, or using officially sanctioned books of prayers, devotional guides, or materials offered in popular magazines like *Ave Maria,* shape some personal devotion and are part of much popular practice. Yet, like other Americans, Catholics are exposed to mass culture in, for example, picking up some ideas to promote reflection from radio and then television. Some programs all along were oriented toward a Catholic audience. Bishop Fulton Sheen's early television endeavor, *Life*

Is Worth Living, proved popular among Protestants as well as Catholics, earning Sheen an Emmy award.[43]

After Vatican II, thousands of Catholic laity explored alternative avenues of popular spirituality, blending practices such as Transcendental Meditation with more traditional ones. Catholics often discovered that the disciplines of contemplation cultivated by traditional piety were not unlike those fostered by various Eastern religions or by faddish New Age gurus. It was easy to fuse them together to create a personal religiosity that gave meaning to life when so much of the trappings of popular Catholicism, like abstaining from eating meat on Fridays, had been discredited or abandoned. Robert Orsi has also shown convincingly how Catholic women, in their devotion to St. Jude, fashioned an idiosyncratic devotion that sanctified their particular experiences as women in a male-dominated religious heritage.[44] Add to this styles of devotion unique to various ethnic and immigrant clusters and it becomes patent that American Catholicism provides fertile ground for cultivating countless highly individualized styles of personal piety and devotion. Pluralism prevails.

Catholicism was not immune from other cultural forces that likewise had caused turmoil within Protestantism. Particularly after the publication of then-Jesuit John McNeill's *The Church and the Homosexual* in 1976, American Catholicism had to respond to the calls of gay and lesbian Catholics for change in the church's official position condemning homosexual activity.[45] Those promoting gay and lesbian concerns formed Dignity, an organization calling for the church to accept the full participation of homosexuals who insisted that they were faithful Catholics. The situation for American Catholicism was complicated as numerous court cases were brought against priests by men who claimed that they had been sexually abused in their adolescent years by gay priests. Officially, the church refused to alter its position. In many dioceses, bishops pressured churches to refuse to allow Dignity chapters to meet in their buildings. But the issue would not go away. In 1993, another Jesuit who has since left the Roman communion, Robert Goss, published *Jesus Acted Up*, with the telling subtitle, *A Gay and Lesbian Manifesto*.[46]

Clearly, the issue would not die. The church's refusal to retreat from its longstanding position received reinforcement in July 1999 when the Congregation for the Doctrine of the Faith in Rome permanently prohibited an American priest, Fr. Robert Nugent, and nun, Sr. Jeannine Grammick, from engaging in pastoral work with homosexuals. The two in the 1970s had started New Ways Ministry, which was basically supportive of gays and lesbians; the decree ordering them to desist claimed that they had not built that ministry on the complete teaching of the church regarding homosexuality, particularly in their omitting the view that homosexual activity was by nature sinful.[47] As with earlier internal conflict over artificial means of birth control, the widely divergent positions taken by faithful Catholics suggested a broader pluralism in belief and practice among the rank and file than church leaders would have welcomed.

American Catholicism entered the twentieth century confronting an unprecedented growth, thanks to immigration, even in the midst of a hostile Protestant culture. That immigrant experience left an enduring ethnic pluralism at the heart of American Catholicism, a pluralism that endures at century's end, though it has taken new aspects as immigrant patterns changed and descendants of earlier immigrants moved to the center of church and cultural life. Catholicism survived those challenges in part because it had a single bureaucratic structure, because it was one church unified around one body of teaching that encapsulated the truth for all ages and places. The Second Vatican Council paved the way for other dimensions of pluralism to shatter that image, as use of the vernacular replaced Latin in celebration of the Mass, parish structure shifted to allow a stronger voice for laity, and millions of Catholic men and women insisted on affirming a Catholic identity even when they jettisoned church teaching on matters such as divorce, remarriage, birth control, abortion, priestly celibacy, and women priests. The ethical pluralism that ran through American Catholicism at century's end left many commentators wondering whether church authority had shattered beyond repair, creating a church that was no longer one beyond sharing a common past. Like mainline Protestantism, by the end of the twentieth century, American Catholicism had taken on many new faces.

CHAPTER 4

The Paradox of Pluralism:
The Jewish Experience

Judaism, America's "third faith," found in the United States fertile ground for growth and development. In the twentieth century, the United States boasted one of the largest Jewish populations of any nation. By 1970, more than 5.75 million Jews called the United States home; a century earlier, the figure was under a quarter of a million.[1] Like Catholicism, American Judaism experienced spectacular growth because of the massive immigration between 1880 and World War I. As with the Catholic experience, that immigration nurtured a pluralism within American Judaism previously unknown, and, as the twentieth century progressed, new dimensions of pluralism came to Jewish life in the United States. Nevertheless, distinctive elements set the Jewish story apart from mainstream Protestant or American Catholic parallels.

Much of that distinctiveness stems from the social location of Judaism in Europe over the centuries. At least since the early Middle Ages, Jews had been cast to the margins of public life in much of Europe. Anti-Semitism is thus central to European religious history.[2] For example, just as the Age of Discovery sparked interest in the New World, Jews refusing to convert to Christianity were expelled from the Iberian peninsula; some made their way to the first European settlements in the Americas. As well, many European powers restricted Jewish participation in political life, prohibited Jews from attending the developing schools and universities, banned Jews from practicing certain vocations outside the Jewish community, and engaged in other forms of recrimination simply on the basis of religious identity. Frequent pogroms or other efforts to eliminate the Jewish presence forced Jews to migrate from place to place. Yet always in the background was a vision of a promised land, often linked to ancient Palestine but sometimes a symbol of liberation from all forms of latter-day bondage.

In Europe, the first inklings of a new day for Jews came around the time of the French Revolution and the heyday of the Age of Reason. The revolution's assault on established religion and reason's rejection of prejudice (along with a concomitant espousal of toleration) undermined efforts to hinder Jewish practice and discriminate against Jews simply because they were Jews. But the further one got from areas under Enlightenment influence, the less likely Jewish fortunes were to improve. Perceptions of the United States as a bastion of personal freedom resonated within Jewish communities, particularly as conditions became more hostile towards Jews in the last decades of the nineteenth century in much of central and eastern Europe.

By then, the earliest expressions of pluralism within American Judaism, the division into Sephardic and Ashkenazic communities, had faded.[3] In the first half of the nineteenth century, the bulk of American Jews were of German ancestry, and exposure to German Enlightenment culture and the American ethos of religious freedom prompted many Jews to reexamine their religious heritage. For example, the American Jewish population became so widely dispersed geographically that few communities could sustain all the apparatus needed to remain strictly observant. The most obvious area was that of diet; in practical terms, a small population could not support a kosher butcher. Nor did Jews want to stand out because of their dietary practice. Most knew the history of persecution in Europe and welcomed an environment where they could "fit in" even at the risk of abandoning much that seemed basic to Jewish life; to stand out was to attract attention that in turn might spur anti-Semitic responses from the larger culture. Some synagogues moved away from services in Hebrew since only a handful knew or understood the language; some pondered whether to abandon Sabbath observance for services on Sunday, like the Christian majority around them. Behind these concerns lurked questions about what was integral to Jewish belief and practice. To abandon a practice peripheral to Jewish faith was one matter, but to cast aside something central to Jewish life and ways of understanding was another, more serious issue. Here is one dimension of the paradox inherent in the American setting for Judaism. The environment that theoretically allowed for free practice and observance brought questions about precisely what practice and observance was basic to Judaism.

Wrestling with all these issues while accommodating to the prevailing culture spurred a fascination with Reform Judaism among American Jews, with early leadership provided by the dynamic Isaac M. Wise.[4] Reform had roots in Germany, but came to dominate organized Jewish life in the United States by the early 1880s, just as immigration began to change the face of American Judaism altogether. The famous Pittsburgh Platform of 1885 summarized Reform principles, and the organization of the Central Conference of American Rabbis in 1889 gave some coherence to Reform efforts. Even so, Judaism was fundamentally different from organized expressions of Christianity in lacking an authoritative hierarchy that could pressure, if not coerce, adherents to accept a particular mode of belief or practice. Each synagogue was basically independent; and even associations of rabbis or conferences that linked synagogues together, like the Central Conference of American Rabbis or the (Reform) Union of American Hebrew Congregations, had only advisory power. This local autonomy allowed small Jewish populations to bring persons of different viewpoints into one synagogue and thus develop viable institutions in many communities. It also left American Judaism without a bureaucracy to oversee dealing with the tremendous influx of Jews from central and eastern Europe after the 1880s. Between 1882 and 1924, when restrictions on immigration went into effect, some 2.3 million Jews came to the United States from Russia alone, swelling the nation's Jewish population.[5] As well, Jews whose American roots stretched back a few generations had accommodated to American ways, encouraged by Reform elements. Many leading Jewish families had carved a place for themselves in the nation's mercantile and banking industries, both of which rapidly gained importance after the Civil War.[6] In a word, much of the American Jewish community belonged to the emerging urban middle or upper middle class when central, southern, and eastern European immigrants began arriving by the thousands.

Immigration Transforms Judaism

This immigration brought new forms of pluralism to American Judaism, rather different forms of pluralism than the same wave of immigration brought to Catholicism. Several dimensions of that pluralism had repercussions still echoing in American Jewish life at the end of the twentieth century. First, alongside Reform Judaism, Orthodox and what became known as Conservative Judaism also flourished. This tripartite division gave American Judaism a pluralistic cast then pretty much unknown in Judaism elsewhere. In time other subgroups, ranging from ultraorthodox Hasidic Jews to very liberal Reconstructionist Jews, would enrich that pluralism.[7] Here is another dimension of paradox. The marginalized position in which Jews found themselves in Europe fostered tight bonds within individual communities. When not forced to the periphery, those bonds loosened, and Jews became diverse rather than united.

Immigrants wishing to adhere to traditional practice, to remain observant Jews in a strict sense, found the more easygoing atmosphere dominated by Reform dangerous. To the Orthodox, Reform Jews abandoned all that was central to being Jewish in order to assimilate into the larger culture. Many who agreed that Reform had sacrificed too many essentials found Orthodoxy aloof and removed from society. It seemed as if Reform Jews had transformed the synagogue into a Jewish version of a Christian church, using English as the language of worship and expecting the rabbi to preach a sermon like a Protestant minister. But strict Orthodox practice seemed anachronistic, perpetuating much that had little relevance to the modern world. Nonetheless, Orthodox Jews followed prevailing patterns to form agencies that would provide networks of communication and association. Among the earliest were the Union of Orthodox Jewish Congregations (1898) and the Union of Orthodox Rabbis (1912). That many Orthodox were of immigrant stock for whom English was an alien language and American ways different comes to the fore as late as 1935 when English-speaking Orthodox rabbis formed their own Rabbinical Council of America.

In many ways, Conservative Judaism represents an effort to mediate between the perceived extremes of Orthodox and Reform Judaism.[8] Like Reform Jews, Conservative Jews also pondered the essentials of Judaism and how best to observe basic practices in the American environment. For example, Conservative Jews might adhere to the requirements of a kosher diet within their own homes, seeing dietary regulations as a matter of religious discipline or obligation, but not essential. Hence they might dine in restaurants or homes of non-Jewish friends where food was not prepared following religious requirements.[9] Some Conservative Jews would always decline to eat foods forbidden by Torah, but others would bend the rules outside their own homes. At service, Conservative Jews might expect a homily in English from the rabbi and assume that rabbis would perform pastoral functions akin to those of Protestant clergy, but some prayers would be recited in Hebrew and Torah readings would be done in Hebrew. In some communities, opting for the Conservative approach was necessary for survival as neither the Orthodox nor Reform had the numerical strength to assure survival.

The Conservative approach became a compromise that brought two struggling communities together for the greater good of Jewish survival. By the end of the 1920s, Conservative Judaism was displacing Reform as the dominant strand in the American Jewish mosaic, helped by the reorganization of the Jewish Theological Seminary in New York City in 1902 to train rabbis in the Conservative style. The rising influence of the Jewish Theological Seminary after 1902 stemmed in part from the powerful leadership and reflective theological voice of Solomon Schechter, who served as president of the school from 1902 until his death in 1915. Schechter was also prominent in establishing the (Conservative) United Synagogues of America in 1913. Conservative rabbis felt a greater need for some organization of their own after Schechter, the main symbol of Conservative Judaism, died. Consequently in 1919 the Rabbinical Assembly of America was formed. That Conservative ways resonated with many who wanted to be both Jewish and American receives testimony in Conservative Judaism's steady growth. By 1960, estimates were that half of all American Jews identified themselves as Conservative.[10]

For Jews, confinement to the ghetto or *stetl* or forced movement from place to place had marked life in Europe for generations, as had threats of extinction through persecution or pogroms. The theoretical lack of any connection between religious identification and access to the public sphere in the United States, from gaining an education through the public schools to participating actively in the political process, created a new ethos. Then, too, the atmosphere of religious freedom the United States provided, thanks to the First Amendment, lured many Jews away from traditional religious life. In some ways, the contours of religious practice within Judaism facilitated this process. In Christianity, corporate worship or "going to church" was basic to religious life. For Judaism, the heart of religious practice came in the home, the private sphere, where men might recite daily prayers and wives signal the Sabbath's arrival by lighting the ritual candles. There were religious institutions, like synagogues, but Judaism never made corporate expression as central as Christianity.

Consequently, during the course of the twentieth century, thousands of American Jews became "secular" Jews, "nonobservant" Jews, or "nonpracticing" Jews—terms denoting those who retained some sense of Jewish identity, but who abandoned even in private virtually all the distinctive religious elements that once formed that identity. To have a religious label that had no religious content set American Judaism apart, infusing it with an internal pluralism of its own.

Two rather different understandings of Judaism that move in this direction are the Reconstructionism advocated by Mordecai M. Kaplan (1881–1983) and the secularism advanced by Horace M. Kallen (1882–1974). Kaplan, born and raised an Orthodox Jew, came to see Judaism as a civilization, the title he gave to one of his better-known books.[11] Religious practice, as in Orthodox observance, was marginal, but Judaism as a source for values that sustained society was central. In a nutshell, Kaplan made ethics, not even belief in God, the defining criterion for meaning in life and affirming a Jewish identity. Always suspect by the Orthodox, whose Union of Orthodox Rabbis condemned him in 1945, Kaplan established several organizations to promote his vision of a Judaism relevant to the times: the Jewish Center (New York City) in 1916, Society for the Advancement of Judaism (1922), and finally the Jewish Reconstructionist Foundation (1935). For many years, Kaplan saw these not as leading to yet another Jewish "denomination" since he believed his perspective could revitalize all Judaism. But by 1954 he recognized that his approach represented an understanding of Judaism different from Conservative, Orthodox, and Reform, and he helped organize the Federation of Reconstructionist Congregations, which set up the Reconstructionist Rabbinical College just over a decade later.

Horace Kallen pushed even further the move away from supernaturalism inherent in Reconstructionism.[12] A rabbi's son, one-time faculty member at Princeton (English) and Harvard (philosophy), and a founder of the New School for Social Research, Kallen was personally drawn to a cultural humanism grounded in science for its intellectual base and democracy for its practical dimension. He recognized that some individuals might espouse traditional religious beliefs, such as life after death, but he also knew there were many alternative systems beckoning for support. Hence Kallen believed that one aspect of Judaism's "adjustment to modernity," as he put it in the subtitle of a 1932 book, was to affirm a religious and cultural pluralism. Kallen did not obscure the history of Judaism that entailed considerable persecution. Here his espousal of democracy propelled him to become a voice for minority rights. Consequently he worked as well with outfits like the American Jewish Congress to support Zionist efforts to establish a Jewish homeland in Palestine and secure civil rights for Jews everywhere. But Kallen also illustrates the paradox characteristic of Jewish life. In the American context, Judaism could flourish as one ethnic identity among many; it did not even have to maintain overt religious trappings.

As well, Judaism also had a cultural dimension, *yiddishkeit*, that added to the pluralism marking its development in the United States in the twentieth century.[13]

That, too, had origins in Europe. Yiddish was first a language, using the Hebrew alphabet but combining Hebrew, German, Aramaic, Italian, and French elements, that began to develop in the tenth century and that in time added Slavic components as Jews from the fourteenth century on migrated from Germany through Poland into Russia and elsewhere. As always, language became a cohesive force among the Jewish communities, but decades of forced migration also brought amalgamation of traditional Jewish ways with German and then local cultural expressions that spawned a unique cultural style. For example, *kasrut* or "keeping kosher" includes what foods one eats and how one prepares them; many of the particular dishes that became associated with Jewish culture in the United States were adaptations of local and regional cuisine from the many places Jews migrated in the long trek eastward in Europe.

In the United States, Yiddish came to denote the distinctive cultural expressions marking Jewish immigrant life in the opening decades of the twentieth century—from language to literature to popular press to theater to styles of clothing. Popular writers such as *Jewish Daily Forward* editor Abraham Cahan early in the century and Isaac Bashevis Singer later echoed the culture of *yiddishkeit*, and vaudeville owed much of its beginnings to performers who came from a Yiddish cultural background. Even after mid-century, in theatrical presentations such as *Fiddler on the Roof,* which debuted on Broadway in 1964 with its exposition of Hasidic life in the *stetl*, the culture of *yiddishkeit* continued to influence the larger society. Of course, the language itself absorbed English words and phrases as Yiddish-speaking Jews settled in the United States; some Yiddish words and phrases made their way into English usage.

The culture of *yiddishkeit* functioned differently than had Latin among American Catholics until Vatican II mandated use of the vernacular. For Catholics, Latin was a religious language used only in the formal liturgical celebrations of worship; it never carried all the trappings of a popular culture with roots in central and eastern Europe that Yiddish did for American Jews. Yiddish bestowed an ethnic identity on Judaism as it developed in the United States, but not one associated necessarily with one particular place of origin. Once more, paradox prevails. If the religion of Judaism fed into a culture of *yiddishkeit*, that culture soon no longer needed the religion itself in order to endure; it had taken on an ethnic cast.

The Image of Israel

The 1920s brought two more dimensions of pluralism within American Judaism into focus. One was primarily positive, although it caused considerable dissension in Jewish circles then and for decades to come, namely Zionism, or the call to establish a Jewish state in the Middle East. The other was an insidious anti-Semitism that reared its head alongside the anti-Catholic sentiment crystallizing in the religious prejudice expressed in the 1928 presidential campaign.

Modern Zionism became a force within Judaism and western political life with the energetic crusades of Theodor Herzl in the 1880s.[14] The era of World War I gave renewed life to Zionism. Prior to the war, Palestine, the geographic area at the eastern end of the Mediterranean regarded by Jews as the land promised in the covenant between Yahweh and Israel, was part of the Ottoman Empire, an Islamic entity leery of Jewish political aspirations. After the Ottoman defeat in the war, the Treaty of Versailles transferred oversight of much of the Middle East, including Palestine, to Great Britain as protectorates. Jews eager again to have the "promised land" under Jewish rule believed they could pressure Britain to declare Israel's independence; such was the essence of the Balfour Declaration of 1917. Zionism thus received renewed vigor, although not without opposition. The American Jewish Congress, organized in 1922, coordinated much of the pro-Israel activity among those whose heritage stretched back to eastern Europe, where pogroms were most common. Some opposition came from the most orthodox Jews, particularly Hasidic communities, who believed that only God's intervention in human history through the Messiah would restore Palestine to the Jews. Any human endeavor to regain the Promised Land usurped the divine prerogative. Other obstacles came with the Great Depression and then World War II. Both drained resources from the Zionist cause, which nevertheless continued to gain ground.

When the atrocities of the Holocaust became evident, calls to establish a Jewish state came even from some who were reluctant to endorse Zionism earlier, although the American Council for Judaism continued to coordinate opposition. Most saw a Jewish state as insurance against a Hitler-like plan to exterminate the Jews. The nation of Israel thus carried a symbolic significance well beyond its becoming an independent entity in 1948.[15] It became a beacon for Jewish identity throughout the world. American Jews overwhelmingly supported the creation of Israel as a national state and for decades represented a potent political lobby urging the government to maintain a staunchly pro-Israel foreign policy. That policy became all the more important as Arabs and Palestinians launched military struggle after military struggle to weaken, if not topple, the nation of Israel.

The image of Israel, however, also illuminates several strands of pluralism integral to American Jewish life in the twentieth century. Some Jews were hesitant to give too overt support to Zionism earlier in the century lest the Protestant majority equate loyalty to a Jewish state with the sort of allegiance to the Pope mistakenly attributed to Catholics. In other words, Jews did not want support for a Jewish state to fuel anti-Semitism the way presumed political loyalty to the Pope fed into anti-Catholicism.

The link to Israel was always more complex. Jewish immigrants often lacked the emotional ties to an ancestral homeland that marked immigrant life among Catholic communities, for example. Pushed to the margins of society by repressive policies and often having to relocate unwillingly to escape persecution, if not extermination, many Jews found it difficult, if not impossible, to celebrate ties to the nations where they resided prior to coming to the United States. For millions, Yiddish culture replaced the culture of nation of origin. As well, since Israel did not exist as a political entity until 1948, there could hardly be a devotion to Israel that competed with or undermined an American patriotism. Then, too, Protestant fundamentalists, while often linked to anti-Catholic endeavors, were ambivalent about the image of Israel. For some Protestant biblical literalists, the restoration of a Jewish state was a necessary precondition for the Second Coming of Christ. Hence some militant Protestants became allies of Zionists and then adamant supporters of a pro-Israel foreign policy.

But the role of Israel in American Jewish life reveals a deeper pluralism and illustrates afresh the paradox that surrounds Jewish identity in the United States. Jews who had abandoned observance of Torah and saw themselves as nonreligious supported Israel and Jewish causes internationally, buttressed by indignation at the abomination of the Holocaust. The result was what Jacob Neusner has called "checkbook Judaism," or the willingness to give financial support for Jewish enterprises, but without engaging in either private or personal religious observance.[16] Neusner saw this expression of a Jewish identity as inadequate, for to him some religious commitment remained essential to authentic Jewish identity. For increasing numbers of American Jews, the explicitly religious dimension was unnecessary. Pluralism took on more complexity as a result, for by the end of the century there was little consensus as to what kind of connection one needed to the Jewish religious tradition in order to call oneself a Jew—or whether any connection was needed. And that was a paradox indeed.

As well, by the end of the twentieth century there was a deepening pluralism within Jewish circles over precisely how best to support Israel as a nation and whether unquestioning support was still in order. Several political and religious phenomena outside the United States helped propel that pluralism. Israel's decisive military victories over Arab Muslim opponents, especially in 1967 and 1970, as well as global support for maintaining a modicum of political stability in the Middle East to assure access to its rich oil supplies, bred a sense of security over Israel's future. Then, too, by the 1990s, many Americans, including significant numbers of Jews, concluded that Israel itself exacerbated political turmoil in the region, particularly in its treatment of and policies toward Palestinians who legitimately claimed a heritage of many generations living within Israel's national borders.[17] Israel's mistreatment of Palestinians mirrored the repression that Jews themselves had experienced throughout European history.

At the same time, the rise in Israel of a strident, ultra-orthodox party with considerable political clout generated a range of responses revealing how diverse were American Jews' views of Israel.[18] On the one hand, some grudgingly recognized that the Orthodox maintained the most thoroughgoing observance of Jewish tradition and Torah. But by the end of the twentieth century, few American Jews believed that rigid orthodoxy should be forced on all. The American ideology of religious toleration meant that many Jews accepted a pluralism in how individuals defined themselves as Jews and saw that as appropriate for Israel as well. Especially among more secularized American Jews, those given to Neusner's "checkbook Judaism," there was little support for Israeli government policy that reflected only the most extreme Orthodox fundamentalist perspective. Pluralism prevailed, and paradox prevailed, for the multifaceted Jewish community in the nation that had been most vocal in support of the nation-state of Israel was now becoming critical of Israel.

An Anti-Semitic Cultural Context

Along with the resurgence of Zionism in the 1920s came anti-Semitism.[19] Flourishing in the midst of a hostile culture was a challenge all too familiar to Jewish immigrants, given their experience over the centuries in Europe. Jewish Americans of German stock, the largest group prior to the 1880s, had assimilated into the larger culture and were ambivalent about how to respond to Jewish immigrants whose ways seemed unsettling to them. They nevertheless established numerous agencies and institutions to assist immigrants in adapting to American society. In this regard, they mirrored the immigrant experience more generally, though without the centralized structures that American Catholics had to assist them in meeting the needs of an immigrant constituency. In particular, Jewish Americans lent their support to health care agencies, with some of the leading hospitals in the nation's urban areas at the end of the twentieth century tracing their founding to Jewish philanthropic activity.[20] So many social welfare organizations emerged from the immigrant years that by mid-century there was a Council of Jewish Federations and Welfare Funds to coordinate support.

Like their Catholic counterparts, Jewish immigrants from southern and eastern Europe entered the industrial workforce and endorsed the nascent labor movement's efforts to improve the workers' situation, especially in the garment industry. Some of the leading labor organizers in the early years of union activity, such as Samuel Gompers, were persons with a Jewish identity. Some, like Emma Goldman, merged the labor struggle with radical politics.[21] Given the different nature of links between labor and politics in Europe, where many believed only a radical political posture—one perhaps informed by socialist or Communist ideology—could undo centuries of abuse, and given the ways many European nations had once prohibited Jews from active engagement in the political process, Jewish immigrants naturally seized the greater liberty in the United States to take on such involvement. As fascination with socialism grew generally in the United States in the years just before entry into World War I, so, too, American Jewish socialism mushroomed. Organizations like the Jewish Socialist Farband and the Jewish Socialist Federation mobilized political support, although the federation's dalliance with communism brought criticism, especially during the Red Scare of the 1920s. All such endeavors stirred anti-Semitism. Prejudice, buttressed by vested interest in preserving the status quo, propelled many Protestant business and industrial magnates to equate Jewish identity with potential treason. Strikes organized by unions, often quashed by brutal force, got construed as dangerous efforts, presumably led by Jewish socialists and Communists, to destroy the American way of life. While there was a radical political dimension to some union activity, little of it was designed to overthrow the government.

In the political sphere, Jewish support invigorated socialist endeavors, especially in New York City. Support for candidates was mobilized, and some, like Morris Hillquit, ran for office. Nevertheless, the animosities fostered by decades of labor-management conflict and Jewish intrigue with socialism in politics early in the century fed undercurrents of anti-Semitism. As early as 1906, from Reform circles came the American Jewish Committee, founded in part to promote better relations between Jews and non-Jews, but also to combat anti-Semitism both in the United States and especially in Russia.

The most insidious anti-Semitism came in the 1920s, but had immediate roots in the Leo Frank case in Georgia in 1914. Frank, owner of a pencil manufacturing company, was accused of murdering a female employee. Although evidence was lacking, Frank was found guilty. After the governor reduced the sentence from hanging to life imprisonment, not only did Christian citizens boycott Jewish businesses, but they seized Frank from prison and lynched him. Had not World War I erupted, that episode might have triggered a more widespread anti-Semitism, such as emerged right after the war. That anti-Semitism resulted in part as a reaction to the success and achievement of Jewish Americans who readily availed themselves of opportunities theoretically open to all in the United States, but from which they had historically been excluded or restricted in Europe. Catholics developed a powerful network of parochial schools to help Americanize an immigrant constituency while nurturing them in their faith; Jewish Americans flocked to the public schools, despite their Protestant character. More significant, Jewish Americans took advantage of state-supported colleges and universities to prepare for professional careers, in many cases careers that had been closed to Jews or laden with restrictions in Europe. Jewish students excelled in academic endeavors and as a group moved extraordinarily quickly from the urban slum and ghetto, from the underpaid laboring class, from the margins of society to the middle and upper socioeconomic groupings. By 1955, more than twice the percentage of Jewish heads of households held college degrees as their white Protestant counterparts and more than three times the percentage as their Roman Catholic counterparts.[22]

As Jewish Americans identified more with the middle and upper classes, they also began to look to the leading private colleges and universities, rather than just state-supported ones, for education, to join clubs and fraternal societies like other professionals, and to take advantage of leisure pursuits offered by resorts and other vacation establishments. In many cases, in the 1920s Jews found their doors closed, with quotas limiting the number of Jewish students admitted to entering classes at Ivy League universities, policies limiting membership in selected societies and clubs to "Christians only," resorts refusing Jewish guests, and homeowners frequently covenanting together to refuse to sell their property to Jewish buyers.[23] Catholic immigrants, particularly the Irish a century earlier, had confronted similar phenomena, but not on the same scale.

In the midst of the 1920s, anti-Semitism received fresh vigor with the republication of *The Protocols of the Elders of Zion*, backed by automobile industrialist Henry Ford. That document, spurious throughout, purported to set out plans for Jewish domination of global political and economic life.[24] The Ford-controlled newspaper, the *Dearborn Independent*, separately printed and distributed inflammatory articles presumably exposing the depth of "Jewish influence" in the nation.[25] Some attributed the stock market crash and the coming of the Great Depression to sinister Jewish activity; the most rabid anti-Semitic voices echoed Hitler and the Nazi movement in their characterization of Jewish persons and unfounded claims of Jewish conspiracies to control international banking and finance, among others. Catholic radio priest Charles Coughlin moved in this direction before church authorities silenced him.[26]

Not until after World War II did strident anti-Semitism abate. Awareness of the extremes of Nazi policy and the devastation of the Holocaust weakened anti-Semitism in some circles. Military service and Jewish support for the Allied cause also contributed to anti-Semitism's decline, as was the case with anti-Catholic sentiment. But by the late 1940s, Jewish Americans had responded by developing a host of social institutions parallel to those from which they were excluded. Cities and towns with a large enough Jewish population to support them had Jewish "community centers" that offered recreational and leisure-time programs.[27] Jewish schools and universities, including institutions like Brandeis University that held great distinction at the close of the twentieth century, offered private alternatives to the exclusionary Ivy League and schools of that ilk. Resorts catering to a Jewish clientele abounded, particularly in New York's Catskill Mountains, that became noted for opulent Jewish-owned establishments such as Grossinger's and the Concord.[28]

All these bring the pluralism and the paradox within Jewish identity into focus. In many locales, for example, Jewish community centers received support not only from Orthodox, Conservative, and Reform Jews, but from those who abandoned all pretense of religious observance. Catskills resorts advertised whether they offered kosher food in their dining rooms in order to attract Jewish guests whose religiosity spanned the spectrum. By the 1950s, legal challenges to quotas had generally succeeded in dismantling them, although some private organizations (ranging from country clubs to college fraternities) still had unofficial quotas or exclusionary policies. Housing covenants began to break down in the movement to the suburbs that brought Americans of diverse religious and ethnic backgrounds together, although some neighborhoods attempted to maintain them. This blending of people together evident in demographics of the post–World War II years gave credence to Will Herberg's claim that Jewish, Catholic, and Protestant labels were functionally equivalent in marking one as a trustworthy citizen.[29] Herberg's own life substantiates that claim; he was for several years a labor organizer thought to entertain radical political views who became a professor of the sociology of religion at a mainline Methodist theological school. But anti-Semitism never entirely disappeared, and the Anti-Defamation League of B'nai B'rith, founded in 1913, at century's end still monitored anti-Semitic activity and still used all legal means to end overt anti-Semitism.[30]

Public Issues Bring Pluralism

The religious climate of the second half of the twentieth century by no means obliterated the various kinds of pluralism characterizing Jewish life in the United States. We have already noted the pluralism that came in attitudes towards the nation of Israel and the concern over conflicts between Palestinians and Jews in Israel itself. At the same time, the social currents that challenged Protestant and Catholic life, spurring new forms of pluralism in both, also had an impact on American Jewish life. For example, the civil rights movement, the women's movement, and social controversy over the status of homosexuals in the United States compounded expressions of pluralism among American Jews.

Until the last quarter of the twentieth century, American Jews had traditionally aligned themselves with the Democratic Party in national politics and stood in the vanguard of efforts to secure the civil rights of African Americans. With a history of forced exclusion from the larger society, Jewish Americans were natural allies in the struggle to assure full civil rights for African Americans. Yet in the late 1960s and the 1970s, Jewish attitudes took a variety of shapes.[31] Some Jewish Americans remained staunch advocates for the civil rights movement; others sounded almost racist, reacting in part to verbal attacks on Jewish-American business people by some civil rights leaders who accused them of racial discrimination in their business practices. Many of the most economically successful Jewish Americans began to rethink their allegiance to the Democratic Party, concluding that the economic policies advocated by Republicans better promoted and protected their financial interests.[32] Ronald Reagan became the first Republican candidate for the presidency to receive a majority of the Jewish vote. Clearly a political pluralism had come to American Judaism.

When feminists, including some with Jewish backgrounds such as Gloria Steinem and Bella Abzug, began to question male dominance of American public and professional life, no strand of the Jewish tradition was left untouched.[33] Jewish women in the United States had rather quietly for decades carved out a place of increasing importance in virtually all strands of the tradition. In the broad revitalization that came to American Judaism in the late nineteenth and early twentieth centuries came the birth of the sisterhood movement, a phenomenon then unknown in Jewish circles elsewhere.[34] By the last third of the twentieth century, Jewish women were less inclined to be content on the margins.

But if anything, Judaism was more intrinsically male-focused than Roman Catholicism with its insistence on an exclusively male priesthood. Orthodox Jewish men, for example, daily offer thanksgiving to God that they were not created women. Historically, the rabbinate was as closed to women as was the Catholic priesthood.

As with other issues that cut to the heart of centuries-old tradition, Jews had to decide what in terms of gender was essential to Judaism and what was peripheral and therefore open to modification. Those of Orthodox persuasion rejected outright any calls for change; Reform Jews were most open. Reform saw its first woman rabbi, Sally Priesand, ordained in 1972. Conservative Jews ordained women rabbis beginning in 1986, but not without much soul-searching and a recognition that because synagogues contracted individually with rabbis, not all Conservative ones would welcome women as spiritual leaders.[35]

The *bar mitzvah*, a Jewish boy's rite of passage into manhood and thus into the religious elite of the synagogue, became adapted outside Orthodox circles as a cognate rite for girls, a *bas mitzvah*.[36] The first documented *bas mitzvah* occurred in 1922 for Judith Kaplan, daughter of Reconstructionist founder Mordecai Kaplan. Divisions over the role and status of women, however, continued to sustain pluralism, not just because the Orthodox seemed hopelessly patriarchal, but because Jewish women were rethinking their own roles within the complex religious and cultural heritage that informed American Judaism.

Similar issues emerged within Judaism over matters concerning homosexual persons. For American Jews, the question of having gay rabbis focused on only one dimension of the dilemma. Judaism's patriarchal history meshed with a tribal consciousness that called for the creation of a people; biologically, peoplehood required reproduction. Since the popular mind assumed that gay persons were disinclined to engage in sexual acts that would lead to the perpetuation of the people, Judaism had a different predicament than Christianity.[37] Christians, both Protestant and Catholic, eager to condemn homosexuality or afraid of what accepting homosexual persons might mean, found in the Jewish Levitical code a basis for classifying homosexual acts as sins. So, too, did Jews. Nonetheless, gay American Jews in the last third of the twentieth century refused to be consigned to the margins. Another face of pluralism came into view as gay and lesbian Jews formed their own synagogues.[38] Most were identified with Reform, which was more open than Conservative Judaism to affirming homosexuals. Orthodox Jews, with a more literal understanding of Torah and tradition and a hesitancy to alter that tradition, had the greatest challenge when confronted by homosexuals who proudly affirmed a Jewish religious identity.

The Multifaceted Interplay of Judaism and Protestantism

American Judaism also had to deal with a more aggressive evangelical Protestantism in the closing decades of the century.[39] Evangelical Protestants were not anti-Semitic in the traditional sense, but had an ambivalent relationship to Judaism as a religious heritage. On the one hand, because of their penchant for a literal interpretation of biblical texts, evangelical Protestants acknowledged Jews as God's chosen people. Therefore they could not easily cast Jews aside or promote anti-Semitic activity. On the other hand, because evangelicals proclaimed that only those who affirmed Jesus as the Christ would attain salvation and because they saw their brand of Christianity as the logical fulfillment of Jewish expectation, they prosely-tized among Jews. Some persons of Jewish ancestry moved into the Christian orbit through groups such as "Jews for Jesus." Other evangelical societies regularly promoted missionary activity among Jews.[40]

Enriching the paradoxical pluralism and reflecting a different intertwining of Judaism and Christianity in the United States is the growth of Messianic Judaism in the closing decades of the century.[41] Messianic Jews, scattered among more than 125 congregations by the early 1990s, regarded themselves as Jews, but Jews who acknowledge Jesus (*Yshua*) as the Messiah. Drawing persons who previously may have been Jewish or Christian, Messianic Judaism adhered to traditional Jewish observance, including the dietary laws, but added a layer of meaning. All traditional practice was linked not only to the early history of the Hebrew people, but to the figure of Jesus and early Christian experience. Messianic Jews believed they were restoring the style of earliest New Testament Christianity that retained some Jewish practice or what New Testament scholars label "Jewish Christianity." The hybrid nature of Messianic Judaism meant that most observant Jews saw Messianic Jews as more Christian than Jewish, while the self-affirmation of most Messianic Jews as Jews, not Christians, meant that most Christians, particularly evangelicals, placed them outside the Christian orbit. Another paradox thus colors Jewish pluralism.

Over the last quarter of the twentieth century, other strains of pluralism came to American Judaism as individuals and groups sought to be faithful to Jewish practice and observance in an industrial, technological culture, but without connecting observance to Christian thinking as did Messianic Jews. In the 1970s, for example, when interest in communitarian religious experiments gained renewed plausibility, several Jewish communes sprang up in the nation's larger cities, bringing together Jewish men and women not in traditional households revolving around a nuclear family, but in some sort of communal arrangement where traditional Jewish life could be celebrated.[42] This approach represented an obvious reshaping of features of the tradition. Communitarians could claim they were imitating the tribal character of early Jewish life, but many outside the groups were apprehensive of communal living that brought unmarried men and women together in such sustained and intimate ways.

Jewish women, responsible for preparing the home for religious observance, began to rethink how to do so when technology had altered family life and fewer women were full-time homemakers. There appeared new guidebooks for Jewish women addressing such fundamental questions as how to use a dishwasher properly to maintain a kosher kitchen.[43]

There was resurgent interest among younger Jews in recapturing Orthodox ways. In one later twentieth-century celebrated episode, some Orthodox undergraduates at Yale University refused to comply with the university's requirement that all first-year students live in campus housing. They argued that dormitory-like living arrangements contaminated their religious observance for they would be forced into close contact with persons whose value structures, ethical codes, and behavior (especially when it came to intimate contact between men and women) countered what Torah and Jewish tradition enjoined.[44]

American Judaism's experience with pluralism presents many paradoxes. Prior to the major waves of immigration that began around 1880, Jewish pluralism echoed primarily the Sephardic or Ashkenazic approaches to religious life with deep roots in different regions of Europe. Numerically small, American Judaism nevertheless exhibited another kind of pluralism as Reform Judaism came to the fore with its reshaping of much Jewish observance and practice. The immigration from central and eastern Europe that increased the American Jewish population more than tenfold in forty years enhanced that pluralism as three major families, Orthodox, Conservative, and Reform, emerged in the American context. At the same time, another face of a paradoxical pluralism came when some Jews abandoned a Jewish religious identity, but affirmed a Jewish cultural or ethnic identity. Having a secular expression set Judaism apart from other religious traditions in the United States. Yet even for Jewish Americans who continued some religious observance, there was an ethnic or cultural dimension, *yiddishkeit*, tied to Judaism itself as much as to the geographic nation of origin. Sifting through what was ethnic, what was cultural, and what was religious gave American Judaism a different experience of pluralism than either mainstream Protestantism or Catholicism experienced.

At the same time, the history of anti-Semitism in Europe and anti-Semitic elements in American society generated other kinds of pluralism as American Jews sought to ensure that they had access to all the opportunities life in the United States offered. Yet another face of pluralism emerged in the convoluted relationships American Jews had with Zionism and with Israel after it came into existence in 1948. How was support for Israel to be expressed? Did it mean Jews were likely to be subject to accusations that they were not trustworthy citizens of the United States if they openly supported the nation of Israel? And what should one do as a Jew if one disagreed with Israel's policies? Responding to other social currents, such as the civil rights movement, the women's movement, and the gay rights movement, exposed additional forms of pluralism, as did groups like Messianic Jews who were neither fully Jewish in a traditional sense, nor fully Christian. For American Judaism, the pluralism that came of age in the twentieth century has been an experience of paradox.

CHAPTER 5

Religion and the Pride of a People: Black Religion in the United States

Forced immigration, the slave experience, and the heritage of racism echoed through African-American religious life at the close of the twentieth century. Until the second half of the century, most analysis of African-American religion overlooked the African past, underestimating the enduring impact of slavery, and constructed a skewed picture beginning with mid-eighteenth-century efforts to convert slaves to Christianity. In the wake of the civil rights movement of the 1950s and 1960s, interpreters questioned conventional understandings. It became apparent, for example, that the Christianity offered to the slaves was often bastardized, emphasizing submission not only to the will of God, but also to the will of the slave owner, and promising a salvation that was exclusively otherworldly, never a transformation of life here and now.[1] At the same time, expressions of that Christianity emerging within the African-American communities carried a different message, one of freedom and liberation, that challenged the dominant white religious culture.[2] The contrast between the Christianity presented to slaves and what was actually received by them gave African-American religion a pluralism all its own long before the twentieth century.

But in the latter half of the twentieth century, it also became increasingly clear that much that was African still coursed through African-American religious expression.[3] At one time, conventional wisdom held that African Americans were drawn more to evangelical Protestantism than other forms of Christianity because of its emphasis on inner experience or emotion, its minimizing of creed and doctrine, and its openness to exuberant demonstration. After all, slaves forbidden to learn to read could scarcely debate the fine points of theology; feeling the Spirit within was somehow more appropriate. That simplistic understanding neglected the role of shout, song, and dance in much African tribal religion.[4] Slaves appropriated from evangelical Protestantism what was compatible with a religious style etched deep in collective memory and history. The call-response cadence giving black preaching its distinctive rhythm and concomitant power likewise echoes a distinctive African mode. It was easier for white commentators to overlook the African dimension in a way they never neglected, for example, the ethnic nuances in the Catholicism or the Judaism of eastern European immigrants, because of the ferocity with which slave traders and owners in the colonial period had attempted to demolish all that was distinctively African in slave culture in order to boost their control over the slaves. Yet this undercurrent sustained a pride in an African heritage that never disappeared.

The enduring African past bequeathed a kind of pluralism to African-American religion that was patently different from the fusion of folk ways with a formal tradition within immigrant Catholicism, for example. Among Italian immigrants in the later nineteenth century, the blending of local custom, pre-Christian religiosity, and the formal tradition of Catholicism had evolved over nearly two millennia, giving that immigrant community a coherent and comprehensive worldview, one that was from the inside authentically Italian and authentically Catholic. In comparison, the mingling of things African with things Christian is still in its early stages. Hence we might expect to see some religious phenomena where there remains vivid contrast between what has tribal roots and what has its genesis in Christianity. Two examples, voodoo and *santeria*, receive fuller consideration in the subsequent discussion of personal spirituality. Here we should note simply that in voodoo, African, Haitian, and Christian elements come together; different African, Caribbean, and Christian strands coalesce in *santeria*.[5] The pluralism pervading African-American religion reveals a syncretism that in and of itself is not uncommon to American religious life. What is unique is its demonstration of how the African past continues to influence black religious life.

Until recently it was rare to find recognition that there were African slaves who were Muslim and who sought at least for a generation or two to maintain the practice of Islam. The occasional references to providing selected slaves with a ration of beef rather than pork (since devout Muslims would abstain from eating pork) offers evidence to the Muslim presence long before the Nation of Islam came on the scene.[6] Small numbers and dispersion among the slave population made perpetuating a Muslim identity impossible over time; by all accounts a vital African-American Islam among slaves disappeared rather quickly.

The Role of Black Denominations

A different sort of pluralism emerged from the movement to establish African-American denominations independent of white groups. The first efforts came early in the nineteenth century with the formal organization of the African Methodist Episcopal Church in 1816 (though its genesis was in 1787).[7] Until after the Civil War, African-American denominations were concentrated in the northern states. When the war ended, these groups moved quickly into the South to start congregations among former slaves, while other African-American denominations, such as the Colored (now Christian) Methodist Episcopal Church, formed.

These denominations provided a church structure that allowed a black Christianity to develop. In those groups, more obviously than among African-American congregations within predominantly white denominations, the blending of African tribal practice with Christian belief continued unfettered by white dominance or influence. They also provided extraordinary opportunities for an oppressed people to take on leadership roles denied them by a racist culture. Until the civil rights movement opened doors to other professions more widely, black clergy pastoring congregations in African-American churches and their denominational leaders (bishops and the like) held positions of unusual power, influence, and respect among large sectors of the African-American population.

The Effects of Geographic Dispersion

Geography had implications for another aspect of religious pluralism among African Americans. In the South, the former slave population was predominantly rural, although there were enclaves of African Americans in cities like Charleston, South Carolina, in some cases embracing persons who were already free as well as former slaves. Elsewhere, the African-American population tended to be urban. Although an incipient racism restricted the economic and career opportunities of African Americans in the cities, there was a small but identifiable black middle class emerging in the latter decades of the nineteenth century.[8] The urban-rural configuration and the greater range of socioeconomic class identification among urban blacks often gave urban and rural churches rather different styles.

Churches in former slave areas also quickly assumed a special status in the African-American community at large. In many cases, the churches began to take on many social welfare responsibilities, since racism meant that blacks were generally denied access to what might be available to others through public or private means. Often the church building and the land on which it stood might be the only property actually owned by African Americans, and the preacher often the most well-educated black in the area, although generally forced to have secular employment in addition to ministerial work. Churches became community centers as well as houses of worship, the pivot of black life in a racist culture.

As Jim Crow became the norm, particularly after receiving legal sanction in the Supreme Court's 1896 *Plessy* v. *Ferguson* decision, the churches became social oases in the midst of a hostile environment. Perhaps the closest analogue comes in the array of social services the Catholic churches and Jewish organizations provided for immigrants. But there is a significant difference. However strong anti-Semitism and anti-Catholicism were, slavery and racial difference compounded the issues for American blacks. As well, the institutions that developed to serve an immigrant constituency were often distinct from the churches or synagogues themselves, adjuncts or supplements to pastoral ministry; for African Americans in the rural South, they were identical with the churches, central to pastoral ministry. Hence the church as an institution assumed an extraordinarily prominent position in southern African-American life, adding to its pluralistic cast because of the range of seemingly secular functions it took on. Supporting a church and its pastor, even on a part-time basis, remained for generations a major source of pride in black communities across the nation.

Within southern African-American communities especially, church pastors thus often had a more expansive role than their counterparts elsewhere. Not only were they preachers with oversight of their flocks, they were also the leaders of their communities, often the only ones with an entree to the white power structure of the larger culture because of their clerical standing.[9] At the same time, many preachers were also renowned for their abilities as root doctors, with knowledge of herbal healing practices, or their skills in conjure, in part because the abilities associated with such practices also elevated their specialists to positions of leadership. On a functional level it mattered little whether the preacher invoked the power of Jesus Christ or conjured some other spiritual entity; each involved calling upon supernatural power for the benefit of others. This preeminence given the clergy lasted until the second half of the twentieth century. Then, as the civil rights movement made it more likely for talented and skilled African Americans to enter high-status professions other than the clergy, fewer of "the best and the brightest" looked to the church for careers. In some areas concern mounted by the end of the century over the ability of African Americans to sustain a quality professional ministry.[10]

Geography brought other forms of pluralism to African-American religious life. With the southern economy in shambles for decades after the Civil War and with sharecropping one of the few means of support open to former slaves in a racist culture, many believed that greater economic opportunities existed in the rapidly industrializing northern cities. Significant migration from the former Confederacy to northern cities was under way by the 1890s, but skyrocketed in the opening decades of the twentieth century.[11] Mass production of automobiles attracted thousands to Detroit and other areas connected with the industry. Additional opportunities came when the nation's economy shifted to supply materials needed for military use during World War I. Lured by jobs and the often mistaken expectation of a less racist environment, African Americans came to the burgeoning northern urban centers, bringing with them the worship styles and religious ways of the rural South.

To some degree, the religious dislocation of these in-migrants paralleled that of Jewish immigrants from Russia and other areas of eastern Europe. They found the African-American congregations in the cities alien space, perhaps more subdued in worship (though still more lively than most white congregations), and serving a constituency that increasingly drew from an emerging black urban middle class. There was frequently a clash of cultures, not unlike the clash between Yiddish-speaking Orthodox Jewish immigrants and the Reform Jews who had established themselves rather comfortably in American society.[12]

The resulting pluralism expressed itself in the proliferation of storefront churches and the emergence of countless small sectarian movements.[13] The storefronts and urban sects shared several features, most notably a charismatic preacher, an exuberant worship expression, and often a syncretistic blend of aspects of Protestant Christianity with folk ways harkening back to African tribal religiosity. All reflected efforts to transplant the religious style of the rural South to a new social context. To be sure, denominations serving a predominantly African-American constituency also saw their numbers grow as a result of this Great Migration, but the proliferation of religious groups and gatherings is even more striking.

Another dimension of pluralism emerging in the early years of the twentieth century had a profound impact on both African-American and Euro-American Christianity in the United States. In 1906, in a building on Azusa Street in Los Angeles formerly used by Methodists, dynamic African-American preacher William J. Seymour sparked a revival marked by powerful manifestations of the Holy Spirit though glossolalia or speaking in tongues.[14] Although Pentecostal stirrings occurred somewhat earlier among African-American congregations around Dunn, North Carolina, the Azusa Street revival attracted extraordinary media attention. While the revival lasted, hundreds came to Azusa Street to see and experience the gifts of the Spirit. The revival, generally credited with giving birth to the modern Pentecostal movement, at first ignored the racial boundaries that divided Americans in their churches as well as their culture. Spiritual ecstasy seized blacks and whites side by side at Azusa Street and in other places where those who had encountered the Spirit established new congregations filled with Pentecostal fervor. For nearly a decade, the Pentecostal excitement held the potential for blossoming into a cross-racial crusade, but as independent congregations of a Pentecostal bent began to coalesce into denominations, as with the formation of the Assemblies of God in 1914, the racial divisions characterizing American society reasserted themselves, and the new Pentecostal denominations tended to be overwhelmingly white or overwhelmingly African-American.[15]

The Pentecostal ethos was clearly consonant with much that was central to African-American religion. The religious ecstasy that came when one was seized by the Spirit had analogues in tribal religious expression that had never disappeared. The enthusiasm and the cadence of Pentecostal worship drew heavily from the fusion of things Euro-Christian and African already characteristic of much African-American religion. The spiritual power evidenced by speaking in tongues and other charismatic gifts remained a power superior to that denied most African Americans on an empirical level, whether political, economic, or social. Predominantly African-American Pentecostal denominations like the Church of God in Christ remained a vital current in black religious life in the United States throughout the twentieth century and continued to offer accessibility to that same realm of sacred power.

Moving Beyond Christianity

The experience of racism, the social dislocation accompanying movement from the rural South, the signal authority of the black preacher, and the class conflict

that haunted some black churches in the North allowed other expressions of pluralism to emerge in African-American religious life between World War I and
World War II. One aspect of this pluralism involved the rejection of Christianity as
a white religion of oppression; another came in the ways some individuals, like
Daddy Grace and Father Divine, fused elements of Christian teaching with their
own world views to create unique religious opportunities for African Americans.

One of the earliest expressions of the rejection of Christianity as a white religion inappropriate for African Americans came from the teachings and followers
of Timothy Drew (Noble Drew Ali).[16] Shortly before the outbreak of World War I,
Drew began street-corner preaching in Chicago, pitching his message to those he
called "Asiatics" (African Americans) and claiming that he was Mohammed III.
For his followers in the Moorish Science Temple, Noble Drew Ali developed a
pamphlet like sacred text that he called the *Holy Koran*, but it bore little resemblance to the sacred text of Islam also known popularly by that name. Not to be
confused with the Nation of Islam or Black Muslims that coalesced a few decades
later around the leadership of Elijah Muhammad, the Moorish Science Temple
insisted that Christianity was a religion exclusively for "Europeans" or Caucasians. It thus represents one of the earliest efforts in the twentieth century to foster
a sense of black pride through a religious approach intentionally separate from Christianity, including the denominations that were predominantly African-American in
their membership or those religious impulses that were highly syncretistic. Maintaining a symbiotic relationship with African-American Christianity but finally seeing
Christianity as an exclusively white religion was another group, the Church of God
founded by Prophet F.S. Cherry and popularly known as the "Black Jews." It attracted many followers in northern cities before the outbreak of World War II.[17]

More on the margins of African-American religious culture was the Universal
Negro Improvement Agency (UNIA), started by Jamaican immigrant Marcus
Garvey in 1916.[18] Generally secular in tone, Garvey's weekly *Negro World* aggressively promoted what later generations called black pride, along with advo-
cating that American blacks migrate to Africa. Garvey recognized the powerful
hold of religion on African Americans when he called on adherents to plant and
cultivate the Temple of God in individual hearts to assure peace and to increase a
spirit of brotherhood. Garvey never sought to lure African Americans away from
their churches; he knew that most who found his teachings plausible were already
church members. But for those who were not, the UNIA offered the African Orthodox Church.[19]

Both the Father Divine Peace Mission Movement and the United House of Prayer
for All People, which emerged from the teachings of Daddy Grace, exerted considerable influence during the Great Depression.[20] Some of Father Divine's followers
embarked on cooperative or communal living arrangements that brought greater economic stability than most outside the movement experienced during those turbulent
years. More than the United House of Prayer, Father Divine's movement also cut
across racial lines, though each remained overwhelmingly African-American. While

both faced government suspicion or investigation not unlike that which televangelists faced in the 1970s and 1980s, the faithful remained steadfast; there was a pride in knowing one possessed a superior truth and was already experiencing the heavenly life. What set these two movements apart was the singular role played by the founder. One early commentator, Arthur Huff Fauset, remarked that in the United House of Prayer in the 1930s it was as if God had disappeared, replaced in theology and practice by Daddy Grace himself.[21] Father Divine's sobriquet indicates directly the supernatural status followers were willing to accord him. Both illustrated another feature of pluralism layered onto the African-American religious experience, the movements that drew from Christianity and other sources but centered around a charismatic individual. Such are not unique to African-American religious life, but they add another dimension to its richness.

By century's end, the Father Divine Peace Mission Movement had dwindled in influence. Followers in the United States were concentrated in the Philadelphia area, where for some years after Father Divine's death in 1965, his widow led the movement. The group has reported organized adherents in several countries outside the United States, but numbers are minimal. In contrast, after the death of Daddy Grace in 1960, the United House of Prayer for All People began to take on the characteristics of a stable sect, placing far less emphasis on the figure of Daddy Grace than in the early days of the movement. It also gradually began to look more and more like a Pentecostal group in worship and general theological approach. In the mid-1970s, the United House of Prayer claimed some four million members; while those numbers are exaggerated, even in the late 1990s the movement was still demonstrating growth in some locales, building new facilities, taking a place as a Pentecostal religious communion alongside countless others.

The Civil Rights Movement Transforms Black Religion

American Christianity, across racial and ethnic lines, has long sustained a tension between that which was religious or spiritual and that which was political or social. In relation to the African-American experience, that tension loomed large in the antebellum period as proslavery and antislavery advocates both looked to the Bible and to the Christian tradition to bolster opposing positions. That tension has been much less prevalent in African-American religion for reasons already noted in other contexts. The pervasive racism in the decades after the Civil War, for example, forced African-American congregations (and denominations) to become the centers of their communities, with social-political roles as vital as patently religious ones. As well, the message of freedom from oppression and bondage that cascaded through African-American religion, alongside beliefs and practices whites hoped would keep African Americans docile and content, had an enduring political message. Black preachers knew that their people had not exchanged slavery for freedom as a result of the Civil War, but had in reality seen racism substituted for slavery. Yet the churches kept alive the message of freedom and liberation.

Hence not surprisingly, when the civil rights movement came to the fore in the latter half of the 1950s, the African-American churches supplied thousands of grassroots supporters and public leaders, offered space for training workers and demonstrators, and made the call for equality a moral imperative. Martin Luther King, Jr., whose name is synonymous with the civil rights movement, was, of course, a preacher, better educated than many of his black colleagues, who possessed extraordinary skill in fusing the religious with the political.[22] Freedom from oppression was, after all, a theological idea; persons were liberated from bondage to sin in the course of salvation, just as the ancient Hebrews had been liberated from slavery in Egypt to freedom in the land God provided for them. But freedom was also a political phenomenon, rooted in the U.S. Constitution and the heritage of liberty that gave meaning to the American experience. Little wonder, then, that King named his civil rights organization the Southern Christian Leadership Conference and sought the endorsement and active support of religious leaders from all denominations and from all regions of the country in his crusade to bring an end to legalized racism. King's speeches to mass crowds rang with the cadence of sermons, resounding with biblical quotation and analogy that stirred audiences not to claim salvation, but to embrace the struggle for political rights and full participation of African Americans in the nation's common life.

Historians generally view King and his work from a social and political perspective, but the civil rights movement also revitalized African-American religion in the United States and brought fresh features of pluralism to black religious life. Some who had dismissed the churches as irrelevant because of their focus on heavenly rewards for the faithful after death, rather than on the social injustice confronting African Americans here and now, were drawn back into the churches. King's version of the social gospel molded religion and daily life into a single whole. Churches breathed with new life as marchers, demonstrators, and those in the movement for the long haul used them as headquarters, training centers, and places of worship. In many communities, once again the church became the center for the common life of the African-American population.

At the same time, however, the surge of black pride and celebration of the African heritage stimulated by the civil rights movement also challenged the centrality of a white-dominated Christianity within black religious circles. Albert Cleage, for example, called for a Christian theological construction centered on a black messiah;[23] the white Jesus of tradition was simply irrelevant to African-American life and reeked of the oppression and paternalism that still penetrated a racist culture.

Perhaps the most compelling voice of black theology emerging from a Christian context was that of James Cone.[24] Cone found powerful parallels between the suffering messiah of Christianity and the experience of oppression that shaped African-American life. But just as the Christian message proclaimed triumph over suffering in resurrection, black power, Cone believed, was the parallel that would bring new life to African Americans politically, economically, and socially. For Cone, the Christian gospel was a message of liberation from oppression in any form. Thus by the end of the twentieth century, Cone urged African Americans to support the cries for social justice and liberation of other oppressed peoples in the United States, particularly Hispanic Americans.

Some oppression was evident in mainline Protestant denominations with a significant African-American membership. Yet here, too, the civil rights movement became a catalyst for change. Methodism provides a good case study, since among the mainline denominations it had the largest proportion of African-American members. In 1939 when the Methodist Church formed through the merger of three denominations (Methodist Episcopal, Methodist Protestant, and Methodist Episcopal, South), congregations for administrative purposes were assigned to geographic units called jurisdictions, with the exception of those congregations that were predominantly black. Regardless of location, black congregations were placed in a jurisdiction that spanned the nation.[25] This administrative segregation came under attack from African-American Methodists from the outset, although white leaders insisted that the arrangement was necessary to bring the former Southern church into the new denomination.[26]

The ethos of the civil rights movement made it impossible for Methodists to remain racially divided structurally. Consequently, in 1964 the Methodist General Conference, which was then also guiding a merger with the Evangelical United Brethren to be consummated in 1968 with the formation of the United Methodist Church, ordered the racial structure dismantled over an eight-year period, with African-American congregations being absorbed into the formerly all-white regional conferences and jurisdictions. In every case, however, African Americans became a minority, and provisions were made on an interim basis to assure that the more inclusive plan would not dilute African-American representation on denominational boards and agencies.[27]

By and large, however, at the end of the twentieth century individual congregations within the United Methodist Church remained overwhelmingly white or overwhelmingly black in membership; not until the 1990s were the first serious efforts made to have African-American pastors serve predominantly white congregations and vice-versa. At the same time, African-American church leaders, while remaining opposed to forced administrative segregation, became increasingly concerned that absorption into a denomination that remained predominantly white would erode what was distinctive to the African-American Methodist experience. In the closing years of the twentieth century as the denomination expanded its ministry among other ethnic communities, particularly Hispanic Americans and Asian Americans, the issues of maintaining separate histories and distinct heritages within a single denomination remained problematic.

Others who rejoiced in the pride that propelled civil rights and black power chose to reject all association with Christianity and the complex African-American religious heritage. Christianity was, after all, the religion of slave owners in the past and the religion of racists in the present. In white hands, the Christianity presented to African Americans had been skewed and diluted of its full power, designed to allow white Christians to retain their positions of dominance and superiority in both church and society. What was needed, said some critics, was a black religion for black Americans.

For growing numbers from the 1960s on, that religion was Islam in one of its myriad forms. The cultural and religious climates were more congenial to non-Christian alternatives than in earlier decades when groups like the Moorish Science Temple, Black Jews, or African Orthodox Church attracted only very small numbers. In the days of the civil rights movement, the Nation of Islam, generally known as the Black Muslims, dominated popular awareness of this facet of African-American religious pluralism. The Nation of Islam had some connections to Noble Drew Ali and the earlier Moorish Science Temple, although by the 1960s it had moved in very different directions. Under the leadership of Elijah Muhammad, the Nation of Islam forged an ideology of racial separatism and black supremacy.[28] White devils, emissaries of Christianity, threatened to destroy the purity of Africans; hence the Nation of Islam called for blacks to work towards self-sufficiency within their own communities, keeping contacts with whites to a minimum. To achieve these social goals, the Nation of Islam encouraged a rather ascetic lifestyle that included abstinence from alcohol, tobacco, and certain foods. Black Muslims also insisted on marital fidelity and promoted a work ethic, ostensibly to allow African Americans to become independent of a white-dominated economic system. Ironically, however, the values endorsed by the Nation of Islam were precisely those that brought success according to the white standards rejected.

Although Elijah Muhammad was the titular head of the Nation of Islam during the era of the civil rights movement, media attention made one of his followers, Malcolm X, the symbol of the movement.[29] A compelling orator, Malcolm X brought hope to thousands of African Americans who heard him speak, but fear to the hearts of white Americans who watched him on the news. The message of hatred and racial separation popularly synonymous with the Nation of Islam seemed to many, both African-American and white, to undercut gains made by the civil rights movement in dismantling legally sanctioned racism.

Yet Malcolm X himself became transformed after being cast into the public eye. Perceived as a rival of Elijah Muhammad and aware that the revered leader of the movement did not personally always adhere to the behavioral codes imposed on others, Malcolm X determined to look more deeply into the religion of Islam that presumably shaped the Nation of Islam. Going on the *hajj*, the pilgrimage to Mecca all devout Muslims are expected to undertake at least once, Malcolm X experienced a classic conversion. Seeing that the Islam based on the *Qur'an* fostered the unity of all humanity across racial and ethnic lines, not the separatism enjoined by the Black Muslims, Malcolm X returned from Mecca proclaiming a message of racial reconciliation as a Muslim, but not as a member of the Nation of Islam. His new work was cut short when he was assassinated in 1965, but since then, thousands of African Americans have come to identify with Islam, not just the Nation of Islam, finding in submission to Allah the key to meaning in life.

When filmmaker Spike Lee released the cinema version of *The Autobiography of Malcolm X* in 1992, a generation born after the civil rights movement and the age of black radicalism became acquainted with Malcolm and indirectly with Islam. Islam found its plausibility again enhanced. At the same time, although Islam is Arabic rather than African in its origins, in the second half of the twentieth century, it experienced astonishing growth in Africa.[30] Hence for many African Americans, exploring an African identity and heritage naturally led to investigation of Islam, often in expressions other than those promoted by the Nation of Islam.

Pride in black identity also fueled interest, still growing at the close of the twentieth century, in another alternative to Christianity, this one originating in Jamaica and initially brought to the United States by Jamaican immigrants. The Rastafarians represent a millenarian-type movement elevating the late Ethiopian emperor Haile Selassie into a near-messianic figure. Selassie, emperor from 1930 until 1974, was previously known as Ras Tafari, Ras meaning prince. Building on some features of the earlier Jamaica-founded Universal Negro Improvement Association of Marcus Garvey, the Rastafarians assert the superiority of blacks to whites, claiming that whites will eventually serve blacks. Ethiopia figures as a promised land to which Africans now scattered will one day return, though some see Ethiopia as both the nation-state by that name and a symbol of the whole African continent. Known more for the hairstyle known as dreadlocks and reggae music, the Rastafarians in the United States have attracted followers outside the Jamaican immigrant community who are disgruntled with Christianity because of its historic ties to slavery and racism, but remain committed to bolstering pride in black identity and strengthening ties between blacks in the United States and Africa.[31]

Increasing pride in being African has taken another religiocultural turn with the growing attention paid to the celebration of *Kwanzaa*.[32] First introduced in the United States by M. Rob Karenga in 1966, *Kwanzaa* is based on an African festival marking the harvest of the first crops. In its contemporary form, however, *Kwanzaa* reflects the importance of both Christmas and Hanukkah in American culture. *Kwanzaa*, like the Jewish Hanukkah, is spread over several days; *Kwanzaa* highlights seven values Karenga believed vital to African-American life, devoting one day to each. Those values are unity, self-determination, collective work and responsibility, cooperative economics, purpose, creativity, and faith. The celebrations, revolving around rituals for home and communal use that extol each of these virtues, begin on December 26, the day following Christmas, a major holiday of the Christian tradition laden with secular import as well. While many of the rituals build on African practices, the holiday itself is distinctly American. Its timing allows thousands of African Americans to combine the Christian and cultural commemoration of Christmas with something ostensibly more African. *Kwanzaa* enables African-American Christians to affirm their African, American, and Christian identities simultaneously, taking pride in how each contributes to individual life and the life of the black community. For the first few decades after *Kwanzaa* celebrations began, the holiday received scant attention outside of those African-American communities where it had taken hold. By the close of the century, however, *Kwanzaa* had clearly made its mark, as stores began carrying merchandise targeted for the festival. Another facet of pluralism accenting pride in black identity became fixed in African-American religious life.

Challenges Confronting African-American Religious Life

Although the civil rights movement provided impetus for many of these expressions of pluralism, particularly those emphasizing pride in racial identity, it had other consequences that brought new challenges to African-American religious life. As *de facto* segregation crumbled, educational, social, and economic opportunities open to African Americans increased dramatically. The church, once the social center for black life, saw its role change; other institutions and agencies provided a greater range of leisure-time activities for African Americans. Professions that had once seemed nearly the exclusive domain of white men slowly became viable career choices for African-American women and men. In the last quarter of the century, it was less and less likely that the preachers would constitute the best educated cohort of the black population.[33] Denominational leaders pondered the implications for the future of the black churches, now facing for the first time some of the challenges that for decades had eroded the centrality of religious organizations to the social and cultural life of white Americans.

When C. Eric Lincoln and Larry Mamiya published their monumental study of the black church in the United States in 1990, much of it read like a lament, for it seemed to them and their research team that the social and cultural shifts that followed in the wake of the civil rights movement left the future of the black churches in jeopardy.[34] A decade later, one cannot yet trumpet the decline of the black church, but it is not too soon to mark the growing pluralism that has come to African-American religious life, often unwittingly undermining traditional black churches. Religious and spiritual concerns remain vital, but they find expression in a multitude of ways that were not options in the opening years of the century.[35]

Other forces, many of them operative in the culture at large, suggest that even greater variety and pluralism will come to African-American life in the first decades of the twenty-first century. As in other religious bodies, African-American denominations, religious communities, and congregations have had to wrestle with the role of women, particularly as feminist issues became more prominent in the larger society.[36] On the one hand, African-American Pentecostal and countless independent storefront churches had long accepted the preaching of charismatic women, but within the historically black Protestant denominations there resounded the same debates about the ordination of women and what Scripture decreed as woman's role in church and society. Like other Protestant bodies, gradually, if reluctantly, African-American denominations came to accept women into the ranks of the professional ministry. Dealing with women's roles in African-American religious groups is compounded by the high proportion of African-American single-parent households headed by women in the larger society. In other words, African-American women's roles are more complex and more nuanced, given the context of an ethnic culture shaped to a large degree by racism. In turn, that has complicated dealing with women's contributions to religious life, personally and professionally. Yet when feminist theology developed among white women, African-American women quickly added a distinctive element, often called womanist theology, that reflected this complex heritage.

Broader cultural currents have also brought issues regarding homosexuality to African-American religious bodies. While homosexuality refers to both lesbians and gay men, as well as bisexuals, within black religious groups there has been a tendency to see homosexuality as a matter involving primarily men.[37] Given the demographics suggesting a higher degree of instability among African-American families because of abandonment by husbands and fathers, the African-American churches have been even more reluctant than their white counterparts to acknowledge the presence of homosexuals within their religious communities. Gay men appear to many religious leaders to undermine even further the sustained efforts to foster deeper commitment to families among African-American men.

Although experts from many disciplines insist that family issues and homosexuality are totally separate matters, it is easy to collapse them, given the historic difficulty in maintaining strong male role models in the nurture of African-American boys. The Million Man March organized by the Nation of Islam's Louis Farrakhan was notable both for its effort to strengthen the commitment of African-American husbands and fathers to their families and its marginalization of African-American gay men.[38] Promise Keepers, while predominantly white, remains committed to building bridges across racial lines, trying to dismantle the racism that runs just below the surface throughout American society, and calls husbands and fathers to commit themselves anew to their families and the responsibilities accompanying family life. It, too, has no place for gay men.[39] Moving into the twenty-first century, African-American religious bodies will continue to confront challenges relating to gender and sexuality as deep as those facing their white counterparts.

African-American religious life in the United States during the twentieth century became increasingly pluralistic. So did virtually all American religious culture. What distinguished the African-American story was the way in which this pluralism reflected the heritage of slavery, the penetration of racism and prejudice to the core of American common life, and the pride of being a people that religion has spurred. A rich amalgam of African styles and dimensions continued to enrich the black Christian experience that had roots in the half-hearted efforts of colonial slave owners to see that the gospel was preached to all. Demographic patterns that saw thousands of African Americans leaving the South for northern urban centers aided in the emergence of alternative religious styles that added to the pluralism already there. The diverse social roles played by religious institutions among African Americans from the slave era to the present brought another feature of the story to the fore, namely the signal role of religion in nurturing and sustaining the civil rights movement. Increasingly, as African Americans fostered a racial and ethnic pride that defied the racism around them, religious perspectives informed by non-Christian understandings (especially Islam) and even a range of Christian viewpoints forged from the distinctive circumstances shaping black life added to the pluralism. At the same time, African-American religious life had to struggle with challenges from the same social currents as the culture at large, from issues of gender to those of sexuality. African Americans entered the twenty-first century with a considerably more pluralistic religious culture to sustain them and to buttress pride in a black identity than was the case at the dawn of the twentieth century.

CHAPTER 6

Syncretism and Pluralism:
Native American Experiences
in the Twentieth Century

For most Americans, the religious cultures of the Native American tribes who peopled the continent before the arrival of Europeans remain unknown or perhaps consigned to an exotic realm of medicine men and rain dances. Much of the ignorance owes its origin to European attitudes towards the indigenous peoples of the New World centuries ago. Spanish *conquistadors* saw native cultures only as targets for subjugation and destruction, despite the many missions established by monks and priests to convert the natives to Christianity.[1] The English were initially not as intent on total destruction, but from the start they, too, assumed the superiority of European ways and especially of European religion to tribal ways. After all, the native tribes, despite hundreds of different spoken languages, had yet to put their words in written form and even in oral usage had no separate word for "religion." Although some Puritan colonists endeavored to bring the Christian gospel to tribes in the northeast, most were as ambivalent about converting Native Americans as they were about converting African slaves. If many feared that baptism of slaves would mean their freedom from the bonds of slavery, they also feared that baptism in the Christian faith would render Native Americans equals of the Europeans. Equality in the faith would make it much more difficult for Europeans to usurp tribal lands or coerce tribes into relocating.

Wherever the Christian message meshed with tribal ways, change followed in the ways native cultures expressed themselves religiously.[2] Change almost always meant that dimensions of pluralism came to Native American experience in ways specific to the tribal heritage. When analysts of American religious life did take account of tribal cultures, until recently most tended to operate with many of the same assumptions that for too long undergirded interpretation of African-American religions. The most important of those assumptions held that much of what was indigenous to tribal religious culture was cast aside or suppressed as Christians gained converts, as tribes were forced from ancestral lands onto reservations, and as events like the removal of many tribes to Oklahoma decimated the integrity of cultures.

The image of the "Trail of Tears" that captures much of that removal also suggests that the very essence of tribal life was destroyed by the Indian policy of the U.S. government. Yet as with the durability of many aspects of African tribal religiosity despite the atrocities of the slave system, much that was vital to Native American tribal religiosity has also endured. If with African Americans a great deal of that earlier heritage persisted in tandem with Christianity, a similar pattern developed among Native Americans. Much of the story of pluralism is one of relating how Native American religiosity interacted with, adapted to, and also altered the styles of Christianity presented by missionaries. It is thus a saga of syncretism.

There is yet another rough parallel between the African-American and Native American stories. The civil rights movement launched a resurgence of pride in the African heritage that spread well beyond the African-American communities of the nation. For example, it helped spur the women's liberation movement and then the gay rights movement, both of which had a profound effect on the religious life of the nation. It also sparked a renewed appreciation of a distinctive identity and heritage among countless ethnic groups, including numerous Native American tribes. While there was no "pure" Native American past to recover any more than descendants of slaves could recover a pure African past, there was a revitalization of tribal spirituality, albeit now in new forms.[3]

Given the variety that has always pervaded Native American tribal life, it is impossible to detail every dimension of pluralism within every tribal society in the twentieth century. Representative examples of the changing face of pluralism within Native American religions in the twentieth century will illuminate the larger picture.

Pluralism as Syncretism: The Encounter with Christianity

At the dawn of the twentieth century, few of the ongoing ministries of various Christian bodies to Native Americans were prospering. Most were mission endeavors in at least two senses of that phrase. The ostensible aim was to convert the indigenous tribal peoples to Christianity, meaning that these efforts had a missionary goal. At the same time, most were heavily subsidized by sponsoring denominations or agencies of larger religious communities; few had either the number of adherents or the financial resources to be self-sustaining. For most Christian groups, the integrity of Native American religions was not apparent, convinced as they were of the superiority of Christianity and the necessity of conversion of tribal peoples to assure their eternal salvation. Many of the ritual practices that interwove religion with every aspect of tribal consciousness were seen by Christians as evidence of a misguided paganism at worst or polytheism at best.

The situation was compounded by the Indian policies of the U.S. government that had forced most tribal cultures from their ancestral lands onto reservations. On the one hand, the consignment of Native Americans to reservations, artificial constructs of land that generally had no sacred character, seriously compromised efforts to maintain tribal traditions. Every tribal heritage was thus undergoing change and transformation because of the necessity of adapting to new circumstances. On the other hand, missionaries and government officials too frequently concluded that in time tribal cultural patterns would die off, rendering the people more pliable targets for conversion by missionaries and less likely to resist or even rebel against governmental authority. Apart from schools set up by the Bureau of Indian Affairs but sometimes run by missionaries and thus offering religious as well as secular instruction, few efforts were made to provide educational opportunities on the reservations. Nor were there employment opportunities that would both enrich tribal consciousness and identity and also link the tribal peoples to the larger society. Countless missionary reports note the poverty that marked reservation life; they and others have documented the extraordinarily high presence of other social problems, such as alcoholism and spousal abuse among some tribal groups. For much of the century, native tribes remained on the periphery of American life, pushed to the margins by hostile government policy and regarded as pagans to be converted by the dominant religious groups.

Nevertheless, the dynamics at work reveal how Christianity and a tribal religious consciousness worked together to create a religious style that was distinctive; in other words, pluralism was expanding within Native American cultures. From the start of Christian missions to the indigenous peoples, the Christian gospel was filtered through tribal culture. Biblical individuals and the saints of Catholic Christianity blended in the received tradition with characters drawn from native mythology and the tribal past. That form of syncretism endured throughout the twentieth century. As Sam D. Gill has noted, "Christian churches are the dominant feature in most Pueblo villages. Not only are these churches attended for the celebration of Mass, but dances and other tribal religious performances may take place in them. At Zuni life-size depictions of Zuni religious figures are painted on the walls of the Catholic mission church. Such murals date from the nineteenth century."[4]

Numerous tribal communities have taken over Christian hymns, first introduced by missionaries as tools to train potential converts in the teachings of the faith. But often the tunes to which the hymns are sung are those rooted in the tribal past, not the Christian tradition. Sometimes changes in imagery incorporated native thinking. Among the Ojibwa in Minnesota, hymns intended to weaken ties to the tribal past by bringing the people into the Christian fold when missions developed there more than a century and a half ago now serve almost exactly the opposite function.[5] By the 1880s, after government Indian policy had brought considerable dislocation to the Ojibwa, guilds of singers at White Earth deftly took the Christian hymns set to Ojibwa musical forms and used them as a means to connect to the tribal heritage in danger of extinction. At the end of the twentieth century, singers from White Earth continue to travel to Ojibwa gatherings, particularly funerals, where performance of Christian hymns promotes tribal cohesion and identity. Ironically, then, what was designed "to root out the indianness [sic] of native peoples . . . has become an emblem of distinctiveness and the stuff of survival . . ."[6]

For generations of students in the twentieth century, however, an introduction to the ethos of tribal religions came through reading *Black Elk Speaks*.[7] In 1931, Black Elk, a Lakota shaman, recounted his experience from childhood visions he had to memories of tribal myths to John G. Neihardt, who presumably transcribed them with the assistance of his daughter and published them the following year. Black Elk was born most likely in the early 1860s. He had thus come of age before the massacre at Wounded Knee in 1890 when government officials authorized the annihilation of the Lakota engaged in the Ghost Dance, which left an indelible imprint in his mind.[8] In Neihardt's recasting of Black Elk's story, the visions, dreams, rituals, and tales that provided meaning and cohesion for the Lakota before the destruction of their culture come to life, ending with a jeremiad for a civilization that seemed about to vanish by the 1930s.

Today there is considerable scholarly debate over the extent to which Neihardt edited or otherwise revamped what Black Elk said in order to present a presumably more "pure" account of Lakota tribal religiosity. What does not come through in any of the printed versions of *Black Elk Speaks* is the Roman Catholic identity of Black Elk, who was confirmed in that faith in 1905.[9] Among the Lakota, Black Elk was renowned as much for being a devout Catholic who trained others in that faith as he was for being a healer and shaman adept at invoking the supernatural powers sustaining traditional Lakota culture. Evidence also suggests that prior to becoming a Roman Catholic, Black Elk had been baptized as a Christian under the aegis of an Episcopal mission. Before the establishment of the Holy Rosary Mission under Roman Catholic auspices, Episcopalians had staffed the only Christian ministry at Pine Ridge, South Dakota, to serve the Lakota; indeed, U.S. government policy fixed in the Grant administration (1869–77) had generally granted permission only to one Christian group to set up a mission on any single reservation where there was a school, a practice in many cases lasting well into the twentieth century. After Neihardt's work appeared, Black Elk signed a statement reaffirming his Catholic identity and suggesting that the portrait given by Neihardt reflected Black Elk's Lakota past, not his then current religious sensibilities. When Black Elk died in 1950, he was buried as a Roman Catholic.

The situation, however, may be more complex. Black Elk likely fused together a Christian identity with a Lakota identity, blending Christian belief and practice with the way of the pipe and the sacred mythology he learned as a child among the Lakota in the decades before Wounded Knee. If so, Black Elk was not unusual among the Lakota or other Native Americans in balancing or combining multiple religious identities. Just as numerous accounts survive of African-American Christian preachers and pastors who were also revered for their knowledge of conjure, so there are numerous Native Americans like Black Elk who fused their tribal heritage with dimensions of Christianity to create a syncretistic religious world view.

A more recent study of the Lakota Sioux, marking the centenary of Catholic missions and schools at Pine Ridge, suggests that this sort of syncretism was close to the norm. Generations of Native American children attended the Catholic schools on the reservation, took religious instruction, and in many cases were baptized and confirmed in the Catholic faith. Yet outside the confines of church and school, they retained a vital connection to their tribal heritage. In home life and in other aspects of their daily routine, the norm was more a combination of tribal ways, transformed through the years of life on the reservation, interaction with the larger culture, and association with Christianity, with the formal aspects of a Catholicism that was learned and appropriated in part because doing so was expected.[10] So, too, the Lakota sweat lodge ritual has changed as a result of a syncretistic relationship with Christianity.[11] A blending of traditional practice with Christian forms, as Randall Balmer has shown, was also the case with the Episcopal mission at the Standing Rock Indian Reservation at Fort Yates, North Dakota.[12]

Scholars have speculated that John Neihardt may have suppressed some of Black Elk's statements where he discussed his Catholic sensibility as well as the way he fused things Catholic with Lakota culture to fashion a syncretistic world view, as Neihardt may have amplified what Black Elk recalled of distinctly tribal ways. Others have argued that Black Elk, for whatever reason, chose not to discuss his Christian beliefs with Neihardt since the latter was interested primarily in learning about Lakota understanding. Neihardt apparently knew that Black Elk was a respected Roman Catholic lay catechist, but either Neihardt again failed to note that or Black Elk again did not emphasize his Christian affiliation when Neihardt returned a few years after *Black Elk Speaks* was published to interview Black Elk for a subsequent volume.[13]

What is significant is how Black Elk and generations of Native Americans were able to craft what in some senses is a new religion or at least a new expression of Native American religion that interacted with, but never totally absorbed, elements of Christianity. Black Elk may have been a baptized and confirmed Christian for decades, but he did not forget the Lakota way or the access it provided to a realm of power that endowed life with spiritual meaning. It may be that the longer such syncretistic interplay occurs, the less that is singularly Native American will endure, for succeeding generations, more distant from a time when tribal cultures were not subject to the constraints of reservation life, will have less collective memory of the earlier heritage. But such also presumes that these traditions were static prior to the assault on tribal integrity that came with reservations and events like Wounded Knee.

That a syncretistic fusion, along with a vibrant substratum of indigenous religiosity that may have defied or minimized syncretism with Christianity, endured provides one theme in some of the writings of novelist Leslie Marmon Silko, a Pueblo. *Ceremony* is instructive in showing the vitality of such syncretism.[14] In the narrative, interspersed with a poetic retelling of much Pueblo mythology, Tayo, the main character, comes to grips with his Pueblo past and his presumed modern identity. The latter bears a marked Christian influence through an aunt who raised him, even if it is not a formal affiliation. After service in Asia during World War II, Tayo returns to a people whose tribal consciousness is in flux. On the one hand,

Tayo's friends, who also have military experience, exemplify what it is like to be trapped between two worlds. They no longer see themselves as Pueblo, for they see the Pueblo traditions as affirming a way of life that is irrelevant to the modern world. Yet, as members of a Native American tribe, they are excluded from the U.S. culture which they believe is the wave of the future. Tayo's aunt, presented as self-consciously Christian (Catholic), likewise seems willing to eschew a tribal sensibility, but her faith and her apparent acceptance of "white" culture also fail to bring any cohesion to Tayo's life.

Through his grandmother, who bridges these multiple religious and cultural worlds more creatively than others, Tayo establishes contact with Betonie, a shaman who understands that the power of Pueblo "witchery," as he calls it, must be remolded, not cast aside, for his people to survive. Moving into that syncretistic realm, Tayo himself experiences the power of the past, but not just as the way of a tribal people who have no real place in the industrialized world. Rather Tayo brings together past and present, tribal culture and white culture, Pueblo religion and facets of Christianity. In doing so, he is able to seize control of his life and gain a sense of wholeness as a Pueblo and an American.

Part of the point of Silko's forceful novel is that neither a tribal religiosity nor a Christian religiosity alone will work. In reappropriating Pueblo mythology, Tayo makes it something which is his own, fusing it with the religious ways of the nontribal world around him. In that lies the hope for the future of his people. Silko should not be read as calling for mere revitalization of a tribal heritage, but as passionately articulating a new way that merges that heritage with the larger religiocultural world to create something new.

Silko's work reinforces what was implicit in the saga of Black Elk, both Lakota shaman and Catholic catechist, and in later studies of Christian missions on the reservations. Even if the Christian message penetrated to the core of Native life, the heritage of a vital tribal consciousness was not forgotten. Those who sought baptism as Christians were not likely to cast aside all of the tribal patterns that had shaped their lives and the collective life of their people. Rather, they were selective in what they chose to incorporate from Christianity into their own world views, just as they were selective in what they chose to retain from tribal religions. The result was a distinctive religiosity, always syncretistic and often idiosyncratic and somewhat inchoate. But through this fusion, pluralism became and remains a key element in Native American religion in the twentieth century.

Peyotism and the Native American Church

In at least one case, this syncretism ultimately led to the formation of a distinctive religious denomination. In 1918, the Native American Church received an official charter from the state of Oklahoma. What set this denomination apart from others was not only its name, suggesting that its primary constituency came from among Native Americans, but its use of peyote in a religious ritual that reflected another aspect of the syncretistic pluralism that has characterized twentieth-century Native American religion. The peyote ritual drew not only from ceremonial practices that had taken deep root among numerous North American tribes, particularly after the demise of the Ghost Dance, but also from some distinctively Christian ideas.[15]

In the background as well was a non-Native American, James Mooney, an ethnographer employed by the Smithsonian Institution who had studied several tribal cultures (especially those where the Ghost Dance had figured prominently). Mooney seemed eager to assure that Native American ways—particularly those of the Kiowa with whom he had developed a close relationship—retained their viability in the artificial context of reservation life. In order to understand the dynamics of the Native American Church and some of the problems it has encountered as the century progressed, it is necessary first to explore how the ceremonial use of peyote became part of Native American religious life.

Precisely when the ritual use of peyote made its way into Native American life in the United States is lost to history. What evidence exists suggests that it appeared first among some Comanche tribes and among the Kiowa in the decades immediately after the suppression of the Ghost Dance and was well established by the dawn of the twentieth century. Most likely the various Plains tribes learned of peyote and adapted the rituals surrounding its use from tribal cultures that flourished in northern Mexico. At least peyote and other substances with hallucinogenic properties were long part of tribal ceremonies among the Yaqui, Tarahumare, and Otomi who populated the Sonoran desert, though apparently they came later to the Yaqui in Arizona. Some tribal stories claim that these groups were introduced to the mysteries of peyote, mescal, and other similar substances centuries earlier by the Aztecs. But early religious use of peyote among tribes in the United States seems relatively contained. Government records show numerous arrests of Native Americans for use of peyote in the early years of the century. At that time, strict regulations limited the sale of alcoholic beverages to Native Americans, largely because those in charge of Indian Affairs assumed that the tribal peoples would in drunken frenzies be likely to foment uprisings against government authority. Authorities used these laws to bring charges against those who used peyote. But because the laws generally spoke only of intoxicants, those arrested for use or possession of peyote were only infrequently prosecuted. Technically the provisions regarding intoxicants did not extend to use of peyote.

Some researchers trace the spread of ritual peyote use to one individual known as Quanah Parker. The son of a Comanche tribesman and an Anglo-American woman who had been taken by Comanches during a confrontation with white Americans when she was a child, Quanah Parker and his mother were forcibly removed from Comanche society by the woman's family following the death of her husband. Neither mother nor son fared well; both became ill when brought back to white culture, and the mother, Cynthia Anne Parker, died. When the same destiny seemed likely to befall the son, family members finally summoned a Comanche *curandera*, a woman skilled in indigenous healing rituals that revolved around use of herbs, chant, and prayer. Her labors succeeded. Once cured, Quanah determined to leave the white culture and society of his mother's family and return to his father's people. However, perhaps out of gratitude for his recovery, Parker determined to promote the understanding of tribal lore that he learned from the *curandera*. He traveled among various Plains tribes, instructing and then initiating men into the ways of peyote. The practice spread relatively quickly. By the time James Mooney helped engineer the incorporation of the Native American Church in 1918, not just the Comanches from which Parker came, but also the Kiowas, Kiowa-Apaches, Arapaho, Cheyenne, Kickapoo, Shawnee, Sac and Fox, and some of the Navajo were all engaged in the ritual use of peyote.

In the peyote ceremony, at least as practiced in the early part of the century, some Christian elements became fused with things Native American. Some of the Road Men, as those who lead the peyote ceremony in some tribes are called, read from the Bible during the nightlong ritual. For many years, the Roman Catholic Douay version was favored, no doubt because of the long presence of Roman Catholic missions in the central and southern Great Plains. The peyote buttons are also handled in much the same way as the Eucharistic elements, placed on an altar and carefully wrapped prior to being ritualistically distributed in a manner akin to the sharing of the bread and cup in the Eucharist. The respect for the sacred character of the Christian symbols and the supernatural power that came to them in their consecration as the body and blood of Christ thus became extended to peyote. In many circles, use of prayer beads was also part of the peyote ceremony; many Native Americans no doubt first learned to use such as Roman Catholic missionaries instructed them in the use of the rosary as a devotional device. Prayer, of course, was common to both Native American and Christian religiosity apart from peyote use, but the language used to address the supernatural power symbolized by peyote (and which was more directly experienced by those participating in the ceremony after ingesting the substance) likely reflected what had been picked up from Christian missions. The power inherent in the peyote is often addressed, for example, as Father, and some practitioners offer prayers to Christ during the peyote rite. For many, it is Christ who is the source of the visions that come once the peyote is ingested.[16]

Other features more obviously echoed the tribal heritage, with some variation in details among the various tribal groups where use of peyote became common. The prominence of birds, especially of Thunder Bird, in some tribal religious practices carried over in the design of the tipi used for peyote ceremonies and later in the use of fans made of bird feathers in the Native American Church. So, too, incorporating the ceremonial presence of water, corn, fruit, and meat also has roots more directly in tribal practice. Altogether, the coming together of Christian and indigenous elements is apparent.

Legal incorporation of the Native American Church did little to halt persecution and prosecution of those who engaged in the peyote ceremony, although since the ceremony was performed at night and lasted until the next morning, often it could be carried out without attracting attention of government authorities. Road Men and tribal leaders early on learned not to publicize the ceremony, which was not performed every week as the Christian Eucharist was celebrated at Catholic mission churches. Many who became part of the Native American Church continued to report their religious affiliation as being one of the Protestant denominations or the Roman Catholic Church, whichever had active missions where they lived, in part to mask their involvement in a practice the government sought to suppress. Of those who did so, a large proportion, it seems, continued to attend Christian services, thus furthering the meshing of Christian and Native American elements that marks the syncretistic pluralism coloring Native religious life in the twentieth century. Even though relatively few of the men, even among those attending the peyote ceremony, were active participants and the role of women, though central, was restricted to bringing water and other materials needed during the execution of the rite, rumors persisted that the ritual was a cover for sexual orgies and therefore not only illegal but immoral. Other outsiders sought to contain, if not prohibit, its use because occasionally participants would have unpleasant physical reactions to the active chemical in the peyote. Some critics always insisted that the practice was nothing other than a form of escape either from the mores of the larger society or from the misery attendant on the poverty that often accompanied reservation life.

For better or worse, much attention became directed to peyote use among Native Americans as a result of the counterculture movement of the 1960s and 1970s. Some segments of the counterculture were absorbed with experimenting with various chemical substances, from marijuana to peyote, that were regarded by the government as "controlled substances," the use of which was illegal. Peyote and its connections to Native American culture came to the fore when anthropologist Carlos Castaneda published his revised doctoral dissertation in 1968 as *The Teachings of Dan Juan: A Yaqui Way of Knowledge*.[17] Castaneda claimed that he had become a student of a Yaqui shaman, who trained him in that northern Mexican tribe's lore. Much of that centered around his ingestion of peyote, mescal, and other substances, with detailed descriptions of his personal experiences while under their influences. According to Castaneda, he was able to enter a realm of power with the help of allies, supernatural powers who were accessed through such substances and the rituals that accompanied their use, as he studied to become a "man of knowledge." At some point in his training to be a shaman, a matter that was remarkable in its own right since he was not a Yaqui and therefore something of an interloper, Castaneda decided to abandon the apprenticeship. The alternate reality represented by Don Juan's teaching, and the ritual apparatus that went with it, had come so close to supplanting empirical reality or life in the "real world" that Castaneda feared he would soon be unable to function in society outside the Yaqui orbit.

Almost as soon as Castaneda's book appeared, scholars raised questions, not because of the structural analysis of the Yaqui world view that Castaneda appended to his study, but because no third party, except for other Yaquis whose identities were unknown, had met Don Juan or had witnessed Castaneda's apprenticeship. In other words, there was no standard academic means to verify or otherwise confirm what Castaneda reported. Nonetheless, the book became a leading seller, especially among college and university students where the so-called "drug culture" had also attracted considerable attention. In that context, however, the commitment to serious study of the way of the Yaqui shaman disappeared, and the book frequently became more a guide to recreational drug use. Castaneda followed *The Teachings of Don Juan* with several sequels where he expanded on the learning he had received, though none achieved the popularity—some would say notoriety—of his initial work.[18] But Castaneda did succeed in drawing attention to the ritual use of peyote and other substances that could alter one's consciousness. In doing so, he unwittingly drew attention to peyote religion among Native Americans in the United States, whether part of the Native American Church or part of other tribal activity.

By the late 1980s and early 1990s, the counterculture seemed long in the past and student fascination with Castaneda had waned. But then some states began to challenge the religious use of peyote among Native Americans. Part of the legal dilemma stemmed from the incorporation of the Native American Church, for within that body, proponents of peyote use claimed that legal standing exempted the group from prosecution on charges of using a controlled substance. In some ways, the claim for exemption was akin to the arguments allowing for use of wine in Christian eucharistic ceremonies during Prohibition when the sale and consumption of alcoholic beverages were illegal; peyote was integral to religious ritual and its use restricted to specific ceremonial occasions. In California, the state supreme court in 1964 ruled (*People* v. *Woody*) that ingestion of peyote was the "theological heart" of Native American Church practice after several Navajo had been arrested for illegal possession of the substance, and therefore in this case was protected under the First Amendment's free exercise clause.[19] In 1990, however, the legal debates reached the U.S. Supreme Court, which decreed in *Oregon* v. *Smith* that states individually could restrict or prohibit the use of peyote in a religious context, despite the legal standing of the Native American Church. Those dismayed by the decision saw an infringement on the free exercise of religion guaranteed by the First Amendment that provided the legal context for pluralism to flourish. Congress chose in 1993 to enact legislation that would assure the right of Native Americans to use peyote in religious rituals, but further court challenges and appeals meant the situation was far from resolved at the end of the century.

For thousands of Native Americans some form of peyote religion has become a key ingredient in their religious identity as the century progressed. All evidence suggested that use of peyote continued to spread not only among people belonging to tribal societies where the practice was introduced a century or so ago, but also among other tribal peoples, despite legal challenges and occasional prosecution by federal or state authorities. In bringing a range of Native American religious expressions together with elements of Christian teaching and practice, peyote religion exemplified one manifestation of pluralism in the religious life of Native

Americans in the twentieth century, one that witnessed the birth of a new practice that combined elements of both and also one that took institutional form in the Native American Church. Much variety remains in peyote rituals, for each individual tribal culture has given the practice its own features, much in the way that there is considerable variation in local practice among congregations identified with the same Protestant denomination. Peyote religion gives evidence of a pluralism that continues to enrich Native American life in the United States.

The Recovery of Old Traditions

The rekindling of interest in ethnic identities that swept through American society as an offshoot of the civil rights movement and the way African Americans pursued their own African roots, including religious dimensions of African tribal life, influenced Native Americans as it did countless others in the nation. Many of the generation of Native Americans who came of age in the wake of the civil rights movement were interested in recovering, if not revitalizing, the mythology, rituals, and related religious practices that had given cohesion and coherence to tribal life before the European conquest and the consequent decimation of tribal life, particularly after the consignment of tribes to reservations often distant from their ancestral lands.

One compelling voice seeking to articulate Native American concerns and place them in the larger social context of liberation and human rights following the civil rights era is that of Vine Deloria. The approach taken by Deloria in some ways echoed that of many African-American theologians who were both activists working for social justice and thinkers seeking to develop a theological posture that reflected their singular experience. In addition to his work as a theological writer, Deloria has served as executive director of the National Congress of American Indians. He has also remained involved in many of the legal battles over the last three decades that have sought redress for past abuses stemming from federal policy.

Deloria's early writing is a summons to Native Americans to recapture the vitality of their tribal traditions.[20] Like so many others, Deloria feared that generations of life on reservations, the increasing numbers of younger tribal members who sought education and employment off the reservations and thus were becoming assimilated into the larger society, and the continued intrusion of Christian missions into Native life spelled the eventual demise of virtually all distinctive tribal religious practice. By recovering what was in danger of eradication, tribal peoples could preserve what had once given shape to individual and collective existence for those yet to come. Revitalization also required changes in the principles that had buttressed government policy, assuring Native Americans of their full rights. There was some naiveté in Deloria's position. Given the transformations of time, the syncretistic pluralism that had emerged in varying degrees among all tribes with extended contact with Christianity, and the history of prolonged separation from lands once central to tribal life, no "pure" traditions and practices from the past could be recovered. Change had been a constant in tribal life such that all indigenous practice bore the marks of transformation.

Like African-American thinkers who saw in their advancement of a black theology an opportunity to recast white Christianity and its theological underpinnings, Deloria also turned attention to constructs within the Native world view that he believed could revitalize the whole of American society, not just the Native American communities. In *God Is Red* (1973), for example, he argued forcefully that Christianity had serious flaws rendering it incapable of responding to some of the critical social issues that were undermining American life.[21] Unlike his African-American theological peers, Deloria did not single out racism as the primary failing of white Christianity, but rather its giving sanction to the heedless exploitation of the land and the natural resources of the nation. In the world view generally espoused by indigenous peoples, the land was itself sacred and thus the basis for sustaining all life. What American Christians could learn from the Native American perspective was an appreciation for the interconnectedness of all living things and their links to the land. By stressing the larger applicability of Native American sensibilities Deloria had moved well beyond tribal boundaries; for normally one was born into a tribe, and one did not assume a tribal identity simply by appropriating Native American views. Although Deloria offered a sophisticated theological approach that had its greatest appeal in intellectual circles, his emphasis on the land and connections to the land had particular congruence with the way of thinking undergirding the developing ecological and environmental movements.

As an activist, Deloria called for assuring that full legal rights were extended to tribes and their members. The issues have been particularly complicated because of claims to land that had been taken over by the government or regarded as private property belonging to others once removal to reservations began more than a century and a half ago. The renewed ethnic consciousness that swept through American society as a consequence of the civil rights movement led several tribal communities to seek compensation for land that had been seized decades earlier, the restoration of such land to tribal collective ownership, or at least guarantees of access to lands regarded as sacred for purposes of celebrating tribal religious rites. Often disputes wound up in the courts, from local to federal levels. In the 1980s, for example, cases involving the Navajo, Hopi, Cherokee, Lakota, Tsistsistas, Inupiat, and several Northwest tribes all came before the courts. In general, so long as reasonable access to land was guaranteed, the courts were reluctant to transfer ownership or provide monetary compensation. What constituted reasonable access remained a source of disagreement. In *Wilson* v. *Block*, for example, the Court of Appeals for the District of Columbia in 1983 rejected a Hopi claim that construction of new facilities for skiing and expansion of existing ones in the Snow Bowl area of the San Francisco Peaks in the Coconino National Forest in northeastern Arizona would impede their free exercise of religion.[22] Certain rites were celebrated at Snow Bowl, and the Hopi argued that the larger ski facilities make it unreasonably difficult for them to carry out these rites. The court dis-

agreed because the Hopi still had access to the sacred space where religious celebrations occurred, albeit not unrestricted access to the entire mountain that they
saw as sacred, and they had managed to mark these rites for the half century that
the original ski operation had been in place.

Other cases revolved around the controversial American Indian Religious Freedom Act, which from 1978 on made it the government's duty to protect and preserve Native American access to sacred sites, the use and possession of sacred
objects (which many thought sanctioned use of peyote), and freedom of worship
using traditional tribal rites.[23] Changes in the law, generally designed to broaden
such protection, continued into the 1990s. Yet no one could claim that returning to
lands once home to tribal peoples and renewed practice of rites in the way they
were performed in a precolonial era could really be accomplished. Simply put, the
pluralism and syncretism that had come to Native American life and the changes
in the cultural context that had come over the centuries rendered any return to the
past impossible.

Often on the periphery of the dominant culture, Native American tribes have
confronted extraordinary challenges in trying to maintain their heritage or even
adapt it to changing circumstances. Whether in a symbiotic relationship with the
various strands of Christianity associated with the many missions to indigenous
peoples, the development of new forms of tribal expression as in the rituals surrounding peyote, the call to extend Native American sensibilities to the larger
culture, or efforts to protect the free exercise of religion and preserve sacred lands
for tribal use, Native American peoples and their religious expressions have moved
in ever more pluralistic directions as the twentieth century progressed. While much
of that pluralism has involved syncretism, it has brought a new richness to Native
American life.

CHAPTER 7

Personal Religious Expression
in a Pluralistic Culture

Religion harbors an inherent tension between the teachings and practices of formal traditions and what David Hall has called the "lived religion" of individuals, the way persons appropriate beliefs and practices for themselves as they seek to make sense out of their own experience.[1] This more personal religion—what bears the label of spirituality, religiosity, or popular religion—is more eclectic and idiosyncratic because of the way individuals respond to church and creed, filter out what they personally do not accept or understand, and combine what remains with other ideas and practices to fashion ways of giving meaning to the world in which they live. The relationship between lived religion and formal tradition receives illustration in historian Robert Orsi's brilliant discussion of how Italian Americans, in what was New York's Italian Harlem, fused aspects of Roman Catholicism with beliefs and customs rooted in Italian peasant life to create a distinctive religious culture and accompanying spirituality neither fully Catholic nor fully Italian. What resulted was a spirituality informed by a Catholic "sensibility," not by the Catholic Church.[2]

Spirituality is very practical. Its goal is to provide individuals with a sense of wholeness through tapping reservoirs of inner strength often linked to what today is popularly called a "Higher Power," what traditional language calls God or the supernatural. Various exercises, from prayer to meditation, provide access to that supernatural realm; some also use objects, such as rosary beads or candles. All spirituality assumes that the empirical world is not the whole of reality, with the spiritual superior to the empirical. Often a healthy suspicion of established religious authority pervades the personal spiritual quest, based on the conviction that priests and churches seek to manipulate the sacred for their own advantage, not for the well-being of ordinary people. While religious authorities may not have malevolent intent, they prefer some control over individual spirituality to assure that it does not become heterodoxy, heresy, or some other dangerous form.

In the nineteenth century, the institutions making up the American religious landscape did not lack interest in individual spirituality. For example, Roman Catholic leaders promoted personal piety that was oriented around devotion to the Virgin Mary and the Blessed Sacrament.[3] Catholic parishes organized confraternities for men and sodalities for women designed to increase personal devotional practice. Popular periodicals such as the *Messenger of the Sacred Heart* or *Ave Maria* offered readers pious stories touting the benefits of devotion. The denominations and agencies, like missionary societies, of Protestant America championed ways of being religious that reflected "official" teaching and doctrine. The Methodist *Christian Advocate*, in addition to denominational news, regularly carried articles to assist laity in the pursuit of piety.[4] Even more personally oriented was material that appeared in such Protestant publications as the *Guide to Holiness*, which—like the Italian-American Catholic spirituality that Orsi studied—was shaped by Methodist sensibilities but not by the denomination per se.[5] In addition, in the later nineteenth century, moral fiction, novels designed to inform spirituality and elevate life, became an increasingly popular literary genre.[6] But Protestant denominations exerted indirect, although powerful, influence over personal spirituality because of the centrality of the church in social and cultural life, particularly in smaller cities, towns, and rural areas before the age of the automobile, film, and television. Leisure time revolved around church activities, allowing individuals to absorb a modicum of spirituality, almost by osmosis. Also in the later nineteenth century, American Jews, whose spirituality always focused on the home more than formal institutions like the synagogue, began to produce literature for the devout in English, since those comfortable with Hebrew were becoming an ever smaller proportion of the Jewish population.

The twentieth century brought astounding proliferation to the expression of personal spirituality. Here, perhaps more than in any other arena of the nation's religious life, pluralism prevailed. Sociologists have long asserted that as societies become increasingly complex, as they industrialize and urbanize, the location of vital religion shifts from religious institutions and traditions to the individual, from the public sphere to the private sphere.[7] The push towards an urban, industrial society that mushroomed in the last decades of the nineteenth century has yet to abate. At the same time, scholars such as Colleen McDannell have demonstrated that, independent of this process, in the Victorian era American Christianity, in its multifaceted Protestant and Roman Catholic expressions, came to see religious nurture as a domestic matter; the home was sacred space where spirituality was cultivated.[8] But the home was also private space, ultimately beyond the control of religious authorities. Denominations prepared materials for home use but could not control how people used them or what they made of their content.

As the twentieth century progressed, mass production of print materials at low cost to consumers made religious materials from many sources readily available to more people. The technological advances resulting in radio, film, and television gave the public visual access to a growing number of religious alternatives. For example, in the 1960s and 1970s when the military conflict in Vietnam came into millions of living rooms on television's nightly news, Asia became less exotic, distant, and alien, as did the spirituality associated with its religious traditions. The massive immigration at the end of the nineteenth and beginning of the twentieth centuries brought an ethnic richness, making the possibilities for personal spirituality more pluralistic as many became familiar with southern, central, and eastern European ways. But as sources of immigration shifted, other possibilities from the life experience of different clusters of immigrants entered public consciousness. By century's end, for example, Hispanic American ways added fresh layers to the possibilities for personal spirituality.

Expanding the Expression of Catholic Spirituality

For American Catholics, the dynamics of spirituality and the greater pluralism in expression that marked the twentieth century come into focus with the peasant people, the *contadini*, who came by the thousands from southern Italy to the United States during that last major wave of immigration.[9] Italian spirituality nurtured a substratum antedating Christianity and Rome's becoming Catholicism's institutional center. Where ancient agrarian civilizations flourished on the Italian peninsula, fertility religions—centered around a Mother Goddess who gave birth to the earth and whose power enabled the earth to bring forth fruit—prevailed. When Christianity replaced the remnants of those religions, the Virgin Mary readily usurped the role of the goddess, echoed today in the hundreds of churches bearing the name of *Santa Maria*. But ancient agrarian people knew, as do farmers today, that nature can be fickle, that the earth does not always produce as we would like. Evil, demonic powers were as prevalent as holy ones and readily dominated unless they were appeased or superior benevolent powers were invoked. They did not disappear when Christianity came to prevail. The people knew better than the priests how to avoid the demonic *malocchio* or evil eye. Church authorities remained suspect as well because the church as an institution was identified with forces of economic or political oppression as much as with a realm of spiritual power.

This rich overlay of spirituality penetrated the Catholicism brought to places like Italian Harlem as the nineteenth century gave way to the twentieth. For ordinary people, there was no contradiction between this spirituality and church teaching, although Irish-American priests were often taken aback. Shrines in the homes of Italian immigrants linked them to places of pilgrimage in the homeland noted as sources of sacred power long before Christianity entered the picture. The *festa*, or street festival, that on the surface honored the Blessed Virgin, recalled veneration of the Mother Goddess, though there lingered a fondness for the Virgin herself, one who knew the hard life of ordinary people through the pain experienced as her son suffered through the agony of crucifixion. Robert Orsi noted how Americans of Italian descent whose forebears came to Italian Harlem, to churches like the one on East 115th Street dedicated to the Madonna of Mount Carmel, returned year after year long after they had moved to the suburbs and entered the middle class because here was a reminder of a spiritual realm, of a personal way to bring order and meaning to daily life.[10]

Similar stories, though details vary, move through other Catholic immigrant communities. A rich eclectic spirituality pervaded Polish immigrant neighborhoods, Czech neighborhoods, and others.[11] The constant in Catholic immigrant spirituality was some form of Marian devotion, but different from that promoted by the church generally in the mid-nineteenth century. After promulgation of the doctrine of the Immaculate Conception in 1854, interest in the Virgin mushroomed. Romantic currents boosted the appeal of the divine Mother, a human but one who transcended the vicissitudes of ordinary life. The Blessed Virgin extolled in immigrant piety became a symbol of survival, of hope for triumph over the hardships of the immigrant experience itself. If the one popularly depicted as cradling in her arms both the infant Jesus and the crucified Christ could become elevated in glory almost as a coredemptor for humanity, immigrants could prevail over the difficulties of uprootedness and adjustment to a new land and identity. This vibrant spirituality flourished alongside the more traditional piety promoted through sodalities and confraternities and echoed in celebrations like the Mount Carmel street procession long after the immigrant generation joined the heavenly host.

In the latter half of the twentieth century, a new wave of Catholic immigrants perpetuated their own eclectic spirituality. Mexican Catholicism, for example, had retained more of a Mediterranean flavor than the Irish-dominated Catholicism that assumed reins of leadership in the United States. As Mexican immigration skyrocketed in the last third of the century, churches in many communities not only had to offer Mass in Spanish, the vernacular of Mexican Americans, but they confronted a panoply of patron saints and a festive style of public expression of spirituality intertwining remnants of indigenous religious practices with "official" Catholicism. For some, the more dramatic expressions of this spirituality seemed an aberration. The *pentitentes* of New Mexico, for example, fused blood rituals and ancient tribal initiation ceremonies with a spirituality centered on the suffering of Jesus in rites of self-flagellation.[12]

Clusters of immigrants from Cuba and other Caribbean areas followed *santeria*, literally "the way of the saints." Yet *santeria* spirituality merged a Catholic understanding of the saints with the world of African spirits, particularly the *orishas* of the Yoruba.[13] In *santeria*, animal sacrifice (the practice generating the greatest media attention), a rich herbal lore, dance, and divination come together along with the sacrifice of Christ in the mystery of the Mass to create a dynamic spiritual realm. *Santeria* appealed to many as a supplement to more traditional piety; many who sought the ministrations of *santeria* priests were not regular practitioners, but simply drawn to the realm of power *santeria* represented. African Americans cognizant of *santeria*'s Yoruba connections, but with no ties to the Roman Catholic Church, frequently explored *santeria* in communities where it flourished.

Historian Thomas Tweed highlighted dimensions of Cuban Catholic immigrant spirituality with a marked resemblance to another feature of earlier Catholic immigrant piety. Tweed unraveled connections between a Cuban nationalism, an ongoing effort to retain a Cuban identity amid diaspora, and devotion to the Blessed Mother manifested in pilgrimage to the shrine dedicated to Our Lady of Charity in Miami, the center of much of the Cuban immigrant population.[14] Among earlier immigrants, those from Poland had also combined nationalistic impulses with Marian devotion.[15]

Currents in African-American Spirituality

African-American spirituality, though heavily influenced by the Christian tradition from the eighteenth century on, also brought together diverse approaches to the religious life. Those drawn to *santeria* represent only a recent example. The exuberance long evident in much public worship among African-American Christians reveals the continuing impact of African tribal religiosity, with its extensive use of chant, song, and dance.[16] The appeal of ecstatic experience, most apparent in African-American Pentecostalism, demonstrates a continuous awareness of the power of an unseen, spiritual world that can take control and transform the life of the faithful in the midst of present reality.

This vital connectedness to a spiritual realm receives confirmation in other ways in African-American spirituality. One is the continuing intrigue with conjure. Conjure itself has a distinguished history, harkening back to the presence of trickster figures in African tribal religiosity.[17] The trickster deceived and effected unexpected outcomes in complex situations because it belonged to a spiritual world. The trickster could invade a human body, endowing that person with extraordinary spiritual power. Often that power manifested itself in an ability to bring healing from disease or to transform ill-fated situations into that which was beneficent. The trickster's spiritual power might be malevolent for those who were "tricked," but remained positive for those on whose behalf it was conjured or invoked. Like *santeria*, conjure also tapped into the world of folk medicine or herbal remedies for various ailments, a substratum of cultural life everywhere.

Conjure doctor and trickster entered the domain of spirituality largely through preachers or other individuals popularly regarded as unusually holy. Prior to the middle of the twentieth century, most African-American Protestant clergy lacked the seminary training many white denominations expected of candidates for ordination. Most evidenced a dynamic, charismatic piety grounded in intense, personal religious experience; so, too, did some extraordinary laypersons. In other words, most preachers owed their power as preachers to the power of their person and personality. This power was exactly the same sort of spiritual energy that for centuries set apart some as technicians of conjure. Many African-American lay folk went to their preachers or specially endowed laypersons to seek physical healing through folk remedies or to tap into a realm of spiritual power they could access or, quite literally, conjure. Decades ago, more in the rural South than elsewhere, some African-American churches offered more traditional fare on Sunday mornings, albeit with the added enthusiasm typical of African-American worship, and something more reflective of conjure at other times. Affinities between the preacher/conjure doctor and the shaman in Native American tribal cultures are patent.

Akin to conjure and drawing on some of the same principles is voodoo, an approach to spirituality more common among African Americans than others. For decades, scholars suggested that voodoo was generally restricted to areas of Louisiana, Georgia, and the Sea Islands off the South Carolina coast, where, in the antebellum period, African slaves arrived after having spent time in Haiti.[18] They rightly saw voodoo as a syncretistic blending of African, Christian, and Haitian elements to create a spiritual realm controlling everything from fertility to the weather. The aim of this voodoo was benign: to harness that power for the benefit of the people. Through dance and ecstatic frenzy, spiritual forces possess those who become conduits of power to be harnessed to accomplish particular ends. But individuals may perform these rituals alone as an expression of personal spirituality. Interest in voodoo enjoyed a resurgence in the later twentieth century, but its ecstatic spirituality stretched back earlier and was always more widespread than formerly assumed.[19] Indeed, it represents almost a constant substratum in much African-American spirituality.

While it is inappropriate to apply the labels of conjure or voodoo to the spirituality fostered by many of the independent storefront African-American churches central to black religious life in urban America during the Great Migration and after, there were points of contact. Many of the independent preachers, male and female, who attracted followings among those displaced from their southern rural roots and not always accepted by the black urban middle class, were those believed to possess extraordinary spiritual power.[20] It was no accident that such storefronts were often nestled between establishments where palms were read or fortunes told; they were all part of a spiritual cosmos where the power of the Other could be brought to bear on daily life.

Strains of Jewish Spirituality

Jewish immigrants from eastern Europe who developed the culture of *yiddishkeit* also evidence strains of a spirituality with features common to other immigrant spirituality. Judaism boasts a formal tradition of spirituality, largely influenced over the centuries by what Americans came to call Orthodox Judaism. Men who recited daily prayers at home or in a *minyan* (a minimum of ten men who gather for prayer in the mornings at a synagogue) followed a practice hallowed by generations. The traditional language for religious ceremonies, whether celebrated in the home or synagogue, was Hebrew, although there was also a popular literature in German, since German was the first language of the bulk of Jewish Americans prior to the influx of immigrants from eastern and central Europe. For many, the adjustment to the American environment meant abandoning Hebrew and then German. Hence there was a need for religious materials in English. The symbolic marker that spurred the development of other literature to sustain a Jewish spirituality was the publication of the *Union Prayer Book* in 1896. It contained no German at all and only a small amount of Hebrew. Within a decade it was standard in more than 225 Reform synagogues.[21] Jewish women, whose gender role included oversight of food preparation, often adhered to the dietary codes longer than their husbands and sons. While this faithfulness to tradition gave a unique dimension to the spirituality of Jewish women, it was increasingly difficult to "keep kosher" in the context of the ghetto tenement.[22]

At the same time, Jewish spirituality shaped by the eastern European heritage also contained an interesting mixture of mysticism, most obvious in Hasidim, and magic.[23] It included the idea, for example, that one could manipulate the names of God for personal benefit. Belief in angels, in antiquity influenced by Persian and other Near Eastern traditions, also had magical aspects. Within the culture of *yiddishkeit* much of this lore infused personal spirituality along with whatever prayers and practices of the formal Jewish heritage might be appropriated. For individuals, it was not a two-track spirituality, one magical and one religious, but an eclectic whole.

The Power of Angels

Awareness of a supernatural realm of power, inhabited perhaps by angels, accessible perhaps through conjure, or revitalized in ethnic festivals, by no means died out as the twentieth century progressed. It remained an ongoing stratum in the spirituality indigenous to much of Appalachia.[24] It had a stunning renaissance in the closing decades of the century when popular belief in angels and the availability of supernatural power mediated by angels swept through much of American Christianity. Religious bookstores reportedly could not stock enough goods, from coffee mugs to jewelry, with artistic designs associated with angels.[25] Books on angels, once rare, became bestsellers in religious circles, spurred by evangelist Billy Graham's *Angels: God's Secret Agents*, which appeared in 1975. The rebirth of interest in angels was sustained into the late 1990s by the likes of James Redfield's *The Celestine Prophecy*, which enjoyed more than two years on the *New York Times* bestseller list.[26] At first, the vitality of belief in angels in late-twentieth-century popular spirituality may seem anachronistic, but it represented much more than reaffirming one strand of belief in the supernatural. It is integral to the baby boomer generation's rejection of rigid scientism and its appreciation for inner-directed religiosity. One critic, however, suggests that popular books on angels and other aspects of personal spirituality marketed for a mass audience are little more than appeals to the vanity of the boomer generation that wants to join a spiritual elite.[27]

For much of the century, mainline Protestant spirituality pushed belief in angels to the periphery. But the denominations eagerly promoted personal spirituality informed by approved denominational teaching. Its roots again stretch back to the late nineteenth century when the domestication of religion generated a literature for use in the home in instructing children and cultivating piety among children and youth.[28] Much had a feminine cast to it, since the age regarded religious nurture as women's domain (though men had a role) and saw women as more naturally religious than men. The rapid expansion of the publishing industry, including religious publishing, between the Civil War and World War I enabled denominations to prepare a broader range of materials oriented toward personal spirituality. From Sunday school literature to pamphlets and magazines intended for use in the home, denominations began to gear content by specific age levels and sometimes by gender for adolescents and adults.[29]

Aids to Devotion

In addition, late-nineteenth-century Protestantism developed two phenomena specifically designed to promote and shape personal spirituality: the daily devotional book or magazine and the distribution by catalogue and direct sales of books and study aids targeted for laypersons. Colleen McDannell, in her *Material Christianity*, tracked the development of the Gospel Trumpet Company, an arm of the Church of God (Anderson, Indiana).[30] McDannell focused on religious objects, from art reproductions to wall plaques, stationery, bookmarks, and postcards with a religious message. Denominational catalogues also generally advertised Bibles, including the familiar "family" Bibles with places for genealogical records, and books containing such inspirational materials as the collected sermons of evangelist Dwight L. Moody or popular British preacher Charles Spurgeon. Clergy may have purchased these for their own edification; laity were encouraged to use them to gain understanding of scripture and doctrine. In other words, such books enriched personal spirituality.

By the dawn of the twentieth century, books with daily devotionals had become popular, with the better selling ones reprinted year after year. A standard format developed: one page for each day in the year containing a brief biblical quote, a three- or four-paragraph meditation applying the biblical message to daily life, and a short prayer. Most were by women such as Mary W. Tileston and Ellen Dyer, unknown to the professional theological world.[31] While the majority were "all purpose," designed for private or family devotions (perhaps led by the husband or father), some targeted particular audiences. Ellen Dyer, for example, in the late 1890s compiled an anthology designed specifically for workers, acknowledging the growing numbers of single women and men employed in urban industries and businesses. In 1925 the first volume of *Streams in the Desert* appeared.[32] Compiled by Mrs. Charles E. (Lettie Burd) Cowman, six years later it was still selling 2 million copies a year. Methodists pushed daily devotional materials in a new direction in 1935 when the *Upper Room* first appeared.[33] Most earlier devotional collections were books covering an entire year and reflecting the work, either as author or compiler, of one person. The *Upper Room* was a pocket-sized magazine with devotions for a two-month period. From the start the Methodist editors solicited contributions from individuals around the world, giving the brief testimonies to faith a personal touch. Just over two decades later, from the Radio Bible Class came a similar magazine, *Our Daily Bread*, with its appeal directed primarily to an evangelical or theologically conservative audience.[34]

In many ways all these materials are cut from the same cloth. All are practical, designed to deal with real situations that individuals confront in daily life, not weighty matters of theology. Sickness, death of a spouse, conflict in the work place, difficulties with children, and a host of other "real life" situations frame the narrative, which also purports to be an exposition of the biblical text cited at the outset. But an implicit theology and understanding of personal spirituality may be equally important. Cheryl Forbes argued that Lettie Cowman's *Streams in the Desert* was directly related to women's spiritual experience. Consigned by male-dominated religious institutions to a spiritual desert, women found in the devotionals—in which many passages were taken from earlier collections by other writers—strength for survival and an ability to cope.[35] There is little difference in the theological framework between these passages and those appearing later in the *Upper Room* or *Our Daily Bread*. All presume the reality of a God vitally interested in the daily affairs of each individual. All suggest that reliance on divine supernatural power helps to solve problems, resolve conflict, and provide a sense of control over the vagaries of routine existence. They promote a spirituality transcending denomination and even doctrine. The expectation is that if one engages in such devotional exercises daily, one will have a greater sense of wholeness and happiness in life. The distinctively feminine cast of the earliest daily devotional materials has become muted. The *Upper Room*, for example, has many male contributors and few direct references to experiences unique to women as women. At century's end, such materials still shaped spirituality. In the early 1990s, for example, the *Upper Room* reported a bimonthly circulation of around 2 million; *Our Daily Bread* claimed a bimonthly circulation of 7 million.

Self-Help and Popular Psychology

The religious reconfiguration following World War II brought another dimension of spirituality to the forefront, one with a rich history, but also one still a major force in personal spirituality at century's end: the ties to popular psychology. Before the close of the century, bookstores boasted "self-help" sections as a result. When Rabbi Joshua Liebman's *Peace of Mind* became a bestseller in 1946,[36] it joined a vast religious literature arguing for the power of the mind over the physical and the ability of the individual to achieve self-improvement and thus greater personal happiness and well-being.[37] Similar concerns had sparked the emergence of Christian Science under Mary Baker Eddy a century before, and later in the century informed Russell Conwell's well-known lecture *Acres of Diamonds*, which was reportedly delivered more than 6,000 times.[38] The most direct forerunner was Ralph Waldo Trine's *In Tune with the Infinite*, published in 1897 and still in print a century later.[39]

What cemented popular psychology to spirituality was the work of Norman Vincent Peale, whose ministerial career revolved around promoting and refining ideas advanced in his *The Power of Positive Thinking* (1952).[40] Since 1968 hundreds of clergy have learned to nurture this spirituality through the Blanton-Peale Graduate Training Institute; more were reached through Peale's monthly magazine *Guideposts* that, while eschewing any denominational stance, went to more than 3 million subscribers even after Peale's death in 1993.[41] Although not a mirror image of Peale, Robert Schuller and his "possibility thinking," brought to millions of private homes through the televised "Hour of Power" from Schuller's Crystal Cathedral in Garden Grove, California, are of the same ilk, arguing that individuals can seize control of their lives, orchestrate personal and material improvements, and achieve an inner peace and happiness once missing. All of them, including Billy Graham whose *Peace with God* (1953) and *The Secret of Happiness* (1955) and Charles L. Allen whose *God's Psychiatry* (1953) are part of the genre, insist that this self-help is possible only if accompanied by trust in God.[42] More controversial was science fiction writer L. Ron Hubbard's use of similar principles in his *Dianetics: The Modern Science of Mental Health* (1950), which forms the basis for Scientology.[43] In whatever guise, this approach represents Arminianism's final triumph over Calvinism in American Protestantism, for it places primary responsibility for one's life and changing its course (redemption, salvation) in the hands of the individual. Ironically, two of its major proponents, Peale and Schuller, held affiliation with the Reformed Church of America, whose theological foundation was staunchly Calvinist.

The 1950s were ripe for a spirituality based on positive thinking. The relocation of many returning World War II veterans and their families to communities where they had no ties and the mushrooming of suburban developments brought a concomitant social dislocation. If the Cold War made it seem as if one had no control over national destiny, the rootlessness of suburban life and the triumph of the "organization man" in business made it seem as if there were no real control over personal life.[44] As well, the materialism and economic prosperity marking the postwar years prior to the 1957 recession left a hollowness for thousands; they basked in the signs of success, but failed to reap inner satisfaction from them. Positive thinking, God's psychiatry, and their cognates provided that satisfaction by giving the individual psychological power. Older forms of spirituality did not disappear; indeed, the year before Peale's *Power of Positive Thinking* topped bestseller lists, Catherine Marshall published her biography of her husband, *A Man Called Peter*, that was so successful it was made into a regular commercial film.[45] Marshall came from a studied Presbyterian background where all revolved around the providence of God, not humans seizing control of their lives.

Secular forces joined with positive thinking to transform spirituality's story. In 1935 Alcoholics Anonymous (AA) pioneered its twelve-step program.[46] Predicated on the conviction that alcoholics were powerless in their present situation, AA claimed that turning to a Higher Power and having a spiritual awakening restored order and happiness to life. Intentionally vague in its notion of a Higher Power to avoid offending those who found traditional belief in God a stumbling block, AA through its meetings also pioneered development of the support group or small group, now a key ingredient of most Protestant churches' endeavors to foster spirituality. AA's success in restoring spiritual and psychological wholeness to recovering alcoholics led others to use its "twelve steps" in different areas. Overeaters Anonymous, Narcotics Anonymous, Adult Children of Alcoholics, and a host of others promoted self-help and improvement through the "twelve-step" approach. For many, the AA group and its parallels became religious groups and the "twelve steps" became a mechanism bringing meaning to life, much like explicit religious belief.

A more public dimension of 1950s spirituality highlighted the underlying desire to cultivate the inner life. In the 1950s, the "prayer breakfast" became a fixture in political circles. Reminiscent of Puritan "fast days" and the like, prayer breakfasts cut across denominational lines, bringing together persons seeking supernatural guidance to lead American common life.[47] Critics noted the vacuous theological content in the prayers and addresses offered at them, but such should be expected. Spirituality is so intensely personal that common language cannot capture its power. More important, the symbolism in a common affirmation of a spiritual dimension and in public events like prayer breakfasts gives legitimacy to spiritual pursuits.

Spiritual Surrender and Inner Power

Central to spirituality are prayer and disciplines of personal meditation to draw individuals closer to the divine. As the 1950s gave way to the 1960s, spirituality found these disciplines enriched with new possibilities. One byproduct of the Pentecostal and charismatic renewal beginning in the late 1960s was a fresh appreciation of ecstatic experience. Surrender to the power of the Holy Spirit became preferable to surrender to the hassles of making a living and coming out on top in an increasingly complex society. Others drawn to spiritual ecstasy followed Timothy Leary's lead by experimenting with hallucinogenic drugs to expand interior consciousness and release spiritual energy. Critics dismissed drug-induced spiritual experience because the drugs used were controlled substances, making experimentation illegal. They also insisted that the resulting experience was artificial, not genuine, because it depended on the chemical reaction generated by the drug. Advocates countered that prolonged fasting and meditation also produced a chemical imbalance that led mystics and others to report similar experiences accepted as genuine.[48]

This frantic search for inner spiritual power turned in other directions as Asian religious groups made a presence for themselves in the United States. In the 1950s, intellectuals typifying the "beat generation" stimulated interest in Zen Buddhism's meditation disciplines that practitioners hoped would bring them to *satori* (a blissful state ending the cycle of rebirth). From then until century's end, the numbers of Americans visiting Zen retreat centers and the number of centers operating grew steadily.[49] The International Society for Krishna Consciousness launched its mission in the United States in 1965, just as American military engagement in Southeast Asia was escalating.[50] Soon it was routine to see persons in saffron robes chanting on street corners or in airports, extolling by example the virtues of meditation techniques nurtured for centuries in the Hindu and Buddhist traditions. When celebrities endorsed the Transcendental Meditation (TM) advocated by the Maharishi Mahesh Yogi, millions sought out local gurus, paid fees to get a personal mantra, and started practicing TM.[51] Most who appropriated these techniques did not abandon a religious identity or spirituality associated with Christianity or some other religious community. They were "add-ons" to enhance pursuit of the inner life, even if not sanctioned by the religious groups with which practitioners were affiliated. This personal blend evidenced the eclectic nature of spirituality; individuals combined elements of Asian discipline with the traditional aids to spirituality to create something uniquely their own.

When fascination with Asian meditation disciplines waned, New Age spirituality filled the void.[52] There was little "new" about New Age. Some recognized its affinity with what others called the "perennial" philosophy, for New Age spirituality looked to age-old techniques to bring the individual in harmony with unseen spiritual forces pervading the universe. The upswing of popular interest in astrology paralleling fascination with New Age likewise drew on the conviction that humans were integrated with the whole of the universe; it seemed logical to assume that the location of stars and planets had an impact on the rest of the whole. Many personal practices that the media classified as New Age had cognates in Asian religiosity. For example, the sense of the world as an integrated whole pervades the Confucian *I Ching*, while more Taoist understandings of astrology and divination and principles of *feng-shui* (a system of geomancy or practices for determining the location of spiritual forces) operate much the same way as some New Age postulates. New Age practitioners often failed to appreciate that their practices, from arranging crystals to lighting incense, revolved around ritual forms functioning much the same way as forms of traditional spirituality. Saying the rosary or repeating prayers to focus spirituality accomplished the same results: a sense of oneness with the spiritual forces of the universe and a concomitant sense of inner wholeness. What set New Age apart in its American manifestations was its highly individualistic nature and its not being readily identified with a recognizable religious tradition. Shorn of the trappings that, for example, tied the rosary to the baggage of Roman Catholicism, New Age seemed purer and less culture-bound. Yet it was inextricably wedded to a culture that valued private devotion more than public worship. The highly individualistic aspect of New Age diverged from more traditional forms of spirituality in another way. One of sociologist Wade Clark Roof's subjects noted that while her eclectic New Age-type spirituality "worked" to provide a framework of meaning for her life, it was too idiosyncratic to pass on to her children to assist them in their religious quests.[53] Traditional spirituality, while personal in expression, emerged from a community of faith with resources to transmit to succeeding generations.

The Neopagan Revival

New Agers were not alone in finding in the spiritual wisdom of the past tools to use in their personal journeys. The last decades of the twentieth century brought a revival of interest in pre-Christian spiritual forms, often dubbed neopaganism and frequently associated with women's quest for forms of spiritual expression speaking to their experience as women.[54] Because some had historical connections to witchcraft and magic, detractors lumped all such practices together as *wicca*. Some American women did return to *wicca* in the last third of the century, not because of its presumed links to the evil and demonic, but because, like other pagan or pre-Christian religious forms, it had rituals highlighting the unique experiences of being female. Ancient fertility religions celebrated the mysteries of birth; the neopagan revival celebrated the mysteries of pregnancy and childbirth, along with other physical aspects of being female. Women gathered to celebrate rituals emerging from specifically female experience, from reaching menopause to invoking the goddess. Claiming the Divine in the form of the goddess not only stripped spirituality of patriarchal dominance and oppression; it also imputed a holiness to the experience of being a woman.

Many of these endeavors supplemented involvement in other, more traditional forms of spirituality. For example, one widely used guide to women's spirituality that called attention to connections with pagan expression was the Unitarian Universalist Association's *Cakes for the Queen of Heaven*, itself a quotation from Jeremiah 7:18 (albeit there it is a reference to idolatry).[55] In the mid-1990s, many mainline Protestant denominations were rent with controversy because of ecumenical women's gatherings that used female symbols for Deity, such as *Sophia* (wisdom). Many expressions of women's spirituality cut across the boundaries dividing religious groups; women gathered in a forest grove to invoke the goddess had formal religious identities spanning the gamut—or none at all. What brought them together was simply their being women.

Many women, however, have developed their own practices of spirituality within the churches. Robert Orsi carefully analyzed the twentieth-century devotion of millions of Roman Catholic women to St. Jude almost as an ancillary to much officially sanctioned devotionalism because the "central political fact of devotionalism is that while it was ostensibly made for women, directed at their hearts and purses, it was made against them, too."[56] On their own, Catholic women had to deal with the oppression and control fostered by formal devotionalism. Within Jewish circles, apart from Orthodoxy, women have developed new rituals marking such events as a miscarriage to enhance their spiritual quest within the parameters of the tradition.[57] Protestant women from a variety of denominational backgrounds have found spiritual nurture through groups like Women's Aglow, which combines psychological and charismatic approaches in a parachurch experience.[58]

Part of what propelled the pursuit of a feminist or women's spirituality was the assumption that the patriarchal Western religions dominant in American religious life modeled the forms of spirituality after what was distinctly male. The assumption harbors truth and falsehood. As the larger culture began to consign spirituality to the domestic realm, already the sphere of women, many of the resources developed to nurture personal spirituality bore a feminine (but not feminist) cast. Hence in the 1990s, there emerged efforts to promote a male spirituality that had roots in the experience of being male. Most had to combat popular perceptions that men were by nature less religious or spiritual than women and that men were therefore less likely to be interested in cultivating the inner life. The "muscular Christianity" touted by early twentieth-century Protestant evangelist Billy Sunday and the mass effort of the Men and Religion Forward Movement (1911–12) to add men to church membership rolls set the stage for promoting a distinctive male spirituality.[59] Many of the later efforts, such as the Promise Keepers movement from 1992 on, sought to bring large groups of men together in environments such as football stadiums or sports arenas that were thought to be quintessentially masculine.[60] Promoters hoped these mass rallies would prompt men to undergo a spiritual reawakening that would in turn spur them to cultivate the spiritual life in private or in the company of a small group of like-minded men. These efforts gave added confirmation to the transdenominational nature of spirituality, for men attending a Promise Keepers rally or some similar event have a variety of religious backgrounds.

Popular Culture Invades the Spiritual Realm

By the 1990s, the pursuit of spirituality moved into the arena of popular culture, further collapsing the boundaries between the sacred and the secular. In the latter part of the decade, the series of inspirational books that began with *Chicken Soup for the Soul* soared to the top of bestseller lists and remained there for months.[61] *Chicken Soup for the Soul*, combining aphoristic-like quotations, one- or two-page stories, and other snippets geared to a readership on the move but seeking a spiritual anchor, enjoyed a few years on paperback bestseller lists and had several sequels; its cognate *Chicken Soup for the Teenage Soul* by the Fall of 1998 had held bestseller status for more than a year.[62] A score of titles using the "chicken soup" label all sold well; at one point in 1998, *Publishers Weekly* had five of the series on its list of ten bestselling paperbacks. All of these books were oriented to particular audiences such as workers, women, or mothers. Of a similar ilk were the several works authored by Leo Buscaglia; of more theological substance, but still oriented to individual spirituality were the bestselling writings of Kathleen Norris.[63] While on the surface they extolled simple virtues, they spoke to the baby boomer generation's yearning to nurture the inner life apart from the trappings of church structure or denominational bureaucracy.

The wildly popular "chicken soup" inspirational books drew on the cultural assumption that chicken soup as a food offered healing possibilities. Connections between spirituality and healing were more overt as a variety of medical personnel reported that persons with religious faith frequently showed a better recovery rate from certain diseases than those without a spiritual base and a greater control when confronting terminal disease. A 1998 study conducted under the auspices of the Duke University medical school provided evidence that individuals who cultivated a spiritual life had lower blood pressure than others and even stronger immune systems. Some persons returned to more traditional exercises of spiritual discipline, such as fasting, to promote health as well as religious growth. Others offered an approach to physical exercise and movement grounded in spirituality, while several writers developed weight loss programs and diet regimens linked to spirituality.[64]

Targeting "Generation X" was the spirituality popularly captured in the "W.W.J.D." or "What Would Jesus Do?" movement in the 1990s. Few adolescents or young adults who sported woven bracelets bearing those four letters realized they represented the subtitle of Charles M. Sheldon's novel, *In His Steps*, initially appearing in the 1890s and still in print a century later.[65] With the wearing of crosses as jewelry so widespread that the practice was devoid of explicit religious symbolism, and the wearing of St. Christopher medals and the like on the decline since Vatican II, "W.W.J.D." emblems provided instant reminders of the spiritual dimension of life and the focus of that spirituality primarily for Protestant Christians. By the end of the 1990s, there was also a growing passion for sacred music, sacred dance, and associated religious phenomena in the performing arts. Performers were attracted to the aesthetic dimensions of the sacred arts; consumers, whether listening to a CD in the privacy of the home or attending a dance performance, sought "spiritual nourishment without the time-consuming efforts of learning a philosophy or, for that matter, making the leap of faith."[66]

At the dawn of the twentieth century, personal spirituality, while often individual and private, was shaped largely by forms and resources supplied by religious communities. By the dawn of the twenty-first century, personal spirituality had become increasingly pluralistic, mingling elements drawn from a variety of religious orientations. Mircea Eliade long ago argued that one of religion's main functions was providing individuals and communities with an axis, a center around which all else revolved and which therefore endowed life with meaning.[67] Personal spirituality has as its end providing individuals with means of access to that axis. If the forms of personal spirituality became ever more pluralistic as the twentieth century progressed, its end goal remained constant.

CHAPTER 8

The Proliferation of Pluralism

The sight of men standing on city street corners, having heads shaved, wearing saffron robes, and chanting mantras in praise of Krishna (a manifestation of the Hindu deva Vishnu) would have been unimaginable at the dawn of the twentieth century. In the early 1970s, it was common. Although within a decade few devotees of Asian religious expression approached travelers in airports or intrigued passersby on the street, by the end of the century Hindu temples were found in most major cities, even in the heart of the Bible Belt. Most who celebrated Hindu festivals at these temples were not youthful American converts, but Indian Americans sustaining and preserving that mix of religion and culture indigenous to their land of origin. By the close of the century as well, those with an eye toward statistics claimed that the number of Muslims in the United States, not just African-American adherents of the Nation of Islam or the Black Muslims, equaled or perhaps surpassed the number of Jews.[1] While none dared suggest a recasting of Will Herberg's classic *Protestant, Catholic, Jew* as *Protestant, Catholic, Muslim*, it was increasingly evident that the contours of religious pluralism were shifting, that the Christian hegemony in American religious life—while still a force to be reckoned with—was not as strong as it had been a century earlier, and that Americans of whatever religious identity were daily contending with a greater array of religious alternatives that were markedly different from one another than ever before in the nation's history.

Many of these alternatives had links to immigrants, as had Protestant groups generations earlier. The difference was that as the twentieth century progressed, again the sources of immigration shifted, bringing millions from Asia, for example, who, like previous generations of immigrants, sought to transplant their own religious style to American soil. More recently, the significant increase in immigrants from the Near East and parts of Africa greatly augmented the ranks of Islam in America, supporting the claim that Islam had replaced Judaism as the nation's "third faith." Some fresh alternatives were connected to traditions with a venerable heritage in the United States, but reflected the unique manifestations of faith associated with different cultural experience. One example, noted in the discussion of American Catholicism, is the vibrant presence of a Hispanic ethos, echoing especially Puerto Rican, Cuban, Mexican, and Latin American ways of being Catholic. Political pundits likened the world to a global village, given gains in communications technology and economic interdependence among nations as the twentieth century progressed; the new pluralism in American religious life mirrored the global consciousness of the American people and the increasingly diverse ethnic and racial foundations of American culture.

Yet not all of the new pluralism had ties to the traditional world religions, even if transplanted to a different cultural environment. Some comprehensive world views that functioned for adherents like more religious belief systems lacked a substantive religious base. For example, the Society for Ethical Culture emerged in 1876 under the leadership of one-time Jewish rabbinical student Felix Adler, promoting a humanistic ethic without the supernatural substructure that buttressed more overtly religious systems.[2] Adler also had ties to the more radical Free Religious Association that sprang from Unitarianism in 1867 and promoted a "religion of humanity" rooted in science, idealism, and reason, not supernatural revelation. In a similar vein, by the 1930s, some thinkers promoted a form of humanism that also eschewed things otherworldly. Many taken with the gains of science and technology in enriching the quality of life and opening new vistas for the future saw in them almost a replacement for traditional religion, more so than had those who shaped the Free Religious Association.[3] Although countless religious leaders expressed fear of "secular humanism" and the "religion of science" or dismissed them as false and heretical, their presence added to the new pluralism transforming American religious culture as the twentieth century ended.

The Lure of the Orient

Until the latter part of the nineteenth century, most Americans with any knowledge of Asian religions were taken by the philosophies supporting them, not the practices of adherents who found in them meaning in life and direction for action. Ralph Waldo Emerson and others in the Transcendentalist circle in antebellum New England, for example, were intrigued especially with the monism of the Hindu *Upanishads* that seemed to them akin to their own brand of Unitarianism.[4] Outside of intellectual and literary circles, letters written to supporters and articles penned for missionary society journals by those carrying the Christian message "from Greenland's icy mountains" to "India's coral strand" (as Anglican missionary bishop of India Reginald Heber put it in a hymn),[5] provided the primary source of information about things Hindu and Buddhist.[6] Often that information was intentionally exaggerated or skewed; missionaries dependent on financial support from American Christians astutely presented their work in such a way as to convince readers of their needs, even when they developed a more sophisticated and realistic appreciation of the religions of those to whom they ministered.

There were immigrants from Asia who made their way to the United States. The larger groups came from China and Japan to areas along the West Coast of the

United States and Canada beginning around 1850.[7] Numbers remained relatively small until the 1870s. But Euro-Americans, whose movement into California and other areas of the Southwest was dramatically increasing, from the start exhibited prejudice more on ethnic than on religious grounds, with hostility towards Chinese immigrant laborers in California often more violent and intense than attacks on southern and eastern European immigrant laborers in the Northeast. For some Christian congregations in places like Los Angeles and San Francisco, Chinese immigrants were objects of evangelization, although those who abandoned traditional ways for Western styles in everything from clothing to religion were generally ostracized by other Chinese Americans. Yet Chinese immigrants established their own religious and social institutions, reflecting the same blend of Buddhist, Confucian, and Taoist aspects that prevailed in Asia.[8] Antagonism toward Chinese laborers became so bitter, however, that in 1882 Congressional legislation banned Chinese immigrants from entering the country for ten years.[9]

The most immediate backgroup for the twentieth-century explosion of interest in Asian religions in the United States, though, was the World's Parliament of Religions, held in Chicago in 1893 in conjunction with the Columbian Exposition.[10] Representatives of faith communities from around the globe had a public forum on American soil to explain to the curious and the critic alike the beliefs and practices of their own traditions. Some, like the Theosophical Society with its fusion of Buddhist, Hindu, Spiritualist, and ancient metaphysical philosophies, already had a small U.S. following in a handful of urban areas.[11] Publicity from the World's Parliament spurred modest growth. But a pluralism pushing beyond the confines of the Judeo-Christian heritage gained impetus when some of the Asian religious teachers chose to stay in the United States for a time, going on lecture tours to cities around the country. Swami Vivekananda (1862–1902; born Narendranath Datta) lectured in Chicago on the philosophical monism advanced by the eclectic mystic and spiritual teacher Ramakrishna (born Gadadar Chatterjee). His subsequent travels around the United States gave birth to the Vedanta Society, and after returning to India, in 1897 Vivekananda organized the Ramakrishna Mission there.[12] Although generally confined to larger cities, the Vedanta Society still offers a program of philosophical lectures based on the *Upanishads*, but has never promoted ritual practices of the Hindu tradition. World War I discouraged other Asian religious leaders from coming to the United States, but in 1920, another Indian religious teacher, Paramahansa Yogananda (born Mukunda Lal Ghosh), came to a conference in Boston and then toured the United States, lecturing on yoga techniques. Out of his teaching came the Self-Realization Fellowship, headquartered in Los Angeles, but maintaining just a handful of temples or religious centers in the country.[13]

There were others, but these illustrate the first infusion of things Asian into twentieth-century American religious life. Their appeal was primarily intellectual, and their constituency drawn from the ranks of more well-educated persons of Euro-American stock. None actively proselytized; most were restricted to the larger cities where lectures would be advertised in newspapers. Relatively few Asian immigrants, even of Hindu inclination, have identified with them. Some adherents reflect the personal eclecticism that has come to mark much American religiosity; not every follower of Vedanta, for example, abandons identification or even affiliation with another religious body.

Other Asian religious currents made their way into American life as an unintended consequence of World War II, the Korean Conflict, and the continued American military presence in Asia during the Cold War. For Asian Americans, the years that brought World War II were unsettling. The internment of thousands of Japanese Americans disrupted efforts to support those religious institutions serving their communities; one, the Honpa Hongwanji, changed its name to the Buddhist Churches of America (except in Hawaii), hoping that the word "church" in its formal designation would help dispel hostility. It remains the largest Buddhist group in the United States.[14] The war years also brought the first sustained contact millions of American had with Asian culture, not only in the course of combat, but in the years of military occupation that followed in some areas. Military personnel brought home Asian spouses eager to continue their own religious ways, as had generations of European and African immigrants earlier.

Japan loomed large in much of this new appropriation of Asian religious ways, sparking another wave of interest in Asian philosophy in intellectual circles. Authors popularly dubbed the "beat generation," including Jack Kerouac and Alan Watts, wove Zen themes into their writing. Some, like Watts, practiced Zen meditation; all were smitten by the metaphysical ethos of Zen.[15] Much of what they learned came not from direct experience in Japan, although hundreds traveled to the East to study meditation at traditional monasteries. The most influential source of information about Zen came in the writings of D.T. Suzuki, who wrote in English, and his American wife.[16] Suzuki's lectures on Zen at Columbia University in the early 1950s were extraordinarily popular and should have served as a signal of things to come to those who touted the so-called "religious revival" of the postwar decade.

Numerous Zen centers were established in the United States, many flourishing initially in the 1950s. But as early as 1930, long before the beat generation's fascination with Zen, the Buddhist Society of America was founded in New York, changing its name after World War II to the First Zen Institute of America.[17] Some Zen centers are linked through formal associations; others have more informal connections. The most well known is the Zen Center of San Francisco, with its popular retreat complex at Tassajara Hot Springs, east of Big Sur in Carmel Valley.[18] Most of the Zen centers around the country have appealed to Euro-Americans, but even if leaders are of Asian extraction or trained in Japanese monasteries, they have had to adapt traditional formats for an American clientele. Few Americans, regardless of ethnic heritage, could devote the hours each day to meditation that authentic practice required. The Southern Dharma Retreat Center, near Asheville, North Carolina, is not unusual in scheduling events that run a single weekend for those just embarking on serious meditation and others for those wishing more intensive study as well as more extended programs for persons pursuing advanced practice and knowledge. There and at Tassajara, as at other centers, devotees experience a vegetarian diet and other activities reminding them that they have broken out of the frenzy of ordinary life to recover inner strength and direction.

Numerous other Japanese groups, several identified with the "new religions" that cropped up in the nineteenth century, but mushroomed in twentieth-century Japan, have also found a niche in the United States, mostly among Japanese Americans and Japanese nationals whose business brings them here. Most well-known is Nichiren Shoshu, sometimes called Soka Gakkai for one movement within Nichiren, but Tenrikyo, Konkokyo, Omoto, Sekai Kyusei Kyo (often called the "Church of World Messianity"), Seicho no Ie ("House of Growth"), PL Kyodan ("Perfect Liberty Order"), numerous sects of Nichiren, and a host of others all have modest American followings.[19] Nichiren Shoshu, rooted in the teachings of the thirteenth-century prophet Nichiren centered on the Lotus Sutra, gained currency in Japan through a lay organization (Soka Gakkai) in the 1930s, but grew rapidly in the 1950s as the Japanese people looked in new directions following the devastation and defeat of World War II.[20] In 1960, the first Soka Gakkai chapter in the United States, first called Nichiren Shoshu of America, formed in California. From there, interest spread quickly, benefiting from the spiritual experimentation and dissatisfaction with established religious patterns that marked the 1960s. For Americans, Nichiren Shoshu was attractive because of its practical side. The rapid chanting, adherents claimed, produced results that ranged from the usual sort of inner peace and serenity to landing better jobs, acquiring specific material possessions, and the like. Critics feared another dangerous cult, largely because they did not understand the dynamics of chanting the *Nam Myoho Renge Kyo* (the Daimoku) and the seemingly militaristic cast of group marching and public exercises that was part of Nichiren's presence. Today priests are organized through the Nichiren Shoshu Temple in Etiwanda, California (east of Los Angeles near San Bernardino), and laity as Nichiren Shoshu Soka Gakkai of America.

As with other Asian expressions that counted on American converts, Nichiren Shoshu in the 1960s and 1970s drew particularly from among those in late adolescence or young adulthood, stages in human development, according to psychologists, when persons are more open to religious alternatives as they seek a spiritual anchor that is theirs, not necessarily one taken over from parents or the larger society.[21] The same was true for the form of Asian meditation practice that had held the greatest attraction for Americans, the World Plan Executive Council known to almost all as Transcendental Meditation (TM). Unlike American manifestations of Zen or Nichiren Shoshu, which received ideological support for meditation and chanting from within the Buddhist orbit, TM looked to Hindu meditation for its origins.[22] In 1959, the Maharishi Mahesh Yogi, a one-time physics student and then a disciple of Hindu yoga master Swami Brahmananda Saraswati, first arrived in the United States. With long hair and a generous beard, wearing a flowing white robe and sandals, and often carrying roses, the Maharishi appeared sent by central casting. He was the very image of a Hindu holy man in the popular mind, and after he employed public relations specialists to promote him and his work, he received enormous media attention. When celebrities such as Mia Farrow, rock sensations like the Beatles, athletes like Joe Namath, and popular pundits like Marshall McLuhan all became practitioners, some photographed for the press as they accompanied the Maharishi on jets to India and other places where he proclaimed his truth, TM became a sensation.

Serious students of Indian religion and culture found TM a sham. For a fee, those wishing to learn its secrets could approach a TM master, receive a personal mantra to chant, and gain instruction on instant meditation techniques that could be employed everywhere from crowded New York subways to the privacy of one's home. TM advocates crowed that one need not devote hours a day to mastering meditation; ten to fifteen minutes of TM could produce the same serenity and inner peace. By the 1970s, TM operated Maharishi International University on the former campus of Parsons College in Fairfield, Iowa, and expanded its organization to include the Student International Meditation Society (SIMS) and the more formal Spiritual Regeneration Movement targeting a much smaller and generally older clientele. It unabashedly claimed to be a scientific means to produce peace of mind, something Americans had long sought, not just a form of spirituality.[23] In some ways, that briefly revitalized TM, for by then the frenzied spiritual experimentation of the 1960s that fueled earlier interest had faded. It became a practical technique, not a spiritual exercise, that anyone could employ without abandoning previous religious identification or affiliation. Like some forms of Buddhism in America, TM became another ingredient in the eclectic personal recipes that millions sampled in their quest for spiritual fulfillment.

Other manifestations of the Hindu tradition that marked the new pluralism coming to reshape American religion as the twentieth century progressed also found the 1960s a ripe time for promulgating their visions of truth. Some benefited from the dissatisfaction many coming into adulthood in the 1960s felt with an American religious culture that they saw as racist. Some no doubt owed intrigue with Asian styles to the easy equation of Western religion with support for the scientific endeavors that produced "the bomb," the symbol of potential universal destruction; by contrast, the religions of Asia seemed purer. Although they were as intertwined with their own indigenous cultures as any American religion was with its own culture, they left that behind when emissaries came to the United States.

The most well-known, and perhaps the most controversial, was the International Society for Krishna Consciousness (ISKCON), better known popularly as Hare Krishna, from the words of chants devotees uttered on street corners across the nation.[24] Like many Asian religious options, Krishna Consciousness benefited from the spiritual malaise of the 1960s. In the wake of social dislocation linked to civil rights and kindred "liberation" endeavors, traditional religion seemed too tied to the status quo. Without recognizing the ways the Hindu tradition was enmeshed in a social and cultural status quo in India, thousands looked to Krishna Consciousness for a new approach to spiritual well-being because in the American context it seemed more pure, more fresh, and less entwined with a morally bankrupt culture. It was also the case that U.S. military involvement in Southeast Asia (the Vietnam War) introduced another generation of Americans to Asian culture; ISKCON benefited from that exposure.

Krishna Consciousness from the start was different. Unlike the earlier Vedanta Society and Self-Realization Fellowship, Krishna Consciousness demanded that adherents engage in traditional Hindu religious practice, only grudgingly and in minor ways altered to fit the American setting. The organizing genius behind the movement, revered by followers as His Grace A.C. Bhaktivedanta Swami Prabhupada (1896–1977; born Adhay Charan De), came to the United States after a Vaishnavite master in a deathbed utterance ordered him to devote his life to promoting devotion to Krishna, an avatar or manifestation of the Hindu deva Vishnu, in English-speaking lands. Prabhupada, according to stories cherished by followers, began his work in the tawdry Bowery district of New York City. From the start, he was adamant that followers pledge absolute obedience to his spiritual mastership and adhere strictly to a regimen banning premarital sex, use of intoxicating beverages or controlled substances, gambling, and eating eggs, meat, or fish. When followers began to live in communal settlements, take on Sanskrit names, and don Indian rather than Western dress, they signaled their total change of identity and devotion.

To outsiders, especially those who saw their college-student children severing family ties for a life of seeming squalor and devotion to a foreign teacher, Hare Krishna epitomized everything negative associated with religious cults. Aggressive proselytizing activities, from button-holing passengers scurrying through airline terminals to selling copies of the *Bhagavad Gita* on city streets, also aroused opposition, although in theory they differed little from those used by groups such as the Jehovah's Witnesses and Mormons. Little matter that devotees followed a daily regimen of devotion to Krishna more rigorous than that of most Hindus in India. Little matter, either, that converts spent a prolonged probationary period, often a minimum of six months, before initiatory rites brought them into the fold.

ISKCON retreated from public view after Prabhupada's death, witnessing greater growth in other nations. In the United States, a prominent ISKCON community, New Vrindaban (near Moundsville, West Virginia), split from the main body after a mysterious killing and reports of other criminal activities brought federal investigation there in the mid- to late 1980s.[25] Some analysts suggest that Krishna Consciousness is following the time-honored progression from being a marginal, emergent religion to an organized, accepted, and established religion, and that its followers, now raising children themselves, demonstrate the stability that comes when transmitting religious teaching to a generation born to believers supersedes the need for securing converts from outside the circle of the faithful. Regardless, the continuing presence of Krishna Consciousness gives proof to the broadening contours of religious pluralism in twentieth-century America.

In the 1960s, Krishna Consciousness was only one of several Hindu-based groups that carved out a place for themselves in American religious life, and TM's Maharishi Mahesh Yogi was only one of numerous gurus who sought to impart Eastern wisdom to an American audience. The Guru Maharaj Ji, a teenager, promoted his teaching through the Divine Light Mission.[26] Maharaj Ji claimed to awaken an inner light in devotees; followers reported that they actually saw a bright light when in the presence of Maharaj Ji or when touched on the forehead by him or another enlightened one. When the fascination with things Asian waned as American military presence in Southeast Asia ended, Maharaj Ji and other gurus also receded into the background, although some still count a handful of followers. The Divine Light Mission, for example, in the 1980s became Elan Vital and dropped most of its Asian trappings. Even as many such gurus declined in public influence, one emerged who created as much controversy as had Bhaktivedanta Prabhupada a couple of decades earlier. In 1981, the Bhagwan Shree Rajneesh arrived in the United States. From a Jain background, Rajneesh combined Hindu, Buddhist, Jain, and Tantric elements with features from a host of other traditions in what he called Dynamic Meditation. Abandoning a career as a philosophy professor to spread his truth, Rajneesh attracted both followers and critics, for he seemed to promote an indulgent approach to life rather than the asceticism characteristic of Indian religion. Especially after American devotees clustered in a commune, Rajneeshpuram, near Antelope, Oregon, reports surfaced of sexual license, regular use of controlled substances supposedly for meditative purposes, and other questionable activities. Legal difficulties led to the deportation of the Bhagwan after he was charged with several breaches of immigration laws in 1985, and conflict ensued over transmission of leadership. Like most earlier Asian manifestations that were short-lived—Krishna Consciousness is an exception—the Rajneesh International Foundation and its Colorado-based successor, the Chidvilas Foundation, quickly dropped from public view.[27]

Virtually all of these expressions of a new pluralism drawing strength from the religious traditions of India, especially the Hindu tradition, have pitched their message primarily to Euro-Americans. But the most vital presence of Hindu religious life in the United States at the dawn of the twenty-first century has few Euro-American followers, but represents the commitment of Indian immigrants to sustaining their religious heritage in an American context. Unlike immigrants of an earlier age popularly portrayed as relatively poor and uneducated, Indian immigrants have often come from the thousands who pursued professional education in the United States and did not return to India. Others have come because of business opportunities; in some areas, the Indian-American community has extended family ties or can trace lineage to the same cities, towns, or regions of India. Regardless, what is most significant for the new pluralism is the sharp increase in the number of Indian Americans. For the decade of the 1950s, the total number of immigrants from India was just under 2,000. The total swelled to slightly more than 260,000 for the decade of the 1980s. The numbers continue to rise; the Immigration and Naturalization Service reported that nearly 45,000 immigrants came to the United States from India in 1996 alone.

In India where Hindu culture dominates, it is impossible to draw sharp lines between sacred and secular, between the religious and the social. Religious practice also differs markedly from what most Americans assume from Christian practice. Hinduism has no fixed day of worship each week, no worship services with sermons or discourses that the faithful are expected to attend, no array of auxiliary programs to attract persons of various demographic groups. Yet Hindus have been inveterate temple builders to provide a place where individuals can make offerings and receive blessings from priests as well as celebrate major festivals; and, as with Judaism, the heart of Hindu practice is in the home. In the United States as in India, Hindu homes will have a room or some space set apart for *puja* or personal devotion and meditation. In the American context, Indian immigrants have had to take conscious responsibility to sustain the tradition since American culture provides no tacit support for the Hindu tradition as does its very pervasiveness in India. They had to be committed to establishing religious institutions in the United States. In most major American cities, Hindus have built temples or converted existing structures into temples; priests have been brought from India to provide ritual leadership. In the midst of an environment offering few props for Hindu identity, Indian Americans can raise families within some familiar religious structures. In many locales, residents are often unaware of the presence of Hindu temples, even if they appreciate the Indian restaurants and other cultural accoutrements accompanying Indian immigration. The reason is simply the nonproselytizing character of the tradition, another trait shared with Judaism. One is simply born into Hindu culture; the word "Hindu" itself means Indian. To be sure, some Hindu Indian Americans have converted to other religious communities, though in relatively small numbers. The Indian Hindu faithful are content to pursue personal devotion without calling attention to distinctive religious practices. By the close of the twentieth century, however, the nation included more than a million Hindus in its population and about 900,000 Buddhists and practitioners of traditional Chinese religions.

Another Asian import, one from Korea, aroused as much controversy as had the appearance of Krishna Consciousness. Known formally as the Holy Spirit Association for the Unification of World Christianity or the Unification Church, the movement was more widely called the Moonies, after its founder, Sun Myung Moon.[28] Moon and his family had become Christians, converted by conservative Presbyterian missionaries in what is now North Korea when Moon himself was a child. Yet Moon's teaching drew from the religious life indigenous to the Korean peninsula as much as it did from Christianity. Unification doctrine, centered around what Moon calls the Divine Principle, reveals an eclectic, idiosyncratic fusion of things Chinese, Buddhist, Christian, and more. The particular mix was also influenced by Moon's unfortunate encounters with Communists, who held him in a forced labor camp for more than two years during their rise to power in North Korea. As early as 1959, some Unification seeds had been planted in the United States when Young Oon Kim came to the West Coast. She was destined to become one of the movement's most influential and articulate theological thinkers. Moon first visited the United States in 1971.

While the Unification Church bears all the marks of a standard "new religion" with an Asian flavor, it quickly aroused suspicion in the United States. What made critics cringe were messianic claims made about Moon and his wife, for Unificationists, assuming a bipolarity that pervades all nature, believed that the male Jesus had ultimately failed as a messiah who could restore a fallen humanity to its right relationship with God because he had no female spouse. Moon and his wife, the True Parents, made up for that. Like Krishna Consciousness devotees, Moonies demanded celibacy before marriage, and, like many new religious movements, they encouraged adherents to live together for mutual support. Particularly controversial were two practices. One was the requirement that new converts engage in fund raising, often by badgering drivers stopped at traffic lights to buy flowers; the practice was designed to teach humility. The other is having Moon identify marriage partners for adherents, followed by group marriage ceremonies, sometimes involving thousands of couples at one time. Because Moonies used the language of Christianity, some American Christians saw them as especially threatening, insisting that those who entered the Moonie ranks were brainwashed and that the group was a dangerous cult.

During the 1980s, Moon and the Unification church tried to counter these criticisms, albeit without complete success. Some devotees completed advanced degrees in various religious disciplines in order to give an intellectually credible base to the religion's ideology, and the group began a seminary. Publications, a staple of twentieth-century new religious movements, presented Moonie teaching and practice to a larger audience, without pressure of conversion. Seminars were held for religion professors and other religious leaders in the hope that once they understood the theological base of Unification teaching, albeit one different from orthodox Christianity, opposition would dwindle. Subsidiary organizations like the International Cultural Foundation, the International Religious Foundation, Project Volunteer, and a host of others targeted specific areas of outreach. When Moon was jailed on charges of income tax evasion, many oldline Protestant bodies filed "friend of the court" briefs on his behalf, recognizing that similar charges could be brought against many of their own clergy who managed a local congregation's finances. At the time, some believed that the government pursued its case against Moon simply because he and the Unification movement were controversial. Conservative Christian critics of the Moonies were often baffled because they share similar views with the Moonies on numerous social issues, such as opposition to abortion and gay rights and a strident patriotism. By the end of the twentieth century, however, the Unification Church had become much less aggressive in its American proselytizing activities, although there were still signs of strength and growth elsewhere, particularly in Japan and in parts of Europe. Many of the arranged marriages failed, leading hundreds to drop out of the movement. If numbers remained small and converts dwindled, the Unification Church continued to illustrate ways that pluralism by the end of the twentieth century had broadened well beyond what it had been earlier.

Islam Becomes an American Religion

Until the twentieth century, the Muslim population of the United States was numerically insignificant. Although evidence reveals that practicing Muslims were among the African peoples brought to North America as slaves in the antebellum period, circumstances worked against the establishment of flourishing Muslim communities.[29] Even at the end of the century, the overwhelming majority of American Muslims were foreign-born, indicating that immigration since the close of World War II has been the primary source of the Muslim population. The first significant Muslim immigration, however, came in the decades immediately following the Civil War. Most were relatively poor and uneducated men from the Ottoman Empire, especially from areas that today constitute Lebanon, Jordan, and Syria. Most who came right after the war were kin to those already here. After laws in the 1920s fixed quotas on immigration based on proportions set in the 1890 census, opportunities for Muslims from other areas to migrate to the United States were minimal.

A shift came after World War II with the upheaval in Europe accompanying the expansion of communism, the unsettledness in the Middle East that ensued after the creation of Israel as a Jewish state, and, to a lesser extent, the division of the Indian subcontinent into the predominantly Hindu nation of India and the predominantly Muslim nation of Pakistan. The first two decades after World War II thus saw an ethnic diversity coming to Islam in America, although those of Near Eastern stock continued to dominate. That ethnic diversity has continued, despite changes in immigration patterns in the last quarter of the twentieth century. Thousands of Muslims from a variety of nations have come to study at American universities, with a large number remaining to pursue professions and careers. Muslims from other parts of Asia—from Indonesia, for example, which boasts the largest Muslim population of any nation—and especially from Africa have also come in ever larger numbers. By the end of the century, more than 5 million Americans were practicing Muslims, leading some analysts to proclaim that if the number of Muslims in the United States in 2000 did not exceed the number of Jews in the United States, it would within the first decade of the twenty-first century. Add to this those who are Black Muslims, despite the insistence of some that the Nation of Islam is not an authentic representative of the teachings of Muhammad, and it becomes clear that Islam gives much credence to the thesis that pluralism has come of age in twentieth-century America.[30]

Yet Muslims have rarely felt accepted as an integral part of American religious life, and persons of other religious persuasions have often looked on American Muslims with suspicion, one nurtured by ignorance of Islam.[31] Given the historic tilt of American foreign policy toward Israel since its creation, Muslims have long felt that Americans misunderstood the convoluted and complex nature of Middle Eastern politics, particularly where Palestinians were concerned. Such apprehensions mounted after the Six Day War of 1967, prompting formation of many non-religious organizations to combat discrimination against Arabs in the United States. At the same time, such organizations have been divisive within the Muslim communities, since not all Muslims are of Arab extraction. The Iranian hostage crisis that ended in 1981 likewise spurred misunderstanding; many Americans assumed that all Muslims identified with the Shi'ite branch dominant in Iran, while most are actually linked to the Sunni tradition. Hence American Muslims, like some other earlier immigrant communities, have felt an ongoing need to educate the non-Muslim population, not so much to gain converts as to alleviate the misunderstandings impeding efforts to create viable Muslim religious institutions to serve the followers of Allah.

Securing a niche within American religious life has also been complicated by the nature of Muslim religious organizations in the United States. Although by the end of the century, most American cities were home to more than one mosque, American Islam lacks the kind of bureaucracy common among Protestant denominations. Mosques are theoretically independent, although federations provide opportunities for networking. Among the larger are the Islamic Society of North America, the Federation of Islamic Associations, the Council of Masajid, and the Islamic Circle of North America.[32] These umbrella organizations also include Muslim communities in Canada. None could speak for all American Islam. Another hindrance has been cultural and religious differences over the role of women. While many Muslim women in the United States appear in public with heads covered, they are not necessarily the abused victims of a patriarchal tradition that much popular perception holds. Historically, Muslim women were often the key figures in the establishment of mosques to serve the larger community, especially in the earlier part of the century.

Like other religious and immigrant communities, American Muslims have established periodicals and other ancillary mechanisms to sustain the faithful. *Muslim World*, for example, targets an intellectual and academic audience.[33] Some interpreters speak of the "Americanization" of Islam and its institutions, much as an earlier generation spoke of the Americanization of Catholicism or the Americanization of Judaism.[34] In the Jewish experience, that process centered around the role of the rabbi, the synagogue, and the Jewish community center; rabbis took on pastoral functions, synagogues expanded their programs after the model of Christian congregations, and community centers emerged to promote social and cultural life shaped by Jewish sensibilities. For American Muslims, especially in the larger cities, the mosques have also taken on a larger role, offering classes for children and youth and a host of social activities, much like a community center.

At the same time, there have been American converts to Islam. Estimates hold that anywhere from one-fifth to one-third of American Muslims are converts; the

proportion varies in part depending on whether one counts those who are tempo-
rary residents of the United States—students and businessmen primarily—in the
tally. Most converts are African Americans; estimates hold that only around 100,000
Euro-Americans have become practicing Muslims. Some African-American converts initially made their way into groups like the Moorish Science Temple and
then the Nation of Islam, but in recent decades, encouraged by the immigration of
Africans who are Muslims, more African-American converts have come into "mainstream" Islamic communities rather than smaller sectarian groups. The appeal of
Islam to converts stems in part from the awareness that Christianity in the United
States for generations fostered first slavery and then discrimination. Islam seems a
purer faith since it has less American cultural baggage. Its long African history
leads some African-American converts to see the move to Islam as one back to
more authentic religious roots. Many Euro-American converts, perhaps even a
majority, come into the ranks of Islam through marriage to a practicing Muslim,
following a pattern repeated countless times among other groups throughout American history.[35]

The measurements developed to gauge the depth of Christian commitment are
as inappropriate for American Muslims as they are for American Jews. As with the
Jewish tradition, Islam is a total way of life, not easily broken down into components.[36] The heart of Muslim practice has long been personal adherence to such
basics as praying five times daily facing in the direction of Mecca, not attendance
at or even membership in a mosque or ancillary organization. Scholars estimate
that probably not more than 10 percent of American Muslims are affiliated with a
mosque.[37] Mosques offer Friday prayer services, often with exposition of passages of the *Qur'an*, the tradition's sacred text. Attendance is sparse, with men and
women separated and only men taking part in leading the prayer service. As in
other religions, more attend on special holidays or festival occasions. Thousands
of American Muslims appear to outsiders as totally secularized, although a substratum of Muslim identity remains. Again one is reminded of the debates among
American Jews whether religious practice is essential to a Jewish identity.

There are signs of increasing acceptance of Muslims in American religious
culture. Although there was residual opposition, over the last two decades of the
twentieth century, many prison systems added Muslim chaplains and began to
accommodate religious and dietary practices of Muslim inmates. The United States
armed forces now includes Muslim chaplains.[38] Of greater symbolic than practical import, in 1991 for the first time a Muslim leader was invited to offer the
opening prayer for a session of Congress. Given current immigration patterns,
American Muslim communities are likely to grow rapidly in the opening decades
of the twenty-first century. If Islam still sparks images of the Ayatollah Khomeini
and anti-American sentiment, Americans of all religious persuasions would do
well to understand the character of Islam as a religion of submission to the will of
Allah, for pluralism today must include the many faces of Islam in America. In
time, too, that pluralism will have an internal ethnic dimension, for there are varia-

tions in the Muslim style from one Muslim culture to another. But creating the institutions to sustain Islam in the American environment has thus far muted some of those ethnic particularities from coming to the fore in the United States.

Emerging from within Islam is another religious movement also experiencing an astonishing rate of growth at the end of the twentieth century, Baha'i.[39] With roots in the teachings of a nineteenth-century Iranian prophet, Baha'u'llah, and his teacher, Mirza Ali Muhammad (known to the faithful as the Bab or "Gate"), Baha'i draws on the Zoroastrianism indigenous to Iran, the Sufi tradition of Islam, and features of other religions to fashion its vision of the ultimate unity of God and humanity. That vision breeds a concern for human rights and equality, a belief in progressive revelation leading to the conviction that there is truth in all religions, an insistence on extraordinarily high moral standards given the cultural milieu of the late twentieth century, and a very practical passion for social justice (giving the movement in the United States an interracial quality) and for the social and ecological environments.

Baha'i was introduced in the United States as early as 1892 in the Chicago area. By 1912, there were enough converts that work began on the Baha'i House of Worship in Willmette, Illinois (near Chicago), which is the American spiritual and administrative headquarters. Most local Baha'i communities have no formal Sunday services, although some, including Willmette House of Prayer, offer weekly lectures. Usually the faithful simply gather for prayer and readings and conversation on an announced theme or topic. Not aggressive in seeking converts, Baha'i remains small, counting probably not more than 100,000 adherents in the United States at the start of the twenty-first century. What is significant, however, is its proportional growth rate, particularly in parts of the country like the Deep South often perceived as religiously homogeneous. The emphasis on the unity of humanity while celebrating diversity made Baha'i increasingly attractive as American society became more culturally and ethnically heterogeneous. Baha'i's presence and growth demonstrate further the way pluralism is expanding beyond its former Judeo-Christian boundaries.

Stretching the Boundaries of Religious Pluralism

Important also for understanding the dynamics of the expanding pluralism in late twentieth-century American religious life are movements and groups that, while remaining numerically small, eschew identification with any of the traditional faith communities. In Protestant theological circles early in the century, liberal currents led to an empirical approach, most often associated with the University of Chicago Divinity School, and a radical modernism that seemed even to other Protestants almost devoid of theistic belief in any supernatural sense.

Perhaps the most radical movement outside traditional religious circles is epitomized by the *Humanist Manifesto*, published in 1933, reflecting a trend to formulate a religious world view rid of all traces of supernaturalism.[40] Signed by eleven prominent educators, journalists, and some Unitarian clergy, the manifesto sought to affirm the teachings of modern science, particularly evolutionary theory. Hence it denied the idea of the divine creation of the universe, rejected the division of human experience into sacred and secular categories, and celebrated achievements in science, technology, and humanitarian endeavors. With humanist groups organizing in local communities, usually around universities or other intellectual centers, religious humanism offered itself as an alternative to traditional forms of religion that were intertwined with supernaturalism. At the same time, the religious humanism that came from this movement was hardly the secular humanism so feared by religious conservatives in the last quarter of the twentieth century. Those who signed the manifesto, like well-known educator John Dewey, held strong moral and ethical views promoting human welfare and well-being. They were not hostile to values, even if a later generation portrayed them that way. Even with the formation in 1941 of the American Humanist Association, publisher of the periodical *The Humanist*, humanism attracted very few followers as an organized alternative to religion. Yet it demonstrates that the pluralistic environment was expanding in unforeseen directions.

More directly related to the surge of confidence in science and scientific progress were several efforts, again primarily in intellectual circles, to rethink the character of religion from a scientific viewpoint. None coalesced into an organization that took on the trappings of religion as had the American Humanist Association. Among the more influential, thanks to its academic journal *Zygon*, has been the Institute on Religion in an Age of Science, formed in 1954 out of a discussion group centered at Harvard.[41] Its early leaders, especially Harlow Shapley and Ralph Burhoe, envisioned using science to mold a new religious consciousness. Many had begun conversations moving in that direction at gatherings of the Conference on Science, Philosophy, and Religion, started in 1939 but in decline by the early 1950s. Like Harlow and Shapley, many also had ties of some sort to Unitarianism; several also associated with a group called the Coming Great Church, a series of annual conferences begun in 1950 by Unitarian and Christian thinkers that speculated about the possibilities of a universal religion, but one rooted in an acceptance of a scientific world view. Because of the heavy involvement of professors and scientists in the Institute, it developed more as a professional academic society than a religious organization. Yet in its first decade or so, many presentations at annual sessions pointed towards fashioning a cosmology that would replace traditional religious ones and thus provide a foundation for a new religion. Like religious humanism, outfits like the Institute on Religion in an Age of Science stretched the contours of pluralism.

Perhaps the most stretching came with what some feared was a dangerous repudiation of religion altogether in the form of atheism. Atheism has never had a structure resembling an organized religion in the United States, although there is American Atheists, Inc., an overarching group that was started by Madalyn Murray O'Hair.[42] For some, to speak of atheism as a religion is oxymoronic. Throughout the twentieth century, once professional pollsters began tracking popular beliefs and practices, only a very small proportion of Americans—somewhere generally between three and eight percent—admitted to atheistic belief. Others would argue that the figure should be somewhat higher, since in a technical sense some formal religions, such as certain strands of Buddhism, are atheistic. Yet beginning in the early 1960s, American atheists received more media coverage than their numbers would warrant. Much of that publicity centered around O'Hair, who remained a controversial figure until her mysterious disappearance in 1995. O'Hair gave much energy to court battles that climaxed in the 1963 Supreme Court decision banning prayer and Bible reading for devotional purposes in the public schools. Critics often mistakenly lumped O'Hair and her fellow atheists together with humanists of various stripes when they insisted that removing devotional Bible reading and prayer from public school classrooms resulted in a decline in moral values through-out the nation. For the story of pluralism, however, what is important about the more public presence of atheists in the later twentieth century is that they force analysts to recognize that pluralism in its extreme must accommodate not only those who reject supernatural theism, as did humanists and some of the scientists associated with the Institute on Religion in an Age of Science, but also those who deny the utility of any form of religious world view.

There are numerous other expressions of a religious orientation that moves well beyond the bounds of standard religious traditions. Since 1966, the Church of Satan, founded by Anton Szandor LaVey, has offered one alternative, although it is rather different from the images of satanism described in the mass media each year at Halloween.[43] The Church of Satan is more properly linked to the resurgence of interest in pre-Christian religions and forms of ritual magic and witchcraft in the neopagan revival than to forces of evil. Some pre-Christian styles have made individual traditions more pluralistic, when given an ethnic dimension. One thinks here, for example, of the long history of fusing indigenous religious elements with Roman Catholic belief and practice that marks much Latin American Catholicism and of how that has brought a pluralism to Catholicism in the United States with the increasing prominence of Hispanic and Latino immigrants. We have already noted the eclectic fusion of features drawn from multiple ethnic and religious traditions in the practice of *santeria* and the rise of interest in voodoo in recent years. Then, too, many Native American tribal religious forms have received renewed life, despite the historic encroachment of Euro-Americans on land held sacred by various tribal societies and the frequent legal challenges to some practices.

The vitality of all of these suggests that pluralism in American religious life in the twentieth century has moved in many new directions. Along the way, the kind of pluralism identified by commentators early in the century—the variety of Protestant denominations—got left behind. Pluralism still includes that variety, but has stretched to encompass a range of world religions, alternatives to Christianity, and many new religious movements. As well, religious communities in the United States that developed later in the century no longer felt the need to identify themselves against a presumed Protestant majority; they simply assumed the right to stake out a place for themselves on the religious landscape of the nation. Simply put, pluralism has come of age. At the start of the twentieth century, there still prevailed a consensus of sorts in the dominance of an evangelical Protestant style that pervaded much of American culture. At the start of the twenty-first century, no such consensus is possible, given the prevalence of pluralism.

CHAPTER 9

The Politics of Religion in a Pluralistic Society

As the twentieth century closed, evangelical Protestants increasingly found voter guides slipped under windshield wipers on cars in church parking lots Sunday mornings near Election Day. Catholic archbishops, like John Cardinal O'Connor of New York, routinely made headlines with pleas for political powers to end legal abortion. If the First Amendment to the Constitution effectively kept government from meddling in the internal affairs of religious communities, except to protect the general welfare, leaders from many different religious traditions did not hesitate to promulgate political agendas and urge legislators to enact bills informed by the perspectives of their faith communities. Many of them, especially those more conservative theologically and politically, had concluded there was no longer a shared vision of the nation—no common moral base shaping public policy and legislation or set of ethical values guiding all Americans. They recognized that pluralism prevailed, but found in it a dangerous mixture of truth and falsehood, right and wrong.

As they moved to muster the coercive power of the state to impose policies and practices resonant with their own understanding of religious truth, they unwittingly affirmed that many competing religious visions sustained American common life, some of which were in direct conflict with each other. The First Amendment aside, American religious life and American political life were never divorced from each other, but intertwined. The interplay between religion and politics at the end of the century meant only that pluralism had come of age, not that suddenly preachers plunged into politics.

The story has major divisions, with numerous subplots, for during the century strategies for bringing religious influence to bear on public life became more pluralistic. For convenience, the approaches most prevalent may be clustered into four categories. One, exemplified in the Prohibition movement early in the century, is the attempt to use the legislative process to enact laws in keeping with the moral and ethical beliefs of a presumed religious majority who felt threatened by a minority with different beliefs. The second emerges from attitudes towards policy or practices endorsed by the government, whether in support or in opposition. A clear example of opposition to government policy is the large-scale movement opposing United States military involvement in Vietnam that marked the 1960s and 1970s, much of it generated by religiously based groups and individuals. For opposition to practice sanctioned by government, the civil rights movement looms large, for it sought to dismantle legal discrimination based on race given sanction by the Supreme Court in *Plessy* v. *Ferguson* (1896). That decision declared the principle of "separate but equal" consonant with the United States Constitution. A patent example of religious support for government policy remains the endorsement of United States support for Israel that continued almost without question for nearly half a century after Israel's creation as an independent nation in 1948. A third is using the courts to secure protection for minorities; those engendering the greatest long-term controversy have concerned public schools and such matters as Bible reading, prayer, religious instruction, and curriculum issues like teaching evolutionary theory and creation science. The fourth concerns direct support for individual candidates for public office whose positions on key issues are in harmony with those of a specific religious perspective, and grassroots, local activity to secure political influence and power. Each has a history spanning the century, revealing that religion and politics have long been connected and that the struggles through which pluralism came of age resound in political life as much as in religious life.

Protecting the Majority in a Pluralistic Milieu

Immigration, urbanization, and industrialization underway in the late nineteenth and early twentieth centuries brought considerable political and social engagement not only on the part of mainline Protestants, who then enjoyed unparalleled cultural influence, but also on the part of some immigrant communities. Mainline Protestants exhibited a range of attitudes that at first seem contradictory. On the one hand, there were moves to use the power of government to protect a Protestant culture from contamination. On the other hand, there were equally powerful endeavors, most readily seen in the Social Gospel movement, recognizing that changes in the social order were irreversible. The world sustaining mainline Protestant hegemony was gone forever.

Josiah Strong, in his popular *Our Country* (1885), identified immigration as one major peril threatening the American way of life.[1] Strong urged Protestants to seize the evangelistic opportunities presented by the millions of Catholics, Eastern Orthodox Christians, and Jews entering the country, intimating that converting non-Protestant immigrants to an evangelical style of Protestantism was a primary step in Americanizing them. What troubled many were the cultural mores of immigrants, for in the popular mind immigrants became linked with a virtually uncontrollable fondness for consuming alcoholic beverages.

To be sure, consumption of alcohol was nothing new in the United States. For much of American history most Protestants did not oppose use of alcohol in moderation.[2] But by the beginning of the twentieth century, alcohol had become for many evangelical Protestants a symbol of the collapse of Protestant culture and a harbinger of doom. In much popular thinking, immigrant laborers, struggling to survive on low wages, neglected their homes and families by squandering their money on alcohol, constantly drinking to excess, and returning home from work drunk to terrorize their inadequately clothed and poorly fed families.[3] While enough abuse of alcohol existed to give credence to these perceptions, reality was different. What Protestants saw were non-Protestants for whom enjoyment of alcoholic beverages was accepted culturally and by no means condemned by the religious leaders.

Reacting to what they felt were real dangers to Protestant ways, many mainline leaders became vigorous supporters of the Prohibition movement. Methodist laywoman Frances Willard, later an advocate of both woman's suffrage and the ordination of women to professional ministry, used her position as head of the Women's Christian Temperance Union (W.C.T.U.), founded in 1874, to urge women to form local chapters in their churches.[4] One goal of the W.C.T.U. was to urge state legislators to restrict the manufacture and sale of alcoholic beverages. Women who were members not only swore off use of alcohol themselves, but also covenanted to raise their children to abstain as well.

The Prohibition movement expanded its focus when the Anti-Saloon League organized in 1895.[5] While not officially linked to any Protestant denomination, the league received tacit endorsement from many mainline groups and owed its genesis to the indefatigable anti-alcohol crusade of a Methodist clergyman and denominational bureaucrat, Alpha J. Kynett. Although Kynett died a few years after the Anti-Saloon League organized, a Congregational minister, Howard Hyde Russell, served as the league's general superintendent. He led the league, with aid from Baptist, Presbyterian, and Methodist clergy and congregations, working for local option laws restricting the sale of alcohol and the location of bars and saloons. Mounting success brought additional efforts, often joined by the W.C.T.U., to pressure state legislators to restrict if not prohibit sale of alcohol. Positive results spurred a concerted campaign for congressional legislation that prohibited not only the manufacture and sale of alcohol, but also its transit across state lines.

The backbone of the Prohibition movement was the Protestant middle class. Whether urban or rural, middle-class white Protestants felt most threatened, for they saw the demise of the American way of life informed by evangelical precepts in the urbanization and industrialization underway. Evangelicals rejoiced when the Volstead Act in 1920 implemented the Eighteenth Amendment to the Constitution (ratified in 1919), formally launching the national experiment with Prohibition. Evangelicals never anticipated the underground criminal networks providing alcohol to the wealthy and opening speakeasies barely one step removed from saloons. When Prohibition ended in 1933, the Anti-Saloon League lost much of its influence, finally becoming part of the National Council on Alcohol Problems in 1964. The W.C.T.U., today also a shadow of its former self, continued to promote abstinence, albeit not very effectively.

While some historians believe Prohibition created more social problems than it remedied, it did not resolve the plight of immigrant laborers living in squalor in urban slums. Some mainline leaders, while not necessarily unsympathetic to Prohibition, believed the federal government needed to begin regulating business and industry to assure that the growing working class received adequate wages to support their families and labored in factories where conditions did not threaten health and safety. The situation of women and child laborers especially, the length of the workday and work week, the housing shortage that forced workers' families into tenements—all fed into the Social Gospel movement, which was, as theologian Walter Rauschenbusch put it, simply an effort to apply the teachings of the Hebrew prophets and of Jesus to real life situations.[6] Rauschenbusch and other Protestant Social Gospel advocates were drawn to emerging liberal theology; that led them to endorse crossdenominational cooperation when the Federal Council of Churches organized in 1908.[7] The council quickly adopted a statement of social principles, adapted largely from the Methodist Episcopal Church's social creed,[8] but also so prolabor that it might have come from leaders of the burgeoning labor union movement.

Catholic officials recognized that thousands of their faithful benefited from labor union activities, despite the violence that accompanied strikes and the patent opposition of Rome, which viewed the American labor movement through European lenses.[9] A distinguished body of Catholic social thought, epitomized in John Ryan's *A Living Wage*, emerged as a cognate to the Protestant-dominated Social Gospel movement.[10] Much of the leadership of the labor unions came from the ranks of Jewish immigrants, many of whom savored opportunities to become involved in the political process and some of whom were drawn to socialist ideology, more so than Protestant or Roman Catholic social thinkers.

By the opening decades of the twentieth century, much of this agenda had political expression in the Progressive movement; many proposals originating with church leaders, denominational assemblies, or theologians like Rauschenbusch and Ryan were taken up by political leaders such as Theodore Roosevelt, William Jennings Bryan, and Woodrow Wilson, who disagreed on many other issues.[11] As a whole, the Social Gospel movement represented a signal effort on the part of religious leaders to bring moral and ethical teachings to bear on public life by using the legislative process. Social reform, change in the very structures of society, could have a religious base.

Even then, pluralism prevailed, for not all evangelical Protestant leaders applauded efforts to plunge into the political process to effect social change. Many still believed that society would always remain sinful and that social problems, whether slum conditions or low wages, resulted from sin. Only through personal salvation could individuals rise above the social morass and be set on a path to economic success without state intervention. Persons of this ilk did not deny that social problems existed; their approach to dealing with them was different. Some formed settlement houses in the nation's cities to help immigrants and workers; others started "rescue missions" where they ministered to both physical and spiritual needs. Chicago's Pacific Garden Mission, opened in 1877, is perhaps the most famous, though in time organizations like the Salvation Army promoted such activity on a national scale.[12]

The thrust of the Social Gospel affected primarily the North. In the South, Protestant denominations demurred from active involvement in political or social issues. That reluctance stemmed in part from how Southern Christians had tried to reconcile religious faith with endorsement of slavery. Seeing society as a sphere distinct from the church distanced the churches from social concerns. Theologians arguing for the "spirituality of the church" offered more sophisticated formulations of an orientation that emphasized personal ethics more than social ethics.[13] Yet Southern Christians, especially women, took the lead in the antilynching movement, even as more reactionary Christians organized the Ku Klux Klan.[14] Both reflect a social ethic.

Some denominational leaders occasionally addressed the sort of issues sustaining the Social Gospel.[15] As industry trickled into the South, to areas like Birmingham with its steel industry, more denominational leaders recognized the need to apply religious teaching to the social order and called on state legislatures to enact laws protecting workers.[16] The Southern Sociological Congress, organized in Nashville, Tennessee, in 1912, and its successor, the Southern Cooperative League of Education and Social Service (1920), likewise called for cooperation among government, churches, and other social agencies to resolve social problems, ranging from child welfare to public health to race relations.[17]

The coming of World War I dampened enthusiasm for a Social Gospel, the swell of Progressivism in politics coopted many of its practical suggestions, and the passage of the Eighteenth Amendment and its implementation in the Volstead Act betokened success for the Prohibition movement. The war also slowed immigration to a trickle, abating concerns that immigrants were undermining the moral core of American society, as did immigration quotas set in the 1920s. Little wonder, then, that the churches lent moral support and provided much volunteer labor for the war effort. Little wonder, too, that there was minimal Protestant opposition to legislation restricting immigration. Nor did Protestant denominations express much concern when the federal government toyed with restricting personal liberty in the wake of the Red Scare following the Bolshevik Revolution in Russia.[18]

Opposing Government Policies on Religious Grounds

The civil rights movement of mid-century exemplifies another paradigm of the interaction of religion and society. Not only does it powerfully demonstrate the first paradigm—use of the legislative process to achieve political-religious ends—it also highlights a second—the active opposition to established government policy on religious and moral grounds. The United States entered the twentieth century a nation where racial segregation enjoyed legal sanction, for in *Plessy* v. *Ferguson* (1896), the Supreme Court ruled that providing "separate but equal" public facilities based on race did not violate the United States Constitution.[19] In many states, particularly those of the former Confederacy, poll taxes and other tests reduced the percentage of African-American citizens registered to vote from what it was during Reconstruction. Segregation effectively created two nations, one with access to social and economic privilege and power, and one, with only a few exceptions, denied access to social and economic privilege and power. Even the Social Gospel movement, with its passion for the rights of labor and the quality of life of the working class, generally failed to address segregation and the immorality of a social system that marginalized one race.[20] Early in the century, some prominent African Americans urged accommodation to racist culture, hoping that gradual improvement in the educational and economic status of African Americans would whittle away at racism.[21]

The "great migration" of African Americans from the rural South to the more urban North in the opening decades of the century complicated the racial situation. They joined immigrants and thousands of Euro-Americans seeking economic advancement in the cities. During the era of World War I, racial tension was almost the order of the day in some urban centers.[22] The Great Depression displaced some, but not all of that undercurrent of racial tension with the sheer struggle for survival.

The turning point came only after World War II. During the war, African Americans had volunteered or been drafted for military service as had others. But the armed forces remained racially segregated. In 1948 President Harry Truman issued an executive order desegregating the American military.[23] Six years later the United States Supreme Court, in *Brown* v. *Board of Education*, reversed the decision made in *Plessy* v. *Ferguson* fifty-eight years earlier, proclaiming the policy of "separate but equal" unconstitutional, for separate had never meant equal.[24]

Resistance to desegregation was widespread and often violent, yet the momentum initiated by *Brown* v. *Board of Education* could not be halted. The churches were at the center, though not all leadership for the civil rights movement came from the churches, particularly in the early days. The most-well known religious advocate of resistance through peaceful means and opposition to unjust policy was one nurtured in the church, the Rev. Martin Luther King, Jr.[25] King offered his church and his leadership to a boycott of the public transportation system in Montgomery, Alabama, after Rosa Parks, an African-American woman, refused to follow segregated practice by standing in the rear of the bus when there were seats, by local law reserved for whites, available in the front.[26]

Earlier discussion of the pluralism developing in African-American religious culture highlighted the significance of the civil rights movement, especially how it revitalized churches, spurred development of black theology, made non-Christian religious options viable for thousands, and brought renewed appreciation for the African past. Also significant was how the political engagement fostered by the civil rights movement affected white religious culture. As clergy, seminary students, and other sympathizers joined protest marches, employed King's use of nonviolence in sit-ins, combed the rural South to register black voters, and otherwise challenged segregation, people in the pews had to take stock. They were not used to seeing their leaders arrested and imprisoned for protesting government policy in a civil rights demonstration. Although the Social Gospel's call for concrete application of faith to common life buttressed the religious rationale for protesting government policy and calling for social change, there was a difference. One was the extent of involvement of religious leaders in civil rights protests; another was their willingness to break the law in peaceful civil disobedience. Nor were most Americans prepared to see black churches firebombed or bishops denied access to services in churches of their own denomination.[27]

Many challenged the way religious professionals immersed themselves in civil rights activity. Some still believed that racial separation and the supremacy of Caucasians were part of the divine plan. Others argued that civil rights were properly the domain of government, not of religion, echoing the claims about the "spirituality of the church" that flourished in the antebellum South. Theologian Charles Marsh has deftly shown how a deep religious faith propelled civil rights activists, segregationists, and those who tried to insist that the church should remain aloof, concentrating on individual salvation, not social transformation.[28] The pluralism of views sustained by faith swept through religious institutions, though it quickly became clear that, particularly in predominantly white religious groups, the rank and file had more reservations about the movement than their clergy. Sociologist Jeffrey Hadden wrote about "the gathering storm in the churches," the growing gap between clergy and laity over political activity as a legitimate expression of faith.[29]

Federal legislation in the 1960s ended *de jure* segregation, at least in public institutions, though it could not demolish *de facto* racism. But even before the civil rights movement began to wind down, U.S. military involvement in Southeast Asia, popularly called the Vietnam War, began to provoke protest and dissent, providing another example of the opposition to policy paradigm. Clergy and other religious leaders were again in the forefront, although the antiwar movement developed a wider base of support than the civil rights movement. From priests such as the brothers Daniel and Philip Berrigan pouring animal blood on draft files in Selective Service System offices to the formation of interfaith protest organizations such as Clergy and Laity Concerned, religiously informed opposition to government policy assumed unprecedented magnitude.[30] It also sparked unprecedented criticism.

Although every war or military action involving the United States aroused some protest on religious grounds beyond that of the so-called "peace churches" or pacifist groups like the Quakers, Mennonites, and Church of the Brethren, by and large religious groups, their leaders, and their bureaucracies helped muster and sustain support for government military policy. Vietnam was different, reflecting the pluralism marking religious involvement in political life as the twentieth century progressed. Those who opposed government policy, supported draft resisters, and led public demonstrations were castigated by some religious leaders not for applying their faith to a social issue, but for being unpatriotic. Hence the style of religious protest moved well beyond what transpired, for example, when religious leaders attempted to influence government policy in the Prohibition movement. The Prohibition effort was regarded as a patriotic endeavor, for it was part of a vision to protect the purity of American society. The antiwar movement in the Vietnam era assumed that society was already contaminated and that the government itself was responsible.[31] At the time, commentators too readily labeled opponents of government policy as liberals, who believed protest a legitimate strategy, and supporters of government policy as conservatives, who rejected protest and affirmed governmental authority on religious grounds.

After the Supreme Court announced its 1973 decision in *Roe* v. *Wade*, the way religion was tied to public life became more pluralistic. *Roe* v. *Wade* made abortion legal in the United States providing certain criteria were met. The years following revealed how deeply divided Americans and denominations were when supporting or protesting *Roe* v. *Wade* on religious grounds.[32] Some of the discussion dealt with the sanctity of life, determining when life began, and whether abortion was murder. Ethicists broadened the argument, debating whether women had a right to choose whether to be pregnant.[33] Some shuddered that abortion was used for birth control and would ultimately be a means of engineering who might be born, since those with physical deformities, certain recessive genes, and the like would be aborted. Others argued that legitimate moral questions emerged when rape or incest resulted in pregnancy, when carrying a child put a woman's life at risk, when physical problems would bring a life of suffering should a fetus be carried to term, and a host of other issues.[34]

While the media cavalierly classified people as "pro-choice" or "pro-life," many individuals whose views fell along a broader spectrum were also often motivated by deep religious faith. On the one hand, those insisting that abortion was morally right under certain conditions (and abortion advocates themselves displayed a range of viewpoints) found themselves forced to sustain a steady campaign to keep *Roe* v. *Wade* in place and to challenge laws passed by state legislatures imposing greater restrictions on access to legal abortion. Abortion foes, on the other hand, used pressure tactics that moved well beyond the nonviolent approach of the civil rights era and even the more aggressive strategies of the antiwar movement.[35] Abortion clinics were bombed and burned, several medical personnel working at such centers were assassinated, and few could provide services without dealing with daily picket lines and protesters trying to keep clients from entering. Arrests and jail sentences proved as ineffective as they had in the civil rights and antiwar movements.

Supporters and opponents of abortion cut across denominational lines, although anti-abortion forces broke with historical precedent. Roman Catholic teaching had long opposed abortion; it was natural to find American Catholic leaders among outspoken "pro-life" voices. Yet among Protestants, the most vocal foes of abortion came from denominations and clusters of churches among the most theologically conservative, groups that in the past frequently harbored anti-Catholic sentiments. The abortion debate made strange bedfellows. Yet in retrospect, the civil rights movement, the antiwar movement, and the controversy surrounding abortion meant that by the last decade of the twentieth century aggressive, direct action to protest laws and government policies on religious grounds had become a way of life.

Using the Courts to Affirm Pluralism

Less dramatic, but no less significant for understanding the many faces of pluralism in twentieth-century American religious life, were efforts of minority religious groups to secure what they regarded as proper protection for their beliefs and practices. Early in the nineteenth century, that prescient commentator on American ways, Alexis de Tocqueville, observed that the greatest danger in the American democratic system was the potential for tyranny of the majority.[36] At the time, he may not have had religious communities in mind, but by the twentieth century, numerous groups argued that tacit government support even for religious assumptions shared perhaps by a majority impinged on their religious freedom, fostering a tyranny of the majority.

The most controversial situation had to do with the religious tone that prevailed in public schools at the dawn of the twentieth century, in many areas continuing well after the close of World War II. The 1925 Scopes trial in Dayton, Tennessee, to some extent epitomized how a religious perspective pervaded public education, for while John Scopes was found guilty of violating Tennessee law by teaching evolutionary theory in a secondary school biology class, at the time the Tennessee law itself was not directly challenged.[37] Decades later, controversy still raged over curricular matters, despite the greater religious pluralism that prevailed. Arkansas's law, for example, banning teaching evolutionary theory in any public school or university, was not declared unconstitutional by the United States Supreme Court until *Epperson* v. *Arkansas* in 1968.[38] That did not end public debate, however. In 1987, the court in *Edwards* v. *Aquillard* declared unconstitutional a Louisiana law that required teaching "creation science" (i.e., presenting the Genesis creation story as a scientific account of the origins of the world) in schools where evolutionary theory was taught.[39] By 1999, Kansas had entered the fray, although moves there to restrict the teaching of evolutionary theory had not reached the United States Supreme Court.

In many American school districts, beginning the school day with a patriotic exercise that included reciting the Pledge of Allegiance to the flag and also with Bible reading and prayer was common practice well into the twentieth century. Some minority religions had difficulty with all such activities. Jehovah's Witnesses, for example, refused to salute the flag, arguing that pledging allegiance to the flag violated their primary allegiance to God.[40] Repeatedly children from Witness families were expelled from school; in many cases, parents were prosecuted. Repeatedly, too, courts sustained the practice of the schools. The first case to reach the

Supreme Court came in 1940, an unpropitious time from a minority perspective. War raged in Europe, and the patriotic support for American entry into World War II was evident. In a case originating in Pennsylvania, *Minersville School District* v. *Gobitis*, the court upheld the school district, arguing that the social cohesion advanced by requiring pupils to salute the flag superseded any religious freedom issues. Three years later, however, in *West Virginia State Board of Education* v. *Barnette*, the court reversed itself, setting a precedent still remaining in force. The reversal represented judicial acknowledgment of the religious pluralism within the nation.

Also hotly debated at the end of the century were court cases ending Bible reading and required prayer in public schools. Two Supreme Court decisions from the early 1960s remained the symbolic center of this controversy. In *Engel* v. *Vitale* (1962), the court struck down a requirement set by the New York State Board of Regents mandating daily recitation of a presumably nonsectarian prayer in the state's public schools. The following year, the court moved further in *Abington* v. *Schempp*, prohibiting both Bible reading for devotional purposes in public schools and recitation of the Lord's Prayer. The court insisted that these moves in no way precluded academic study of religion, or even of sacred texts, in the schools, but only that promoting practices associated with one religious tradition, in this case Christianity, implied government establishment of a particular religion.[41] Throughout the rest of the century, political action groups and, in many cases, local school boards attempted to get around these provisions. But in reality, the court cases simply affirmed the depth of religious pluralism that characterized American life. No longer could school districts assume that an overwhelming majority of students shared evangelical Protestant or even Christian beliefs.

Almost forgotten in time were other court challenges to the religious tenor of the public schools. If the Protestant ethos of public schools in the later nineteenth century encouraged Roman Catholics to establish a church school in every parish, the United States Supreme Court as early as 1948 in *McCollum* v. *Board of Education* forbade use of school time and facilities for direct religious instruction designed to train school children in a particular faith tradition, even if attendance was voluntary. Four years later (*Zorach* v. *Clausen*), the court sanctioned early dismissal of children on a voluntary basis to receive religious instruction held off school property. Here the issue concerned whether it was appropriate to use school facilities for programs intended to inculcate the beliefs and practices of any one religion; such also seemed to cross the line set in the First Amendment.[42]

By the end of the century, critics railed that removal of any explicit religious activity from the schools contributed to a general erosion of moral standards and increased discipline problems. Individual congregations often started their own schools so that children could receive religious instruction and nurture in a setting that promoted a particular understanding of morality.[43] The Christian school movement also had roots in residual racism; with gradual desegregation of schools following the 1954 *Brown* v. *Board of Education* decision, some churches, especially in the South, organized schools in order to maintain racial separation. As well, in the last quarter of the twentieth century, increasing numbers of parents chose to educate their children at home where they could more directly control curriculum, within guidelines set by the state, while maintaining a moral or religious educational environment and minimizing exposure to ideas thought dangerous.[44] Ironically, the Christian school and home schooling movements drew greatest support from sectors of the population once the most enthusiastic advocates of public education and most critical of Roman Catholics and others who established private school systems. Yet those who decried moves of courts to end religious practices in the schools unwittingly gave credence to the extent of religious pluralism in the larger society in their efforts to avoid its implications for public education.

Other issues coming before the courts highlighted different facets of pluralism, particularly how to secure free exercise of religion for minority groups. A few examples illustrate the range of concerns and challenges pluralism presents to a society striving to maintain social cohesion. One arena already received passing mention: securing exemption from military service, especially that involving combat, for persons who as individuals or as members of so-called "peace churches" maintain a strict pacifism. The Vietnam War era broadened the scope of exemption in another grudging acknowledgment of pluralism. Prior to this time, to receive exemption from military service one had to be a member of a religious group that required all members to abstain from combat or recognized strict pacifism as an acceptable posture for members. Those without religious affiliation or who held pacifist principles on philosophical rather than religious grounds were excluded. The courts finally had to accept the validity of their positions as a basis for conscientious objector status. Unsuccessful were efforts to secure recognition for "selective conscientious objection," a position that claimed individuals might choose to participate in combat if the military endeavor met certain moral criteria, but refuse to participate if it did not.[45]

A second cluster of cases centers on those refusing certain types of medical assistance on religious grounds, usually blood transfusions or particular medical procedures, but sometimes all professional medical service.[46] The most well-known have involved Jehovah's Witnesses and Christian Scientists, but there are many others. The greatest controversies have debated whether parents had the right to withhold treatment from children not of legal age. The record here is itself diverse, with the courts tending to affirm the right of mentally competent adults to refuse medical treatment on religious grounds and to intervene when the treatment of minor children was at stake. Similar ethical issues surrounded discussion of euthanasia, physician-assisted suicide, and withholding life support from persons whose condition made it impossible for them to make decisions regarding treatment.[47] That such issues have come into the public forum reflects the depth of religious pluralism and the range of positions all supported on religious grounds that became commonplace by the end of the twentieth century.

A third cluster of legal questions arose when the states and courts have declared particular religious practices illegal. Since the opening decades of the century, some congregations, primarily in Appalachia, have engaged in the practice of handling serpents and ingesting poisonous liquids (usually strychnine). States have wrestled with making such practices illegal on the grounds that the responsibility of government to promote the general welfare superseded the right to free exercise of religion when such might result in injury or death (since most handlers also refuse medical treatment when bitten). Some states did make serpent handling illegal, but enforcement was both sporadic and impossible. Court challenges generally resulted in the striking down of such laws, especially when adults engaged in such practices voluntarily.[48] Kindred issues of religious freedom came when states moved against Native Americans whose religious practice involved ingestion of peyote or other controlled substances in ritual contexts. In the 1990s, congressional efforts to enact legislation protecting the rights of Native Americans also ran into difficulty, for the Supreme Court more than once found particular provisions problematic.[49] Yet vital questions remained. Could persons break the law if doing so were mandated by their religion? How much pluralism could be celebrated before government intervention crushed the free exercise of religion?

Promoting a Religious-Political Agenda

The last quarter of the twentieth century witnessed a more widespread use of yet another strategy by which the religiously faithful sought to influence public life. Groups organized to promote a broad political agenda, but they garnered support from individuals who came from a range of denominational backgrounds. Such groups served as political lobbies, sometimes in an informal sense, to push passage of legislation consonant with their religious or moral objectives. But they also campaigned for individual candidates for public office from the local to national levels. The most well-known groups developed in evangelical circles. Independent Baptist pastor and televangelist Jerry Falwell started the Moral Majority in 1979, though it disbanded a decade later as a discrete entity, and charismatic Baptist televangelist and presidential candidate Pat Robertson established the Christian Coalition in 1989.[50] Together with a host of smaller organizations, many with narrower goals such as eliminating presumed pornography from network television, they constituted what became known as the New Religious Right or New Christian Right. Usually identified with more conservative political stances and personnel from the Republican Party, the Moral Majority and Christian Coalition both sought to make abortion illegal once again, eliminate pornography, restore prayer and Bible reading in public schools, undermine efforts to secure full legal rights for homosexuals, and refocus American life on what the age called "family values."

At the national level, the groups had mixed success. Often throwing support to political candidates whose platforms matched their own, the Moral Majority and Christian Coalition faced repeated disappointment when candidates, once elected, could not implement what they wanted. Simply put, even politically and religiously conservative officials recognized how pluralistic the nation had become and how much dissension would follow, should the wishes of such groups become the law of the land. The Christian Coalition had greater success pursuing political activity at the local level, frequently succeeding in gaining control of local school boards or of county Republican Party organizations. Under the leadership of Ralph Reed, executive director of the Christian Coalition prior to becoming an independent political consultant, the group trumpeted achievements that probably exceeded actual accomplishment. Even among the rank and file, the efforts of such groups to coerce persons of faith to hew to a particular political line reeked of unwarranted intrusion into the private sphere. As leaders like Reed, Robertson, and Falwell cast their message in extreme terms, they alienated even their own followers. Many sympathetic to what the Moral Majority and Christian Coalition promoted also recognized that the nation was too pluralistic religiously and politically for any one moral perspective to be imposed on all. Frequently, too, there were calls from groups like People for the American Way or Americans United for the Separation of Church and State to investigate such groups and their leaders on grounds that their overt political activity was inconsistent with the tax-exempt status some enjoyed as religious or charitable organizations.[51]

At the same time, this strategy, perhaps because it was more open-ended and cast a wider net in attempting to bring religious influence to bear on public life, brought occasional interfaith cooperation, sometimes among unlikely parties. Because the Roman Catholic Church had long officially rejected abortion under almost any circumstances, its leaders frequently worked with evangelical Protestants who in other contexts would have nurtured anti-Catholic sentiments. The Catholic Alliance, an unofficial conservative political action group, was criticized by some for being almost an arm of the Christian Coalition, so closely did leaders work together and so similar did goals and objectives appear.[52]

In the midst of this broad-based political activity prompted by religious belief and often led by clergy, the meaning of the First Amendment and the principle of separation of church and state came under repeated scrutiny. At the dawn of the twenty-first century, political perspectives shaped by religious belief were more the rule than the exception. If separation of church and state prohibited government from interfering in matters of doctrine internal to religious communities and required protection of rights of religious minorities so long as the general welfare was not endangered, it did not prohibit persons of faith from seeking to use the political process to gain legal sanction for policies and practices consistent with their faith. Throughout the century, religion and politics were intertwined, but the emergence of new strategies reflected the pluralism in both religious faith and political perspective that came to maturity in the twentieth century.

CHAPTER 10

Pluralistic Turns in American Religious Thought

People in the United States from the colonial epoch on were a people on the move, expanding from the Atlantic to the Pacific, shifting from a rural to an urban population base, and developing an industrial economy to supersede an agricultural one. There was little time for the sustained reflection that produces systematic religious thought or theology. For generations, historians proclaimed eighteenth-century Puritan divine Jonathan Edwards was the only great philosopher-theologian the nation produced.[1] No other theologians attained the stature of medieval Christianity's Thomas Aquinas, the Reformation era's John Calvin, or even Jonathan Edwards. Yet in the twentieth century, there was an explosion in religious thought. American theology moved in many directions as the century progressed, revealing how pluralism had both entered the domain of religious thought and prompted tremendous creativity. Much twentieth-century American religious thought echoed trends in theological circles elsewhere, but how American thinkers worked and the fresh approaches and particular emphases they gave reflected the religious and cultural pluralism of U.S. society.

The Diffusion of Protestant Thought

In part because Protestantism historically dominated American religious culture, Protestant thinkers explored the widest range of theological concerns in the twentieth century. At the dawn of the century, one of the more creative modes of thought, the Social Gospel or Social Christianity, sought to respond to the same cluster of social phenomena—urbanization, industrialization, and immigration—that were undermining Protestantism's hegemony.[2] The most systematic treatments came from Baptist pastor and then seminary professor Walter Rauschenbusch (1861–1918), although Congregationalist pastor Washington Gladden (1836–1918), economist Richard T. Ely (1854–1943), and even Evangelical Alliance official Josiah Strong (1847–1916) all offered significant works to advance the Social Gospel cause.[3] Their work paralleled similar efforts in Europe, especially in Germany and Britain.

At the heart of the Social Gospel lay the conviction, inspired by German thinkers identified with emerging liberal theology, that Christianity was not a complicated metaphysical system, but a simple set of moral and ethical postulates with
direct relevance for daily life. Also in the background lay the increasing acceptance among biblical scholars and theologians of a historical-critical approach to
scripture that regarded sacred writ as divinely inspired, but properly understood
only in its own context. Thus Rauschenbusch, for example, held up the Hebrew
prophets and the teachings of Jesus summarized in the Sermon on the Mount as
containing the core doctrines of the Christian faith. Love of one's neighbor, affirmation of a common humanity, and a conviction that government and even business and industry existed to serve the common good were built on that ethical
foundation. The age's belief in progress and an optimism regarding human knowledge and technological advances led Social Gospel proponents to believe that humanity was on the brink of erecting the kingdom of God on earth.

Scorning the position popularly associated with steel magnate Andrew Carnegie,
the Gospel of Wealth, which insisted wealth was a divine gift to be used responsi-
bly but that social class distinctions would always exist,[4] Rauschenbusch and others sought to transform the social order, to Christianize its very foundations. To do
so, Social Gospel advocates took up the cause of labor in the bitter conflicts with
industrialists that marked the last decades of the nineteenth century and the first of
the twentieth, making better working conditions one sign of how the social order
could reflect Christian values.[5] Then and later, Social Gospelers reaped criticism
for seeming to downplay the individual experience of salvation fueling so much of
evangelical Protestantism in the United States,[6] but they argued that until human
beings were assured of access to the basic necessities of life, an otherworldly salvation had little relevance. Poorly paid immigrant factory workers laboring under
unsafe conditions, for example, would be more open to calls for personal salvation
once their social situation was Christianized.

In retrospect, the Social Gospel was overly optimistic. Yet it fed into the Progressive movement in politics that in turn promoted some of its specific proposals
for a more Christian social order, such as the eight-hour workday and the five-day
work week. As well, many denominations took up social causes; for example,
beginning in 1908 the Methodist Episcopal Church adopted a social creed reflecting positions identified with the Social Gospel.[7] When the Federal Council of
Churches organized that same year, it, too, embraced many Social Gospel positions.[8] But the optimism that buttressed the movement vanished with World War I.
The ravages of war and the national greed that spurred them were powerful reminders that humans would not always direct knowledge and technology toward
the common good. At the same time, the years immediately after the war saw
American Protestantism caught up in the controversy surrounding fundamentalism. Indeed the deep divide between fundamentalists and modernists gives evidence that even greater pluralism was making its way into American religious
thought.

To fundamentalists, Social Gospel advocates and others who erected theological positions on a liberal foundation had jettisoned Scripture as the foundation for Christian doctrine. While fundamentalists insisted that they were merely preserving the historic teachings of the Christian church, they were in reality creating a new understanding of the past. Yet few fundamentalist thinkers emerged to shore up the intellectual foundations of their perspective. They defined themselves more in terms of what they were not—they were not modernists—than in terms of what they were. In the later nineteenth century Benjamin Breckinridge Warfield (1851–1921) of Princeton Theological Seminary was among the more prominent thinkers committed to giving rational credibility to traditional notions of biblical authority.[9] In the early twentieth century, the mantle passed to J. Gresham Machen (1881–1937).[10] But fundamentalists then seemed on the defensive, trapped in defending an approach to Christian faith that seemed at odds with scientific and other rational ways of constructing belief systems. Modernism became the byword of a new generation of intellectuals; a viable theological stance shaped by orthodoxy and the evangelical style prevailing for generations did not emerge with force until the last third of the century.

The Social Gospel was modernist in that it celebrated the achievements of science and technology to advance the commonweal. Other Protestant thinkers were less practically oriented, but nevertheless smitten with the possibilities of a scientific base for theological speculation. Personalism, centered in the theological faculty of Boston University, and theological empiricism, identified with the University of Chicago Divinity School, represent two of the most significant attempts to reconcile a scientific-rational approach with Christian faith. At Boston, Borden Parker Bowne (1847–1910), Albert C. Knudson (1873–1953), and Edgar S. Brightman (1884–1953) began their theological enterprise not with the claims of scripture or tradition, but with the human personality.[11] Reasoning from the human to the divine, the Boston Personalists saw in human life a reflection of the being or personality of God. Humans had freedom to make choices, but because they were finite, they could misuse their freedom. Humanity thus still needed redemption offered by a Christ who completely manifested the personality and character of God. Critics castigated Personalists for downplaying the extent of sin and the qualitative difference (and distance) between the human and the divine, but Personalists believed they were recasting Christian doctrine to keep faith relevant for a scientific age.

At Chicago, Shailer Mathews (1863–1941), Shirley Jackson Case (1872–1947), and Henry Nelson Wieman (1884–1975) also cast aside the traditional starting point of theological speculation; for the empirical school, the main issue was method.[12] The Chicago school was particularly taken with sociohistorical method. That approach revealed the complex ways beliefs and religious institutions like the church evolved over time. Doctrine always emerged in a specific historical context; Christianity in its myriad manifestations had restated and reshaped its core message continuously as social and historical circumstances shifted. Critics claimed that this scientific modernism, as it was also known, denied the absolute character of the Christian faith and thus dangerously relativized eternal truth.

Even more radical were those who concluded that any theological position based on revelation, whether of the divine personality in human life or of evolving truths rooted in scripture, was anachronistic. By the 1930s, humanism had a rebirth, and the "Humanist Manifesto" endorsed by John Dewey and others seemed to dismiss the relevance of religious faith altogether for those in step with the intellectual advances of the day.[13] The ascendancy of scientific method in intellectual circles thus variously challenged the plausibility of Protestant understandings of Christian doctrine, but likewise revealed the pluralism in approaches ranging from those that sought to sustain faith to those that abandoned it altogether.

If the devastation of world war had a sobering effect in some circles informed by liberalism, like the Social Gospel, it also spurred the development of one of the century's more creative theological ventures. In Europe during the war years, Karl Barth (1886–1968) had called for a fresh appreciation of the depth of human sin and of the transcendence of God, arguing that liberals, in emphasizing human possibility and the immanence of God, had forgotten the absolute otherness of the Almighty.[14] As Barth's thought gained a hearing in the United States, it became one force among many prompting the development of a new orthodoxy (neoorthodoxy) that received its most well-known expression in the Christian realism of Reinhold Niebuhr (1892–1971), his brother H. Richard Niebuhr (1894–1962), and ethicist John C. Bennett (1902–1995).[15] Reinhold Niebuhr, who moved from a pastorate in Detroit in the 1920s to a long-time professorship at New York's Union Theological Seminary, provided the most thoroughgoing exposition of his position in his well-known Gifford Lectures, published as *The Nature and Destiny of Man*. Mindful of the gap between the divine and the human but appreciative of human potential, Niebuhr insisted that human beings could make advances in their common life when guided by biblical ethical ideals. Human finitude and sin, however, meant that such gains were always flawed and proximate at best.

Niebuhr believed his stance more realistic than that of either earlier liberalism or the rigid orthodoxy popularly associated with fundamentalism. It was more realistic than liberalism because it did not glorify human achievement and progress; every advance still fell short, revealing how much distance separated the human from the divine ideal rather than closing the gap. At the same time, it was more realistic than the orthodoxy associated with fundamentalism since it applauded the partial gains made through science, technology, and other human achievement. As well, realism responded to concrete circumstances in efforts to apply biblical ideals. Hence Reinhold Niebuhr espoused pacifism in theory since it mirrored biblical ethical standards, but called for Allied support in World War II in the struggle to defeat Hitler. Hitler posed a greater threat to humanity than temporarily abandoning pacifist principles. Some therefore saw Niebuhr as inconsistent and a proponent of the old Social Gospel liberalism in a fresh disguise; he argued that his position was simply realistic. Others believed that Niebuhrian realism too readily became a prop to justify American self-interest.

American neoorthodoxy's philosophical underpinnings received tremendous support when the rise of Hitler and the Nazis in Germany forced philosophical theologian Paul Tillich (1886–1965) to come to the United States, where he became a colleague of Reinhold Niebuhr and John Bennett at New York's Union Theological Seminary.[16] Moving in the orbit of existentialist thought that captivated many European thinkers in the first half of the twentieth century, Tillich was a prolific writer, producing a three-volume systematic theology that became a bulwark of the intersection of existentialism and neoorthodoxy.

In time, however, a new pluralism began to emerge from neoorthodoxy. While not completely rejecting the more somber assessment of human nature advanced by Niebuhr and the Christian realists, some wondered whether it was possible to give any credence to traditional theological formulations in a world where a Hitler could come to power and heap destruction on millions. Had God created humanity and then set humanity completely free? With science and technology seeming to march ever onward, was God the Creator allowing humanity to fend for itself? In the words of German pastor-theologian Dietrich Bonhoeffer (1906–1945), who lost his life at the hands of Nazis, did a humanity now come of age need to stand before God *as if* God did not exist?[17] Was a stark secularism the next stage in human development?

Drawing on Bonhoeffer and on some logical implications in Barth's thought, Harvard Divinity School professor Harvey Cox (1929–) trumpeted the religiosity of a humanity freed from the shackles of moribund theology in his best selling *The Secular City* (1965).[18] If urbanization had once challenged Protestant theology, now it was celebrated as promoting a way of life shorn of superstition and myth. Some, such as Gabriel Vahanian (1927–), Thomas J. Altizer (1927–), William Hamilton (1924–), and Paul Van Buren (1924–), went even further and proclaimed the "death of God" or at least the death of certain notions of a transcendent divine entity, considered incompatible with modes of thought favored by an educated, rational, scientifically informed humanity.[19] More traditional church folk shrank back in horror, but "death of God" thinking was never as radical as it appeared on the surface. Coming in the 1960s as the nation faced civil rights turmoil, upheaval over military engagement in Southeast Asia, experimentation with drugs, fascination with new religious movements, and seeming rejection of all that reeked of tradition and authority, it was really just another marker of the growing pluralism that characterized not just American religious life, but the larger culture as well.

Little wonder, then, that in the midst of theological and social unsettledness, there would be an effort to revitalize the values presumed at the heart of the American experience. In a penetrating and widely reprinted 1967 essay entitled "Civil Religion in America," University of California sociologist Robert N. Bellah (1927–) sought to recapture the sense of religious power that he believed integral to the democratic experiment that became the United States.[20] Following eighteenth-century French *philosophe* Jean Jacques Rousseau in believing that some set of core values, some common mythology, must undergird social order,[21] Bellah posited a civil religion existing alongside traditional religions, not competing with them, but forming a substructure that knit together the varied peoples making up the American nation. With sacred texts like the Declaration of Independence and sacred places such as the battlefields of the Revolution and Civil War, this civil religion presumed an amorphous but providential deity who acted in the events of American history, setting the nation apart much the way seventeenth-century Massachusetts Bay Puritans believed God had chosen them to inhabit a "city on a hill" as an exemplar for all humanity.[22] Bellah later joined with colleagues in producing one of the first studies of the religious sensibilities of the baby boomer generation that revealed how reluctant that generation was to make enduring commitments to all social institutions, including religious ones.

Bellah was struggling to affirm a common set of values and beliefs amid the increasing ethnic and religious pluralism of American society. But his civil religion was also a product of the white Protestantism long dominant in public religious discourse. Few African Americans could celebrate an American past that sanctioned chattel slavery; few Native Americans could rejoice in a civil religion that had demolished their own cultures; few women could attach sacred qualities to a social and economic order grounded in patriarchy. Yet Bellah's work generated considerable conversation in academic and religious circles.[23] That response revealed precisely how pluralistic American religion and culture had become. Perhaps there were no common values, but multiple theological and ethical systems sustaining a diverse people. Pluralism come of age sparked the quest for a civil religion.

The voices silent in Bellah's rendering of an American civil religion were making themselves heard in other quarters, as discussed more fully in previous chapters. Influenced in part by the liberation theology developing among Latin American Roman Catholic advocates for the poor and powerless, African Americans generated a black theology that also responded to the history of slavery, racism, and discrimination in the United States. As noted already, James Cone (1938–) became one of the most vital advocates of a theology rooted in the black experience of suffering that could bring spiritual freedom even to whites strangled by their own racism. Because most American blacks identified with the Christian tradition were Protestants, virtually all African American theology came from within Protestantism.[24]

The same was not true for other previously silent clusters within the population influenced by liberation thinking. Among women, as noted earlier, many of the first proponents of a feminist theology had ties to the Roman Catholic heritage. Both Mary Daly and Rosemary Radford Ruether (1936–), who issued some of the earliest calls for a theology grounded in the particular experience of being female, came from within the Catholic fold; in time they were joined by countless others, including Carol P. Christ, Judith Plaskow, Letha Dawson Scanzoni, and Nancy Hardesty (1941–), who sought to begin the theological journey with the biological and social manifestations of being women.[26] Likewise cutting across the Protestant-Roman

Catholic divide were those who took sexual identity as the springboard for theological reflection. From Catholic priest John McNeill's *The Church and the Homosexual* and his more sustained theological meditation *Taking a Chance on God* to lesbian Episcopal theologian Carter Heyward's numerous pieces, Christians with gay, lesbian, or bisexual orientations articulated a theology affirming their sexual identity and also identifying with others who encountered hostility and rejection at the hands of both church and society.[26]

By taking personal experience, whether that of race, gender, or sexual orientation, as the foundation for theological speculation, all these augmented the pluralism that increasingly characterized Protestant thinking in the United States as the twentieth century progressed. Personal experience replaced biblical revelation as the starting point for theological discourse; personal experience likewise superseded the community of the faithful as the buttress for belief. By century's end one could not presume a common launching point for Protestant theology, much less a common core of essential doctrines.

In academic circles, however, some still attempted to construct theological positions based on a particular philosophical scheme or a particular methodological focus. In the twentieth-century United States, among the more rigorous were those who advanced "process theology," an ideological cousin of the philosophical school bearing the same label.[27] Process theology, like earlier modernism, took scientific theories seriously. In this case, the implications of evolutionary theory were especially important, for process theory assumed that everything, from God to humanity and the natural world, was evolving, still in process in moving towards an as yet unrealized completion. Humans confronted evil and suffering not because of fundamental flaws in the nature of things or because of the influence of supernatural demonic powers, but as necessary birth pains in the process of becoming something more. Even God was in process, responding to human need in guiding the cosmos towards a meaningful end. Process thinkers argued that human experience demonstrates growth and development and extrapolated that all else did, too. As well, process theologians accepted the idea that everything that exists develops in relation to all else. Thus the being of God was developing in relationship with humanity and vice versa. Among American thinkers in the middle and later twentieth century, Charles Hartshorne (1897–), Daniel Day Williams (1910–1973), Schubert Ogden (1928–), and John Cobb (1925–) all proposed theologies grounded in process thought.[28] Critics of process theology pounced on its failure to attribute omnipotence and absoluteness to God. Even though process theologians countered that there remained a teleological providence guiding the cosmos, detractors insisted that such an abstraction was a far cry from the biblical God who called the world into being by the power of divine utterance.

As an academic enterprise, theology has always faced challenges in influencing how ordinary folk in the pew formulated their own understanding of faith and doctrine. Indeed, intellectuals have often been perceived as divorced from the currents of common life.[29] Process thinking's following was thus confined largely to intellectual circles. Even liberation theologians often found their work limited in influence to the particular groups they addressed. None shifted the course of theological discussion altogether. Theologians who spoke to ordinary people, however, were often scorned and dismissed by systematicians and philosophers for their lack of logical and rational rigor as well as for their failure to be systematically comprehensive. Hence another dimension of the theological pluralism that came of age in twentieth-century America, especially among Protestants, concerns the gap between professional theologians and popularizers.

One example, briefly discussed earlier, must suffice. In the 1950s, few religious thinkers were as widely read in the United States as Norman Vincent Peale (1898–1993), whose theology drew on a heritage of self-help and popular psychology that itself had a distinguished history in American culture.[30] Ralph Waldo Trine's (1866–1958) *In Tune with the Infinite*, first published in 1897 and still in print more than a century later, kept alive for the twentieth century the conviction that individuals could summon the psychological and spiritual strength from within themselves to seize control of their own lives and destinies.[31] Peale's bestselling *The Power of Positive Thinking*, first appearing in 1952, made much the same case, though Peale used more explicit theological language in urging readers to pray as they visualized their lives and then actualized control over their circumstances.[32] Scorned by the intellectual and religious elite for masquerading popular psychology as theology and for downplaying everything from sin to human finitude, Peale reached millions through his books, his magazine called *Guideposts*, and his preaching ministry at New York City's Marble Collegiate Church.

Peale's heritage lived on after his death, for his basic viewpoint had clear echoes, for example, in the "possibility thinking" of Robert Schuller (1926–), himself a widely published writer and religious television personality, and in the less well-known *God's Psychiatry* of Charles Allen.[33] A few still sought to speak to those alienated from Christianity on rational and scientific grounds. Episcopal Bishop John Shelby Spong (1931–), for example, wrote several books targeted to a lay audience estranged from Christian faith because faith was equated with fundamentalism.[34] Spong in writing style was as acerbic as fundamentalists who criticized him, for each saw the other as the "enemy" bent on destroying authentic faith. Spong insisted, however, that he was merely rescuing Christianity from those who distorted it and thus renewing its vitality for a postmodern, postscientific age.

Protestant evangelical theologians were as disgusted with the lack of an orthodox theological base in positive thinking and the work of someone like Spong as they were with process theology and even the earlier neoorthodox ideologies that shaped Christian Realism. But decades elapsed after the fundamentalist-modernist controversy before Protestant evangelicals set forth an orthodox theology that was intellectually respectable, though they were building a network of schools, publishing enterprises, and other agencies that connected them together to lay a solid framework for the evangelical resurgence in the latter third of the century.[35] In mid-century, among the first to articulate an evangelical theology that would pass intellectual muster were Edward John Carnell (1919–1967) and Carl F.H. Henry (1913–). Reaching more towards a mass audience with both a theology and an interpretation of history shaped by evangelicalism was the more fundamentalist-inclined Francis Schaeffer (1912–1984), who spent much of his career in Switzerland. Some of the impetus for developing a fresh evangelical theology came from revivalist Billy Graham (1918–) and his associates who launched the periodical *Christianity Today* in the mid-1950s.[36] In the postwar years, Graham had seen audiences respond favorably to his strident reassertion of claims about biblical truth. Consequently, he and several other leading evangelicals sought to provide vehicles to revitalize evangelical thinking.

The founding of Fuller Theological Seminary, named for the father of Charles E. Fuller (one of the century's leading radio evangelists), symbolizes another aspect of that endeavor.[37] Aware that the nation's leading Protestant seminaries favored neoorthodoxy and more liberal theological postures, Graham, Carnell, Henry, Boston pastor and later Fuller president Harold John Ockenga (1905–1985), and some associates determined to support an evangelical divinity school with a faculty whose academic credentials matched those of any more liberal institution and whose theologians developed lines of thought as readily and as rigorously defensible as any other. Fuller was that school.

Carnell's 1948 *Introduction to Christian Apologetics* masterfully argued that the biblical understanding of creation and of human nature was more internally consistent than nontheistic (or even nonevangelical) alternatives in part because it shed greater insight into lived human experience than other theories.[38] Henry, who edited *Christianity Today* for a time and also taught at Fuller, attempted what few outside evangelical circles dared in the later twentieth century: writing a comprehensive, systematic theology in his six-volume *God, Revelation, and Authority,* which appeared between 1976 and 1984.[39] Henry was particularly concerned about the erosion of objective authority in Protestant thinking, attributable in part to the expanding pluralism within the Protestant experience and the concomitant privatization of religious expression. Neither would do in his mind, for at the center of Christian proclamation was an objective truth that could be neither relativized by pluralism nor subjectified by privatization. Both Henry and Carnell were careful to distinguish their positions from the fundamentalism of an earlier age; both eschewed the separatist tendencies within fundamentalism, the peremptory dismissal of other positions simply because they were different. Closer in spirit to earlier fundamentalists was Francis Schaeffer, who always remained apprehensive of those who did not subscribe to his personal theological position.[40] Through popular works and films, Schaeffer helped provide much of the theological underpinning for the evangelical surge into political life, exemplified by the so-called "new religious right" that became a public force from the 1970s on.

In different ways, these evangelical theologians and popularizers added to the pluralism marking Protestant theological life. By their renewed emphasis on objective biblical truth and the authority of scripture, evangelicals kept alive the traditional starting point for Christian theological speculation, even as others turned to personal experience, gender, social experience, and the like to launch the theological enterprise.

As the twentieth century closed, no single voice dominated Protestant theology in the United States. Pluralism prevailed. Many analysts despaired that anyone would attempt, let alone complete, a comprehensive, systematic theology as had evangelical Carl Henry in the 1970s and 1980s or neoorthodox German-American Paul Tillich in the 1950s and 1960s. So diverse was the range of theological starting points that consensus on method, let alone content, was impossible. A pluralistic Protestant theology meant that truth was subjective and privatized, despite the insistence of those, like Carl Henry, who saw in such trends the demise of Christian faith. As well, the movement of the postwar generations away from commitment to the mainline traditions and the way that movement granted preeminence to spirituality and feeling over religion and doctrine added to an environment rarely conducive to sustained theological reflection. By the end of the twentieth century, much of the same could be said of Roman Catholic theology in the United States, though at the start of the century, the Catholic theological story was very different.

A Sleeping Giant Awakens

From the turmoil produced by the Protestant Reformation of the sixteenth century until the era of the Second Vatican Council (1962–65), much Roman Catholic theological reflection was hampered by the official position of the church regarding Thomas Aquinas and the hostility that marked relationships between Protestants and Catholics, first in Europe and then in the United States. In fixing boundaries after the Reformation, the Catholic Church latched onto the magisterial thought of thirteenth-century philosopher-theologian Thomas Aquinas and made his system the norm for all official Catholic theology. That imprimatur granted to Thomistic thinking still prevailed as American Catholics entered the twentieth century. For Catholics, that norm created a bulwark of truth to counter Protestant falsehood. As Protestantism itself became more pluralistic, it looked to Catholic leaders as if Protestants had no clear standards for determining right belief. Grounding theology in Thomism gave Catholicism a certainty, an ideological security, even as new intellectual and theological currents swirled around its borders. But it also isolated Catholic theology and made it difficult for creative Catholic thinkers to develop fresh ways of doing theology as the intellectual and ideological climates shifted.

There were other reasons why Catholic thought seemed less fertile than Protestant thought in the early decades of the twentieth century. The massive immigration from central, southern, and eastern Europe that swelled the ranks of Catholicism in just a few decades meant that higher priority went to meeting the needs of a rapidly expanding constituency than to the fine points of theological speculation. Just as American Protestants were slow to shed their misplaced fears of Catholicism, so American Catholic leaders had to struggle with a Vatican hierarchy suspicious of democracy and convinced that Catholicism and the religious environment of the United States were mutually incompatible. American Catholic bishops and church leaders, at least until after the American church was no longer regarded as a missionary endeavor (1908), had devoted considerable energy to convincing top church officials in Rome that a vital Catholicism could flourish in the United States. In the twentieth century, Jesuit theologian Gustave Weigel (1906–1964) nudged his fellow Catholics into a more ecumenical posture, one that was confirmed by the Second Vatican Council.[41] Weigel wrote about Protestant theology for a Catholic lay audience, convinced that the ecumenical movement of his day was a force equal in significance to the Reformation, although Weigel himself doubted that the Protestant-Catholic divide could be closed—in part because of the pluralism that had come to American Protestantism economically, socially, and culturally as well as theologically.

Sensitive in other ways to the unique circumstances of American public life and the tradition of separation of church and state was the Jesuit John Courtney Murray (1904–1967), regarded by many as the most distinguished American Catholic theologian of the twentieth century.[42] During his formative years, Murray recognized the import of New Deal public policies for American Catholics who were then overwhelmingly clustered into the blue-collar working classes. Consequently, he sought to develop a stance that would link official Catholic doctrine to public policy issues while at the same time engaging in conversation with non-Catholics who also were affected by and responding to the same public policy matters. To some, Murray seemed to sell out to the American ethos, and in the 1950s he was officially silenced for a time. Yet his views emerged largely triumphant at the Second Vatican Council, particularly in the Council's 1965 "Declaration on Religious Freedom."

To a large extent, Murray and Weigel were addressing both the Catholic faithful and a Protestant audience inherently suspicious of Catholicism. With Thomistic thought still officially the norm, neither ventured far into areas of theology outside the public domain, although both sought to show the relevance of theism and a Catholic understanding of God for a culture that no longer simply assumed the truths of Christianity in any form. Nor did the better-known Catholic social activists of the 1960s and 1970s offer doctrinal reformulation. But in the wake of Vatican II, some of the same forces that moved American Protestant theology in a more pluralistic direction also prodded American Catholicism in creative ways. As noted earlier, feminist theologians like Mary Daly and Rosemary Radford Ruether challenged the patriarchal orientation of their own tradition. Ethicists nudged American Catholics to develop fresh responses to social issues, particularly in the wake of Pope Paul VI's reassertion of the traditional Catholic ban on artificial means of birth control. Some American Catholic ethicists, such as Charles Curran, found themselves in difficulty with church authorities, for often the questions they raised seemed to undermine traditional authority, especially the teaching authority of the papacy.[43] Fashioning a speculative, systematic American Catholic theology was still on the back burner.

One twentieth-century immigrant convert to Catholicism, however, was destined to have a profound impact on a popular level among both Protestants and Catholics because of his concern for spirituality and for linking spirituality to other aspects of life. Thomas Merton (1915–1968), born in France and educated at Cambridge, became a Roman Catholic while a graduate student at Columbia University and then in 1942 a Trappist novice at the Gethsemani Abbey in Kentucky. Merton's autobiography of his conversion, *The Seven Storey Mountain*, became a bestseller, but his real genius lay in making the essence of monastic life come alive for a lay audience.[44] Convinced that monastic wisdom and the life of contemplation provided resources for Christian living in the twentieth century, Merton expanded his vision to embrace Zen approaches to meditation, along with classic Christian ones. Merton was also a poet and translator; through his fascination with the poetry of Latin American authors influenced by liberation theology, he sought to wed contemplative ideals and a passion for social justice, certain that the monastic life itself was a protest against injustice and prevailing cultural norms. But Merton was not a systematic theologian. If American Protestants at the close of the twentieth century despaired of finding one outside of evangelical circles who would attempt to build a comprehensive, systematic theology speaking across denominational lines, American Catholics likewise had yet to produce one inclined to systematic construction, even after the Second Vatican Council and subsequent papal pronouncements had ended the primacy given to Thomistic thought. That pluralism had come to American Catholic thought comes into focus in the subtitle University of Chicago Roman Catholic theologian David Tracy (1939–) gave to his 1979 book, *Blessed Rage for Order: The New Pluralism in Theology*.[45]

Pluralism was apparent in other ways, too, for many of the Catholic theologians whose writings the American faithful read avidly were Europeans, such as Karl Rahner and Hans Kung. They seemed to wrestle more with matters of faith and belief, perhaps because unlike their American contemporaries they were freed from the need to continue justifying the compatibility of Catholicism and the social-religious context provided by the United States. And, like Protestants, Catholics had to confront the challenges brought by feminist theology, since some of the earliest efforts to construct theology from a feminist perspective came from Catholic women, as discussed earlier. The roots of feminist theology in liberation thought also demonstrate a dimension of pluralism internal to Catholicism in a vital way, for much of the antecedents of liberation theology in the United States relied on the work of Latin American Roman Catholic theologians. Similar challenges came from Catholic thinkers who advanced a theological position reflecting the experience of lesbian and gay persons.

The Search for Tradition amid Pluralism

Immigrant voices from other strands of the Christian heritage as well as those from the Jewish heritage added yet other dimensions to American religious thought in the twentieth century, reflecting the pluralism that prevailed even as they reacted to the prevalence of a Protestant ethos that was internally pluralistic. The most influential thinkers rooted in the Eastern Orthodox wing of Christianity, Georges Florovsky (1893–1979) and John Meyendorff (1926–1992), were both born in Europe, Florovsky in Russia and Meyendorff in France, the son of Russian emigrants there. Yet both had distinguished careers in the United States. So, too, with Judaism. The twentieth-century theological giants of that tradition in the United States were born overseas. Solomon Schechter (1847–1915) came from England in 1902 to assume leadership of the fledgling Jewish Theological Seminary in New York City. A generation later, Abraham Joshua Heschel (1907–1972), born in Poland, immigrated from Germany via London in 1940, teaching first at Hebrew Union in Cincinnati and then from 1945 until his death at the Jewish Theological Seminary.

Florovsky devoted his career to articulating what he believed the eternal truths of Orthodox Christianity, treating most of the classical doctrines of the faith, and combating trends that he believed undermined them.[46] In his early work, much of it published before he came to the United States in 1948, Florovsky sought to demonstrate that Enlightenment rationalism had distorted the foundation of Russian Orthodox thought, which for him was grounded in what he regarded as a far better synthesis of reason and revelation, the synthesis of Hellenistic philosophy's rationalism and biblical revelation found in patristic thought. Florovsky boldly defended the traditional Eastern christological creedal statements, particularly the formula adopted at Chalcedon in 451 on the perfect union of the human and divine in the figure of Christ, two natures joined without confusion or separation. This construction, Florovsky argued, avoided the pitfalls of both the neoorthodoxy and the liberalism informing American Protestant thought. Protestant liberalism bordered on the ancient heresy of Nestorianism, for it elevated the historical Jesus, the human nature, to primacy as an exemplar for human life and conduct. Neoorthodoxy, on the other hand, by stressing the infinite gap between the Almighty and humanity, stood on the brink of the ancient monophysite heresy in its emphasis on the divine nature. In some ways, Florovsky sustained the traditional theological task, for he directed his message to a community of faith and addressed matters of doctrine. While American Protestant thought had many starting points, ranging from social issues to gender (along with sacred writ) and thus made the theological enterprise increasingly diffuse, Florovsky stuck more with pure doctrine. But part of his reason for doing so was the pluralistic environment in which he worked, with its dangers for relativizing or jettisoning the essential truths of the tradition.

Florovsky, however, was long engaged in conversation with those outside the Orthodox fold, as was Meyendorff. Both served, for example, on the Central Committee and on the Faith and Order Commission of the World Council of Churches. If such venues provided Florovsky with opportunities to criticize perceived weaknesses in the ever more pluralistic Protestant theological tradition, they provided

Meyendorff with opportunities to explain the contours of Orthodox belief and history to those for whom it seemed strange and exotic. Central to Meyendorff's approach was his insistence that the Eucharist, the sacrament common to Christians, was basic to Orthodox understanding of both the church and the character of human life.[47] In the eucharist, the individual experienced not only the presence of Christ, but also the unity of the one body of Christ. As well, gathering around the Eucharistic table reminded the faithful that human life was meant to be lived in communion with God; that was the point of divine creation. In this way, Meyendorff sought to revitalize the Orthodox tradition in America, shifting from an arid appropriation of the past to a living experience of the tradition itself, and also to avoid the excessive individualism and self-reliance that Americans held in such high esteem. But, like Florovsky, Meyendorff shunned active engagement in social issues outside ecclesiastical structures. Faithful to Orthodox understanding, he also believed that such action was impossible apart from grounding in the eternal truths of the tradition. Hence he, too, was reacting to the prevailing pluralistic trends in the larger culture in which he worked.

Like Orthodox Christianity, Judaism places great stock in tradition. In twentieth-century America, Judaism likewise confronted trends in the larger culture that worked against sustaining a vital appreciation of ways hallowed by centuries of tradition. But Jewish theologians moved in different directions in responding to their heritage and the world around them. Solomon Schechter, for example, arrived in the United States when Reform was poised to become the dominant strand of Judaism. With its willingness to accommodate to all things modern and to jettison the trappings of tradition that seemed relics of the past rather than essentials of Jewish identity, Reform stood in sharp contrast to Orthodox practice, which seemed hopelessly anachronistic and doomed to die out in the American setting. Schechter's theology and the leadership he provided through the Jewish Theological Seminary reversed those trends, laying the foundation for the growth of Conservative Judaism as the leading expression of Judaism in America.[48] For Schechter, Conservative Judaism was not a middle ground, a compromise, or an amalgamation of elements drawn from its Orthodox and Reform cousins. Rather, it was the way to affirm a Judaism faithful to the biblical tradition in the midst of ethnic pluralism within and cultural pluralism without. Schechter understood that the great immigration that brought millions of Jews from central, southern, and eastern Europe to the United States around the turn of the century gave American Judaism an internal pluralism. The common foundation was scripture and centuries of rabbinic interpretation.

For Schechter, Conservative Judaism meant preserving and celebrating what was common to Jewish experience. That entailed recapturing the essence of biblical revelation, not simply through rational learning, but through lived experience. Biblical truth must be felt as well as analyzed. Then tradition came alive as a basis for ethical decision; it took on a practical dimension for Jewish life in the alien religious and cultural world of the United States. Schechter believed his approach was fully in keeping with the American ethos as well as faithful to Jewish tradition. American Protestant immigrants generations earlier had also been people who took the Bible seriously; most Protestant theologians of his own day would have insisted that they were simply seeking to understand biblical principles in order to apply them in the world in which they lived. This parallel with Protestant experience enabled Schechter to regard the Conservative posture as simultaneously American and Jewish and thus the most viable means for sustaining Jewish identity in a religiously and ethnically pluralistic society.

Abraham Heschel also took the Bible seriously. Even before leaving Germany for London and then the United States, he had published his now classic study of the Hebrew prophets.[49] Like those prophets, Heschel believed that faithfulness to Torah required a passion for social justice and a humility before the Divine. Heschel also sought to demonstrate how Jewish practice, epitomized in sabbath observance, was essential to being fully human in a culture propelled by industry and technology. The sabbath, after all, sacralized time itself and allowed the divine presence to penetrate human life. It was a gift, a reminder that God had chosen humanity to be agents of divine love in concrete ways. Influenced as well by the Jewish mystical tradition, Heschel wrote like a poet; critics frequently cautioned readers not to be carried away by the grandeur of Heschel's style, finding his approach lacking in rigorous, logical argumentation.

Heschel himself insisted that he must personally live what he proclaimed. If the biblical prophets proclaimed that faith mandated social justice, the faithful must work for social justice in their own societies. Hence, in the 1960s, as more and more Americans questioned the moral validity of United States military involvement in Southeast Asia, Heschel became active in the antiwar effort. In doing so, he joined forces with like-minded Protestant and Catholic figures who also saw themselves as committed to living justice. Through social action, Heschel believed his life offered a Jewish witness to biblical prophetic truth, which could in turn recall Christian activists and American Christianity to the Jewish foundation of the Christian tradition itself. Heschel thus lived the pluralism that prevailed in American common life while remaining devoted to his own tradition.

If much American Protestant theology outside evangelical circles by the end of the twentieth century had abandoned a biblical starting point, looking instead to human experience, the work of Heschel and Schechter reminded Americans of the vitality of the biblical heritage. So, too, did evangelical Protestants who insisted on the authority of scripture for all theological speculation. If Protestant thinkers were increasingly inclined to minimize doctrinal particularity, Orthodox Christian theologians of the ilk of Meyendorff and Florovsky prompted renewed appreciation of the importance of doctrine and the implications of doctrine for action in the world. American Catholic thinkers joined with many Protestant theologians in trying to articulate a public faith, a religious stance in harmony with the spirit of democracy yet faithful to a longstanding heritage. Yet all these varied approaches suggest the deep inroads made by pluralism, for there were many ways of doing theology, many starting points, many approaches to scripture, many views of doctrine and tradition. By the dawn of the twenty-first century, other forces exposed how pervasive that pluralism had become, for by then American Muslims were beginning to expound a theology rooted in Islamic teaching yet tempered by the American experience.[50] The increasing numbers of Asian Americans who remained practitioners of their native traditions, such as Hinduism or Buddhism, signaled that it would not be long before yet other voices tried to explain the ways of God to humanity, adding to that pluralism. In theology as in all other areas of American religious life, in the twentieth century pluralism came of age.

CHAPTER 11

The Persistence of Pluralism

At the start of the twentieth century, what analysts call "mainline Protestantism" dominated American religious life, for its influence penetrated every aspect of American common life, in some cases exceeding what numbers alone might suggest. Episcopalians and Presbyterians, whose membership rolls were significantly smaller than those of the Methodists and Baptists although all were part of mainline Protestantism, were in one sense overrepresented in political and business life. There were proportionately more Episcopalians serving in Congress, for example, than there were in the population as a whole. Even though Roman Catholics constituted the largest single religious community in the United States as early as the middle of the nineteenth century, there were still more Protestants, when all the denominations were lumped together, than there were Catholics. At the start of the twentieth century, American Catholicism was changing, as the massive immigration of the last few decades of the nineteenth century brought millions of Catholics from southern, central, and eastern Europe to American shores. While Irish Catholics continued to control the hierarchy of the church in the United States, they constituted an increasingly smaller proportion of the American Catholic population as the century progressed.

At the start of the twentieth century, too, Jews were barely on the way to becoming the third body in the celebrated American triad of Protestantism, Catholicism, and Judaism. Yet it was not long into the twentieth century before the influence of the Jewish presence far exceeded the proportion of the Jews in the population at large. If pluralism had once denoted the multiplicity of Protestant groups—denominations to some, sects to others—seeds of a new pluralism that had to embrace at least Roman Catholicism and Judaism were in place as the century began.

When those seeds of that new pluralism began to sprout, however, the result was far beyond what even the most prescient observers could have foreseen at the start of the century. No one at the dawn of the century could have fathomed the profound changes to American life that would come especially from two world wars. World War I, despite the backlash of 1920s isolationism, moved the United States onto a global stage where it has remained. The transformation of the economic base of the nation from agriculture to business and industry during the same epoch reinforced the new role of the United States as a leader in international affairs.

For domestic developments, World War II was equally important, if not more so. The boom in suburban development, the rapid growth of higher education, the mobility of American families both geographically and socially—all these and more began to alter American religious life. Denominational switching among Protestants, once the exception, became almost the norm as families raising children found themselves changing locations several times before their offspring reached adulthood rather than remaining in the place of origin for generations. Selecting a new congregation in each locale became a matter of convenience, programming, and prestige more than it did a matter of doctrine, previous affiliation, or traditional commitment.

One result, as noted earlier, was the gradual homogenization of mainline Protestantism. That is, the Protestant denominations accustomed to dominance increasingly downplayed what made each distinct from the other, doctrine and creed became more a matter of personal preference than a fixed body of belief unique to a denomination, and even worship (outside the liturgical denominations) began to seem the same regardless of denominational label. The ecumenical movement furthered that homogenization as it celebrated cooperation across denominational lines, promoted mergers within denominational families, and, with the Consultation on Church Union, brought consideration of merger across denominational lines. By the latter third of the twentieth century the homogenization process had proceeded to such an extent that in many cases it was almost impossible to tell one mainline Protestant congregation from another, were it not for the name on a sign outside.

Add to this mix the spirit of freedom and adventure long celebrated in popular American lore and the religious freedom presumably guaranteed in the First Amendment to the Constitution. Although few Americans have ever really understood the meaning of the First Amendment clauses dealing with religion, virtually all have glorified the so-called "separation of church and state" the amendment promoted. Well before the twentieth century, that freedom had made the United States fertile ground for religious experimentation. There has never been an epoch when new religious movements were not emerging in significant numbers, always arousing some consternation. Most faded quickly, for many centered around a dynamic leader able to draw followers into the fold, but crumbled when the founder died or moved on to something else. Some endured, often seeming less threatening to the majority outside the longer they were around. A few in time became vital contenders in the larger religious picture.

The Church of Jesus Christ of Latter-day Saints, more popularly known as the Mormons, illustrates this process. In the 1830s, when founder Joseph Smith gathered around him a handful of followers, the Mormons attracted much suspicion. They experimented with communal living, for decades practiced a form of polygamy, and based much of their unique doctrine on a sacred text other than the

Bible. By the end of the twentieth century, Mormons were more numerous than Episcopalians; indeed, by most methods of counting, the Church of Jesus Christ of Latter-day Saints ranked in the "top ten" in membership among all United States religious bodies. Of course, the fear attached to Mormons and their practices had also dissipated; there may have been fewer Mormons than Episcopalians in the United States Congress, but they were there and elsewhere in high elected public office, serving not only Mormon-dominated Utah. Mormonism had arrived.

The proliferation of religious communities, either through the emergence of new religious movements or the arrival in the United States of religious groups with origins in other lands, continued throughout the twentieth century. As in earlier periods, many were short-lived. Many also aroused suspicion. When David Koresh led his handful of followers in a showdown with United States government officials that led to the community's destruction in a tragic conflagration outside Waco, Texas, in 1993, and when, a few years later in 1997, those known as Heaven's Gate engaged in group suicide, all the old fears of cults came to the surface. Those fears had been stirred earlier during the 1960s and 1970s when young Americans seemed fascinated with Asian gurus, and the media promoted images of thousands unwillingly leaving biological families to join religious communes and being brainwashed into accepting alien beliefs promoted by religious hucksters. Others made claims about the legitimacy and illegitimacy of the hundreds of radio and television preachers, whose formal religious affiliations spanned the pluralistic spectrum, seeing many of them as more committed to receiving donations from unsuspecting listeners and viewers than to proclaiming any religious gospel. But the "separation of church and state" and the long heritage of religious experimentation helped create and sustain an environment where one dimension of pluralism was the sheer explosion in the number of religious groups flourishing among the American people.

The Impact of Immigration

Repeatedly the story of pluralism come of age has called attention to the impact of immigration. Immigration patterns in the later nineteenth and early twentieth centuries brought internal pluralism to American Catholicism by adding to its ethnic base even as they assured the position of Roman Catholicism as the nation's largest religious group. Immigration at the turn of the last century guaranteed the survival of Judaism in a social environment where there was little to support *yiddishkeit* or a distinctive Jewish identity, while it also brought internal pluralism as Reform, Orthodox, Conservative, and Reconstructionist wings developed. That last major wave of immigration likewise secured a place for Eastern Orthodox Christianity in locales other than Alaska and the far West, where Russian Orthodoxy had long had a vibrant presence. Immigration quotas that went into effect in the 1920s, along with the Great Depression and World War II, severely reduced the number of immigrants entering the nation each year.

When immigration laws were changed in the 1960s, new patterns emerged, adding fresh dimensions to religious pluralism in the United States. Even before the laws changed, immigration from Latin America was on the increase. Add to that the arrival of a significant number of Cubans in the late 1950s in reaction to Castro's coming to power, the movement to the mainland of American citizens from Puerto Rico, and the steady influx of Mexicans both legally and illegally, and the stage was set for the infusion of a Hispanic presence throughout American religious life. Protestant and Catholic congregations in many communities began to provide services in Spanish as well as English; in larger cities with a concentration of Hispanic Americans, independent Spanish-language congregations flourished as well. Many, especially the independent ones, had a Pentecostal flavor.

By the last two decades of the twentieth century, immigration from Asia and from the Near East was adding yet other features to American religious pluralism. If many Americans associated fascination with Asian religions with the hippie generation of the 1960s and 1970s, those making up this new wave of Asian immigrants were anything but dropouts from society looking for a religious alternative. They were a people intent on transplanting and practicing the religious traditions that had given meaning to their lives in their lands of origin. Hindu temples began to appear next to Baptist churches as Indian Americans planted their tradition on American soil. Most spectacular was the rapid growth of Islam, which, as noted earlier, was well on the way to surpassing Judaism as the third major faith tradition even before the end of the twentieth century.

If trends in place at the end of the twentieth century continue even for a few decades into the twenty-first century, the shape of American religious life will change radically. As Americans of European descent become an ever-dwindling proportion of the American population, the religious groups and traditions with which they have been identified will diminish, although their influence will remain strong for a time. Most directly affected is Christianity, particularly the white Protestantism vital to much of the nation's history in an earlier era. The forms Protestantism takes over the next half century are more likely to draw on the rich heritage of African-American religious culture and Hispanic-American life than the Euro-American ways of the past. Even within Catholicism, which still claims to be a single tradition wherever it exists around the world, there are ample signs of a pluralism that will permanently alter the face of the Roman heritage. The Catholic church may maintain its headquarters in Rome, looking back to the days of its ascendancy with the demise of the Roman Empire centuries ago, but within the next two to three decades at the most, estimates hold that a majority of the world's Roman Catholics will live in Latin America. Hispanic Catholicism will become the majority ethnic style; given the spurt in Hispanic immigration to the United States, it is likely to become the dominant style in United States Catholicism as well. At the dawn of the twenty-first century, the erosion of Irish dominance within the hierarchy and bureaucracy of American Catholicism seems a given, even though the Irish presence remains formidable.

Islam's stunning growth, while to date primarily the result of immigration, has also reaped some benefit from the conversion of Americans from other traditions to Islam. The largest concentration of converts has come from among African Americans, many into the Muslim subcommunity of the Nation of Islam, though an increasing number have made their way into groups closer to the Muslim mainline. The number of white Americans attracted to Islam was on the increase by the end of the century, although raw numbers remained small. Over the next half century, Islam could easily become the second largest religious community in the nation, lagging behind only Roman Catholicism. The total number of Protestants would still be larger, but it seems likely that by 2050 there will be more Muslims in the United States than Southern Baptists.

Asian traditions like Hinduism do not aggressively recruit members, except for a very few guru types who broke out of that mold over the last half century. But as Hindu temples establish a full range of festivals and programs and offer the ministrations of a priest thoroughly entrenched in Sanskrit ways, they also begin to draw a small number of Euro-Americans and others into their ranks. Intermarriage brings some into the fold, much more for Islam than for Hinduism. Within Hindu immigrant communities, the traditional practice of arranged marriages has by no means disappeared. Ethnic pluralism will be slower to come to Hinduism in America than to many other traditions, but the seeds are already planted.

Enduring Ethnicity

In the culture at large, controversy ensued in the 1990s over multiculturalism and over offering instruction in public schools in more than one language. On the one hand, multiculturalism was nothing new in the United States, for since the arrival of the first Europeans and then Africans there had been a mix of cultural and ethnic backgrounds. Even if later generations lost some of the direct relationship with a culture of origin, elements endured. A common example has been the way those drawn to Reform Judaism readily shed overt trappings of a religious and cultural tradition that would have set them apart from others in society. Even though that accommodationism routinely involved abandoning a kosher diet, in the homes of Reform Jews generations later one could still find dishes served that harkened back to the German Jewish culture from which many of their ancestors came. On the other hand, the myth of the melting pot presumed that various cultural and ethnic traditions merged together into an amalgam that was somehow uniquely American. Careful analysts suggest now that not as much melted in that cultural pot as idealists like to believe.

In retrospect, the melting pot was little more than the imposition of a dominant northern European-American, white Protestant understanding of both authentic religion and the nation on later immigrant peoples. Evangelical Alliance executive secretary Josiah Strong's call for the conversion of Catholic immigrants (and Jewish and Orthodox Christian immigrants as well) to some brand of evangelical Protestantism in order to Americanize them echoes this misleading understanding of a melting pot. Indeed, ethnic and cultural particularities often retained their greatest vitality in the religious sector.

Tracking the merger of various Lutheran denominations over the course of the twentieth century provides ample evidence, since most had their roots in particular ethnic communities. But as long as all were "Lutheran" in some form and as long as Lutheranism was regarded as a socially acceptable expression of Protestantism, it was easy to overlook the ethnic twists and turns within a single denomination.

As the century progressed, while some of the ethnic pluralism with roots in northern and western European cultures may have become muted, a new ethnic pluralism—Hispanic, Asian, and Middle Eastern—came to the fore. Once again the religious sector provided a powerful lens through which to view the continuing power of the cultures of origin. But there was a difference that was becoming increasingly clear as the nation moved into the twenty-first century. That difference, simply put, was that these cultures and the religions identified with them had such a fundamentally different cast from those of earlier European immigrants, especially, that they would be much less likely to be absorbed into any religious or cultural melting pot.

It was not simply that Roman Catholic churches offered the Mass in Spanish to accommodate Spanish-speaking parishioners. The Catholicism practiced by Hispanic immigrants was itself rather different from what the Irish-dominated American Catholic hierarchy had nurtured and even from the more festive Mediterranean and Slavic Catholicism of those immigrants arriving in the late nineteenth and early twentieth centuries. Hispanic Catholicism in the Western hemisphere reflects centuries of fusing together pre-Christian elements with European elements, and in some cases African elements, to produce a unique style of Roman Catholicism.

Then, too, the vast majority of earlier generations of immigrants had ties to some form of Christianity or to Judaism, the tradition from which Christianity emerged. With Asian immigrants nurturing forms of both the Buddhist and Hindu traditions and Near Eastern and Asian immigrants cultivating a distinctive American Islam, other global religions come into the picture, religions that are likely to resist amalgamation or absorption into even a polyglot religious culture. Ethnicity was central to American religious life at the start of the century; it was central at the end. But many more ethnic groups had found a home in the United States, intent on preserving ethnic particularity, often in religious forms, than was the case one hundred years earlier. Pluralism had come of age.

Even within ethnic communities, the forces of pluralism left their mark. With a history stretching back to the arrival of slave ships in the early seventeenth century, African-American religious life may demonstrate this facet of pluralism more compellingly than other ethnic cultures. At the dawn of the century, most African-American churches were part of denominations that had split off from larger, predominantly white Protestant groups. In organization and polity, they reflected that earlier association. Perhaps the most obvious arena where distinctive African-

American elements came to the fore was in worship, which remained more exuberant and continued to have echoes, sometimes rather distant, of the earlier African past. Except for a handful of Roman Catholic congregations, African Americans identified with denominations were overwhelmingly Protestant.

Yet throughout the century, several movements sought to elevate a religious style that was thought more characteristically African, whether through something like the Moorish Science Temple or, later, the Nation of Islam. During the first three-quarters of the century or so, there was a steady migration of African Americans from the South to urban areas in other parts of the country. The countless storefront churches and short-lived sects that emerged in the cities to respond to the religious needs of these in-migrants represent another strand of pluralism coming to African-American religious life.

With the civil rights movement came a reawakening of a black Christianity, shaped by the long history of slavery, racism, and discrimination, but also propelled now by the liberation theology with its own roots among the poor and oppressed in Latin America. No longer would African-American Protestant thought simply mimic or repeat ideas of white Protestant theology; there would be a theology that emerged directly from the way the lived experience of African Americans engaged scripture and Christian tradition. There would also be renewed interest in other forms of religious expression, such as voodoo and *santeria*, which themselves had a basis in the coming together of many religious forces. African Americans who had a formal religious affiliation at the close of the twentieth century were still likely to be Protestant, but like the rest of the American population, African Americans were taking many paths to find personal fulfillment in their spiritual quest.

Among Native Americans, the indigenous tribal peoples of the nation, syncretism with Christianity brought its own form of pluralism and led in the case of the Native American Church to the emergence of a new denomination when the religious use of peyote spread. As with other ethnic communities, Native Americans sought to revitalize their own traditions in the wake of the civil rights movement, but a century and more of change made easy return to the ways of the past impossible. Pluralism was evident even in the efforts to recapture the spirit that had once given coherence to tribal communities.

Constructing Worlds of Meaning

Religious pluralism in the United States at the dawn of the twenty-first century is about far more than numbers, whether of members or the total number of religious groups with a home in America or even of how many global traditions or ethnic communities have made a place for themselves in the United States. It is also about the myriad ways individuals construct a world of meaning through which they understand and interpret their own human experience. Earlier discussion highlighted the increasing privatization of religious experience and the growing eclecticism that marked spirituality, once spirituality had replaced religion as the locus for talking about meaning in life, personal values, and the like.

At the start of the century, many of the resources for cultivating personal spirituality still came from denominational publishing houses, often with some sort of imprimatur from denominational leaders. Consequently, most of these resources reflected the doctrinal teaching of the particular denomination that sponsored or endorsed them. For Christians, whether Protestant, Catholic, or Orthodox, that connection to a denomination meant that devotional materials or other tools for fostering the life of piety had some sort of biblical foundation. By the end of the twentieth century, most materials available for individuals to use in building a personal spiritual life were independent of denominational label. Many reflected an amalgamation of traditional religious thinking with everything from what was popularly called "New Age" to a glorified form of nature mysticism. The radical individualism in belief and practice commonly seen as a benefit of the First Amendment became an "I can believe and do whatever I want when it comes to my own religion" perspective. Hence the biblical basis of traditional spirituality ebbed as other concerns, ranging from the unique experience of being female (or male) to sexual orientation, became the starting point for an individual's spiritual journey.

As a result, spirituality became the arena where the extent of pluralism in U.S. religious life was most apparent. In the extreme, the idiosyncratic and eclectic nature of spirituality or lived religion, as some scholars called it, meant that there were in theory as many forms of spirituality as there were Americans. But some common elements endured, however differently they might be expressed. Some sense of the Other, of a Higher Power, of something more than human penetrated spirituality, even as the baby boomer generation and Generation X shied away from traditional God-language. On a functional level, what individuals expected from the spiritual quest also remained constant. Men and women embarked on spiritual journeys because they continued to be convinced that there was more to life than empirical reality and that their own life experience, as well as that of all humanity, had meaning. Endowing experience with transcendent meaning was as vital to spirituality at the end of the twentieth century as it was at the beginning. The difference was that religious institutions and their leaders, the theologians and the clergy, had provided the framework within which a personal world of meaning was constructed. By century's end, building a framework of meaning was very much a private, personal enterprise.

The same forces that made personal spirituality more pluralistic likewise infected theological reflection as the century progressed. Again, because of Protestantism's historic dominance of American religious culture, the developments come into sharp focus when one examines the history of Protestant religious thought in the United States in the twentieth century. If thinkers at the beginning of the century, like Social Gospel advocates, were caught up in a fascination with liberal theology as it developed in Germany, they insisted that their message was grounded in faithful exposition of scripture, particularly the ethical teachings of Jesus and the Hebrew prophets. By the end of the century, especially among Protestants, the starting point for theological speculation had shifted away from scripture. As with spirituality, for some the defining base for theology was gender or sexual orientation. For others, especially those who saw the intimate ties between the civil rights movement and theological reflection, race became the starting point. Consequently, the pursuit of a comprehensive, systematic theology was all but abandoned by Protestant thinkers, except within the evangelical fold. There, where the authority of scripture remained the central issue, building a comprehensive, coherent, systematic theology remained a vital endeavor. For Catholics, the situation was similar, especially after Vatican II removed the restriction that all theology build on a Thomistic foundation.

With such a range of starting points, pluralism had come of age in theological circles. The pluralistic environment was potentially dangerous to religious minority groups, for it was harder to articulate a single theological perspective when so many others competed for allegiance. Yet Orthodox Christian and American Jewish thinkers did just that, adding even more to the pluralistic mix that made up American religious thought in the twentieth century.

Pluralism in the Public Sector

The ways religion related to public life during the twentieth century also became more pluralistic. Less and less as the century moved on did Americans accept the notion that separation of church and state meant that religion and public life were not connected, if indeed that idea had ever really been widely accepted. Early in the century, religious folk sought to impress values and a particular conception of what American society should be through organizing groups like the Anti-Saloon League to work in the public arena; by the end of the century, there were groups like the Christian Coalition that promoted a particular religious agenda in political life without organizing separate agencies for every issue.

Another way to see the ongoing connection between religion and public life is to scrutinize legal cases that had to be adjudicated in the courts. Many had as their ostensible aim the protection of the constitutional right to freedom of religion for minority groups. The courts, especially in cases that restricted required prayer and Bible reading in the public schools, may well have recognized the extent of religious pluralism that prevailed in the United States long before the rank and file did. Indeed, the continuing efforts of some to restore such practices, in the belief that doing so will be almost a panacea for the nation's problems, suggest that many do not yet realize that the proportion of Americans identified with the old Protestant-Catholic-Jewish triad is shrinking.

Other faces of pluralism in the arena of religion and common life come to light in the ways both individuals and groups have demonstrated support of or opposition to particular government policies. The most significant during the twentieth century was the civil rights movement that undermined the legally sanctioned practices of racial separation and discrimination. The churches provided not only much of the leadership for the civil rights movement among both African Americans and Euro-Americans, but also much of the most strident opposition.

Finally, it became more common, as the century went on, for religious leaders willingly to be associated with politicians, often endorsing the candidates whose views seemed in harmony with their own. As well, sometimes religious leaders attempted to enter political life. Pat Robertson, founder of the Christian Coalition, sought the presidential nomination of the Republican Party on more than one occasion. Such would have been most unlikely at the start of the century.

Looking back, it becomes increasingly clear that the pluralism that came of age in the twentieth century was a natural development emerging from forces that had long shaped American religious life. The Europeans who embarked on colonial settlement brought diverse understandings of Protestant Christianity with them, laying the groundwork for the development of the denomination as a form of religious organization and the multiplicity of denominations that long constituted most approaches to pluralism. Yet those European colonists confronted an indigenous pluralism, but one they largely ignored, for there were numerous tribal societies already flourishing on North American soil. They added early on to the heritage of pluralism that came of age in the twentieth century. The history of openness to immigration from diverse sources, prevalent through most of American history (with one major exception being the period in the twentieth century when rigid quotas were in place), paved the way for other forms of pluralism to come to life. Immigration helped bring an ethnic pluralism to American Catholicism and American Judaism. The shifting sources of immigrants helped make Islam one of the largest single religious traditions in the United States at the start of the twenty-first century. The legal arrangements of the First Amendment to the Constitution also helped sustain an environment where pluralism would prevail in granting individuals and religious communities considerable latitude in matters of belief and practice. As American society became increasingly industrialized and ever more complex during the century, yet other features of an expanding pluralism came to light, particularly in the area of personal spirituality.

On balance, it may well be that the greatest contribution made by the United States to global religious life is its demonstrating that, however vast the pluralism, a vital religious culture can flourish. Pluralism does not undermine common life, but seems to enrich it. The seeds planted by diverse tribal cultures and by European colonists centuries ago came to full growth in the twentieth century, for it was the century when pluralism—religious pluralism—came of age.

Notes

Chapter 1. Planting Pluralism in the United States

1. Alexis de Tocqueville, *Democracy in America*, p. 318.

2. Sidney Mead expounds on this theme in several of the essays in *The Lively Experiment*.

3. I discuss these matters and several of the themes in the following paragraphs in greater detail in Charles H. Lippy, Robert Choquette, and Stafford Poole, *Christianity Comes to the Americas, 1492–1776*, chaps. 16–21.

4. A recent, solid study is Edwin S. Gaustad, *Liberty of Conscience*.

5. Older, but still valuable, is Joseph Moss Ives, *The Ark and the Dove*.

6. There is some discussion of the "holy experiment idea" in Hans Fantel's popularly written *William Penn*.

7. See Richard W. Pointer, *Protestant Pluralism and the New York Experience*.

8. Ira Rosenwaike, "The Jewish Population in the United States as Estimated from the Census of 1829," in *The Jewish Experience in America*, Abraham Karp, ed., 2:9.

9. The persistent presence of pluralism is evident in the title of Peter Williams's recent survey text, *America's Religions*.

10. A good exposition and analysis of issues during the age of independence and drafting of the Constitution is Edwin S. Gaustad, *Neither King nor Prelate*. For Washington's remarks in his famous "Farewell Address," see *The Writings of George Washington from the Original Manuscript Sources, 1745–1799*, 35:229–30. For Franklin, see *The Autobiography of Benjamin Franklin*, pp. 101–3.

11. See Roger Finke and Rodney Stark, *The Churching of America, 1776–1990*.

12. The interplay of a consistent, inchoate religious undercurrent identified with nineteenth-century evangelical Protestantism in the midst of pluralism is seen in the title Catherine L. Albanese gave to her textbook: *America: Religions and Religion*.

13. Albanese discusses these matters in *America: Religions and Religion*. William Warren Sweet first drew sustained attention to the transdenominational evangelical dominance in the nineteenth century in *The Story of Religion in America* and in greater detail in the anthologies of primary materials he edited under the rubric *Religion on the American Frontier*.

14. Recent studies of anti-Catholicism and anti-Semitism in the United States include Mark J. Hurley, *Anti-Catholicism in the American Experience*, and Leonard Dinnerstein, *Antisemitism in America*.

15. On the convent burning, see Wilfrid J. Bisson, *Countdown to Violence*. See also Maria Monk, *Awful Disclosures of the Hotel Dieu Nunnery of Montreal*.

16. Immigration figures are available through the U.S. Department of Justice, Immigration and Naturalization Service.

17. See Robert T. Handy's classic study, *A Christian America*.

18. Josiah Strong, *Our Country*, esp. chaps. 4 and 5.

19. Features of the impact of ethnic pluralism within American Catholicism are one focus of the following studies, among others: Josef L. Barton, "Religion and Cultural Change in Czech Immigrant Communities, 1850–1920," in *Immigrants and Religion in Urban Culture*, Randall M. Miller and Thomas D. Marzik, eds., pp. 3–24; John Bukowczyk, "'Mary the Messiah': Polish Immigrants, Heresy, and the Malleable Ideology of the Roman Catholic Church in America, 1860–1930," in *Disciplines of Faith: Studies in Religion, Politics, and Patriarchy*, Jim Obelkevich, Lyndal Roper, and Raphael Samuel, eds., pp. 371–89; Paul Wrobel, *Our Way*; William H. Galush, "Faith and Fatherland: Dimensions of Polish-American Ethno-Religion, 1875–1975," in *Immigrants and Religion in Urban Culture*, pp. 84–102; Robert M. Orsi, *The Madonna of 115th Street*; Silvano M. Tomasi, *Piety and Power*; Rudolph J. Vecoli, "Prelates and Peasants: Italian Immigrants and the Catholic Church," and his "Cult and Occult in Italian-American Culture: The Persistence of a Religious Heritage," in *Immigrants and Religion in Urban Culture*, Miller and Marzik, eds., pp. 25–47.

20. A brief, but solid overview of Jewish developments is Abraham J. Karp, "The Emergence of an American Judaism," in *Encyclopedia of the American Religious Experience*, Charles H. Lippy and Peter W. Williams, eds., 1:273–90.

21. This point is one theme of Sandra Sizer Frankiel, *California's Spiritual Frontiers*.

22. See Richard Hughes Seager, *The World's Parliament of Religions*.

23. Two studies, now dated, remain valuable for the early years of the YMCA and YWCA: C. Howard Hopkins, *History of the Y.M.C.A. in North America*, and Mary S. Sims, *The Y.W.C.A.: An Unfolding Purpose*.

24. See Robert D. Cross, ed., *The Church and the City*.

25. See the classic study by Arthur H. Fauset, *Black Gods of the Metropolis*, for one dimension of this pluralism.

26. The dichotomy between "rescue" and "reform" approaches forms the heart of Jean Miller Schmidt, *Souls or the Social Order*.

27. The most thorough treatment of this complex of ideas is Ann Douglas, *The Feminization of American Culture*. But see also two earlier essays by Barbara Welter: "The Cult of True Womanhood, 1820–1860" and "The Feminization of American Religion, 1800–1860," in *Clio's Consciousness Raised*, Mary S. Hartman and Lois Banner, eds., pp. 136–57.

28. Colleen McDannell, *The Christian Home in Victorian America, 1840–1900* and idem, *Material Christianity*.

29. A forceful statement about the push for privatization in complex societies is Thomas Luckmann, *The Invisible Religion*. On its import for American religious life in the later twentieth century, see Wade Clark Roof and William McKinney, *American Mainline Religion*, and Robert Wuthnow, *The Restructuring of American Religion*.

30. The explosion of periodical literature is evident in the founding dates or dates of expansion in content of those covered in *Popular Religious Magazines of the United States*, P. Mark Fackler and Charles H. Lippy, eds.

31. See my discussion of these matters in Charles H. Lippy, *Being Religious, American Style*, pp. 147–54.

32. Mark C. Carnes, *Secret Ritual and Manhood in Victorian America*.

33. See Fergus MacDonald, *The Catholic Church and the Secret Societies in the United States*, p. 100.

34. For a case study of the move towards more decorum in worship, see Paul Harvey, *Redeeming the South*, chaps. 3 and 4.

35. Will Herberg, *Protestant, Catholic, Jew*.

Chapter 2. The Shifting Public Presence of Mainline Protestantism

1. This was the name he gave to the journal he started in the 1880s. See Mark G. Toulouse, "Christian Century," in *Religious Periodicals of the United States*, Charles H. Lippy, ed., pp. 109–14; Annalee Ward, "Christian Century," in *Popular Religious Magazines of the United States*, P. Mark Fackler and Charles H. Lippy, eds., pp. 110–15; Linda-Marie Deloff, Martin E. Marty, Dean Peerman, and James M. Wall, *A Century of the Century*; and Linda-Marie Deloff, "The Century in Transition."

2. See Robert T. Handy's book by that title.

3. I derived this percentage from figures provided by Edwin S. Gaustad, *A Historical Atlas of Religion in America*, and the U.S. Bureau of the Census.

4. See Josiah Strong, *Our Country*.

5. Membership figures for 1990 were taken from Kenneth B. Bedell, comp., *Yearbook of American and Canadian Churches, 1993*.

6. See E. Digby Baltzell, *The Protestant Establishment*. See also Kit Konolige and Frederica Konolige, *The Power of Their Glory*.

7. Figures provided by the Princeton Religion Research Center, based on Gallup Polls, showed 73 percent of Americans claiming religious membership in 1937 and 69 percent in 1995; between 1937 and 1995, the average was around 69.9 percent. Lowest figures reported were for 1988 and 1990; highest figures reported were for 1943 and 1947. George H. Gallup, Jr., comp., *Religion in America 1996*, p. 41.

8. Thomas E. Frank, *Polity, Practice, and the Mission of the United Methodist Church*, chap. 1, persuasively argues that numerical decline does not mean demise because of social changes present in the larger culture.

9. Helpful here is Nathan O. Hatch, *The Democratization of American Christianity*.

10. See Charles H. Lippy, "The Camp Meeting in Transition."

11. Paul Harvey, *Redeeming the South*, tracks this process among both white and African American Baptists in the southern states.

12. Thomas E. Frank, *Polity, Practice, and the Mission of the United Methodist Church*, chap. 1, emphasizes how the birth rate among Methodists declined as the denomination moved to the center. No doubt the same holds for others.

13. Within the Christian tradition, "Pentecostal" refers to gifts of the Spirit, particularly glossolalia or speaking in tongues, described first in the New Testament book of Acts. Fuller discussion of these gifts in 1 Corinthians also includes healing and prophecy, among others.

14. Standard accounts of modern Pentecostalism's emergence include Robert Mapes Anderson, *Vision of the Disinherited*; W.J. Hollenweger, *The Pentecostals*; and idem, *Pentecostalism*.

15. On Seymour, see Douglas Nelson, "For Such a Time as This," and James Tinney, "William J. Seymour." On Parham, see James R. Goff, *Fields White unto Harvest*, and Sarah Parham, *The Life of Charles Fox Parham*.

16. For the Assemblies of God, see Edith L. Blumhofer, *Restoring the Faith*, and idem, *The Assemblies of God*. On the Church of God (Cleveland), see Mickey Crews, *The Church of God*, and Charles W. Conn, *Like a Mighty Army*, a more triumphalist study. The Church of God in Christ awaits scholarly analysis, but see James Courts, comp., *The History and Life Work of Elder C.H. Mason*. Vinson Synan discusses the beginnings of the Pentecostal-Holiness Church in the revised *The Holiness-Pentecostal Tradition*.

17. See chaps. 2 and 3 of H. Richard Niebuhr, *The Social Sources of Denominationalism*.

18. The best recent study of the Scopes Trial and its long-range impact on American religious and cultural life is Edward J. Larson, *Summer for the Gods*.

19. Joel Carpenter brilliantly tracks this networking in *Revive Us Again*.

20. For the Presbyterians, see Bradley J. Longfield, *The Presbyterian Controversy*. Still valuable for the overall story is Part III of Norman P. Furniss, *The Fundamentalist Controversy*, on the various denominations.

21. Robert Moats Miller painstakingly traces Fosdick's involvement in the controversy in *Harry Emerson Fosdick*.

22. See Fosdick, "Shall the Fundamentalists Win?"

23. The Evangelical Alliance was a prototype for some later ecumenical organizations.

24. On the American ecumenical movement overall, see the now dated studies by Samuel McCrea Cavert, *Church Cooperation and Unity in America* and *The American Churches in the Ecumenical Movement*. More detail on the emergence of the FCC and its antecedents is found in even older studies: Harlan Paul Douglass, *Church Unity Movements in the United States*, and Charles Stedman Macfarland, *Christian Unity in the Making*.

25. On the early days of religious radio, see George H. Hill, *Airwaves to the Soul*, and Dave Beckman, "Long Before Falwell."

26. See L. David Lewis, "Charles E. Fuller," in *Twentieth-Century Shapers of American Popular Religion*, Charles H. Lippy, ed., pp. 148–55. The only complete biography is that by Fuller's son: Daniel P. Fuller, *Give the Winds a Mighty Voice*.

27. See Charles H. Lippy, *Being Religious, American Style*, pp. 170–71.

28. A classic account of the impact of the "great migration" on one northern city, Chicago, is given in St. Clair Drake and Horace R. Cayton, *Black Metropolis*.

29. Among the earliest studies of this phenomenon is Arthur Huff Fauset, *Black Gods of the Metropolis*.

30. See Charles Hamilton, *The Black Preacher in America*; Henry H. Mitchell, *Black Preaching*; and William C. Turner, "The Musicality of Black Preaching."

31. The United Methodist Church provides a convenient case study. The hymnal in use when the Methodist Episcopal Church, the Methodist Protestant Church, and the Methodist Episcopal Church, South, merged in 1939 had no source entries for spirituals or even folk hymns. The hymnal produced in 1964, just prior to the merger with the Evangelical Brethren Church which created the United Methodist Church, listed eight spirituals under "folk hymns." In 1981, a supplementary worship resource called *Songs of Zion* appeared; spirituals and songs of African-American origin were its primary components. The most recent hymnal of the United Methodist Church (1989) lists no less than 30 African-American spirituals, now its own category rather than a subset of "folk hymns." All were published in Nashville by the Methodist Publishing House; its successor, the United Methodist Publishing House; or Abingdon Press, a Publishing House subsidiary.

32. Robert T. Handy, "The Great American Religious Depression, 1925–35."

33. Virtually all the sources on which Handy drew came from predominantly white denominations and agencies.

34. Handy expands or revises his views on these in chaps. 7 and 8 of *A Christian America*.

35. See, for example, Keith A. Roberts, *Religion in Sociological Perspective*, pp. 130–35.

36. In the mid-1980s, the pastor of a Presbyterian congregation in Clemson, South Carolina, commented to the author that for one year, not one adult who had joined his church had previously been a Presbyterian.

37. A contemporary statement that tries to recast a positive role for Christianity to assure that higher education and religious faith remain compatible is Harold K. Schilling, *The University and the Church*.

38. By 1970, more than twice as many Americans were likely to marry outside their own religious group as at the start of the twentieth century. See Larry Bumpass, "The Trend of Interfaith Marriage in the United States."

39. Will Herberg, *Protestant, Catholic, Jew*.

40. Quoted in Herberg, rev. ed., p. 95, from *The New York Times*, December 23, 1952.

41. A contemporary example filled with the spirit of optimism over ecumenical possi-

bilities comes from the Lutheran Franklin Clark Fry in "The Unity of the Church." On the ecumenical movement in the United States more generally, see Samuel McCrea Cavert, *The American Churches in the Ecumenical Movement*, and idem, *Church Cooperation and Unity in America*.

42. Among the few challenges to the prevailing self-satisfaction of Protestant denominations in the 1950s are Peter Berger, *The Noise of Solemn Assemblies*; Martin Marty, *The New Shape of American Religion*; and Gibson Winter, *The Suburban Captivity of the Churches*.

43. Both James Hudnut-Beumler, *Looking for God in the Suburbs*, and Mark A. Noll, *A History of Christianity in the United States and Canada*, p. 437, call attention to the building boom among Protestant churches.

44. On the New York crusade, see chap. 3 ("God in the Garden") of William A. Martin, *A Prophet with Honor*.

45. See Weldon T. Johnson, "The Religious Crusade."

46. See Norman Vincent Peale, *The Power of Positive Thinking*, and Billy Graham, *Peace with God*.

47. On early religious television, see Ben Armstrong, *The Electric Church*, chaps. 6 and 7.

48. The best contemporaneous account is Ralph Lord Roy, *Communism and the Churches*, but see also Charles L. West, *Communism and the Theologians*. The anticommunist stance of the churches finds emphasis in Robert S. Ellwood, *The Fifties Spiritual Marketplace*. Its stridency is somewhat ironic given what Gerald Sittser calls the "cautious patriotism" Protestant churches embraced during World War II. See Sittser, *A Cautious Patriotism*. See also Warren L. Vinz, *Pulpit Politics*, passim.

49. The debates within Methodist circles that brought the creation of the all-black Central Jurisdiction in 1939 when merger created the denomination receive the best contemporary treatment in John M. Moore, *The Long Road to Methodist Union*. But see also Willis J. King, "The Central Jurisdiction," in *The History of American Methodism*, Emory Stevens Bucke, ed., vol. 3; Frederick A. Norwood, *The Story of American Methodism*, pp. 406–10; Willis J. King, "The Negro Membership of the (Former) Methodist Church in the (New) United Methodist Church"; and my case study of the dismantling of a Central Jurisdiction annual conference, "Towards an Inclusive Church: South Carolina Methodism and Race, 1972–1982."

50. Jeffrey K. Hadden, *The Gathering Storm in the Churches*.

51. Two of the first women priests provided contemporary accounts of the controversy within the Episcopal Church when they were ordained: Emily C. Hewitt and Suzanne R. Hiatt, *Women Priests: Yes or No?*, and Carter Heyward, *A Priest Forever*.

52. See Nancy A. Hardesty, *Inclusive Language in the Church*. For more recent debates over use of gender-specific language in biblical translations and the lectionary or book of lessons used by many mainline Protestant bodies (and others), see Richard J. Clifford, "The Rocky Road to a New Lectionary"; Timothy C. Morgan, "Biblical Feminists Press for Gender-Inclusive NIV"; and Aida Besancon Spencer, "Power Play."

53. On a fundamentalist understanding of the role and status of women at century's end, see Nancy Tatom Ammerman, *Bible Believers*, esp. chaps. 8 and 10.

54. The Universal Fellowship of Metropolitan Community Churches awaits a solid scholarly history. But see founder Troy D. Perry's early autobiography, *The Lord Is My Shepherd and He Knows I'm Gay*; the now very dated work of Ronald M. Enroth and Gerald E. Jamison, *The Gay Church*; and the more recent "Gays and the Gospel: An Interview with Troy Perry."

55. The issues are probed in Letha Dawson Scanzoni and Virginia Ramey Mollenkott, *Is the Homosexual My Neighbor?* On one of the better-known "ex-gay" ministries, Exodus International, see Justin Chin, "Our Reporter Survives the Ex-Gay Ministries."

56. On the trial of Episcopal Bishop Walter Righter, see "It's Official: Ordaining Gays Is Not Heresy"; Bruce Bawer, "Who's on Trial—the Heretic or the Church?"; "Church Trial Slated for Episcopal Bishop"; William L. Sachs, "Testing Church Doctrine"; Kenneth L. Woodward and Anne Underwood, "A Bishop in the Dock"; and Randy Frame, "Heresy Charges Dismissed."

57. On the first stages of the controversy surrounding Rev. Jimmy Creech, see "Pastor Found Innocent in Lesbian Ceremony"; Gustav Niebuhr, "Trial Opens for Methodist Minister" and "Pastor's Church Trial Attests to Divisiveness of Gay Issue."

58. See Wade Clark Roof, *A Generation of Seekers*, and Benton Johnson, Donald A. Luidens, and Dean R. Hoge, *Vanishing Boundaries*.

59. Roof, *A Generation of Seekers*, repeatedly calls attention to the popular distinction baby boomers made between "spirituality" and "religion."

60. Robert N. Bellah, William M. Sullivan, Ann Swidler, and Steven M. Tipton, *Habits of the Heart*.

61. The 1920 census, as reported by the U.S. Bureau of the Census, showed that the nation had finally become majority urban, not rural, with a majority of the population living in urban metropolitan areas. See also Arthur S. Link and William B. Cotton, *American Epoch*, 1:244–47, on the significance of the demographic changes evident by 1920.

62. The importance of Protestant forces in helping bring about the eight-hour workday, the five-day work week, and other improvements in labor conditions finds solid appraisal in Robert Moats Miller, *American Protestantism and Social Issues*, Part III, and Donald B. Meyer, *The Protestant Search for Political Realism*, pp. 76–106.

63. On changes in Sunday observance among Protestants, see Randall Higgins, "South's Sundays Far from Old Days," *Chattanooga Times* (March 21, 1998): A1, A5.

64. There is a growing literature about Willow Creek and its approach to church life. From the inside, see Lynne Hybels and Bill Hybels, *Rediscovering Church*. For a more analytic perspective, see Donald S. Luecke, "Is Willow Creek the Wave of the Future?"; Gregory Allen Pritchard, "The Strategy of Willow Creek Community Church"; and Kimon Howland Sargeant, "Faith and Fulfillment."

65. New resources for contemporary Christian worship are provided regularly in *Worship Leader*, offered since 1992 by CCM Publishers in Nashville. See also Marva J. Dawn, *Reaching Out Without Dumbing Down*, and Robert Webber, *Signs of Wonder*.

66. This came as no surprise to those who track the networks that allowed fundamentalism to flourish even when the mainstream consigned it to the periphery. See Joel Carpenter, *Revive Us Again*.

Chapter 3. Pluralism's Promise and Perils: American Catholicism in the Twentieth Century

1. On the third plenary, see Peter Guilday, *A History of the Councils of Baltimore*. On the immigrant character of the church, see James J. Hennesey, *American Catholics*, chap. 15.

2. The standard biography remains John Tracy Ellis, *Life of James Cardinal Gibbons*. But see also Gerald P. Fogarty, *The Vatican and the American Hierarchy*.

3. Robert D. Cross, "Origins of the Catholic Parochial Schools in America." On problems with public schools from a then contemporary perspective, see Edwin D. Mead, *The Roman Catholic Church and the School Question*. On a well-known attempt at compromise by renting parochial schools to public school systems for the regular school day and providing "after hours" religious instruction (as a way to gain state financial support), see Daniel F. Reilly, O.P., *The School Controversy, 1891–1893*. For developments in the first half of the twentieth century, see Henry J. Browne, "The American Parish School in the Last Half Century."

4. Valuable primary sources are excerpted in Part 2 of Aaron I. Abell, ed., *American Catholic Thought on Social Questions*. See also Abell, *American Catholicism and Social Action*.

5. Ryan's support for labor is well expressed in his *A Living Wage* and "The Laborer's Right to a Living Wage" and a work he coauthored with Joseph Husslein, *The Church and Labor*. Another powerful contemporary call for the church to stand with labor is Peter E. Dietz, "The Metamorphosis."

6. Much of this misunderstanding, though not entirely without basis, accounted for the "Americanism" condemned by Pope Leo XIII in his 1899 apostolic letter to Cardinal Gibbons, "Testem Benevolentiae," reprinted in John Tracy Ellis, *Documents of American Catholic History*. See also Thomas T. McAvoy, *The Great Crisis in American Catholic History*, and Gerald P. Fogarty, *The Vatican and the Americanist Crisis*.

7. On the change of status for the American church, see Debra Campbell, "Catholicism from Independence to World War I," in *Encyclopedia of the American Religious Experience*, Charles H. Lippy and Peter W. Williams, eds., 1:372.

8. On the National Catholic War Council, see Michael Williams, *American Catholics in the War*, and Elizabeth K. McKeown, *War and Welfare*.

9. Hennesey, pp. 315–26, discusses the major structural changes resulting from Vatican II.

10. See Joan Bland, S.N.D., *Hibernian Crusade: The Story of the Catholic Total Abstinence Union of America*.

11. Attacks on Smith were spurred by the likes of James Scott Vance, *Proof of Rome's Political Meddling in America*. Also widely known is the exchange between Gov. Smith and Charles C. Marshall: Marshall, "An Open Letter to the Honorable Alfred E. Smith," and Smith, "Catholic and Patriot." There is solid discussion of the 1928 campaign and the developing Catholic subculture in William M. Halsey, *The Survival of American Innocence*. For the overall story, see Edmund Arthur Moore, *A Catholic Runs for President*. Published just four years before John Kennedy's election, Moore's work at the time was regarded as overly optimistic in its conclusion that prejudice against a Catholic candidate for the presidency had abated so much as to make the election of a Catholic in the near future highly probable. See also Martin E. Marty, *The Noise of Conflict*, pp. 241–49.

12. Ryan's autobiography, *Social Doctrine in Action*, is instructive, as is Francis L. Broderick, *Right Reverend New Dealer: John A. Ryan*.

13. See Sheldon Marcus, *Father Coughlin*, and Charles J. Tull, *Father Coughlin and the New Deal*. Andrew M. Greeley, *The Catholic Experience*, chap. 7, contrasts Ryan and Coughlin in terms of their significance for American Catholics.

14. Donald F. Crosby, *God, Church, and Flag*.

15. The movement of Catholics toward the demographic center is noted in two helpful studies from the 1950s: John J. Kane, "The Social Structure of American Catholics," and Andrew M. Greeley, *The Church and the Suburbs*. Gallup polls revealed that by the late 1980s for the first time the proportion of "upscale" American Catholics equalled the proportion of "upscale" Protestants. See George Gallup, Jr., and Jim Castelli, *The People's Religion*, p. 75.

16. Herberg, *Protestant, Catholic, Jew*.

17. On the significance for American Catholics of Kennedy's election, see Greeley, *Catholic Experience*, chap. 9.

18. The literature on the impact of Vatican II is huge. Helpful in preparing this chapter were Giuseppe Alberigo, Jean-Pierre Jossua, and Joseph A. Komonchak, eds., *The Reception of Vatican II*; Penelope A. Ryan, *Practicing Catholic*, chap. 2; and countless articles appearing from the 1960s through the 1990s in journals such as *Commonweal* and *America*. The key primary sources are collected in Walter M. Abbott, ed., *The Documents of Vatican II*.

19. While not critical in a scholarly sense, both John Cooney, *American Pope*, and Robert I. Gannon, *Cardinal Spellman Story*, provide the contours of Spellman's life and career.

20. The heart of Murray's thought comes out in John Courtney Murray, *We Hold These Truths*, and *Bridging the Sacred and the Secular*. Helpful interpretive works include Thomas P. Ferguson, *Catholic and American*; Thomas Hughes, *The Believer as Citizen*; and Keith J. Pavlischek, *John Courtney Murray and the Dilemma of Religious Toleration*.

21. O'Connor's essential conservatism is evident in his *Essential Catholic Handbook* and *A Moment of Grace*. See also the best selling debate with former New York City mayor Ed Koch: O'Connor and Koch, *His Eminence and Hizzoner*.

22. On the Berrigan brothers, see William Van Etten Casey and Philip Nobile, eds., *The Berrigans*; Francine duPlessix Gray, *Divine Disobedience*; and William O'Rourke, *The Harrisburg 7 and the New Catholic Left*.

23. There is a considerable literature on Day and her work. Her two autobiographical volumes, *From Union Square to Rome* and *Loaves and Fishes*, are essential; a helpful collection of her writings is *By Little and by Little*. Interpretive works include Robert Coles, *Dorothy Day*; William D. Miller, *Dorothy Day* and *A Harsh and Dreadful Love*; and Nancy Roberts, *Dorothy Day and the Catholic Worker*. For bibliography of works by and about Day, see Anne Klejment and Alice Klejment, *Dorothy Day and the Catholic Worker*.

24. See Robert J. McClory, *Turning Point*; Janet E. Smith, *Humanae Vitae*; Russell E. Smith, ed., *Trust the Truth*; and Morris, *American Catholic*, chap. 14.

25. The text of the *Pastoral Constitution on the Church in the Modern World* is found in Abbott, *Documents*, pp. 199–308.

26. The Gallup poll organization reported in 1989 that two-thirds of American Catholic priests under the age of 40 and 70 percent of the laity under 40 disapproved of the church's position on birth control. See Gallup and Castelli, *People's Religion*, p. 12. See also Penelope Ryan, *Practicing Catholic*, chap. 5. For the long view, see John T. Noonan, Jr., *Contraception*.

27. On how priests resolve some of these dilemmas in the pastoral context, see James Walsh et al., *Grace Under Pressure*. See also Philip S. Kaufman, *Why You Can Disagree and Remain a Faithful Catholic*.

28. See Penelope Ryan, *Practicing Catholic*, chap. 6. See also Theodore Mackin, S.J., *Divorce and Remarriage*.

29. Mark Chaves and James C. Cavendish, "More Evidence on U.S. Catholic Church Attendance."

30. See, for example, C. Kirk Hadaway and Penny Long Marler, "Did You Really Go to Church This Week?"

31. I draw here on both Richard A. Schoenherr and Lawrence A. Young, *Full Pews and Empty Altars*, and Dean R. Hoge, *The Future of Catholic Leadership*.

32. See Elizabeth Durkin and Julie Durkin Montague, "Surveying U.S. Nuns."

33. On the drop in support for parochial schools more generally, see Andrew M. Greeley et al., *Catholic Schools in a Declining Church*.

34. See Penelope Ryan, *Practicing Catholic*, chap. 4, and Raymond J. Gunzel, *Celibacy*.

35. See Philip Jenkins, *Pedophiles and Priests*, and Jason Berry, *Lead Us Not into Temptation*.

36. Among the more controversial Catholic feminist writers is Mary Daly, whose early book, *Beyond God the Father*, became something of a classic. Influential among Protestants as well as her fellow Catholics is Rosemary Radford Ruether. See, for example, her *Sexism and God-Talk*, and *Women-Church*.

37. On women, lay and religious, serving churches, see Philip J. Murnion, *New Parish Ministers*.

38. Garry Wills, *Bare, Ruined Choirs*. On problems in maintaining a Catholic identity, see Robert P. Lambelli, "Vatican II—Twenty Years Later" and "Catholic Identity After Vatican II."

39. Mary McCarthy, *Memories of a Catholic Girlhood.*

40. A helpful early study of the charismatic resurgence in Catholic circles is Rene Laurentin, *Catholic Pentecostalism.*

41. See Robert Anthony Orsi, *The Madonna of 115th Street.* See also Rudolph J. Vecoli, "Prelates and Peasants," and Vecoli, "Cult and Occult in Italian-American Culture: The Persistence of a Religious Heritage," in *Immigrants and Urban Culture*, Randall M. Miller and Thomas D. Marzik, eds., pp. 25–47.

42. Thomas A. Tweed, *Our Lady of the Exile.* See also Ana Maria Diaz-Stevens, *Oxcart Catholicism on Fifth Avenue*, and Jay P. Dolan and Allan Figueroa Deck, *Hispanic Catholic Culture in the U.S.*

43. See Sheen's autobiography, *Treasure in Clay*, and also D.P. Noonan, *The Passion of Fulton Sheen.* Tapes of Sheen's telecasts are available through the Sheen Institute, Victor, NY, and videocassettes through Trinity Communications, Manassas, VA. A recent study (Christopher Owen Lynch, *Selling Catholicism*) is not especially helpful.

44. Robert A. Orsi, *Thank You, St. Jude.* See also Charles H. Lippy, *Being Religious, American Style*, pp. 117–20.

45. John J. McNeill, S.J., *The Church and the Homosexual.*

46. Robert Goss, *Jesus Acted Up.*

47. For early reports and commentary on the silencing of Grammick and Nugent appearing in the American Catholic press, see Teresa Malcolm, "Pair Dealt a Lifetime Ban on Ministry to Homosexuals"; "Vatican Ban Ends Years of Investigation"; Mary E. Hunt, "Despite Silencing, Holy Spirit Prevails"; and Gerald D. Coleman, "Ministry to Homosexuals Must Use Authentic Church Teaching."

Chapter 4. The Paradox of Pluralism: The Jewish Experience

1. Figures are derived from Robert Gutman, "Demographic Trends and the Decline of Anti-Semitism," in *Jews in the Mind of America*, Charles Herbert Stember et al., eds., p. 314 (which gives a figure of 229,087 Jews in the U.S. in 1877), and Alvin Chenhin, "Jewish Population in the United States, 1967," p. 283, which gives a figure of 5,779,845 Jews in the U.S. that year.

2. On anti-Semitism generally, see Gavin Langmuir, *History, Religion, and Antisemitism.* For connections to Christian belief, see Charles Y. Glock and Rodney Stark, *Christian Beliefs and Anti-Semitism.* The best study of anti-Semitism in the United States is Leonard Dinnerstein, *Antisemitism in America.*

3. For the early story, see Nathan Glazer, *American Judaism*, chaps. 2 and 3, and Jacob R. Marcus, *Early American Jewry.*

4. Two helpful early studies are Beryl Harold Levy, *Reform Judaism in America*, and David Philipson, *The Reform Movement in Judaism.* More recent scholarly works include Michael A. Meyer, *Response to Modernity*, and Marc Lee Raphael, *Profiles in American Judaism.* The latter also includes solid discussion of the Conservative, Orthodox, and Reconstructionist traditions. See also Arnold M. Eisen, *The Jewish People in America.*

5. Deborah Dash Moore, "Social History of American Judaism," in *Encyclopedia of the American Religious Experience*, Charles H. Lippy and Peter W. Williams, eds., 1:292. For the overall story, Charles Wyszkowski, *A Community in Conflict*, is most helpful.

6. Both entertaining and informative on this point is Stephen Birmingham, *"Our Crowd."*

7. On Hasidim in the United States, see Janet S. Belcove-Shalin, ed., *New World Hasidim*; Edward Hoffman, *Despite All Odds*; and George Kranzler, "The Jewish Community of Williamsburg, Brooklyn."

8. The classic work remains Marshall Sklare, *Conservative Judaism.* See also Moshe Davis, *The Emergence of Conservative Judaism*; Arthur Hertzberg, "The American Jew and

His Religion," in *The American Jew*, Oscar I. Janowsky, ed., pp. 101–19; and Eisen, *Jewish People in America*, chap. 5. Schechter deserves a contemporary critical biography; among the better older studies is Norman DeMattos Bentwich, *Solomon Schechter*.

9. Jacob Neusner, *American Judaism*, p. 120.

10. Ibid.

11. Kaplan's views are summarized well in Mordecai M. Kaplan, *Judaism as a Civilization* and *The Religion of Ethical Nationhood*. On Kaplan and the Reconstructionist movement, see Richard Libowitz, *Mordecai M. Kaplan and the Development of Reconstructionism*; Mel Scult, *Judaism Faces the Twentieth Century*; and Eisen, *Jewish People in America*, chap. 4.

12. See Horace M. Kallen, *Culture and Democracy in the United States*, and idem, *Secularism Is the Will of God*.

13. On the culture of *yiddishkeit*, see Irving Howe, *The World of Our Fathers*, part 3. For a different perspective, see Jonathan D. Sarna, "The Making of an American Jewish Culture," in *When Philadelphia Was the Capital of Jewish America*, Murray Friedman, ed., pp. 145–55.

14. See Melvin Urofsky, *American Zionism from Herzl to the Holocaust*. On one strand of Jewish opposition to Zionism, see Thomas A. Kolsky, *Jews Against Zionism*. For the convoluted Protestant attitudes, given the ambivalence to Jews as the chosen people, see Hertzel Fishman, *American Protestantism and a Jewish State*.

15. See Zvi Ganin, *Truman, American Jewry, and Israel*, and Michael J. Cohen, *Truman and Israel*.

16. See Neusner, *American Judaism*, and idem, "Judaism in Contemporary America," in *Encyclopedia of the American Religious Experience*, Charles H. Lippy and Peter W. Williams, eds., 1:311–23.

17. One example is Jon Weisberger, "American Jews and Israeli Policy."

18. Helpful in understanding Israeli Jewish fundamentalism and American Jewry's reactions are Ehud Sprinzak, *The Ascendance of Israel's Radical Right*; Samuel C. Heilman, *Defenders of the Faith*; and numerous essays in Martin E. Marty and R. Scott Appleby, eds., *Fundamentalisms Observed*.

19. An interesting contemporary statement is Lewis S. Gannett, "Is America Anti-Semitic?" but see also Naomi Cohen, *Not Free to Desist*.

20. See Marshall Sklare, *America's Jews*, pp. 143–51. Many essays in Michael N. Dobkowski, ed., *Jewish American Voluntary Organizations*, illuminate the numerous agencies, health-related and otherwise, that make up the larger complex. See also Charles S. Levy, "Jewish Communal Service: Health, Welfare, Recreational and Social," in Janowsky, ed., *American Jew*, pp. 253–66; Herman D. Stein, "Jewish Social Work in the United States, 1654–1954"; and National Association of Jewish Center Workers, *Aspects of the Jewish Community Center*.

21. There is an immense literature on Jewish involvement in the early labor movement and in early socialist political endeavors in the United States. See, for example, Selig Pearlman, "Jewish-American Unionism"; Louis Levine, *The Women's Garment Workers*; Melvin Dubofsky, "Organized Labor and the Immigrant in New York City"; Will Herberg, "The Jewish Labor Movement in the United States"; Bernard Bloom, "Yiddish-Speaking Socialists in America"; Moses Rischin, *The Promised City*; and Jewish socialist politician Morris Hillquit's autobiography, *Loose Leaves from a Busy Life*. There are extracts from cognate primary sources in Irving Howe and Kenneth Libo, eds., *How We Lived*.

22. See Michael R. Olneck and Marvin Lazeron, "The School Achievement of Immigrant Children"; C. Bezalel Sherman, "Demographic and Social Aspects," in Janowsky, ed., *American Jew*, pp. 27–51; and Nathan Glazer, "Social Characteristics of American Jews, 1654–1954," the most relevant section of which is excerpted as "The American Jew and the Attainment of Middle-Class Rank: Some Trends and Explanations," in *The Jews*, Marshall Sklare, ed., pp. 138–46.

23. On Jewish quotas, especially in colleges and universities, see Heywood Broun and George Britt, *Christians Only*; Stephen Steinberg, *The Academic Melting Pot*, chap. 1; and Norman Hapgood, "Jews and College Life."

24. The first U.S. edition was issued as *Praemonitus Praemunitus: The Protocols of the Wise Men of Zion* in 1920. See also Garry Wills, *Reagan's America*, pp. 371–77, and Marty, *Noise of Conflict*, pp. 133–35.

25. One 1921 series of articles appeared as *Jewish Influences in America*.

26. On Coughlin's role in promoting the idea of a Jewish conspiracy, see Tull, *Father Coughlin*, pp. 196–98, and Marty, *Noise of Conflict*, pp. 274–78.

27. On the community center phenomenon, see Sklare, *America's Jews*, pp. 135–43, and "Symposium on the Relation Between the Synagogue and the Center."

28. Early advertisements in the *Jewish Daily Forward* are instructive. See also Howe, *World of Our Fathers*, pp. 215–18, and Alf Evers, *The Catskills*.

29. See Herberg, *Protestant, Catholic, Jew*.

30. Jill Donnie Snyder and Eric K. Goodman, *Friend of the Court*. See also Gregg Ives, *To Build a Wall*.

31. V.P. Franklin et al., eds., *African Americans and Jews in the Twentieth Century*.

32. For patterns in the first half of the century, see Lawrence Fuchs, *Political Behavior of American Jews*. On the diversity within Jewish political attitudes later, see Charles S. Liebman, "Jewish Liberalism Revisited."

33. There is a growing literature on Jewish feminism. See Sylvia Barack Fishman, *A Breath of Life*, and Ann Braude, "Women and Religious Practice in American Judaism," in *In Our Own Voices*, Rosemary Radford Ruether and Rosemary Skinner Keller, eds., pp. 109–52. For an early statement, see Gail B. Shulman, "View from the Back of the Synagogue: Women in Judaism," in *Sexist Religion and Women in the Church*, Alice L. Hageman, ed. But see especially Ellen M. Umansky and Dianne Ashton, eds., *Four Centuries of Jewish Women's Spirituality*, and Jacob R. Marcus, ed., *The American Jewish Woman*.

34. Jenna Weissman Joselit, "The Special Sphere of the Middle-class American Jewish Woman: The Synagogue Sisterhood, 1890–1940," in *The American Synagogue*, Jack Wertheimer, ed., pp. 206–30. The movement was aided by the formation of the National Council of Jewish Women in 1893 as a result of the Columbian Exposition. See Faith Rogow, *Gone to Another Meeting*.

35. Curiously, the more radical Reconstructionist tradition did not ordain its first woman rabbi until two years later (1974). On the debate within Conservative circles, see Simon Greenberg, ed., *The Ordination of Women as Rabbis*. There are many relevant essays in Catherine Wessinger, ed., *Religious Institutions and Women's Leadership*. Stirring Orthodox discussion is Blu Greenberg, "Is Now the Time for Orthodox Women Rabbis?"

36. Sklare, *Conservative Judaism*, pp. 154–55.

37. To get a flavor of historic and contemporary understanding of homosexuality within the various Jewish traditions, see Saul M. Olyan and Martha C. Nussbaum, eds., *Sexual Orientation and Human Rights in American Religious Discourse*; Jonathan Magonet, ed., *Jewish Explorations of Sexuality*; and Christie Balka and Andy Rose, eds., *Twice Blessed*.

38. For the story of one such synagogue, see Moshe Shokeid, *A Gay Synagogue in New York*.

39. On changing views of Jews among Protestant evangelicals, see David A. Rausch, "Chosen People"; Marvin R. Wilson, "Changing Christian Perceptions of Jews in America," in *Jews in Unsecular America*, Richard John Neuhaus, ed., pp. 20–40; and idem, "An Evangelical View of the Current State of Evangelical-Jewish Relations."

40. See Julienne G. Lipson, *Jews for Jesus*; idem, "Jews for Jesus"; and Moishe Rosen with William Proctor, *Jews for Jesus*.

41. See Paul Liberman, *The Fig Tree Blossoms*; David A. Rausch, *Messianic Judaism*; Shoshanah Feher, "Managing Strain, Contradictions, and Fluidity: Messianic Judaism and

the Negotiations of a Religio-Ethnic Identity," in *Contemporary American Religion*, Penny Edgell Becker and Nancy L. Eiesland, eds., pp. 25–49; and Carol Harris-Shapiro, "Syncretism or Struggle."

42. For a broad contemporary statement on American Jews and the counterculture of the times, see James A. Sleeper and Alan L. Mintz, eds., *The New Jews*.

43. One example of modern adaptation is Blu Greenberg, *How to Run a Traditional Jewish Household*.

44. For the larger context, see M. Herbert Danzger, *Returning to Tradition*. The controversy at Yale received extensive coverage in the popular press. See, for example, E.V. Kontorovich, ". . . And at Yale," and William F. Buckley, Jr., "Shock Time at Yale."

Chapter 5. Religion and the Pride of a People: Black Religion in the United States

1. Joseph R. Washington, Jr.'s *Black Religion*, one of the early works to analyze the African-American religious experience, emphasized how the Christianity offered to slaves became a folk religion because it overstressed features like obedience and submission.

2. Washington's sequel to *Black Religion*, *The Politics of God*, argued that white Christianity's failure to emphasize freedom and liberation as essential to the gospel not only distorted the message presented to African Americans, but also consigned white Christianity to the category of folk religion. In *Black Sects and Cults*, Washington suggested further that recovery of a vital Christianity informed by African religious sensibilities came in sectarian movements rather than in the black denominations that mirrored their white counterparts. Gayraud Wilmore's now classic *Black Religion and Black Radicalism* sees much of black religion as a freedom movement. James Cone, *Black Theology and Black Power*, startled many when it first appeared because of its claim that Jesus would identify with black radicalism and its more dramatic calls for liberation and power (political, economic, and social) that had nudged the civil rights movement from a more moderate center by the late 1960s.

3. An early statement on the African substratum in American black religion is Leonard E. Barrett, *Soul-Force*. See also Melville J. Herkovitz's now classic *The Myth of the Negro Past*, and Washington, *Black Sects and Cults*, chap. 2. The best overall study is Albert J. Raboteau, *African-American Religion*.

4. Studies that introduce relevant features of African tribal religiosity include Geoffrey Parrinder, *West African Religion*; Noel O. King, *Religions of Africa*; and J.S. Mbiti, *African Religions and Philosophy*.

5. Fuller discussion of voodoo and *santeria* follows in Chapter 6 above.

6. See Clyde Ahmad Winters, "African American Muslims from Slavery to Freedom," and Allen D. Austin, ed., *African Muslims in Antebellum America*.

7. Still valuable on the origins of independent black denominations, especially AME, is Carol V.R. George, *Segregated Sabbaths: Richard Allen and the Rise of Independent Black Churches, 1760–1840*. See also Will B. Gravely, "The Rise of African Churches in America (1786–1822): Re-examining the Context," in *African-American Religion*, Timothy E. Fulop and Albert J. Raboteau, eds., pp. 133–51, and Edward D. Smith, *Climbing Jacob's Ladder*.

8. Controversial when published and covering a broader period is E. Franklin Frazier, *Black Bourgeoisie*.

9. Early studies on the larger role of black clergy, especially in the rural South, include Ralph Felton, *Go Down Moses*, and Harry V. Richardson, *Dark Glory*. More recent, but still culminating in the later days of the civil rights movement, are Randall Burkett and Richard Newman, eds., *Black Apostles*, and Charles Hamilton, *The Black Preacher in America*.

10. Concern for the shortage of qualified African-American clergy in the later twentieth

century is found in C. Eric Lincoln and Lawrence H. Mamiya, *The Black Church in the African American Experience*, pp. 401–2, and Julian Austin Watson, "Challenging Black College Students to Explore the Ordained Ministry in the United Methodist Church as a Profession." See also Burkett and Newman, *Black Apostles*, passim.

11. Contemporary studies of the migration of southern blacks to northern urban areas include Thomas J. Woofter, *Negro Migration*, and Emmett J. Scott, *Negro Migration During the War*. Also helpful is Arna Bontemps and Jack Conroy, *Anyplace but Here*. More recent studies include Rex R. Campbell, *Black Migration in America*; Jacqueline Jones, *"To Get Out of This Land of Sufring"*; Marcus E. Jones, *Black Migration in the United States*; and Joe William Trotter, Jr., ed., *The Great Migration in Historical Perspective*. The best study of the religious dimensions of the Great Migration is Milton C. Sernett, *Bound for the Promised Land*. On the role of religion in responding to in-migrants, Robert Gregg, *Sparks from the Anvil of Oppression*, provides a case study for Philadelphia. Chicago became the new "promised land" in much popular African-American thinking of the day. See James R. Grossman, *Land of Hope*, and Nicholas Lemann, *The Promised Land*.

12. On the clash of religious cultures and styles African Americans from the rural South found in the urban North, see E. Franklin Frazier, *The Negro Church in America*, pp. 39–52, and St. Clair Drake and Horace R. Cayton, *Black Metropolis*, part III (esp. chaps. 15, 19, 21, and 22), for now classic statements. Drake and Cayton focus on Chicago. Especially perceptive on Chicago is Wallace Best, "Passionately Human, No Less Divine: Racial Ideology and Religious Culture in the Black Churches of Chicago, 1815–1955."

13. The classic early study of storefronts and urban sects is Arthur Huff Fauset, *Black Gods of the Metropolis*. See also Frazier, *Negro Church*, chap. 4.

14. See, for example, Iain MacRobert, "The Black Roots of Pentecostalism," in *African-American Religion*, Timothy E. Fulop and Albert J. Raboteau, eds., pp. 295–309. See also Arthur Paris, *Black Pentecostalism*, and Douglas J. Nelson, "For Such a Time as This."

15. On the move within Pentecostal circles from biracial churches to congregations and denominations serving primarily one race, see Vinson Synan, *The Holiness-Pentecostal Tradition*, pp. 167–86; Iain MacRobert, *The Black Roots and White Racism of Early Pentecostalism in the USA*, and Edith L. Blumhofer, *The Assemblies of God*, 1:197–213.

16. On Timothy Drew (Noble Drew Ali) and the Moorish Science Temple, still helpful are sections of Bontemps and Conroy, *Anyplace but Here*. More current is the discussion in Yvonne Yazbeck Haddad and Jane Idleman Smith, *Mission to America*, pp. 79–104. For a biographical profile of Drew, see J. Gordon Melton, ed., *Religious Leaders of America*, pp. 275–76. See also Frank T. Simpson, "The Moorish Science Temple and Its 'Koran.'"

17. There is little scholarly analysis of the Black Jews of Harlem, but see Howard Brotz, *The Black Jews of Harlem*.

18. Some of the religious dimensions of the Universal Negro Improvement Association and the ideology of Marcus Garvey receive discussion in Robert A. Hill and Barbara Bair, eds., *Marcus Garvey*; Randall Burkett, *Garveyism as a Religious Movement*; Tony Martin, *Race First*; Theodore G. Vincent, *Black Power and the Garvey Movement*; and E. David Cronin, *Black Moses*.

19. Burkett, *Garveyism as a Religious Movement*, sheds some insight on the African Orthodox Church. See also Arthur Cornelius Terry-Thompson, *History of the African Orthodox Church*; Morris R. Johnson, *Archbishop Daniel William Alexander and the African Orthodox Church*; and Karl Pruter, *The Strange Partnership of George Alexander McGuire and Marcus Garvey*.

20. For Father Divine and the Peace Mission Movement, see Jill Watts, *God, Harlem U.S.A.*; William M. Kephart and W.W. Zellner, *Extraordinary Groups*; Kenneth E. Burnham, *God Comes to America*; and the brief statement in Melton, *Religious Leaders*, p. 271. On Daddy Grace, see Lenwood G. Davis, *Daddy Grace: An Annotated Bibliography*; see also Melton, *Religious Leaders*, pp. 359–60.

21. Fauset, *Black Gods*, p. 26.

22. Perhaps the best discussion of the religious dimensions of the Southern Christian Leadership Conference and the impact of religion on the work of Martin Luther King is David J. Garrow, *Bearing the Cross*. But see also Taylor Branch, *Parting the Waters*.

23. Albert B. Cleage, Jr., *The Black Messiah*.

24. The following works of Cone provide a good introduction to what became the pivot for much African-American theology: *Black Theology and Black Power*, *A Black Theology of Liberation*, *For My People*, *God of the Oppressed*, *Speaking the Truth*, and *The Spirituals and the Blues*.

25. For the background, see Dwight W. Culver, *Negro Segregation in the Methodist Church*, and Willis J. King, "The Central Jurisdiction," in *History of American Methodism* 3, Emory Stevens Bucke, ed.

26. Seventeen of the nineteen African-American annual conferences had voted against the organizational structure that went into effect with the creation of the Methodist Church in 1939. As well, the bishops of the Central Jurisdiction condemned the structure almost as soon as it was in place. See *Journal of the Central Jurisdictional Conference of The Methodist Church, 1944*, p. 112. See also Philip J. Wogaman, "Focus on the Central Jurisdiction."

27. For a case study, see Charles H. Lippy, "Towards an Inclusive Church: South Carolina Methodism and Race, 1972–1982," in *Rethinking Methodist History*, Russell E. Richey and Kenneth E. Rowe, eds., pp. 220–27.

28. The standard introduction to the Nation of Islam remains C. Eric Lincoln, *The Black Muslims in America*. See also Aminah Berry McCloud, *African American Islam*. Several essays in Yvonne Yazbeck Haddad and Jane Idleman Smith, *Muslim Communities in North America*, discuss the Nation of Islam since the death of founder Elijah Muhammad, various splinter groups emerging from the Nation, and also the role of Louis Farrakhan as the primary successor to Elijah Muhammad. Also helpful is Anthony B. Pinn, *Varieties of African American Religious Experience*, chap. 3.

29. There is a growing literature appraising the work of Malcolm X. Still basic, however, is Malcolm Little, *The Autobiography of Malcolm X*. As well, see Louis Anthony Decaro, Jr., "Malcolm X and the Nation of Islam"; Peter L. Goldman, *The Death and Life of Malcolm X*; and Joe Wood, ed., *Malcolm X: In Our Own Image*. For a comparative interpretation, see James H. Cone, *Martin & Malcolm & America*.

30. Helpful in understanding the growth of Islam in Africa are M. Hiskett, *The Course of Islam in Africa*, and Islam in Africa Conference, *Islam in Africa*. On the appeal of Muslim groups other than the Nation of Islam to African Americans, see Richard Brent Turner, *Islam in the African American Experience*, and Anthony B. Pinn, *Varieties of African American Religious Experience*, chap. 3.

31. Rastafaria deserves more scholarly scrutiny since most studies are now dated. See Barry Chevannes, *Rastafari*; Leonard E. Barrett, *The Rastafarians*; and George E. Simpson, *Black Religion in the New World*.

32. There is a growing literature on *Kwanzaa*, much of it directed to a juvenile and adolescent audience in an effort to instill racial pride. See Maulana Karenga, *Kwanzaa*; Cedric McClester, *Kwanzaa*; Darwin McBeth Walton, *Kwanzaa*; and Sule Greg Wilson, *Kwanzaa*.

33. See note 10 above.

34. Lincoln and Mamiya, *The Black Church in the African American Experience*.

35. We shall look at this more closely in the next chapter.

36. On challenges for African American women seeking ordination in the historic black denominations, see Barbara Brown Zikmund, "Women and Ordination," in *In Our Own Voices*, Rosemary Radford Ruether and Rosemary Skinner Keller, eds., pp. 303–5, and Lincoln and Mamiya, *Black Church*, pp. 285–97. For examples of theological constructions emerging from African-American women's experience, see Katie Cannon, *Black Womanist Ethics*, and Jacqueline Grant, "Womanist Theology."

37. The historic black denominations have not faced internal debates over homosexuality to the extent of their white counterparts like the Episcopal Church, United Methodist Church, or Presbyterian Church in the United States. For the larger context, see the *Ecumenical Review* 50:1 (January 1998), which was devoted to the churches and homosexuality.

38. Much of what has been written on the Million Man March lacks critical analysis since it was intended for a mass audience and produced almost instantaneously. But see Garth Kasimu Baker-Fletcher, *Black Religion after the Million Man March*; LaRon D. Bennett, *The Million Man March*; and Justin W. Fenwick, *A Million Under One*.

39. All of the standard literature produced internally to promote the Promise Keepers movement stresses the necessity of building racial bridges. Some includes condemnation of homosexuality; that position has received greater articulation in interviews with founder Bill McCartney and speeches made at rallies. See Bob Horner, Ron Ralston, and David Sunde, *Applying the Seven Promises*; Bill McCartney, Greg Laurie, and Jack Hayford, comps., *Seven Promises of a Promise Keeper*; and Philip Porter, *Better Men*.

Chapter 6. Syncretism and Pluralism: Native American Experiences in the Twentieth Century

1. The following have informed my general understanding of Native American religions: Sam D. Gill, *Native American Religions*; Ake Hultkrantz, *The Study of American Indian Religions*; Ake Hultkrantz, *Belief and Worship in Native North America*; Joseph Epes Brown, *The Spiritual Legacy of the American Indian*; Christopher Vecsey, *Imagine Ourselves Richly*; and Christopher Vecsey, ed., *Religion in Native North America*. Two accessible collections of primary materials are Sam D. Gill, ed., *Native American Traditions*, and Alice Marriott and Carol K. Rachlin, eds., *American Indian Mythology*. On missions to the tribal peoples, see especially Henry Warner Bowden, *American Indians and Christian Missions*; idem, "North American Indian Missions," in *Encyclopedia of the American Religious Experience*, Charles H. Lippy and Peter W. Williams, eds., 3:1671–82; and Robert F. Berkhofer, Jr., *Salvation and the Savage*.

2. For a broad look, see Carl F. Starkloff, *The People of the Center*.

3. For discussion of the ongoing transformation of Native American religions, see Michael D. McNally, "Religion and Cultural Change in Native North America," in *Perspectives on American Religion and Culture*, Peter W. Williams, ed., pp. 270–85. More generally, see Calvin Martin, ed., *The American Indian and the Problem of History*.

4. Sam D. Gill, "Native American Religions," in *Encyclopedia of the American Religious Experience*, Charles H. Lippy and Peter W. Williams, eds., 1:149–50.

5. See especially Michael McNally, "The Uses of Ojibwa Hymn-Singing at White Earth: Toward a History of Practice," in *Lived Religion in America*, David D. Hall, ed., pp. 133–57. For another tribal culture, see Thomas McElwain, "'The Rainbow Will Carry Me': The Language of Seneca Christianity as Reflected in Hymns," in *Religion in Native North America*, Christopher Vecsey, ed., pp. 83–103.

6. McNally, "Uses of Ojibwa Hymn-Singing," in *Lived Religion*, David D. Hall, ed., p. 146.

7. John G. Neihardt, ed., *Black Elk Speaks*. For interpretation and some discussion of the controversy over the extent to which Neihardt recast what Black Elk actually said to him or the extent to which Black Elk chose to downplay his Christian identity, see Raymond Demaille, ed., *The Sixth Grandfather*; Joseph Epes Brown, ed., *Sacred Pipe*; and Sally McCluskey, "Black Elk Speaks and So Does John G. Neihardt." On the impact of *Black Elk Speaks* and its interpretation, see William K. Powers, "When Black Elk Speaks, Everybody Listens," in *Religion in Native North America*, Christopher Vecsey, ed., pp. 136–51, and reprinted in several anthologies. On Neihardt, see Blair Whitney, *John G. Neihardt*.

8. The devastation at Wounded Knee was brought back to popular consciousness in Dee Brown, *Bury My Heart at Wounded Knee.*

9. See Clyde Holler, *Black Elk's Religion.*

10. Christopher Vecsey, "A Century of Lakota Sioux Catholicism at Pine Ridge," in *Religious Diversity and American Religious History*, Walter H. Conser, Jr., and Sumner B. Twiss, eds., pp. 262–95. For more background on the Holy Rosary Mission, see Ross Enochs, "Lakota Mission."

11. Raymond A. Bucko, *The Lakota Ritual of the Sweat Lodge.*

12. Randall Balmer, *Mine Eyes Have Seen the Glory*, pp. 171–87.

13. John G. Neihardt, *When the Tree Flowered.*

14. Leslie Marmon Silko, *Ceremony.* Works by Silko include *Almanac of the Dead, Gardens in the Dunes, Sacred Water, Storyteller*, and *Yellow Woman and a Beauty of the Spirit.* Not all her writings are fiction.

15. On the Native American Church and other religious use of peyote, see David F. Aberle, *The Peyote Religion Among the Navaho*; Silvester J. Brito, *The Way of a Peyote Roadman*; Weston LaBarre, *The Peyote Cult*; Alice Marriott and Carol K. Rachlin, *Peyote*; Carol K. Rachlin, *The Native American Church*; J. S. Slotkin, *The Peyote Religion*; Huston Smith and Reuben Snake, eds., *One Nation Under God*; Paul B. Steinmetz, *Pipe, Bible, and Peyote Among the Oglala Lakota*; Omer C. Stewart, *Peyote Religion*; and idem, *Peyotism in the West.*

16. See Paul B. Steinmetz, "Shamanic Images in Peyote Visions," in *Religion in Native North America*, Christopher Vecsey, ed., pp. 104–16.

17. Carlos Castaneda, *The Teachings of Don Juan.*

18. Most directly related to his first work are the following by Carlos Castaneda: *Journey to Ixtlan, Tales of Power, A Separate Reality, The Power of Silence*, and *The Second Ring of Power.* Castaneda has written widely, but the following amplify themes developed in the books about Don Juan's teachings or deal with related issues: *Magical Passes, Silent Knowledge, The Fire from Within, Eagle's Gift*, and *The Active Side of Infinity.*

19. See John T. Noonan, Jr., *The Believer and the Powers that Are*, pp. 291–92.

20. Among those writings of Vine Deloria, Jr., that deal with civil rights for Native Americans or the relations of tribal peoples with the U.S. government are *Behind the Trail of Broken Treaties; A Better Day for Indians; Custer Died for Your Sins; The Indian Affair; We Talk, You Listen*; the edited volumes, *American Indian Policy in the Twentieth Century* and *Of Utmost Good Faith*; two volumes coauthored with Clifford M. Lytle, *American Indians, American Justice* and *The Nations Within*; and one coauthored with David E. Wilkins, *Tribes, Treaties, and Constitutional Tribulations.*

21. Vine Deloria, Jr., *God Is Red.*

22. See Noonan, *Believer and the Powers that Are*, pp. 292–97.

23. See also Robert Michaelsen, "American Indian Religious Freedom Litigation."

Chapter 7. Personal Religious Expression in a Pluralistic Culture

1. David D. Hall, ed., *Lived Religion in America.*

2. Robert Anthony Orsi, *The Madonna of 115th Street*, chap. 8.

3. See Ann Taves, *The Household of Faith.* On Ave Maria, see Judith Wimmer, "Ave Maria," in *Religious Periodicals of the United States*, Charles H. Lippy, ed., pp. 38–43.

4. Robert H. Krapohl, "Christian Advocate," in *Popular Religious Magazines of the United States*, P. Mark Fackler and Charles H. Lippy, eds., pp. 101–9.

5. Steven D. Cooley, "Guide to Holiness," in ibid., pp. 256–62. See also George Hughes, *Fragrant Memories of the Tuesday Meeting*, for a contemporary account of the magazine's significance.

6. Ruth Miller Elson, *Myths and Mores in American Best Sellers*, chap. 1.

7. Thomas Luckmann, *The Invisible Religion*.

8. Colleen McDannell, *The Christian Home in Victorian America*.

9. In addition to Orsi, *Madonna*, see Rudolph J. Vecoli, "Prelates and Peasants"; idem, "Cult and Occult in Italian-American Culture: The Persistence of a Religious Heritage," in *Immigrants and Religion in Urban Culture*, Randall M. Miller and Thomas D. Marzik, eds., pp. 25–47; and Silvano M. Tomasi, *Piety and Power*.

10. Orsi, *Madonna*.

11. For example, see John Bukowczyk, "'Mary the Messiah': Polish Immigrants, Heresy, and the Malleable Ideology of the Roman Catholic Church in America, 1860–1930," in *Disciplines of Faith: Studies in Religion, Politics, and Patriarchy*, Jim Obelkevich, Lyndal Roper, and Raphael Samuel, eds., pp. 371–89; Paul Wrobel, *Our Way*; William H. Galush, "Faith and Fatherland: Dimensions of Polish-American Ethnoreligion, 1875–1975," in *Immigrants and Religion in Urban Culture*, Miller and Marzik, eds., pp. 84–102; and Josef L. Barton, "Religion and Cultural Change in Czech Immigrant Communities, 1850–1920," in ibid., pp. 3–24.

12. Marta Weigle, *Brothers of Light, Brothers of Blood*, is helpful on the Penitentes.

13. A good introduction is Joseph M. Murphy, *Santeria*. See also Juan Sosa, "Popular Religiosity and Religious Syncretism," and Anthony B. Pinn, *Varieties of African American Religious Experience*, chap. 2.

14. Thomas A. Tweed, *Our Lady of the Exile*.

15. The fusion of spirituality and nationalism may be seen in the title of a popular newspaper serving Chicago's Polish community for many years: *Faith and Fatherland*. Sometimes nationalist feelings came into such heady conflict with the institution of the Roman Catholic Church that schism resulted, as it did in Scranton, PA. See also Bukowczyk, "Mary the Messiah," in Obelkevich et al., eds.

16. On the vitality of a continuing African presence, see Robert M. Calhoon, "The African Heritage, Slavery, and Evangelical Christianity Among American Blacks, 1700–1870."

17. On conjure, magic, and trickster, see Lawrence Levine, *Black Culture and Black Consciousness*, pp. 121–33, and Bruce Jackson, "The Other Kind of Doctor: Conjure and Magic in Black American Folk Medicine," in *African-American Religion*, Timothy E. Fulop and Albert J. Raboteau, eds., pp. 415–31.

18. A good understanding of voodoo is conveyed in Jean Price-Mars, *So Spoke the Uncle*. The African background is conveyed well in the popularly written "The African Roots of Voodoo" by Carol Beckwith and Angela Fisher. See also Anthony B. Pinn, *Varieties of African American Religious Experience*, chap. 1.

19. Some of the interest has resulted from an influx of Haitian immigrants. See Karen McCarthy Brown, "Systematic Remembering, Systematic Forgetting: Ogou in Haiti," in *African-American Religion*, Fulop and Raboteau, eds., pp. 433–61, but especially pp. 453–55. Also see Anthony B. Pinn, *Varieties of African American Religious Experience*, pp. 34–55.

20. Two older studies, both classics, emphasize this dimension of African-American religious life: St. Clair Drake and Horace Cayton, *Black Metropolis*, and Arthur Huff Fauset, *Black Gods of the Metropolis*.

21. Beryl Levy, *Reform Judaism in America*, p. 12.

22. Ann Braude, "Women and Religious Practice in American Judaism," in *In Our Own Voices*, Rosemary Radford Ruether and Rosemary Skinner Keller, eds., pp. 116–17.

23. Peter W. Williams, *Popular Religion in America*, p. 82. See also Wayland D. Hand, "Jewish Popular Beliefs and Customs in Los Angeles," in *Studies in Biblical and Jewish Folklore*, Raphael Patai, Francis Lee Utley, and Dov Noy, eds., pp. 309–26, and Joshua Trachtenberg, *Jewish Magic and Superstition*.

24. Charles H. Lippy, "Popular Religiosity in Central Appalachia," in *Christianity in Appalachia*, Bill J. Leonard, ed., pp. 40–51.

25. See, for example, Trudy Bush, "On the Tide of the Angels," and Philip Yancey, "Angel Envy."

26. Billy Graham, *Angels*.

27. Wendy Kaminer, "The Latest Fashion in Irrationality."

28. See McDannell, *Christian Home*, pp. 99–103, and Christa Ressmeyer Klein, "Literature for America's Roman Catholic Children."

29. A contemporary case for age-graded materials is Simeon Gilbert, *The Lesson System*. A major advocate was John Heyl Vincent, the moving force behind the Chautauqua Institute. See Leon H. Vincent, *John Heyl Vincent*.

30. On the Gospel Trumpet Company, see Colleen McDannell, *Material Christianity*, pp. 229–46.

31. Ellen Dyer, *Daily Suggestions for Workers*; Mary W. Tileston, *Daily Strength for Daily Needs*.

32. Mrs. Charles E. Cowman, *Streams in the Desert*.

33. John Kloos, "The Upper Room," in P. Mark Fackler and Charles H. Lippy, eds., *Popular Religious Magazines*, pp. 478–82; Leif Sevre, *The Story of the Upper Room*.

34. Cynthia L. Beach, "Our Daily Bread," in Fackler and Lippy, eds., *Popular Religious Magazines*, pp. 367–72.

35. Cheryl Forbes, "Coffee, Mrs. Cowman, and the Devotional Life of Women Reading in the Desert," in David Hall, ed., *Lived Religion in America*, pp. 116–32.

36. Joshua Liebman, *Peace of Mind*.

37. On self-help generally, see especially Donald Meyer, *The Positive Thinkers*. But see also Roy M. Anker, "Popular Religion and Theories of Self-Help," in *Handbook of American Popular Culture*, M. Thomas Inge, ed., 2:287–316; Patricia Braus, "Selling Self Help"; Wendy Kaminer, "Saving Therapy"; Frank Riesman, "The New Self-Help Backlash"; and Steven Starker, *Oracle at the Supermarket*. For an earlier bibliography, see Elise Chase, *Healing Faith*.

38. Russell Conwell, *Acres of Diamonds*.

39. Ralph Waldo Trine, *In Tune with the Infinite*.

40. Norman Vincent Peale, *The Power of Positive Thinking*. See also Carol V.R. George, *God's Salesman*, chap. 5.

41. Lawrence Thompson, "Guideposts," in Fackler and Lippy, eds., *Popular Religious Magazines*, pp. 252–55; George, *God's Salesman*, chap. 4.

42. Billy Graham, *Peace with God*; idem, *The Secret of Happiness*; Charles L. Allen, *God's Psychiatry*.

43. L. Ron Hubbard, *Dianetics*.

44. William H. Whyte, *The Organization Man*.

45. Catherine Marshall, *A Man Called Peter*.

46. See especially Ernest Kurtz, "Alcoholics Anonymous: A Phenomenon in American Religious History," in *Religion and Philosophy in the United States*, Peter Freese, ed., 2:447–62, and J. Keith Miller, *Hunger for Healing*. See also Vernon Bittner, "Taking the Twelve Steps to Church," and Tim Stafford, "The Hidden Gospel of the 12 Steps."

47. Now generally known as the National Prayer Breakfast and held in February each year, the first "White House" or "presidential" prayer breakfast was held in 1953 at the beginning of the Eisenhower administration.

48. On drug-induced religious experience, see Walter Houston Clark, *Chemical Ecstasy*; William Braden, *The Private Sea*; and Jean-Claude Barreau, *Drugs and the Life of Prayer*.

49. Carl T. Jackson, "The Counterculture Looks East"; Stephen Prothero, "On the Holy Road"; and Thomas A. Tweed, "Asian Religions in the United States: Reflections on an Emerging Subfield," in *Religious Diversity and American Religious History*, Walter H. Conser, Jr., and Sumner B. Twiss, eds., pp. 189–217. See also Don Morreale, *Buddhist America*.

50. E. Burke Rochford, Jr., *Hare Krishna in America*; David G. Bromley and Larry D. Shinn, eds., *Krishna Consciousness in the West*.

51. See Anthony Campbell, *Seven States of Consciousness*, for an overview of Transcendental Meditation teaching.

52. For overviews of New Age spirituality, see James R. Lewis and J. Gordon Melton, eds., *Perspectives on the New Age*; Ted Peters, *The Cosmic Self*; and Catherine L. Albanese, "Fisher Kings and Public Places: The Old New Age in the 1990s," in *Religion in the Nineties*, Wade Clark Roof, ed., pp. 131–43.

53. Wade Clark Roof, *A Generation of Seekers*, p. 86. Chap. 3, "Mollie's Quest," addresses several of these points.

54. The best overview is Margot Adler, *Drawing Down the Moon*. For rituals reflecting women's experience as women, see Starhawk, *The Spiral Dance*; Z Budapest, *Grandmother Moon*, *The Grandmother of Time*, and *The Holy Book of Women's Mysteries*. On the renewed interest in the goddess, see Richard N. Ostling, "When God Was a Woman," and Mary Jo Neitz, "In Goddess We Trust," in *In Gods We Trust*, Thomas Robbins and Dick Anthony, eds., 1991, pp. 353–72.

55. Shirley A. Ranck, *Cakes for the Queen of Heaven*. See also Shirley A. Ranck, ed., *Cakes for the Queen of Heaven: Readings*.

56. Orsi, *Thank You, St. Jude*, p. 93.

57. Susan Grossman, "Finding Comfort after a Miscarriage," in *Daughters of the King*, Susan Grossman and Rivka Haut, eds., pp. 285–90.

58. The best study is R. Marie Griffith, *God's Daughters*.

59. See Gail Bederman, "The Women Have Had Charge of the Church Work Long Enough," and Gary Scott Smith, "The Men and Religion Forward Movement of 1911–1912." On "muscular Christianity," see Evelyn A. Kirkley, "Is It Manly to Be Christian?" in *Redeeming Men*, Stephen B. Boyd et al., eds., pp. 80–88, and Donald E. Hall, ed., *Muscular Christianity*.

60. For an "insider" perspective, see John Trent et al., *Go the Distance*. For analysis, see Mary Stewart Van Leeuwen, "Servanthood or Soft Patriarchy?" and Charles H. Lippy, "Miles to Go."

61. Jack Canfield and Mark Victor Hansen, comps., *Chicken Soup for the Soul*.

62. Jack Canfield, Mark Victor Hansen, and Kimberly Kirberger, comps., *Chicken Soup for the Teenage Soul*.

63. Leo Buscaglia was a prolific writer. See, for example, his *Love*; *Living, Loving, and Learning*; *Loving Each Other*; and *Born for Love*. Three books by Norris have attracted a wide following for their spiritual content: *Dakota*, *The Cloister Walk*, and *Amazing Grace*.

64. On connections between spirituality and healing, see, for example, Larry Dossey, M.D., *Prayer Is Good Medicine*. On exercise as a spiritual discipline, see Gabrielle Roth, *Sweat Your Prayers* and *Maps to Ecstasy*. On weight loss and spirituality, see Victoria Moran, *Love Yourself Thin*. On the return to the discipline of fasting, see Laurie Goodstein, "In Hope of Spiritual Revival, A Call to Fast." The 1998 Duke University study was the subject of the "Eye on Health" segment telecast on Chattanooga's Channel 3 news, August 11, 1998.

65. Charles M. Sheldon, *In His Steps*.

66. Jon Pareles, "Music Moved by the Spirit Thrives," p. 27.

67. Mircea Eliade, *The Sacred and the Profane*.

Chapter 8. The Proliferation of Pluralism

1. One reliable estimate held that in 1995, there were 5,518,000 Jews in the United States and 5,167,000 Muslims (including Black Muslims), with the number of Muslims expected to surpass the number of Jews in mid-2000. *Time Almanac 1999 with Information Please*, p. 403.

2. On Adler, see Horace Leland Friess, *Felix Adler and Ethical Culture*. On the emergence of Ethical Culture, see Benny Kraut, *From Reform Judaism to Ethical Culture*. The society produced a celebratory volume, *The Fiftieth Anniversary of the Ethical Movement*.

3. The classic work on the Free Religious Association remains Stow Persons, *Free Religion*. One of the best introductions to the thinking behind the movement was written by one of its early presidents; see Octavius Brooks Frothingham, *The Religion of Humanity*.

4. Helpful is Carl T. Jackson, *The Oriental Religions and American Thought*, especially chap. 2 on Emerson and chap. 6 on the interest of the Free Religious Association in Eastern philosophy. See also Arthur Versluis, *Transcendentalism and Asian Religions*; Thomas A. Tweed, *The American Encounter with Buddhism*, pp. 1–25; Roger Chester Mueller, "The Orient in American Transcendental Periodicals"; Arthur Christy, *The Orient in American Transcendentalism*; and Frederick I. Carpenter, *Emerson and Asia*.

5. Heber's hymn text was first published in 1823 in the *Christian Observer* and appeared in many Protestant denominational hymnals until the middle of the twentieth century with only minor modifications in the wording.

6. See Jackson, *Oriental Religions*, chap. 5; William R. Hutchison, *Errand to the World*; Clifton J. Philips, *Protestant America and the Pagan World*; and Sydney E. Ahlstrom, *The American Protestant Encounter with World Religions*.

7. Polynesian, Chinese, and Japanese influences pervaded Hawaiian culture, home to the nation's only Shinto shrine, but Hawaii did not become U.S. territory until 1898. On Chinese immigration, primarily to California, see Gunther Barth, *Bitter Struggle*, and Shin-Shan Tsai, *The Chinese Experience in America*.

8. On efforts to maintain traditional Chinese religions and Protestant counterefforts to convert Chinese immigrants, see Michael E. Engh, S.J., *Frontier Faiths*, chap. 6.

9. Congress originally proposed a twenty-year ban on Chinese immigration that President Chester Alan Arthur vigorously opposed. The ban, however, was extended after the initial law expired, and in 1902 legislation attempted to exclude Chinese immigrants permanently. The Asian Exclusion Act of 1917 was the final effort, remaining in force until it was repealed in 1965.

10. See Richard Hughes Seager, *The World's Parliament of Religions*; Eric Ziolkowski, ed., *A Museum of Faiths*; Larry Fader, "Zen in the West"; Jackson, *Oriental Religions*, pp. 243–61; and Kent Druyvesteyn, "The World's Parliament of Religions." Some addresses presented at the Parliament are included in Richard Hughes Seager, ed., *The Dawn of Religious Pluralism*.

11. Many of the groups discussed in the following pages receive treatment in Robert S. Ellwood, *Alternative Altars*, and Robert S. Ellwood and Harry B. Partin, *Religious and Spiritual Groups in Modern America*. Especially helpful as overviews are two essays in Walter H. Conser, Jr., and Sumner B. Twiss, eds., *Religious Diversity and American Religious History*: Catherine L. Albanese, "Dissident History: American Religious Culture and the Emergence of a Metaphysical Tradition," pp. 157–88, and Thomas A. Tweed, "Asian Religions in the United States: Reflections on an Emerging Subfield," pp. 189–217; and three essays in Jacob Neusner, ed., *World Religions in America*: Gerald James Larson, "Hinduism in India and America," pp. 177–202; Malcolm David Eckel, "Buddhism in the World and in America," pp. 203–218; and Robert S. Ellwood, "East Asian Religions in Today's America," pp. 219–48. See also Raymond Brady Williams, *Religions of Immigrants from India and Pakistan*. The Theosophical University Press keeps the major works of Theosophy's founder, Helena P. Blavatsky, in print. See Helena P. Blavatsky, *Isis Unveiled*, and idem, *The Secret Doctrine*. A recent secondary study is Sylvia Cranston, *H.P.B.*

12. See *The Complete Works of Swami Vivekananda*. The best scholarly appraisal is Carl T. Jackson, *Vedanta for the West*.

13. There are no current critical studies of the Self-Realization Fellowship, although the group itself publishes numerous works presenting its theological and philosophical posi-

tions. For the basic teachings of the founder, see Paramahansa Yogananda, *Autobiography of a Yogi* and *Descriptive Outlines of Yogoda*.

14. All studies available come from within the Buddhist Churches of America. See *Buddhist Churches of America 75 Year History*; *Buddhist Handbook for Shin-Shu Followers*; *Shin Buddhist Handbook*; and *Traditions of Jodoshinshu Hongwanji-Ha*. The group publishes two English-language periodicals: *Wheel of Dharma* and *Pacific World*. On Buddhism in the United States more generally, see Charles Prebish, *American Buddhism*; and Emma McCloy Layman, *Buddhism in America*.

15. On Zen, see Philip Kapleau, *Three Pillars of Zen*; Emma McCloy Layman, *Buddhism in America*; and D. T. Suzuki, *Zen Buddhism*. The Zen influence is particularly evident in Jack Kerouac, *The Dharma Bums*. Alan Watts was a prolific writer. Although he died in 1973, many of his works promoting a Zen perspective are still available. Among the more central of Watts's works examining Zen are: *In My Own Way*; *Beat Zen, Square Zen, and Zen*; *Zen and the Beat Way*; *Myth and Religion*; *Buddhism*; *The Philosophies of Asia*; *Talking Zen*; *The Spirit of Zen*; *The Art of Contemplation*; and *The Way of Zen*. See also Carl T. Jackson, "The Counterculture Looks East."

16. Suzuki died in 1966, but his key writings are still available. In addition to *Zen Buddhism*, see his *Buddha of Infinite Light*; *Living by Zen*; *The Zen Doctrine of No-Mind*; *An Introduction to Zen Buddhism*; *Zen and Japanese Culture*; *The Training of the Zen Buddhist Monk*; *The Chain of Compassion*; *Japanese Spirituality*; *The Awakening of Zen*; and the classic *Mysticism, Christian and Buddhist*.

17. On the First Zen Institute of America, see *Cat's Yawn*; and Ruth Fuller Sasaki, *Zen*.

18. The approach of the Zen Center is detailed in Shunryu Suzuki, *Zen Mind, Beginner's Mind*. There is also solid discussion, though now dated, in Jacob Needleman, *The New Religions*, pp. 37–73. See also the Zen Center's periodical, *Wind Bell*.

19. The following are helpful for gaining understanding of the Japanese new religions in their own context, more than in their American counterparts, although both are dated: H. Byron Earhart, *The New Religions of Japan*, and Harry Thomsen, *The New Religions of Japan*. For American expressions, see Robert S. Ellwood, *The Eagle and the Rising Sun*.

20. On Nichiren Shoshu and Soka Gakkai, the following have been helpful: Masaharu Anesaki, *Nichiren*; Noah S. Brannen, *Soka Gakkai*; James Allen Dator, *Soka Gakkai*; Hideo Hashimoto and William McPherson, "Rise and Decline of Sokagakkai in Japan and the United States"; Yasuji Kirimura, *Fundamentals of Buddhism*; *Soka Gakkai*; James W. White, *The Sokagakkai and Mass Society*; and George M. Williams, *Freedom and Influence*.

21. The propensity for conversion to occur among those in late adolescence and early young adulthood was discerned as early as E.D. Starbuck's pioneering psychological studies in 1899. It was also widely discussed at the time that many in those age cohorts seemed drawn to Asian religions; see, for example, Gordon W. Allport, *The Individual and His Religion*; Walter H. Clark, *Psychology of Religion*; Walter E. Conn, ed., *Conversion*; and David Elkind, "Age Changes in the Meaning of Religious Identity."

22. TM generated a vast polemical literature not included here. Among the Maharishi's works, see *The Science of Being and Art of Living* and *Love and God*. See also Anthony Campbell, *Seven States of Consciousness*; Martin Ebson, ed., *Maharishi, the Guru*; M.B. Jackson, *Transcendental Meditation as Taught by Maharishi Mahesh Yogi*; William Jefferson, *The Story of the Maharishi*; and Jacob Needleman, *New Religions*, pp. 128–42. Somewhat critical is William Sims Bainbridge and Daniel H. Jackson, "The Rise and Decline of Transcendental Meditation," in *The Social Impact of New Religious Movements*, Bryan Wilson, ed.

23. Ellwood and Partin, *Religious and Spiritual Groups*, p. 196.

24. Some of ISKCON's founder's thought can be discerned in his edition of the ever-popular *Bhagavad Gita*: A.C. Bhaktivedanta Prabhupada, *Bhagavad-Gita as It Is*. On the movement, see Larry D. Shinn, *The Dark Lord*; Edmund Burke Rochford, Jr., *Hare Krishna in America*; Steven J. Gelberg, ed., *Hare Krishna, Hare Krishna*; Francine J. Daner, *The*

American Children of Krsna; idem, "Conversion to Krishna Consciousness: The Transformation from Hippie to Religious Ascetic," in *Sectarianism*, Roy Wallis, ed.; and Milton B. Singer, ed., *Krishna*. A perceptive local study is Gregory Johnson, "The Hare Krishna in San Francisco," in *The New Religious Consciousness*, Charles Y. Glock and Robert N. Bellah, eds.

25. The leader of the Moundsville group at the time it basically went its own way, Kiritananda Swami Bhaktipada, has written several books. Among them are *Christ and Krishna*, *Eternal Love*, *On His Ardor*, and *Song of God*.

26. On the Guru Maharaj Ji and the Divine Light Mission, see Guru Maharaj Ji, *The Living Master*; Charles Cameron, *Who Is Guru Maharaj Ji?*; and James V. Downton, Jr., *Sacred Journeys*.

27. The controversy surrounding the Oregon commune and Rajneesh received extensive coverage in the popular press. For the particular slant on Asian religious teaching of this group, see Bhagwan Shree Rajneesh, *The Great Challenge*, and the community's own *Rajneeshism*. See also Vasant Joshi, *The Awakened One*; Ram Chandra Prasad, *Rajneesh*. Critical is Hugh Milne, *Bhagwan*. Frances FitzGerald, in *Cities on a Hill*, suggests that, despite its Asian appearance, Rajneeshism was very American.

28. The fundamental guide to Unification teaching is *Divine Principle*. On the movement, see Eileen Barker, *The Making of a Moonie*; idem, "Who'd Be a Moonie?" in *The Social Impact of New Religious Movements*, Bryan Wilson, ed.; John T. Biernans, *The Odyssey of New Religious Movements*; David G. Bromley and Anson D. Shupe, Jr., *"Moonies" in America: Cult, Church, and Crusade*; M. Darrol Bryant and Herbert W. Richardson, eds., *A Time for Consideration*; Michael T. Mickler, *The Unification Church in America*; and Frederick Sontag, *Sun Myung Moon and the Unification Church*. Many of these studies were prepared with assistance from the Unification Church.

29. The foremost interpreter of the Islamic experience in the United States is Yvonne Yazbeck Haddad. See especially her *A Century of Islam in America*; her "Make Room for the Muslims?" in *Religious Diversity and American Religious History*, Walter H. Conser, Jr., and Sumner B. Twiss, eds., pp. 218–61; and her edited volume, *The Muslims of America*. A recent, solid study that immediately became the standard single volume on American Islam is Jane I. Smith, *Islam in America*. Another brief overview is provided in John L. Esposito, "Islam in the World and in America," in *World Religions in America*, Jacob Neusner, ed., pp. 243–57. On Muslim slaves in the antebellum period, see Clyde Ahmed Winters, "Afro-American Muslims from Slavery to Freedom"; idem, "Origins of Muslim Slaves in the U.S."; and Allan D. Austin, ed., *African Muslims in Antebellum America*.

30. Yvonne Yazbeck Haddad, "Make Room," pp. 219–20; John L. Esposito, "Islam in the World," pp. 253–55. See also Yvonne Yazbeck Haddad and Adair T. Lummis, *Islamic Values in the United States*; Yvonne Yazbeck Haddad and Jane Idleman Smith, *Mission to America*; and Abdo A. Elkholy, *The Arab Moslems in the United States*.

31. Yvonne Yazbeck Haddad, "Make Room," pp. 255–57. Specific issues, including the suspicion most Americans have of Islam, are treated in Yvonne Yazbeck Haddad, "Islamists and the 'Problem of Israel'"; idem, "The Anguish of Christians in the Middle East and American Foreign Policy"; idem, "American Foreign Policy in the Middle East and Its Impact on the Identity of Arab Muslims in the United States," in *The Muslims of America*, Yvonne Yazbeck Haddad, ed., pp. 217–35; idem, "Nationalism and Islamic Tendencies in Contemporary Arab-American Communities," in *Arab Nationalism*, Hani Faris, ed.; Hatem I. Hussaini, "The Impact of the Arab-Israeli Conflict on Arab Communities in the United States," in *Settler Regimes in Africa and the Arab World*, Ibrahim Abu Lughod and Baha Abu-Laban, eds., pp. 201–22; Jacqueline S. Ismael and Tareq Ismael, "The Arab Americans and the Middle East"; Judith Miller, "The Challenge of Radical Islam"; and Edward W. Said, *Covering Islam*.

32. Oldest is the Federation of Islamic Associations, founded in 1952 primarily by Canadians and Americans of Lebanese stock. The Islamic Society of North America serves

students in American and Canadian universities and offers help to graduates who seek to settle in North America. The Council of Masajid, an offshoot of the Muslim World League, has as its aim fostering cooperation among mosques and overseeing the building and maintenance of the physical structures of the mosques.

33. Published since 1911, *Muslim World*, formerly called *Moslem World*, has been produced under the auspices of the Hartford Seminary Foundation since 1938.

34. Yvonne Yazbeck Haddad, "Make Room," pp. 230–32. See also Gisella Webb, "Tradition and Innovation in Contemporary American Islamic Spirituality: The Sawwa Muhaiyaddeen Fellowship," in *Muslim Communities in North America*, Yvonne Yazbeck Haddad and Jane Idleman Smith, eds., pp. 75–108; Muhammad Abdul-Rauf, "The Future of the Islamic Tradition in North America," in *The Muslim Community in North America*, Earle H. Waugh, Baha Abu-Laban, and Regula B. Qureshi, eds.; Earle H. Waugh, "The Imam in the New World: Models and Modifications," in *Transitions and Transformations in the History of Religions*, Frank E. Reynolds and Theodore M. Ludwig, eds., pp. 124–49; and 'Abdur Rahman Shad, *Duties of an Imam*.

35. On Islam's appeal to American women, see Carol L. Anway, *Daughters of Another Path*. More generally, see Yvonne Yazbeck Haddad, "Make Room," pp. 220–22.

36. See Yvonne Yazbeck Haddad and Adair Lummis, *Islamic Values in the United States*. Among Muslim American thinkers, in different ways both Seyyed Hossein Nasr (an immigrant from Iran) and Fazlur Rahman (an immigrant from Pakistan) have argued that American culture undermines the Muslim way of life. Nasr urges rejection of American cultural styles; Rahman has argued more for the modernization of Islam. For Nasr, see, among others, his *Traditional Islam in the Modern World, Islam and the Plight of Modern Man*, and *Ideals and Realities of Islam*. Rahman has also written extensively. See, for a sample, his *Prophecy in Islam, Islam and Modernity*, and *Major Themes in the Qur'an*.

37. Yvonne Yazbeck Haddad, "Make Room," p. 218.

38. John L. Esposito, "Islam in the World and in America," p. 256.

39. For the flavor of Baha'i, see Joel Bjorling, *The Baha'i Faith*; J.E. Esslemont, *Baha'u'llah and the New Era*; Jessyca Gaver, *Baha'i Faith*; William Hatcher and James D. Martin, *The Baha'i Faith*; Mary Perkins and Philip Hainsworth, *The Baha'i Faith*; and William McElwee Miller, *The Baha'i Faith*.

40. See especially the *Humanist Manifestos I and II*. The association still publishes a periodical, *The Humanist*. See also Paul Kurtz, ed., *The Humanist Alternative*; and Curtis W. Reese, ed., *Humanist Sermons*.

41. The interaction of science and religion, including the formation of the Institute on Religion in an Age of Science, is told in James Gilbert, *Redeeming Culture*. Writings of many of the key figures in the movement at midcentury are included in Harlow Shapley, ed., *Science Ponders Religion*. The institute has published *Zygon: A Journal of Religion and Science* since 1966.

42. Little has been written about O'Hair and the American Atheists. O'Hair advanced her perspective in *What on Earth Is an Atheist?* and told the story of her work to have the courts ban prayer and devotional Bible reading in her *Bill Murray, the Bible, and the Baltimore Board of Education*.

43. Anton Szandor LaVey's writings are the best introduction to the Church of Satan. See his *The Satanic Bible, The Compleat Witch*, and *The Satanic Rituals*. See also Arthur Lyons, *The Second Coming*, and Randall H. Alfred, "The Church of Satan," in *The New Religious Consciousness*, Charles Y. Glock and Robert N. Bellah, eds.

Chapter 9. The Politics of Religion in a Pluralistic Society

1. Josiah Strong, *Our Country*.
2. On changing attitudes about consumption of alcohol, see Ian R. Tyrrell, *Sobering*

Up; Daniel L. Swinson, "American Methodism and Temperance"; Donald B. Chitsey, *On and Off the Wagon*; and W.J. Rorabaugh, *The Alcoholic Republic*.

3. Images that immigrants and persons who were not evangelical Protestant were more taken with alcohol carried over into popular literature. See, for example, the widely known *The Damnation of Theron Ware* (1896) by Harold Frederic.

4. On the contribution of women to the temperance and Prohibition movements, see Ruth Bordin, *Women and Temperance*; Ian R. Tyrrell, *Women's Word/Women's Empire*; and the chapter on the W.C.T.U. in Alison M. Parker, *Purifying America*.

5. The story of Prohibition continues to generate a plethora of scholarly and popular analyses. Among them are John A. Krout, *The Origins of Prohibition*; John J. Rumbarger, *Profits, Power, and Prohibition*; Herbert Asbury, *The Great Illusion*; Thomas M. Coffey, *The Long Thirst*; John Koller, *Ardent Spirits*; Jack S. Blocker, *Retreat from Reform*; David E. Kyvig, *Repealing National Prohibition*; and Daniel Cohen, *Prohibition*. On the Anti-Saloon League, see K. Austin Kerr, *Organized for Prohibition*. Accounts contemporary with the movement include James Lithgow Irwin, *The Birth of the Anti-Saloon League*; William H. Anderson, *The Church in Action Against the Saloon*; and Peter H. Odegard, *Pressure Politics*.

6. Standard introductions to the Social Gospel include C. Howard Hopkins, *The Rise of the Social Gospel in American Protestantism*; Robert T. Handy, ed., *The Social Gospel in America, 1870–1920*; Henry F. May, *Protestant Churches and Industrial America*; and Donald K. Gorrell, *The Age of Social Responsibility*.

7. See John Alexander Hutchison, *We Are Not Divided*, on the early years of the Federal Council of Churches.

8. Much background information on the Social Creed developed by the Methodist Episcopal Church is found scattered throughout Richard M. Cameron, *Methodism and Society in Historical Perspective*, and Walter G. Muelder, *Methodism and Society in the Twentieth Century*. They are excerpted in Georgia Harkness, *The Methodist Church in Social Thought and Action*. Also see A. Dudley Ward, *The Social Creed of the Methodist Church*. The social creed underwent thorough revision in 1972, following merger of the Methodist Church and the Evangelical United Brethren Church.

9. Three older studies still provide a solid introduction to Roman Catholic social involvement: Aaron I. Abell, *American Catholics and Social Action*; Robert D. Cross, *The Emergence of Liberal Catholicism in America*; and Henry J. Browne, *The Catholic Church and the Knights of Labor*.

10. Two of Ryan's most influential works have recently been excerpted as *Economic Justice: Selections from Distributive Justice and A Living Wage*. On Ryan, see Francis L. Broderick, *Right Reverend New Dealer*.

11. The social reform movements of the 1960s sparked enormous scholarly interest in Progressivism since it seemed to some extent a parallel effort to use government to effect social transformation; another wave of reinvestigation came in the 1980s and 1990s, when "big government" was no longer in fashion. Among the earlier studies, especially helpful are William L. O'Neill, *The Progressive Years*; David M. Kennedy, ed., *Progressivism*; Lewis L. Gould, *The Progressive Era*; and John D. Buenker, *Urban Liberalism and Progressive Reform*. More recent contributions include John D. Buenker, *Historical Dictionary of the Progressive Era*; Elizabeth Sanders, *Roots of Reform*; James J. Connolly, *The Triumph of Ethnic Progressivism*; and Leon Fink, *Progressive Intellectuals and the Dilemmas of Democratic Commitment*. See also the provocative study that in part seeks to apply principles associated with Progressivism to political and economic issues of the 1990s: Roberto Mangabeira Unger and Cornel West, *The Future of American Progressivism*.

12. More general studies include Norris Magnuson, *Salvation in the Slums*, and John P. McDowell, *The Social Gospel in the South*. On settlement houses and rescue missions, see Domenica M. Barbuto, *American Settlement Houses and Progressive Social Reform*, and

James R. Adair, *The Old Lighthouse* (which tells the story of the first several decades of the Pacific Garden Mission from a rather triumphalist perspective). On the Salvation Army, see Herbert A. Wisbey, *Soldiers Without Swords*, and the fairly recently revised and expanded *Marching to Glory* by Edward H. McKinley.

13. Benjamin Morgan Palmer offered a classic statement of the "spirituality of the church" in his "The Church, a Spiritual Kingdom." See also Ernest Trice Thompson, *The Spirituality of the Church*; James Oscar Farmer, Jr., *The Metaphysical Confederacy*, pp. 256–60; and H. Shelton Smith, "The Church and the Social Order as Interpreted by James Henley Thornwell." Thornwell advanced the doctrine in part as a way to avoid dealing with the ethical issues surrounding slavery in the antebellum period.

14. Two early studies of the Klan that stress the religious element are John Moffatt Mecklin, *The Ku Klux Klan* (1924), and Stanley Frost, *The Challenge of the Klan* (1923). See also David M. Chalmers, *Hooded Americanism*, and Kenneth T. Jackson, *The Ku Klux Klan in the City, 1915–1930*. On the role of women in opposing lynching, see Jacquelyn Dowd Hall, "A Truly Subversive Affair: Women Against Lynching in the Twentieth-Century South," in *Women of America*, Carol Ruth Berkin and Mary Beth Norton, eds., pp. 360–88.

15. Historian Wayne Flynt has been the most insistent that there was a social ethic in Southern evangelical Protestantism. See, for example, his "Alabama White Protestantism and Labor" and his "Organized Labor, Reform, and Alabama Politics, 1920." See also Hugh C. Bailey, "Edgar Gardner Murphy and the Child Labor Movement"; Ronald C. White, Jr., "Beyond the Sacred"; Thomas A. Becnel, *Labor, Church, and the Sugar Establishment*; John O. Fish, "The Christian Commonwealth Colony"; Paul D. Bolster, "Christian Socialism Comes to Georgia"; John L. Eighmy, "Religious Liberalism in the South During the Progressive Era"; Charles P. Johnson, "Southern Baptists and the Social Gospel Movement"; John W. Storey, "Thomas Buford Maston and the Growth of Social Christianity Among Texas Baptists"; and Dale E. Soden, "The Social Gospel in Tennessee."

16. See Wayne Flynt, *Alabama Baptists*, pp. 339–44; Jean Miller Schmidt, *Souls or the Social Order*; Susan Curtis, *A Consuming Faith*; John L. Eighmy, *Churches in Cultural Captivity*; and Paul A. Carter, *The Decline and Revival of the Social Gospel*.

17. The most recent scholarly assessment of the Southern Sociological Congress is Ida Harper Simpson, *Fifty Years of the Southern Sociological Society*. But see also E. Charles Chatfield, "The Southern Sociological Congress: Organization of Uplift"; idem, "The Southern Sociological Congress: Rationale of Uplift"; and Lee M. Brooks and Alvin L. Bertrand, *History of the Southern Sociological Society*.

18. On Protestant support for World War I, see John F. Piper, Jr., *The American Churches in World War I*, and the classic study of Ray Abrams, *Preachers Present Arms*. On the Red Scare of the 1920s and Protestant response, see Robert K. Murray, *Red Scare*; Robert Moats Miller, *American Protestantism and Social Issues*; and relevant sections of Ralph Lord Roy, *Communism and the Churches*.

19. The best study remains C. Vann Woodward, *The Strange Career of Jim Crow*.

20. On the Social Gospel and race, see Ralph E. Luker, *The Social Gospel in Black and White*, and Ronald C. White, Jr., *Liberty and Justice for All*.

21. The most prominent contemporary advocate of accommodationism was Booker T. Washington, while W.E.B. DuBois was the most outspoken critic from within the African-American communities. See August Meir, *Racial Ideologies in the Age of Booker T. Washington*, and William Toll, *The Resurgence of Race*.

22. Among the more well-known episodes were outbursts of racial conflict in East St. Louis in 1917 and in Chicago in 1919, although racial tension was high in Chicago from the 1890s on. See William M. Tuttle, Jr., *Race Riot*; idem, "Labor Conflict and Racial Violence"; and Elliott Rudwick, *Race Riot at East St. Louis*.

23. For the larger context of Truman's executive order, see William C. Berman, *The Politics of Civil Rights in the Truman Administration*.

24. The story leading up to the Supreme Court's decision in *Brown v. Board of Education* is the basis of Richard Kluger, *Simple Justice*.

25. On King, see especially David Garrow, *Bearing the Cross*, and Taylor Branch, *Parting the Waters*.

26. A splendid local history looking at the role of the church in Montgomery where Martin Luther King, Jr., was pastor at the time of the bus boycott is Houston B. Roberson, "Fighting the Good Fight."

27. An infamous episode occurred at the Galloway Memorial Methodist Church in Jackson, Mississippi, when a group of Methodist bishops, white and African-American, were denied admission to Easter Sunday worship services. See W.J. Cunningham, *Agony at Galloway*.

28. Charles Marsh, *God's Long Summer*.

29. Jeffrey K. Hadden, *The Gathering Storm in the Churches*.

30. The Berrigan brothers were prolific writers. Among their works from the era of their protest activity are Daniel Berrigan, *Night Flight to Hanoi*; idem, *No Bars to Manhood*; idem, *The Trial of the Catonsville Nine*; idem, *The Dark Night of Resistance*; Philip Berrigan, *A Punishment for Peace*; idem, *Prison Journals of a Priest Revolutionary*; idem, *Widen the Prison Gates*. There was also a considerable literature about the Berrigans and others on the "Catholic left" at the time. See, for example, William Van Etten Casey and Philip Nobile, eds., *The Berrigans*; Francine duPlessix Gray, *Divine Disobedience*, pp. 45–228; Eugene C. Bianchi, *The Religious Experience of Revolutionaries*, pp. 55–81; Jack Nelson and Ronald J. Ostrow, *The FBI and the Berrigans*; and William O'Rourke, *The Harrisburg 7 and the New Catholic Left*. More recent is Murray Polner and Jim O'Grady, *Disarmed and Dangerous*.

31. Perhaps the best way to chart the story of religious protest of American involvement in Vietnam is simply to read reports in newspapers such as *The New York Times* or the *Washington Post*. Stories about protest also figured prominently in the religious news commentary magazines such as *Christianity and Crisis*, *Christianity Today*, *Commonweal*, and the *Christian Century*. One central coordinating group for religious protest was Clergy Concerned about Vietnam, later expanded to Clergy and Laity Concerned. Articulating reasons for opposition to the American posture from the perspectives of the nation's tripartite faith heritage (Protestant, Jewish, Catholic) is Robert McAfee Brown, Abraham J. Heschel, and Michael Novak, *Vietnam*. See also Thomas E. Quigley, ed., *American Catholics and Vietnam*. Summaries, not altogether sympathetic, of the religious protest are found in Thomas C. Reeves, *The Empty Church*, pp. 140–43, and A. James Reichley, *Religion in American Public Life*, pp. 250–54.

32. Position statements of many denominations issued through the early 1980s are contained in *Biomedical-Ethical Issues*. Much of the debate is capsuled in the following: Joel Feinberg, ed., *The Problem of Abortion*; James K. Hoffmeier, ed., *Abortion*; Penelope J. Ryan, *Practicing Catholic*, pp. 114–21; John T. Noonan, *A Private Choice*; and Lisa Sowle Cahill, "Notes on Moral Theology." The official Roman Catholic position was set forth in Pope John Paul II, *The Gospel of Life (Evangelium Vitae)*.

33. The most forceful and reasoned "pro-choice" argument is found in Beverly Wildung Harrison, *Our Right to Choose*.

34. The larger historical, legal, and ethical context of the abortion debates may be found in John T. Noonan, ed., *The Morality of Abortion*, and Sydney Callahan and Daniel Callahan, eds., *Abortion*.

35. Pro-life tactics, often identified with groups such as Operation Rescue and anti-abortion advocates such as Randall Terry, became increasingly violent in the 1990s, involving the murder of clinic physicians and fire bombings of facilities where abortions were performed. Such should not have been unexpected. Syndicated conservative columnist Cal Thomas, in a 1982 interview when he was still the public relations director for Jerry Falwell's Moral Majority, remarked that if the abortion controversy were not solved legally to the

satisfaction of pro-life advocates, "it will be necessary to take some form of radical action." See Reichley, *Religion in American Public Life*, p. 328. Two reviews of the pro-life position, which suggest that there was consistency rather than diversity in the thinking of anti-abortion leaders, are Faye D. Ginsburg, *Contested Lives*, and Kristen Luker, *Abortion and the Politics of Motherhood*. On Operation Rescue, mostly from an "insider" perspective, see Joseph L. Foreman, *Shattering the Darkness*; Philip F. Lawler, *Operation Rescue*; and Samuel E. Waldron, *We Must Obey God*.

36. Alexis de Tocqueville, *Democracy in America*, pp. 145–58 (from Book I, chap. 14 of the original).

37. Edward J. Larson, *Summer for the Gods*. See also Jon H. Roberts, *Darwinism and the Divine in America*.

38. Many of the controversies have received scholarly treatment in the quarterly *Journal of Church and State*. Especially helpful is the bibliographical guide edited by John F. Wilson, *Church and State in America*; the second volume covers the period from the Civil War to the present. For an historical overview, see John F. Wilson and Donald L. Drakeman, eds., *Church and State in American History*. Also useful is the series, *Studies in Church and State*, issued under the auspices of the Project on Church and State at Princeton University, directed by John F. Wilson, in the 1980s and 1990s. Among the relevant titles in that series are Robert T. Handy, *Undermined Establishment*; N.J. Demerath and Rhys H. Williams, *A Bridging of Faiths* (a case study of Springfield, MA); Peter Iver Kaufman, *Redeeming Politics*; and Robert Wuthnow, *The Restructuring of American Religion*. Still classic is Anson Phelps Stokes and Leo Pfeffer, *Church and State in the United States*. On debates over the meaning of the "free exercise" of religion more generally, see especially Bette Novit Evans, *Interpreting the Free Exercise of Religion*; Philip B. Kurland, ed., *Church and State*; and Leonard W. Levy, *The Establishment Clause: Religion and the First Amendment*, 2nd rev. ed. An older, but helpful, study on cases and controversies relating to public schools is Sam Duker, *The Public Schools and Religion*. The texts, with commentary, of most of the relevant U.S. Supreme Court decisions through 1986 are contained in Robert T. Miller and Ronald B. Flowers, *Toward Benevolent Neutrality*.

39. Helpful are Ron L. Numbers, "Creationism in Twentieth-Century America," and Henry M. Morris, *History of Modern Creationism*.

40. For the relevant decisions, see Miller and Flowers, *Toward Benevolent Neutrality*, pp. 55–104.

41. For the relevant cases, see Miller and Flowers, *Toward Benevolent Neutrality*, pp. 378–82, 397–428. See also Rodney K. Smith, *Public Prayer and the Constitution*. For the larger background, see Robert Michaelsen, *Piety in the Public School*. Over the years, the journal *Religion and Public Education* has contained numerous articles dealing with the issues discussed here.

42. For relevant decisions, see Miller and Flowers, *Toward Benevolent Neutrality*, pp. 382–97.

43. Most insightful are the following works by Melinda Bollar Wagner: *God's Schools*; "Christian Schools: Walking the Christian Walk the American Way," in *Religion in the Contemporary South*, O. Kendall White Jr., and Daryl White, eds.; and "Generic Conservative Christianity." See also Susan D. Rose, *Keeping Them Out of the Hands of Satan*; George E. Ballweg, Jr., "The Growth in the Number and Population of Christian Schools Since 1966"; James C. Carper and Thomas C. Hunt, eds., *Religious Schooling in America*; Paul F. Parsons, *Inside America's Christian Schools*; and Alan Peshkin, *God's Choice*. The American Association of Christian Schools from time to time publishes a directory of institutions affiliated with the association.

44. There is a growing body of literature on home schooling. See, for example, J. Richard Fugate, *Successful Home Schooling*; Mary Griffith, *Homeschooling Handbook*; Christopher J. Klicka, *The Right to Home School*; and Rebecca Rupp, *Getting Started on Home Learning*.

45. For relevant Supreme Court decisions, see Miller and Flowers, *Toward Benevolent Neutrality*, pp. 104–42. On controversies through World War II, see Mulford Q. Sibley and Philip E. Jacob, *Conscription of Conscience*. On selective conscientious objection, see James Finn, ed., *A Conflict of Loyalties*, and Kent Greenawald, "All or Nothing at All: The Defeat of Selective Conscientious Objection," in *Church and State*, Philip B. Kurland, ed., pp. 168–231.

46. Most of the court cases dealing with refusal of medical treatment on religious grounds and especially those involving parents acting on behalf on their minor children have come at the state level. The legal and ethical controversies come into focus in Committee on Bioethics of the American Academy of Pediatrics, "Religious Objections to Medical Care"; idem, "Religious Exemptions from Child Abuse Statutes"; *Jehovah's Witnesses and the Question of Blood*; J. Lowell Dixon and M. Gene Smalley, "Jehovah's Witnesses"; Harold L. Hirsh and Howard Phifer, "The Interface of Medicine, Religion, and the Law"; and Mark Sheldon, "Ethical Issues in the Forced Transfusion of Jehovah's Witness Children." There is a good overview of the debate in Carol Levine, ed., *Taking Sides*, pp. 176–89.

47. Long before debates over physician-assisted suicide and Dr. Jack Kevorkian emerged in the 1990s, there was discussion of the legal and ethical issues surrounding "voluntary" or "active" euthanasia; see A.B. Downing, ed., *Euthanasia and the Right to Death*, and Marvin Kohl, ed., *Beneficent Euthanasia*. A host of studies and anthologies provide insight into the controversy that mushroomed in the last decade of the century. Among them are Robert L. Barry, *Breaking the Thread of Life*; Vigen Guroian, *Life's Living Toward Dying*; Ron P. Hamel and Edwin R. DuBose, eds., *Must We Suffer Our Way to Death?*; John F. Kilner, *Life on the Line*; Edward J. Larson and Darrell W. Amundsen, *A Different Death*; Charles F. McKhann, *A Time to Die*; Michael Manning, *Euthanasia and Physician Assisted Suicide*; and William F. May, *Active Euthanasia and Health Care Reform*.

48. John T. Noonan Jr., *The Believer and the Powers That Are*, pp. 290–91, catalogues the cases dealing with serpent handling.

49. Relevant cases are listed in Noonan, *Believer and the Powers That Are*, pp. 291–92. See also Charles H. Lippy, *Being Religious, American Style*, p. 128.

50. Many works dealing with the rise of the "religious right" in American political life are annotated in Charles H. Lippy, *Modern American Popular Religion*, chap. 4. See also Randall Frame and Alan Tharpe, *How Right Is the Right?*; Samuel S. Hill and Dennis E. Owen, *The New Religious Political Right in America*; Erling Jorstad, *The Politics of Moralism*; Robert C. Liebman and Robert Wuthnow, eds., *The New Christian Right*; William C. Martin, *With God on Our Side*; Albert J. Menendez, *Evangelicals at the Ballot Box*; Duane M. Oldfield, *The Right and the Righteous*; Corwin E. Smidt, *Contemporary Evangelical Political Involvement*; and Clyde Wilcox, *Onward, Christian Soldiers*. A clear statement of the aims of the Christian Coalition is found in a work by its former executive director, Ralph Reed, *Active Faith*.

51. There is a dearth of secondary analysis of People for the American Way. Americans United publishes a periodical, *Church and State*, that reports on current controversies and court cases. On Americans United and its predecessor, Protestants and Other Americans United for Separation of Church and State, see Glenn L. Archer and Albert J. Menendez, *The Dream Lives On*; Harold E. Fey, *With Sovereign Reverence*; C. Stanley Lowell, *Embattled Wall*; and the more narrowly focused work of Lawrence P. Creedon and William D. Falcon, *United for Separation*, which deals with the group's rather disputatious early anti-Catholic posture.

52. For the Catholic Alliance, see G.W. Gerner, "Catholics and the 'Religious Right'"; Matthew G. Monahan, "The Christian Coalition's New 'Catholic Alliance' Crass and Unnecessary"; Heidi Schlumpf, "How Catholic Is the Catholic Alliance?"; and John M. Swomley, "Catholics and the Religious Right."

Chapter 10. Pluralistic Turns in American Religious Thought

1. A brief, but solid assessment is Stephen J. Stein, "Jonathan Edwards," in *Makers of Christian Theology in America*, Mark G. Toulouse and James O. Duke, eds., pp. 55–63.

2. Studies of the Social Gospel abound. See Charles H. Lippy, "Social Christianity," in *Encyclopedia of the American Religious Experience*, Charles H. Lippy and Peter W. Williams, eds., 2:917–31; Paul A. Carter, *The Decline and Revival of the Social Gospel*; James Dombrowski, *The Early Days of Christian Socialism in America*; C. Howard Hopkins, *The Rise of the Social Gospel in American Protestantism*; Ralph Luker, *The Social Gospel in Black and White*; Henry F. May, *Protestant Churches and Industrial America*; and Ronald C. White, Jr., and C. Howard Hopkins, *The Social Gospel*. For an early, contemporary positive assessment, see Shailer Mathews, *The Social Gospel*.

3. A good introduction to primary materials is Robert T. Handy, ed., *The Social Gospel in America*. Rauschenbusch's key works are *Christianity and the Social Crisis*, *Christianizing the Social Order*, and *A Theology for the Social Gospel*. Paul M. Minus, *Walter Rauschenbusch*, supersedes Dores R. Sharpe, *Walter Rauschenbusch*. Representative of Gladden's writings are his *Social Salvation*, *Tools and the Man*, and *Applied Christianity*. The most complete secondary work is Jacob Henry Dorn, *Washington Gladden*, but see also Richard D. Knudten, *The Systematic Thought of Washington Gladden*. Ely's Social Gospel stance can be seen in his *The Labor Movement in America* and *Social Aspects of Christianity*. Strong's corpus, somewhat more conservative in the minds of many, includes *Our Country*, *The New Era*, and *Religious Movements for Social Betterment*.

4. Andrew Carnegie, *The Gospel of Wealth*.

5. See May, *Protestant Churches and Industrial America*, pp. 204–34; Robert Moats Miller, *American Protestantism and Social Issues*, pp. 203–90; and Dorothea R. Muller, "The Social Philosophy of Josiah Strong."

6. Some of this criticism is made by Susan Curtis, *A Consuming Faith*, and R. Laurence Moore, *Selling God*. On the long-term impact of the style of the Social Gospel and its later impact on feminist and liberation thinking, see Gary J. Dorrien, *Soul in Society*.

7. See A. Dudley Ward, *The Social Creed of the Methodist Church*.

8. The Federal Council preferred the designation "social ideals of the churches" to "social creed." See Hopkins, *Rise of the Social Gospel*, pp. 306–17, and Elias B. Sanford, *The Federal Council of the Churches of Christ in America*.

9. See *The Works of Benjamin Breckinridge Warfield* (10 vols.). Especially influential was an essay Warfield wrote with his Princeton colleague Archibald Alexander Hodge; see Hodge and Warfield, "Inspiration." For analysis of Warfield's thought, see Mark A. Noll, *The Princeton Theology*; W. Andrew Hoffecker, *The Princeton Piety*; and idem, "Benjamin B. Warfield," in *Reformed Theology in America*, David F. Wells, ed., pp. 65–91.

10. Representative of Machen's work are his *Christianity and Liberalism* and *The Origin of Paul's Religion*. For analysis, see Darryl G. Hart, *Defending the Faith*.

11. On Personalism in general, see Paul Deats and Carol Robb, eds., *The Boston Personalist Tradition in Philosophy, Social Ethics, and Theology*. Representative of Bowne are his *Personalism, Philosophy of Theism*, and *Studies in Theism*; secondary studies include Francis J. McConnell, *Borden Parker Bowne*, and Charles B. Pyle, *The Philosophy of Borden Parker Bowne*. The flavor of Knudson's thought comes through well in his *The Philosophy of Personalism*, *The Doctrine of God*, and *The Doctrine of Redemption*. See also Edgar S. Brightman, ed., *Personalism in Theology*. Characteristic of Brightman's works are his *The Problem of God*, *Personality and Religion*, and *The Future of Christianity*. For interpretation, see James John McLarney, *The Theism of Edgar Sheffield Brightman*.

12. For an overview of the Chicago school, see Charles H. Arnold, *Near the Edge of Battle*, and W. Creighton Peden and Jerome A. Stone, eds., *The Chicago School of Theol-*

ogy: Pioneers in Religious Inquiry. Characteristic of Mathews's work are *The Faith of Modernism, The Atonement and the Social Process, Christianity and Social Process*, and *The Growth of the Idea of God*. For Case, representative are his *The Evolution of Early Christianity, The Social Origins of Christianity*, and *The Social Triumph of the Ancient Church*. On Case, see William J. Hynes, *Shirley Jackson Case and the Chicago School*. The tenor of Wieman's thought can be ascertained in his *Religious Experience and the Scientific Method, The Intellectual Foundation of Faith*, and *The Wrestle of Religion with Truth*. On Wieman, see Marvin Shaw, *Nature's Grace*; William S. Minor, *Creativity in Henry Nelson Wieman*; and Robert W. Bretall, ed., *The Empirical Theology of Henry Nelson Wieman*.

13. See John Dewey, *A Common Faith*. On the implications of Dewey's position, see Steven C. Rockefeller, *John Dewey*. For an early negative reaction to this surge of religious humanism, see William P. King, ed., *Humanism*. See also the citations in Chapter 8, n. 40 above.

14. On Barth's early influence, see Dennis N. Voskuil, "America Encounters Karl Barth, 1919–1939."

15. A good general statement of the neo-orthodox position is William Hordern, *The Case for a New Reformation Theology*. On the beginnings of neoorthodoxy in the United States, see Dennis N. Voskuil, "American Protestant Neo-Orthodoxy and Its Search for Realism (1925–1939)." A recent appreciative assessment is Douglas John Hall, *Remembered Voices*. The Niebuhr brothers and Bennett were all prolific writers. Representative of Reinhold Niebuhr are several classic works, cited here in the order of publication: *Moral Man and Immoral Society, An Interpretation of Christian Ethics, The Nature and Destiny of Man, The Children of Light and the Children of Darkness, The Irony of American History*, and *Christian Realism and Political Problems*. For interpretation and analysis, see Robin Lovin, *Reinhold Niebuhr and Christian Realism*, and Ronald H. Stone, *Reinhold Niebuhr*. For a biography, see Richard Fox, *Reinhold Niebuhr*. For a sample of H. Richard Niebuhr's writing, see (in order of publication): *The Social Sources of Denominationalism, The Kingdom of God in America, The Meaning of Revelation, Christ and Culture, Radical Monotheism and Western Culture*, and *The Responsible Self*. Appraisals of H. Richard Niebuhr's work are found in Jon Diefenthaler, *H. Richard Niebuhr*, and James W. Fowler, Jr., *To See the Kingdom*. To sample Bennett's thought, always less theoretical and more practical than that of either Niebuhr, see his *Christian Realism, Christians and the State, Christianity and Communism Today*, and *Foreign Policy in Christian Perspective*. On Bennett, see David H. Smith, *The Achievement of John Coleman Bennett*.

16. Tillich left a huge corpus. For scholars, his three-volume *Systematic Theology* is indispensable. Three collections of sermons brought his more philosophically based neoorthodoxy to ordinary folk: *The Shaking of the Foundations, The New Being*, and *The Eternal Now*. The secondary literature on Tillich is enormous; I have found two older volumes to be helpful introductions: Alexander J. McKelway, *The Systematic Theology of Paul Tillich*, and Charles W. Kegley and Robert W. Bretall, eds., *The Theology of Paul Tillich*.

17. Dietrich Bonhoeffer, *Letters and Papers from Prison*, pp. 218–19.

18. Harvey Cox, *The Secular City*. The controversy in religious circles that followed publication is summarized in Daniel Callahan, ed., *The Secular City Debate*.

19. On the "death of God" movement, see Thomas W. Ogletree, *The Death of God Controversy*, and Jackson Lee Ice and John J. Carey, *The Death of God Debate*. Representative works from theologians in the movement include Thomas J.J. Altizer, *The Gospel of Christian Atheism*; Thomas J.J. Altizer and William Hamilton, *Radical Theology and the Death of God*; Gabriel Vahanian, *The Death of God*; and Paul Van Buren, *The Edges of Language*.

20. Robert N. Bellah, "Civil Religion in America." See also Robert N. Bellah et al., *Habits of the Heart*.

21. Jean Jacques Rousseau, *The Social Contract*, pp. 129–40.

22. See John Winthrop, "A Modell of Christian Charity," in *The Puritans*, Perry Miller and Thomas H. Johnson, eds., pp. 198– 99.

23. At its peak, the civil religion provoked many commentaries and critiques. For example, see Russell E. Richey and Donald G. Jones, eds., *American Civil Religion*, and Elwyn A. Smith, ed., *The Religion of the Republic*. Bellah expanded his own discussion, almost in jeremiad form, in *The Broken Covenant*, and put the proposal in crosscultural context in a work coauthored with Phillip E. Hammond, *Varieties of Civil Religion*.

24. See Chapter 5, n. 23 and n. 24, above.

25. Mary Daly's classic is *Beyond God the Father*; Ruether's early contribution is *Sexism and God-Talk*. Letha Dawson Scanzoni and Nancy A. Hardesty, *All We're Meant to Be*, 3rd ed., contains a very helpful bibliography (pp. 391–409). A broader religious studies context for feminist theology is offered in Carol P. Christ and Judith Plaskow, *Womanspirit Rising*. See also Chapter 6, n. 54–57, above.

26. See John J. McNeill, *The Church and the Homosexual*, and idem, *Taking a Chance on God*. Among Heyward's works relevant here are *Staying Power*, *Touching Our Strength*, and *Our Passion for Justice*.

27. For helpful general discussions of process thought see Delwin Brown, Ralph E. James, Jr., and Gene Reeves, eds., *Process Philosophy and Christian Thought*, and George R. Lucas, Jr., *The Genesis of Modern Process Thought*.

28. Works by Charles Hartshorne include *Man's Vision of God and the Logic of Theism*, *Creative Synthesis and Philosophic Method*, and *Wisdom in Moderation*. Among Daniel Day Williams's writings, helpful here are *God's Grace and Man's Hope*, *The Spirit and the Forms of Love*, and *Essays in Process Theology*. Representative of the work of John B. Cobb are *The Structure of Christian Existence*, *Process Theology as Political Theology*, and a volume written with David R. Griffin, *Process Theology*. For Schubert Ogden, see his *On Theology*, *The Reality of God and Other Essays*, and *The Point of Christology*.

29. See Russell Jacoby, *The Last Intellectuals*, and William D. Dean, *The Religious Critic in American Culture*, on this point.

30. The classic analysis of the self-help tradition is Donald Meyer, *The Positive Thinkers*.

31. See Ralph Waldo Trine, *In Tune with the Infinite*.

32. In addition to *The Power of Positive Thinking*, the following works by Norman Vincent Peale are representative of his perspective: *The Amazing Results of Positive Thinking*, *You Can If You Think You Can*, and *Positive Thinking for a Time Like This*. On Peale's career, see Carol V.R. George, *God's Salesman*.

33. A sampling of works by Robert Schuller includes: *Move Ahead with Possibility Thinking*, *The Greatest Possibility Thinker that Ever Lived*, *Peace of Mind Through Possibility Thinking*, *Self-Esteem*, *Be Happy You Are Loved*, *Turning Hurts into Halos*, and *Pearls of Power*. On Schuller, see Dennis Voskuil, *Mountains into Goldmines*, and the insider account of Michael Nason and Donna Nason, *Robert Schuller*. For Charles Allen, in addition to *God's Psychiatry*, see his *Roads to Radiant Living*.

34. Among Bishop Spong's works are *Born of a Woman*, *Rescuing the Bible from Fundamentalism*, and *Why Christianity Must Change or Die*.

35. See chap. 9 on modern evangelical views of scripture in Robert H. Krapohl and Charles H. Lippy, *The Evangelicals*. See also Mark A. Noll, *Between Faith and Criticism*. That pluralism was also coming into evangelical theology becomes evident in Millard J. Erickson, *The Evangelical Left*.

36. On *Christianity Today* and its role in neoevangelicalism, see John G. Merritt, "Christianity Today," in *Religious Periodicals of the United States*, Charles H. Lippy, ed., pp. 134–40; and Douglas A. Sweeney, "Christianity Today," in *Popular Religious Magazines of the United States*, P. Mark Fackler and Charles H. Lippy, eds., pp. 144–51.

37. On Fuller Seminary, see George M. Marsden, *Reforming Fundamentalism*.

38. The flavor of Carnell's thought comes through in his *The Case for Orthodox Theology* and *Introduction to Christian Apologetics*. On Carnell, see Rudolph Nelson, *The Making and Unmaking of an Evangelical Mind*.

39. Henry was among those evangelicals attempting a comprehensive systematic theology. See his six-volume *God, Revelation, and Authority*. See also Carl F.H. Henry, *The Uneasy Conscience of Modern Fundamentalism*, and idem, *Confessions of a Theologian*. On Henry, see Bob E. Patterson, *Carl F.H. Henry*.

40. All of Schaeffer's classic works, such as *A Christian Manifesto* and *How Should We Then Live?*, are included in the five-volume *Complete Works of Francis A. Schaeffer*. Most writing about Schaeffer is hagiographic; the most helpful of those is Louis Parkhurst, Jr., *Francis Schaeffer*.

41. Representative of Weigel's writing are *A Survey of Protestant Theology in Our Times*, *A Catholic Primer on the Ecumenical Movement*, and *The Modern God*. For analysis of Weigel's contribution, see Patrick W. Collins, *Gustave Weigel, S.J.*

42. A sampling of Murray's work includes *We Hold These Truths*, *The Problem of God*, and *Religious Liberty*. Secondary studies include Robert W. McElroy, *The Search for an American Public Theology*, and Donald E. Pelotte, *John Courtney Murray*.

43. Curran has been an unusually prolific writer. In the last decade, his single-authored works have included *The Catholic Moral Tradition Today*, *History and Contemporary Issues*, *The Origins of Moral Theology in the United States*, *The Living Tradition of Catholic Moral Theology*, *The Church and Morality*, *Catholic Higher Education, Theology, and Academic Freedom*, and *Moral Theology at the End of the Century*. On the controversy surrounding Curran, see Kenneth Briggs, *Holy Siege*.

44. Among Merton's better-known works are *The Seven Storey Mountain*, *No Man Is an Island*, and *Zen and the Birds of Appetite*. Lawrence S. Cunningham has edited a useful anthology, *Thomas Merton, Spiritual Master*. Analyses include Lawrence Cunningham, *Thomas Merton*; James T. Baker, *Thomas Merton, Social Critic*; Dennis Q. McInerny, *Thomas Merton*; and Michael Mott, *The Seven Mountains of Thomas Merton*.

45. David Tracy, *Blessed Rage for Order*.

46. See the five volumes in *The Collected Works of Georges Florovsky*. There is little secondary literature on Florovsky, but see Andrew Blane, ed., *Georges Florovsky*.

47. Representative of Meyendorff's thought are *Byzantine Theology*, *Christ in Eastern Christian Thought*, and *Living Tradition*. There is also a dearth of secondary works about Meyendorff. See Dimitri Obolensky, "John Meyendorff (1926–92)."

48. For Schechter, most helpful are the three series in his *Studies in Judaism* and his *Aspects of Rabbinic Theology*. See also Adolph S. Oko, *Solomon Schechter, M.A., LITT.D.* Also helpful are Norman D. Bentwich, *Solomon Schechter*, and idem, *Solomon Schechter, 1847–1915*.

49. One gets a good sense of the thrust of Heschel's thought in his *The Prophets*, *Man Is Not Alone*, *God in Search of Man*, *The Sabbath*, and *Who Is Man?* Heschel deserves serious scholarly study.

50. On Muslim religious thought in the United States, see Chapter 8, n. 36 above.

Bibliography

Abbott, Walter M., S.J., ed. *The Documents of Vatican II*. New York: America Press, 1966.

Abell, Aaron I. *American Catholicism and Social Action: A Search for Social Justice, 1865–1950*. Garden City, NY: Doubleday, 1960.

———, ed. *American Catholic Thought on Social Questions*. Indianapolis: Bobbs-Merrill, 1968.

Aberle, David F. *The Peyote Religion Among the Navaho*. Chicago: Aldine, 1956.

Abrams, Ray. *Preachers Present Arms*. New York: Round Table, 1933.

Adair, James R. *The Old Lighthouse: The Story of the Pacific Garden Mission*. Chicago: Moody, 1966.

Adler, Margot. *Drawing Down the Moon: Witches, Druids, Goddess-Worshippers, and Other Pagans in America Today*. rev. ed. Boston: Beacon, 1986.

Ahlstrom, Sydney E. *The American Protestant Encounter with World Religions*. Beloit, WI: Beloit College, 1962.

Albanese, Catherine L. *America: Religions and Religion*. 2d ed. Belmont, CA: Wadsworth, 1992.

Alberigo, Giuseppe, Jean-Pierre Jossua, and Joseph A. Komonchak, eds. *The Reception of Vatican II*. Washington, DC: Catholic University of America Press, 1987.

Allen, Charles L. *God's Psychiatry*. Old Tappan, NJ: Fleming H. Revell, 1953.

———. *Roads to Radiant Living*. Old Tappan, NJ: Fleming H. Revell, 1968.

Allport, Gordon W. *The Individual and His Religion*. New York: Macmillan, 1957.

Altizer, Thomas J.J. *The Gospel of Christian Atheism*. Philadelphia: Westminster, 1966.

Altizer, Thomas J.J., and William Hamilton. *Radical Theology and the Death of God*. Indianapolis: Bobbs-Merrill, 1966.

American Association of Christian Schools. *Directory of the American Association of Christian Schools*. Fairfax, VA: AACS, date varies.

Ammerman, Nancy Tatom. *Bible Believers: Fundamentalists in the Modern World*. New Brunswick, NJ: Rutgers University Press, 1987.

Anderson, Robert Mapes. *Vision of the Disinherited: The Making of American Pentecostalism*. New York: Oxford University Press, 1979.

Anderson, William H. *The Church in Action Against the Saloon*. Westerville, OH: American Issue, 1910.

Anesaki, Masaharu. *Nichiren: The Buddhist Prophet*. Cambridge: Harvard University Press, 1916.

Anway, Carol L. *Daughters of Another Path: Experiences of American Women Choosing Islam*. Lee's Summit, MT: Yawna, 1996.

Archer, Glenn L., and Albert J. Menendez. *The Dream Lives On: The Story of Glenn L. Archer and Americans United*. Washington, DC: R.B. Luce, 1982.

Armstrong, Ben. *The Electric Church*. Nashville: Thomas Nelson, 1979.

Arnold, Charles H. *Near the Edge of Battle: A Short History of the Divinity School and the Chicago School of Theology, 1866–1966*. Chicago: University of Chicago Divinity School Association, 1966.

Asbury, Herbert. *The Great Illusion: An Informal History*. 1950. New York: Greenwood, 1968.

Austin, Allan D., ed. *African Muslims in Antebellum America: A Sourcebook*. New York: Garland, 1984.

Bailey, Hugh C. "Edgar Gardner Murphy and the Child Labor Movement." *Alabama Review* 18 (1965): 47–59.

Baker, James T. *Thomas Merton, Social Critic: A Study*. Lexington: University Press of Kentucky, 1971.

Baker-Fletcher, Garth Kasimu. *Black Religion After the Million Man March: Voices on the Future*. Maryknoll, NY: Orbis, 1998.

Balka, Christie, and Andy Rose, eds. *Twice Blessed: On Being Lesbian, Gay and Jewish*. Boston: Beacon, 1989.

Ballweg, George Edward, Jr. "The Growth in the Number and Population of Christian Schools Since 1966: A Profile of Parental Views Concerning Factors Which Led Them to Enroll Their Children in a Christian School." Ed.D. diss., Boston University, 1980.

Balmer, Randall. *Mine Eyes Have Seen the Glory: A Journey into the Evangelical Subculture in America*. New York: Oxford University Press, 1989.

Baltzell, E. Digby. *The Protestant Establishment: Aristocracy and Caste in America*. New York: Vintage, 1966.

Barbuto, Domenica M. *American Settlement Houses and Progressive Social Reform*. Phoenix: Oryx Press, 1999.

Barker, Eileen. *The Making of a Moonie: Choice or Brainwashing*. New York: Basil Blackwell, 1984.

Barreau, Jean-Claude. *Drugs and the Life of Prayer*. Translated by Jeremy Mosier. London: Darton, Longman, and Todd, 1974.

Barrett, Leonard E. *The Rastafarians: Sounds of Cultural Dissonance*. Boston: Beacon, 1977.

———. *Soul-Force: African Heritage in Afro-American Religion*. Garden City, NY: Doubleday, 1974.

Barry, Robert L. *Breaking the Thread of Life: On Rational Suicide*. New Brunswick, NJ: Transaction, 1994.

Barth, Gunther. *Bitter Strength: A History of the Chinese in the United States, 1850–1870*. Cambridge: Harvard University Press, 1964.

Bawer, Bruce. "Who's on Trial—the Heretic or the Church?" *The New York Times Magazine*, April 7, 1996, 38ff.

Becker, Penny Edgell, and Nancy L. Eiesland, eds. *Contemporary American Religion: An Ethnographic Reader*. Walnut Creek, CA: AltaMira, 1997.

Beckman, Dave. "Long Before Falwell: Early Radio and Religion." *Journal of Popular Culture* 21, no. 4 (1988): 1–11.

Beckwith, Carol, and Angela Fisher. "The African Roots of Voodoo." *National Geographic* 188, no. 2 (August 1995): 102–13.

Becnel, Thomas A. *Labor, Church, and the Sugar Establishment: Louisiana, 1887–1976*. Baton Rouge: Louisiana State University Press, 1980.

Bedell, Kenneth B., comp. *Yearbook of American and Canadian Churches, 1993*. Nashville: Abingdon, 1993.

Bederman, Gail. "'The Women Have Had Charge of the Church Work Long Enough': The Men and Religion Forward Movement of 1911–1912 and the Masculinization of Middle-Class Protestantism." *American Quarterly* 41, no. 3 (September 1989): 432–65.

Belcove-Shalin, Janet S., ed. *New World Hasidim: Ethnographic Studies of Hasidic Jews in America*. Albany: State University of New York Press, 1995.

Bellah, Robert N. *The Broken Covenant: American Civil Religion in Time of Trial*. New York: Seabury, 1975.

———. "Civil Religion in America." *Daedalus* 96 (Winter 1967): 1–21.

Bellah, Robert N., William M. Sullivan, Ann Swidler, and Steven M. Tipton. *Habits of the Heart: Individualism and Commitment in American Life*. Berkeley: University of California Press, 1985.

Bellah, Robert N., and Phillip E. Hammond. *Varieties of Civil Religion*. San Francisco: Harper, 1980.

Bennett, John Coleman. *Christian Realism*. New York: Scribners, 1941.

———. *Christianity and Communism Today*. rev. ed. New York: Association Press, 1960.

———. *Christians and the State*, New York: Scribners, 1958.

———. *Foreign Policy in Christian Perspective*. New York: Scribners, 1966.

Bennett, LaRon D. *The Million Man March*. Brunswick, GA: BHouse, 1996.

Bentwich, Norman DeMattos. *Solomon Schechter: A Biography*. Philadelphia: Jewish Publication Society of America, 1938.

———. *Solomon Schechter, 1847–1915: Scholar, Sage, and Visionary*. London: Hillel Foundation Education Committee, 1959.

Berger, Peter L. *The Noise of Solemn Assemblies: Christian Commitment and Religious Establishment in America*. Garden City, NY: Doubleday, 1961.

Berkhofer, Robert F., Jr. *Salvation and the Savage: An Analysis of Protestant Missions and American Indian Response, 1787–1862*. Westport, CT: Greenwood, 1977.

Berkin, Carol Ruth, and Mary Beth Norton, eds. *Women of America: A History*. Boston: Houghton Mifflin, 1979.

Berman, William C. *The Politics of Civil Rights in the Truman Administration*. Columbus: Ohio State University Press, 1970.

Berrigan, Daniel. *Night Flight to Hanoi*. New York: Macmillan, 1968.

———. *No Bars to Manhood*. Garden City, NY: Doubleday, 1970.

———. *The Dark Night of Resistance*. Garden City, NY: Doubleday, 1971.

———. *The Trial of the Catonsville Nine*. Boston: Beacon, 1970.

Berrigan, Philip. *Prison Journals of a Priest Revolutionary*. New York: Macmillan, 1969.

———. *A Punishment for Peace*. New York: Holt, 1970.

———. *Widen the Prison Gates: Writings from Jails, April 1970–December 1972*. New York: Simon & Schuster, 1973.

Berry, Jason. *Lead Us Not into Temptation: Catholic Priests and the Sexual Abuse of Children*. Garden City, NY: Doubleday, 1992.

Best, Wallace. "Passionately Human, No Less Divine: Racial Ideology and Religious Culture in the Black Churches of Chicago, 1915–1955." Ph.D. diss., Northwestern University, 2000.

Bhaktipada, Kiritananda Swami. *Christ and Krishna*. Moundsville, WV: Bhaktipada Books, 1985.

———. *Eternal Love*. Moundsville, WV: Bhaktipada Books, 1985.

———. *On His Ardor*. Moundsville, WV: Bhaktipada Books, 1987.

———. *Song of God*. Moundsville, WV: Bhaktipada Books, 1984.

Bianchi, Eugene C. *The Religious Experience of Revolutionaries*. Garden City, NY: Doubleday, 1972.

Biernans, John T. *The Odyssey of New Religious Movements*. New York: Edwin Mellen, 1986.

Biomedical-Ethical Issues: A Digest of Law and Policy Development. Valley Forge, PA: United Ministries in Higher Education, 1983.

Birmingham, Stephen. *"Our Crowd": The Great Jewish Families of New York*. New York: Harper, 1967.

Bisson, Wilfrid J. *Countdown to Violence: The Charlestown Convent Riot of 1834.* New York: Garland, 1989.

Bittner, Vernon. "Taking the Twelve Steps to Church." *Christianity Today*, December 9, 1988, 31.

Bjorling, Joel. *The Baha'i Faith: A Historical Bibliography.* New York: Garland, 1985.

Bland, Joan, S.N.D. *Hibernian Crusade: The Story of the Catholic Total Abstinence Union of America.* Washington, DC: Catholic University of America Press, 1951.

Blane, Andrew, ed. *Georges Florovsky: Russian Intellectual and Orthodox Churchman.* Crestwood, NY: St. Vladimir's Seminary Press, 1993.

Blavatsky, Helena P. *Isis Unveiled.* New York: J.W. Boughton, 1877.

———. *The Secret Doctrine.* New York: William Q. Judge, 1888.

Blocker, Jack S., Jr. *Retreat from Reform: The Prohibition Movement in the United States, 1890–1913.* Westport, CT: Greenwood, 1976.

Bloom, Bernard. "Yiddish-Speaking Socialists in America." *American Jewish Archives* 12 (April 1960): 34–68.

Blumhofer, Edith L. *The Assemblies of God: A Chapter in the Study of American Pentecostalism.* 2 vols. Springfield, MO: Gospel Publishing House, 1989.

———. *Restoring the Faith: The Assemblies of God, Pentecostalism, and American Culture.* Urbana and Chicago: University of Illinois Press, 1993.

Bolster, Paul D. "Christian Socialism Comes to Georgia: The Christian Commonwealth Colony." *Georgia Review* 26 (1972): 60–70.

Bonhoeffer, Dietrich. *Letters and Papers from Prison.* New York: Macmillan, 1953.

Bontemps, Arna, and Jack Conroy. *Anyplace but Here.* 1966. Reprint, Columbia: University of Missouri Press, 1997. First published as *They Seek a City.* Garden City, NY: Doubleday, 1945.

Bordin, Ruth. *Women and Temperance: The Quest for Power and Liberty, 1873–1900.* 1981. Reprint, New Brunswick, NJ: Rutgers University Press, 1990.

Bowden, Henry Warner. *American Indians and Christian Missions: Studies in Cultural Conflict.* Chicago: University of Chicago Press, 1981.

Bowne, Borden Parker. *Personalism.* Boston: Houghton, Mifflin, 1908.

———. *The Philosophy of Theism.* New York: Harper, 1887.

———. *Studies in Theism.* New York: Phillips and Hunt, 1879.

Boyd, Stephen B., Merle Longwood, and Mark W. Muesse, eds. *Redeeming Men: Religion and Masculinities.* Louisville: Westminster John Knox, 1996.

Braden, William. *The Private Sea: LSD and the Search for God.* Chicago: Quadrangle Books, 1967.

Branch, Taylor. *Parting the Waters: America in the King Years, 1954–1963.* New York: Simon & Schuster, 1988.

Brannen, Noah S. *Soka Gakkai: Japan's Militant Buddhism.* Richmond: John Knox, 1968.

Braus, Patricia. "Selling Self Help." *American Demographics* 14 (March 1992): 48–53.

Bretall, Robert W., ed. *The Empirical Theology of Henry Nelson Wieman.* New York: Macmillan, 1963.

Briggs, Kenneth. *Holy Siege: The Year that Shook Catholic America.* San Francisco: Harper, 1992.

Brightman, Edgar Sheffield. *The Future of Christianity.* New York: Abingdon, 1937.

———. *Personality and Religion.* 1934. Reprint, New York: AMS Press, 1979.

———. *The Problem of God.* 1930. Reprint, New York: AMS Press, 1979.

———, ed. *Personalism in Theology: A Symposium in Honor of Albert Cornelius Knudson.* 1943. Reprint, New York: AMS Press, 1979.

Brito, Silvester J. *The Way of a Peyote Roadman.* New York: Peter Lang, 1989.

Broderick, Francis L. *Right Reverend New Dealer: John A. Ryan.* New York: Macmillan, 1963.

Bromley, David G., and Anson D. Shupe, Jr. *"Moonies" in America: Cult, Church, and Crusade*. Beverly Hills: Sage, 1979.

Bromley, David G., and Larry D. Shinn, eds. *Krishna Consciousness in the West*. Lewisburg, PA: Bucknell University Press, 1989.

Brooks, Lee M., and Alvin L. Bertrand. *History of the Southern Sociological Society*. University, AL: University of Alabama Press, 1962.

Brotz, Howard. *The Black Jews of Harlem*. New York: Schocken Books, 1964.

Broun, Heywood, and George Britt. *Christians Only: A Study in Prejudice*. New York: Vanguard, 1931.

Brown, Dee. *Bury My Heart at Wounded Knee: An Indian History of the American West*. New York: Holt, 1970.

Brown, Delwin, Ralph E. James, Jr., and Gene Reeves, eds. *Process Philosophy and Christian Thought*. Indianapolis: Bobbs-Merrill, 1991.

Brown, Joseph Epes. *The Spiritual Legacy of the American Indian*. New York: Crossroad, 1990.

————, ed. *Sacred Pipe: Black Elk's Account of the Seven Rites of the Oglala Sioux*. Norman: University of Oklahoma Press, 1989.

Brown, Robert McAfee, Abraham J. Heschel, and Michael Novak. *Vietnam: Crisis of Conscience*. New York: Association Press, 1967.

Browne, Henry J. "The American Parish School in the Last Half Century." *Bulletin of the National Catholic Education Association* 50 (August 1953): 323–34.

————. *The Catholic Church and the Knights of Labor*. Washington, DC: Catholic University of America Press, 1949.

Bryant, M. Darrol, and Herbert W. Richardson, eds. *A Time for Consideration: A Scholarly Appraisal of the Unification Church*. New York: Edwin Mellen, 1978.

Bucke, Emory Stevens, ed. *The History of American Methodism*. 3 vols. Nashville: Abingdon, 1964.

Buckley, William F., Jr. "Shock Time at Yale." *National Review* 49, no. 19 (October 13, 1997): 82.

Bucko, Raymond A. *The Lakota Ritual of the Sweat Lodge: History and Contemporary Practice*. Norman: University of Oklahoma Press, 1998.

Budapest, Z [Zsuzsana]. *Grandmother Moon*. San Francisco: Harper, 1991.

————. *The Grandmother of Time: A Women's Book of Celebrations, Spells, and Sacred Objects for Every Month of the Year*. San Francisco: Harper, 1989.

————. *The Holy Book of Women's Mysteries*. Oakland: Wingbow, 1989.

Buddhist Churches of America, 75 Year History, 1899–1974. 2 vols. Chicago: Norbet, 1974.

Buddhist Handbook for Shin-shu Followers. Tokyo: Hokuseido Press, 1969.

Buenker, John D. *Historical Dictionary of the Progressive Era, 1890–1920*. New York: Greenwood, 1988.

————. *Urban Liberalism and Progressive Reform*. New York: Norton, 1978.

Bumpass, Larry. "The Trend of Interfaith Marriage in the United States." *Social Biology* 17 (1970): 253–59.

Burkett, Randall. *Garveyism as a Religious Movement*. Metuchen, NJ: Scarecrow, 1978.

Burkett, Randall, and Richard Newman, eds. *Black Apostles: Afro-American Clergy Confront the Twentieth Century*. Boston: G.K. Hall, 1978.

Burnham, Kenneth E. *God Comes to America: Father Divine and the Peace Mission Movement*. Boston: Lambeth, 1979.

Buscaglia, Leo F. *Born for Love*. Thorofare, NJ: Slack, 1992.

————. *Living, Loving, and Learning*. Thorofare, NJ: Slack, 1982.

————. *Love*. Thorofare, NJ: Slack, 1972.

————. *Loving Each Other*. Thorofare, NJ: Slack, 1972.

Bush, Trudy. "On the Tide of the Angels." *Christian Century* 112, no. 7 (March 1, 1995): 236–38.

Cahill, Lisa Sowle. "Notes on Moral Theology: Abortion." *Theological Studies* 46, no. 1 (March 1985): 64–80.

Calhoon, Robert M. "The African Heritage, Slavery, and Evangelical Christianity Among American Blacks, 1700–1870." *Fides et Historia* 21 (June 1989): 61–66.

Callahan, Daniel, ed. *The Secular City Debate*. New York: Macmillan, 1966.

Callahan, Sydney, and Daniel Callahan, eds. *Abortion: Understanding Differences*. New York: Plenum, 1984.

Cameron, Charles. *Who Is Guru Maharj Ji?* New York: Bantam, 1973.

Cameron, Richard M. *Methodism and Society in Historical Perspective*. New York: Abingdon, 1961.

Campbell, Anthony, M.D. *Seven States of Consciousness: A Vision of Possibilities Suggested by the Teaching of Maharishi Mahesh Yogi*. New York: Harper, 1973.

Campbell, Rex R. *Black Migration in America: A Social Demographic History*. Durham: Duke University Press, 1991.

Canfield, Jack, and Mark Victor Hansen, comps. *Chicken Soup for the Soul*. Deerfield Beach, FL: Health Communications, 1993.

Canfield, Jack, Mark Victor Hansen, and Kimberly Kirberger, comps. *Chicken Soup for the Teenage Soul*. Deerfield Beach, FL: Health Communications, 1997.

Cannon, Katie G. *Black Womanist Ethics*. Atlanta: Scholars Press, 1988.

Carnegie, Andrew. *The Gospel of Wealth*. London: F.C. Hagen, 1889.

Carnell, Edward J. *The Case for Orthodox Theology*. Philadelphia: Westminster, 1959.

———. *Introduction to Christian Apologetics*. Grand Rapids: Eerdmans, 1948.

Carnes, Mark C. *Secret Ritual and Manhood in Victorian America*. New Haven: Yale University Press, 1989.

Carpenter, Frederick I. *Emerson and Asia*. Cambridge: Harvard University Press, 1930.

Carpenter, Joel A. *Revive Us Again: The Resurgence of American Fundamentalism*. New York: Oxford University Press, 1997.

Carper, James C., and Thomas C. Hunt, eds. *Religious Schooling in America*. Birmingham: Religious Education Press, 1984.

Carter, Paul A. *The Decline and Revival of the Social Gospel*. 1956; Reprint, Hamden, CT: Archon, 1971.

Case, Shirley Jackson. *The Evolution of Early Christianity: A Genetic Study of First-Century Christianity in Relation to Its Religious Environment*. 1914. Reprint, Chicago: University of Chicago Press, 1960.

———. *The Social Origins of Christianity*. Chicago: University of Chicago Press, 1923.

———. *The Social Triumph of the Ancient Church*. New York: Harper, 1933.

Casey, William Van Etten, S.J., and Philip Nobile, eds. *The Berrigans*. New York: Avon Books, 1971.

Castaneda, Carlos. *The Active Side of Infinity*. San Francisco: HarperCollins, 1998.

———. *Eagle's Gift*. New York: Simon & Schuster, 1981.

———. *The Fire from Within*. New York: Simon & Schuster, 1984.

———. *Journey to Ixtlan: The Lessons of Don Juan*. New York: Simon & Schuster, 1991.

———. *Magical Passes: The Practical Wisdom of the Shamans of Ancient Mexico*. San Francisco: HarperCollins, 1998.

———. *The Power of Silence: Further Lessons of Don Juan*. New York: Simon & Schuster, 1987.

———. *The Second Ring of Power*. New York: Simon & Schuster, 1977.

———. *A Separate Reality: Further Conversations with Don Juan*. New York: Simon & Schuster, 1971.

———. *Silent Knowledge*. Los Angeles: Cleargreen, 1996.

————. *Tales of Power*. New York: Simon & Schuster, 1974.

————. *The Teachings of Don Juan: A Yaqui Way of Knowledge*. Berkeley: University of California Press, 1968.

Cat's Yawn. New York: First Zen Institute in America, 1947.

Cavert, Samuel McCrea. *The American Churches in the Ecumenical Movement, 1900–1968*. New York: Association Press, 1968.

————. *Church Cooperation and Unity in America: A Historical Review, 1900–1970*. New York: Association Press, 1970.

Chalmers, David M. *Hooded Americanism: The First Century of the Ku Klux Klan, 1865–1965*. Garden City, NY: Doubleday, 1965.

Chase, Elise. *Healing Faith: An Annotated Bibliography of Christian Self-Help Books*. Westport, CT: Greenwood, 1985.

Chatfield, E. Charles. "The Southern Sociological Congress: Organization of Uplift." *Tennessee Historical Quarterly* 19 (1960): 328–47.

————. "The Southern Sociological Congress: Rationale of Uplift." *Tennessee Historical Quarterly* (1961): 51–64.

Chaves, Mark, and James C. Cavendish. "More Evidence on U.S. Catholic Church Attendance." *Journal for the Scientific Study of Religion* 33 (December 1994): 376–81.

Chenhin, Alvin. "Jewish Population in the United States, 1967." *American Jewish Yearbook* 69 (1968): 283.

Chevannes, Barry. *Rastafari: Roots and Ideology*. Syracuse: Syracuse University Press, 1994.

Chin, Justin. "Our Reporter Survives the Ex-Gay Ministries." *The Progressive* 59, no. 12 (December 1995): 32ff.

Chitsey, Donald B. *On and Off the Wagon: A Sober Analysis of the Temperance Movement from the Pilgrims Through Prohibition*. New York: Cowles, 1969.

Christ, Carol P., and Judith Plaskow, eds. *Womanspirit Rising: A Feminist Reader in Religion*. San Francisco: Harper, 1989.

Christy, Arthur. *The Orient in American Transcendentalism*. New York: Columbia University Press, 1932.

"Church Trial Slated for Episcopal Bishop." *Christian Century* 112, no. 27 (September 1995): 878ff.

Clark, Walter Houston. *Chemical Ecstasy: Psychedelic Drugs and Religion*. New York: Sheed and Ward, 1969.

————. *Psychology of Religion*. New York: Macmillan, 1958.

Cleage, Albert B., Jr. *The Black Messiah*. New York: Sheed and Ward, 1968.

Clifford, Richard J. "The Rocky Road to a New Lectionary." *America* 177, no. 16 (August 1997): 18ff.

Cobb, John B., Jr. *Process Theology as Political Theology*. Philadelphia: Westminster, 1982.

————. *The Structure of Christian Existence*. Philadelphia: Westminster, 1967.

Cobb, John B., Jr., and David R. Griffin. *Process Theology: An Introductory Exposition*. Philadelphia: Westminster, 1976.

Coffey, Thomas M. *The Long Thirst: Prohibition in American 1920–1933*. New York: Norton, 1975.

Cohen, Daniel. *Prohibition: America Makes Alcohol Illegal*. Brookfield, CT: Millbrook, 1995.

Cohen, Michael J. *Truman and Israel*. Berkeley: University of California Press, 1990.

Cohen, Naomi. *Not Free to Desist: The American Jewish Committee, 1906–1966*. Philadelphia: Jewish Publication Society of America, 1972.

Coleman, Gerald D. "Ministry to Homosexuals Must Use Authentic Church Teaching." *America* 181, no. 4 (August 14, 1999): 12.

Coles, Robert. *Dorothy Day: A Radical Devotion*. Reading, MA: Addison-Wesley, 1987.

Collins, Patrick W. *Gustave Weigel, S.J.: A Pioneer of Reform*. Collegeville, MN: Liturgical Press, 1992.

Committee on Bioethics of the American Academy of Pediatrics. "Religious Exemptions from Child Abuse Statutes." *Pediatrics* 81, no. 1 (1988): 169–71.

———. "Religious Objections to Medical Care." *Pediatrics* 99, no. 2 (1997): 279–80.

Cone, James H. *Black Theology and Black Power*. 1969. Reprint, Maryknoll, NY: Orbis, 1997.

———. *A Black Theology of Liberation*. Philadelphia: Lippincott, 1970.

———. *For My People: Black Theology and the Black Church*. Maryknoll, NY: Orbis, 1984.

———. *God of the Oppressed*. Maryknoll, NY: Orbis, 1997.

———. *Martin & Malcolm & America: A Dream or a Nightmare*. Maryknoll, NY: Orbis, 1991.

———. *Speaking the Truth: Ecumenism, Liberation, and Black Theology*. 1986. Reprint, Maryknoll, NY: Orbis, 1999.

———. *The Spirituals and the Blues*. New York: Seabury, 1972.

Conn, Charles W. *Like a Mighty Army; Moves the Church of God, 1886–1955*. Cleveland, TN: Church of God Publishing House, 1955.

Conn, Walter E., ed. *Conversion*. New York: Alba House, 1978.

Connolly, James J. *The Triumph of Ethnic Progressivism: Urban Political Culture in Boston, 1900–1925*. Cambridge: Harvard University Press, 1998.

Conser, Walter H., Jr., and Sumner B. Twiss, eds. *Religious Diversity and American Religious History: Studies in Traditions and Cultures*. Athens: University of Georgia Press, 1997.

Conwell, Russell. *Acres of Diamonds*. New York: J.Y. Huber, 1890.

Cooney, John. *The American Pope: The Life and Times of Francis Cardinal Spellman*. New York: Times Books, 1984.

Courts, James, comp. *The History and Life Work of Elder C.H. Mason, Chief Apostle, and His Co-Laborers*. Memphis: Howe Printing, 1920.

Cowman, Mrs. Charles E. (Lettie Burd Cowman). *Streams in the Desert*. Los Angeles: Oriental Missionary Society, 1925.

Cox, Harvey. *The Secular City: Secularization and Urbanization in Theological Perspective*. New York: Macmillan, 1965.

Cranston, Sylvia. *H.P.B.: The Extraordinary Life and Influence of Helena Blavatsky, Founder of the Modern Theosophical Movement*. New York: Jeremy P. Tarcher, 1993.

Creedon, Lawrence P., and William D. Falcon. *United for Separation: An Analysis of POAU Assaults on Catholicism*. Milwaukee: Bruce, 1959.

Crews, Mickey. *The Church of God: A Social History*. Knoxville: University of Tennessee Press, 1990.

Cronin, E. David. *Black Moses*. Madison: University of Wisconsin Press, 1955.

Crosby, Donald F. *God, Church and Flag: Senator Joseph R. McCarthy and the Catholic Church, 1950–1957*. Chapel Hill: University of North Carolina Press, 1967.

Cross, Robert D. *The Church and the City*. Indianapolis: Bobbs-Merrill, 1967.

———. *The Emergence of Liberal Catholicism in America*. Cambridge: Harvard University Press, 1958.

———. "Origins of the Catholic Parochial Schools in America." *American Benedictine Review* 16 (1965): 194–209.

Culver, Dwight W. *Negro Segregation in the Methodist Church*. New Haven: Yale University Press, 1953.

Cunningham, Lawrence S. *Thomas Merton: Monastic Wisdom as Witness to the World*. Grand Rapids: Eerdmans, 1999.

Cunningham, W.J. *Agony at Galloway: One Church's Struggle with Social Change*. Jackson: University Press of Mississippi, 1980.

Curran, Charles E. *Catholic Higher Education, Theology, and Academic Freedom.* Notre Dame: University of Notre Dame Press, 1990.

————. *The Catholic Moral Tradition Today: A Synthesis.* Washington, DC: Georgetown University Press, 1999.

————. *The Church and Morality: An Ecumenical and Catholic Approach.* Minneapolis: Fortress, 1993.

————. *History and Contemporary Issues: Studies in Moral Theology.* New York: Continuum, 1996.

————. *The Living Tradition of Catholic Moral Theology.* Notre Dame: University of Notre Dame Press, 1992.

————. *Moral Theology at the End of the Century.* Milwaukee: Marquette University Press, 1999.

————. *The Origins of Moral Theology in the United States: Three Different Approaches.* Washington, DC: Georgetown University Press, 1997.

Curtis, Susan. *A Consuming Faith: The Social Gospel and Modern American Culture.* Baltimore: Johns Hopkins University Press, 1991.

Daly, Mary. *Beyond God the Father: Toward a Philosophy of Women's Liberation.* 2d ed. Reprint, Boston: Beacon, 1985.

Daner, Francine J. *The American Children of Krsna: A Study of the Hare Krishna Movement.* New York: Holt, 1976.

Danzger, M. Herbert. *Returning to Tradition: The Contemporary Revival of Orthodox Judaism.* New Haven: Yale University Press, 1989.

Dator, James Allen. *Soka Gakkai, Builders of the Third Civilization: American and Japanese Members.* Seattle: University of Washington Press, 1969.

Davis, Lenwood G. *Daddy Grace: An Annotated Bibliography.* Westport, CT: Greenwood, 1992.

Davis, Moshe. *The Emergence of Conservative Judaism: The Historical School in 19th Century America.* Philadelphia: Jewish Publication Society of America, 1953. Reprint, New York: Burning Bush, 1963.

Dawn, Marva J. *Reaching Out Without Dumbing Down: A Theology of Worship for the Turn-of-the-Century Culture.* Grand Rapids: Eerdmans, 1995.

Day, Dorothy. *By Little and by Little: The Selected Writings of Dorothy Day,* ed. Robert Ellsberg. New York: Knopf, 1983.

————. *From Union Square to Rome.* 1933. Reprint, New York: Arno, 1978.

————. *Loaves and Fishes.* San Francisco: Harper, 1983.

Dean, William D. *The Religious Critic in American Culture.* Albany: State University of New York Press, 1994.

Deats, Paul, and Carol Robb, eds. *The Boston Personalist Tradition in Philosophy, Social Ethics, and Theology.* Macon, GA: Mercer University Press, 1986.

Decaro, Louis Anthony, Jr. "Malcolm X and the Nation of Islam: Two Moments in His Religious Sojourn." Ph.D. diss., New York University, 1994.

Deloff, Linda-Marie. "The Century in Transition: 1916–1922." *Christian Century,* March 7, 1984, 243–46.

Deloff, Linda-Marie, Martin E. Marty, Dean Peerman, and James M. Wall. *A Century of the Century.* Grand Rapids: Eerdmans, 1987.

Deloria, Vine, Jr. *Behind the Trail of Broken Treaties: An Indian Declaration of Independence.* Austin: University of Texas Press, 1985.

————. *A Better Day for Indians.* New York: Field Foundation, 1976.

————. *Custer Died for Your Sins: An Indian Manifesto.* 1969; Reprint, Norman: University of Oklahoma Press, 1988.

————. *God Is Red.* New York: Grosset and Dunlap, 1973.

————. *The Indian Affair.* New York: Friendship Press, 1974.

————. *We Talk, You Listen: New Tribes, New Turf.* New York: Macmillan, 1970.

————, ed. *American Indian Policy in the Twentieth Century.* Norman: University of Oklahoma Press, 1985.

————, ed. *Of Utmost Good Faith.* San Francisco: Straight Arrow Books, 1971.

Deloria, Vine, Jr., and Clifford M. Lytle. *American Indians, American Justice.* Austin: University of Texas Press, 1983.

————. *The Nations Within: The Past and Future of American Indian Sovereignty.* Austin: University of Texas Press, 1998.

Deloria, Vine, Jr., and David E. Wilkins. *Tribes, Treaties, and Constitutional Tribulations.* Austin: University of Texas Press, 1999.

Demaille, Raymond, ed. *The Sixth Grandfather: Black Elk's Teachings Given to John G. Neihardt.* Lincoln: University of Nebraska Press, 1984.

Demerath, N.J., and Rhys H. Williams. *A Bridging of Faiths: Religion and Politics in a New England City.* Studies in Church and State. Princeton: Princeton University Press, 1992.

De Tocqueville, Alexis. *Democracy in America.* New York: Random House Modern Library, 1981.

Dewey, John. *A Common Faith.* 1934; Reprint, New Haven: Yale University Press, 1991.

Diaz-Stevens, Ana Maria. *Oxcart Catholicism on Fifth Avenue: The Impact of Puerto Rican Migration upon the Archdiocese of New York.* Notre Dame: University of Notre Dame Press, 1992.

Diefenthaler, Jon. *H. Richard Niebuhr: A Lifetime of Reflections on the Church and the World.* Macon, GA: Mercer University Press, 1986.

Dietz, Peter E. "The Metamorphosis." *Central-Blatt and Social Justice* 2 (July 1909): 7–10.

Dinnerstein, Leonard. *Antisemitism in America.* New York: Oxford University Press, 1984.

Divine Principle. New York: Holy Spirit Association for the Unification of World Christianity, 1973.

Dixon, J. Lowell, and M. Gene Smalley. "Jehovah's Witnesses: The Surgical/Ethical Challenge." *Journal of the American Medical Association* 246, no. 27 (November 1981): 2471–72.

Dobkowski, Michael N., ed. *Jewish American Voluntary Organizations.* Westport, CT: Greenwood, 1986.

Dolan, Jay P., and Allan Figueroa Deck. *Hispanic Catholic Culture in the U.S.: Issues and Concerns.* Notre Dame: University of Notre Dame Press, 1994.

Dombrowski, James. *The Early Days of Christian Socialism in America.* New York: Columbia University Press, 1936.

Dorn, Jacob Henry. *Washington Gladden: Prophet of the Social Gospel.* Columbus: Ohio State University Press, 1967.

Dorrien, Gary J. *Soul in Society: The Making and Renewal of Social Christianity.* Minneapolis: Fortress, 1995.

Dossey, Larry, M.D. *Prayer Is Good Medicine: How To Reap the Healing Benefits of Prayer.* San Francisco: Harper, 1996.

Douglas, Ann. *The Feminization of American Culture.* New York: Knopf, 1978.

Douglass, Harlan Paul. *Church Unity Movements in the United States.* New York: Institute of Social and Religious Research, 1934.

Downing, A.B., ed. *Euthanasia and the Right to Death: The Case for Voluntary Euthanasia.* New York: Humanities Press, 1969.

Downton, James V., Jr. *Sacred Journeys.* New York: Columbia University Press, 1979.

Drake, St. Clair, and Horace R. Cayton. *Black Metropolis: A Study of Negro Life in a Northern City.* 2 vols. rev. ed. New York: Harper, 1962.

Druyvesteyn, Kent. "The World's Parliament of Religions." Ph.D. diss., University of Chicago, 1976.

Dubofsky, Melvin. "Organized Labor and the Immigrant in New York City, 1900–1918." *Labor History* 2, no. 2 (April 1961): 182–201.

Duker, Sam. *The Public Schools and Religion: The Legal Context*. New York: Harper, 1966.

Durkin, Elizabeth, and Julie Durkin Montague. "Surveying U.S. Nuns." *America*, February 11, 1995, 8–12.

Dyer, Ellen. *Daily Suggestions for Workers: Many Thoughts Borrowed from Many Minds*. New York: Harper, 1898.

Earhart, H. Byron. *The New Religions of Japan: An Annotated List of Books Published in English, 1971 Through 1975*. 2d ed. Michigan Papers in Japanese Studies 9. Ann Arbor: University of Michigan Center for Japanese Studies, 1983.

Ebson, Martin, ed. *Maharishi, the Guru*. New York: New American Library, 1968.

Ecumenical Review 50, no. 1– (January 1998–).

Eighmy, John L. *Churches in Cultural Captivity: A History of the Social Attitudes of Southern Baptists*. Revised by Samuel S. Hill, Jr. Knoxville: University of Tennessee Press, 1987.

———. "Religious Liberalism in the South During the Progressive Era." *Church History* 38 (1969): 359–72.

Eisen, Arnold M. *The Jewish People in America: A Study in Jewish Religious Ideology*. Bloomington: Indiana University Press, 1983.

Eliade, Mircea. *The Sacred and the Profane*. Translated by Willard R. Trask. New York: Harcourt, 1959.

Elkholy, Abdo A. *The Arab Moslems in the United States*. New Haven: College and University Press, 1966.

Elkind, David. "Age Changes in the Meaning of Religious Identity." *Review of Religious Research* 6, no. 1 (1964): 36–40.

Ellis, John Tracy. *The Life of James Cardinal Gibbons, Archbishop of Baltimore, 1834–1921*. 1952. Reprint, Westminster, MD: Christian Classics, 1987.

———, ed. *Documents of American Catholic History*. 2 vols. rev. ed. Wilmington: Michael Glazier, 1987.

Ellwood, Robert S., Jr. *Alternative Altars: Unconventional and Eastern Spirituality in America*. Chicago: University of Chicago Press, 1979.

———. *The Eagle and the Rising Sun: Americans and the New Religions of Japan*. Philadelphia: Westminster, 1974.

———. *The Fifties Spiritual Marketplace: American Religion in a Decade of Conflict*. New Brunswick, NJ: Rutgers University Press, 1997.

Ellwood, Robert S., Jr., and Harry B. Partin. *Religious and Spiritual Groups in Modern America*. 2d ed. Englewood Cliffs, NJ: Prentice-Hall, 1988.

Elson, Ruth Miller. *Myths and Mores in American Best Sellers, 1865–1965*. New York and London: Garland, 1985.

Ely, Richard T. *The Labor Movement in America* 1886. New York: Arno, 1969.

———. *Social Aspects of Christianity, and Other Essays*. New York: T.Y. Crowell, 1889.

Engh, Michael E., S.J. *Frontier Faiths: Church, Temple, and Synagogue in Los Angeles, 1846–1888*. Albuquerque: University of New Mexico Press, 1992.

Enochs, Ross. "Lakota Mission: Jesuit Missionary Method and the Lakota Sioux, 1885–1945." Ph.D. diss., University of Virginia, 1993.

Enroth, Ronald M., and Gerald E. Jamison. *The Gay Church*. Grand Rapids: Eerdmans, 1974.

Erickson, Millard J. *The Evangelical Left: Encountering Postconservative Evangelical Theology*. Grand Rapids: Baker, 1997.

Esslemont, J.E. *Baha'u'llah and the New Era*. Wilmette, IL: Baha'i Publishing Trust, 1970.

Evans, Bette Novit. *Interpreting the Free Exercise of Religion: The Constitution and American Pluralism*. Chapel Hill: University of North Carolina Press, 1997.

Evers, Alf. *The Catskills: From Wilderness to Woodstock.* 2d ed. Woodstock, NY: Overlook Press, 1982.

Fackler, P. Mark, and Charles H. Lippy, eds. *Popular Religious Magazines of the United States.* Westport, CT: Greenwood Press, 1995.

Fader, Larry A. "Zen in the West: Historical and Philosophical Implications of the 1893 Chicago World's Parliament of Religions." *Eastern Buddhist* n.s. 15 (Spring 1982): 122–45.

Fantel, Hans. *William Penn: Apostle of Dissent.* New York: Morrow, 1974.

Faris, Hani, ed. *Arab Nationalism and the Future Arab World.* Belmont, MA: AAUG Press, 1987.

Farmer, James Oscar, Jr. *The Metaphysical Confederacy: James Henley Thornwell and the Synthesis of Southern Values.* Macon, GA: Mercer University Press, 1986.

Fauset, Arthur H. *Black Gods of the Metropolis: Negro Religious Cults in the Urban North.* 1944. rev. ed. Philadelphia: University of Pennsylvania Press, 1944.

Feinberg, Joel, ed. *The Problem of Abortion.* Belmont, CA: Wadsworth, 1984.

Felton, Ralph. *Go Down Moses: A Study of 21 Successful Negro Rural Pastors.* Madison, NJ: Drew Theological Seminary, the Rural Church, 1952.

Fenwick, Justin W. *A Million Under One.* Lanham, MD: TPFS Press, 1996.

Ferguson, Thomas P. *Catholic and American: The Political Theology of John Courtney Murray.* Kansas City, MO: Sheed and Ward, 1994.

Fey, Harold E. *With Sovereign Reverence: The First Twenty-Five Years of Americans United.* Rockville, MD: R. Williams Press, 1974.

The Fiftieth Anniversary of the Ethical Movement, 1876–1926. New York: Appleton, 1926.

Fink, Leon. *Progressive Intellectuals and the Dilemmas of Democratic Commitment.* Cambridge: Harvard University Press, 1997.

Finke, Roger, and Rodney Stark. *The Churching of America, 1776–1990: Winners and Losers in Our Religious Economy.* New Brunswick, NJ: Rutgers University Press, 1992.

Finn, James, ed. *A Conflict of Loyalties: The Case for Selective Conscientious Objection.* New York: Pegasus, 1969.

Fish, John O. "The Christian Commonwealth Colony: A Georgia Experiment, 1896–1900." *Georgia Historical Quarterly* 59 (1973): 213–26.

Fishman, Hertzel. *American Protestantism and a Jewish State.* Detroit: Wayne State University Press, 1973.

Fishman, Sylvia Barack. *A Breath of Life: Feminism in the American Jewish Community.* New York: Free Press, 1993.

FitzGerald, Frances. *Cities on a Hill: A Journey Through Contemporary American Cultures.* New York: Simon & Schuster, 1986.

Florovsky, Georges. *The Collected Works of Georges Florovsky.* 5 vols. Belmont, MA: Nordland, 1972–79.

Flynt, Wayne. *Alabama Baptists: Southern Baptists in the Heart of Dixie.* Tuscaloosa: University of Alabama Press, 1998.

———. "Alabama White Protestantism and Labor, 1900–1914." *Alabama Review* 25 (1972): 192–217.

———. "Organized Labor, Reform, and Alabama Politics, 1920." *Alabama Review* 23 (1970): 163–80.

Fogarty, Gerald P. *The Vatican and the American Hierarchy from 1870 to 1965.* Stuttgart, Germany: Hiersemann, 1982.

———. *The Vatican and the Americanist Crisis: Denis J. O'Connell, American Agent in Rome, 1885–1903.* Rome: Gregorian University Press, 1974.

Foreman, Joseph Lapsley. *Shattering the Darkness: The Crisis of the Cross in the Church Today.* Montreat, NC: Cooling Spring Press, 1992.

Fosdick, Harry Emerson. "Shall the Fundamentalists Win?" *Christian Work,* June 10, 1922, 716–19, 722.

Fowler, James W., Jr. *To See the Kingdom: The Theological Vision of H. Richard Niebuhr.* Nashville: Abingdon, 1974.

Fox, Richard. *Reinhold Niebuhr: A Biography.* New York: Pantheon, 1985.

Frame, Randall, and Alan Tharpe. *How Right Is the Right? A Biblical and Balanced Approach to Politics.* Grand Rapids: Zondervan, 1996.

Frame, Randy. "Heresy Charges Dismissed." *Christianity Today* 40, no. 7 (June 1996): 57.

Frank, Thomas E. *Polity, Practice, and the Mission of the United Methodist Church.* Nashville: Abingdon, 1997.

Frankiel, Sandra Sizer. *California's Spiritual Frontiers: Religious Alternatives in Anglo-Protestantism, 1850–1910.* Berkeley: University of California Press, 1988.

Franklin, Benjamin. *The Autobiography of Benjamin Franklin.* Introduced by Jackson W. Wilson. New York: Modern Library, 1981.

Franklin, V.P., Nancy Grant, Harold M. Kletnick, and Geena Rae McNeil, eds. *African Americans and Jews in the Twentieth Century: Studies in Convergence and Conflict.* Columbia: University of Missouri Press, 1998.

Frazier, E. Franklin. *Black Bourgeoisie.* Glencoe, IL: Free Press, 1957.

———. *The Negro Church in America.* New York: Schocken, 1964.

Frederic, Harold. *The Damnation of Theron Ware.* 1896. Reprint, San Francisco: Rinehart, 1958.

Freese, Peter, ed. *Religion and Philosophy in the United States.* 2 vols. Essen, Germany: Verlag die Blaue Eule, 1987.

Friedman, Murray, ed. *When Philadelphia Was the Capital of Jewish America.* Philadelphia: Balch Institute, 1993.

Friess, Horace Leland. *Felix Adler and Ethical Culture: Memories and Studies.* New York: Columbia University Press, 1981.

Frost, Stanley. *The Challenge of the Klan.* Indianapolis: Bobbs-Merrill, 1923.

Frothingham, Octavius Brooks. *The Religion of Humanity.* New York: D.G. Francis, 1873.

Fry, Franklin Clark. "The Unity of the Church." *Lutheran World* 3 (1956–57): 322–28.

Fuchs, Lawrence. *Political Behavior of American Jews.* Glencoe, IL: Free Press, 1956. Reprint, Westport, CT: Greenwood, 1980.

Fugate, J. Richard. *Successful Home Schooling.* Tempe, AZ: Alethia Division of Alpha Omega Publications, 1990.

Fuller, Daniel P. *Give the Winds a Mighty Voice: The Story of Charles E. Fuller.* Waco, TX: Word, 1972.

Fulop, Timothy E., and Albert J. Raboteau, eds. *African-American Religion: Interpretive Essays in History and Culture.* New York and London: Routledge, 1997.

Furniss, Norman P. *The Fundamentalist Controversy, 1918–1931.* New Haven: Yale University Press, 1954.

Gallup, George H., Jr. *Religion in America 1996.* Princeton: Princeton Religion Research Center, 1996.

Gallup, George H., Jr., and Jim Castelli. *The People's Religion: American Faith in the 90's.* New York: Macmillan, 1989.

Ganin, Zvi. *Truman, American Jewry, and Israel, 1945–1948.* New York: Holmes and Meier, 1979.

Gannett, Lewis S. "Is America Anti-Semitic?" *Nation* 116 (1923): 330–31.

Gannon, Robert I. *The Cardinal Spellman Story.* Garden City, NY: Doubleday, 1962.

Garrow, David J. *Bearing the Cross: Martin Luther King, Jr., and the Southern Christian Leadership Conference.* New York: Morrow, 1986.

Gaustad, Edwin Scott. *A Historical Atlas of Religion in America.* rev. ed. New York: Harper, 1976.

———. *Liberty of Conscience: Roger Williams in America.* Grand Rapids: Eerdmans, 1991.

————. *Neither King nor Prelate: Religion and the New Nation, 1776–1826*. Grand Rapids: Eerdmans, 1993. First published 1987 as *Faith of Our Fathers*.

Gaver, Jessyca. *Baha'i Faith*. New York: Award Books, 1968.

"Gays and the Gospel: An Interview with Troy Perry." *Christian Century* 113, no. 27 (September 1996): 896ff.

Gelberg, Steven J., ed. *Hare Krishna, Hare Krishna: Five Distinguished Scholars on the Krishna Movement in the West*. New York: Grove, 1983.

George, Carol V.R. *God's Salesman: Norman Vincent Peale and the Power of Positive Thinking*. New York: Oxford University Press, 1993.

————. *Segregated Sabbaths: Richard Allen and the Rise of Independent Black Churches, 1760–1840*. New York: Oxford University Press, 1973.

Gerner, G.W. "Catholics and the 'Religious Right.'" *Commonweal*, May 5, 1995, 15–20.

Gilbert, James. *Redeeming Culture: American Religion in an Age of Science*. Chicago: University of Chicago Press, 1997.

Gilbert, Simeon. *The Lesson System*. New York: Phillips and Hunt, 1879.

Gill, Sam D. *Native American Religions: An Introduction*. Belmont, CA: Wadsworth, 1981.

————, ed. *Native American Traditions: Sources and Interpretations*. Belmont, CA: Wadsworth, 1983.

Ginsburg, Faye D. *Contested Lives: The Abortion Debate in an American Community*. Berkeley and Los Angeles: University of California Press, 1989.

Gladden, Washington. *Applied Christianity: Moral Aspects of Social Questions*. Salem, NH: Ayer, 1977.

————. *Social Salvation*. Boston: Houghton, Mifflin, 1902.

————. *Tools and the Man: Property and Industry Under the Christian Law*. Westport, CT: Hyperion, 1975.

Glazer, Nathan. *American Judaism*. Chicago: University of Chicago Press, 1957.

————. "Social Characteristics of American Jews, 1654–1954." *American Jewish Year Book* 56 (Philadelphia: Jewish Publication Society of America, 1955): 3–41.

Glock, Charles Y., and Rodney Stark. *Christian Beliefs and Anti-Semitism*. New York: Harper, 1966.

Glock, Charles Y., and Robert N. Bellah, eds. *The New Religious Consciousness*. Berkeley: University of California Press, 1976.

Goff, James R. *Fields White unto Harvest: Charles F. Parham and the Missionary Origins of Pentecostalism*. Fayetteville: University of Arkansas Press, 1988.

Goldman, Peter L. *The Death and Life of Malcolm X*. 2d ed. Urbana: University of Illinois Press, 1979.

Goodstein, Laurie. "In Hope of Spiritual Revival, A Call to Fast." *The New York Times*, February 8, 1998, Sect. 1, 1.

Gorrell, Donald K. *The Age of Social Responsibility: The Social Gospel in the Progressive Era, 1900–1920*. Macon, GA: Mercer University Press, 1988.

Goss, Robert. *Jesus Acted Up: A Gay and Lesbian Manifesto*. San Francisco: Harper, 1993.

Gould, Lewis L. *The Progressive Era*. Syracuse: Syracuse University Press, 1973.

Graham, Billy. *Angels: God's Secret Agents*. Garden City, NY: Doubleday, 1975.

————. *Peace with God*. Garden City, NY: Doubleday, 1953.

————. *The Secret of Happiness: Jesus' Teachings on Happiness as Expressed in the Beatitudes*. Garden City, NY: Doubleday, 1955.

Grant, Jacqueline. "Womanist Theology: Black Women's Experience as a Source for Doing Theology, with a Special Reference to Christology." *Journal of the Interdenominational Theological Center* 13, no. 2 (Spring 1986).

Gray, Francine duPlessix. *Divine Disobedience: Profiles in Radical Catholicism*. New York: Knopf, 1970.

Greeley, Andrew M. *The Catholic Experience*. Garden City, NY: Doubleday, 1969.

————. *The Church and the Suburbs*. New York: Sheed and Ward, 1959.

Greeley, Andrew M., William C. McReady, and Kathleen C. Court. *Catholic Schools in a Declining Church*. Kansas City, MO: Sheed and Ward, 1976.

Greenberg, Blu. *How to Run a Traditional Jewish Household*. New York: Simon & Schuster, 1983.

————. "Is Now the Time for Orthodox Women Rabbis?" *Moment: The Magazine of Jewish Culture and Opinion* 18 (December 1993): 50–53, 74.

Greenberg, Simon, ed. *The Ordination of Women as Rabbis: Studies and Response*. New York: Jewish Theological Seminary of America, 1988.

Gregg, Robert. *Sparks from the Anvil of Oppression: Philadelphia's African Methodists and Southern Migrants, 1890–1940*. Philadelphia: Temple University Press, 1993.

Griffith, Mary. *Homeschooling Handbook, From Preschool to High School: A Parent's Guide*. rev. 2d ed. Rocklin, CA: Prima, 1999.

Griffith, R. Marie. *God's Daughters: Evangelical Women and the Power of Submission*. Berkeley: University of California Press, 1997.

Grossman, James R. *Land of Hope: Chicago, Black Southerners, and the Great Migration*. Chicago: University of Chicago Press, 1989.

Grossman, Susan, and Rivka Haut, eds. *Daughters of the King*. Philadelphia: Jewish Publication Society of America, 1992.

Guilday, Peter. *A History of the Councils of Baltimore, 1796–1884*. 1932. Reprint, New York: Arno, 1969.

Gunzel, Raymond J., S.J. *Celibacy: Renewing the Gift, Releasing the Power*. Kansas City, MO: Sheed and Ward, 1988.

Guroian, Vigen. *Life's Living Toward Dying: A Theological and Medical-Ethical Survey*. Grand Rapids: Eerdmans, 1996.

Hadaway, C. Kirk, and Penny Long Marler. "Did You Really Go to Church This Week? Behind the Poll Data." *Christian Century* 115, no. 14 (May 1998): 472–75.

Haddad, Yvonne Yazbeck. "The Anguish of Christians in the Middle East and American Foreign Policy." *American-Arab Affairs* 26 (Fall 1988): 56–74.

————. *A Century of Islam in America*. Washington, DC: Middle East Institute, 1986.

————. "Islamists and the 'Problem of Israel': The 1967 Awakening." *Middle East Journal* 46, no. 2 (Spring 1992): 266–85.

————, ed. *The Muslims of America*. New York: Oxford University Press, 1991.

Haddad, Yvonne Yazbeck, and Adair T. Lummis. *Islamic Values in the United States: A Comparative Study*. New York: Oxford University Press, 1987.

Haddad, Yvonne Yazbeck, and Jane Idleman Smith. *Mission to America: Five Islamic Sectarian Communities in North America*. Gainesville: University of Florida Press, 1993.

Haddad, Yvonne Yazbeck, and Jane Idleman Smith, eds. *Muslim Communities in North America*. Albany: State University of New York Press, 1994.

Hadden, Jeffrey K. *The Gathering Storm in the Churches: A Sociologist Looks at the Widening Gap Between Clergy and Laymen*. Garden City, NY: Doubleday Anchor, 1970.

Hageman, Alice L., ed. *Sexist Religion and Women in the Church*. New York: Association Press, 1974.

Hall, David D., ed. *Lived Religion in America: Toward a History of Practice*. Princeton: Princeton University Press, 1997.

Hall, Donald E., ed. *Muscular Christianity: Embodying the Victorian Age*. Cambridge, UK: Cambridge University Press, 1994.

Hall, Douglas John. *Remembered Voices: Reclaiming the Legacy of "Neo-Orthodoxy."* Louisville: Westminster/John Knox, 1998.

Halsey, William M. *The Survival of American Innocence: American Catholicism in an Era of Disillusionment, 1920–1940*. Notre Dame: University of Notre Dame Press, 1980.

Hamel, Ron P., and Edwin R. DuBose, eds. *Must We Suffer Our Way to Death? Cultural and Theological Perspectives on Death by Choice.* Dallas: Southern Methodist University Press, 1996.

Hamilton, Charles. *The Black Preacher in America.* New York: William Morrow, 1972.

Handy, Robert T. *A Christian America: Protestant Hopes and Historical Realities.* 2d ed. New York: Oxford University Press, 1984.

―――. "The Great American Religious Depression, 1925–35." *Church History* 29 (1960): 3–16.

―――. *Undermined Establishment: Church-State Relations in America, 1880–1920.* Studies in Church and State. Princeton: Princeton University Press, 1991.

―――, ed. *The Social Gospel in America, 1870–1920.* New York: Oxford University Press, 1966.

Hapgood, Norman. "Jews and College Life." *Harper's Weekly,* January 15, 1916, 53–55.

Hardesty, Nancy A. *Inclusive Language in the Church.* Atlanta: John Knox, 1987.

Harkness, Georgia. *The Methodist Church in Social Thought and Action.* New York: Abingdon, 1964.

Harris-Shapiro, Carol. "Syncretism or Struggle: The Case of Messianic Judaism." Ph.D. diss., Temple University, 1992.

Harrison, Beverly Wildung. *Our Right to Choose.* Boston: Beacon, 1983.

Hart, Darryl G. *Defending the Faith: J. Gresham Machen and the Crisis of Conservative Protestantism in Modern America.* Baltimore: Johns Hopkins University Press, 1994.

Hartman, Mary S., and Lois Banner, eds. *Clio's Consciousness Raised.* New York: Harper, 1974.

Hartshorne, Charles. *Creative Synthesis and Philosophic Method.* LaSalle, IL: Open Court, 1970.

―――. *Man's Vision of God and the Logic of Theism.* 1941. Reprint, Hamden, CT: Archon, 1964.

―――. *Wisdom as Moderation: A Philosophy of the Middle Way.* Albany: State University of New York Press, 1984.

Harvey, Paul. *Redeeming the South: Religious Cultures and Racial Identities Among Southern Baptists, 1865–1925.* Chapel Hill: University of North Carolina Press, 1997.

Hashimoto, Hideo, and William McPherson. "Rise and Decline of Sokagakkai in Japan and the United States." *Review of Religious Research* 17, no. 2 (Winter 1976): 83–92.

Hatch, Nathan O. *The Democratization of American Christianity.* New Haven: Yale University Press, 1989.

Hatcher, William, and James D. Martin. *The Baha'i Faith: The Emerging Global Religion.* New York: Harper, 1984.

Heilman, Samuel C. *Defenders of the Faith: Inside Ultra-Orthodox Jewry.* New York: Schocken Books, 1992.

Hennesey, James J., S.J. *American Catholics: A History of the Roman Catholic Community in the United States.* New York: Oxford University Press, 1981.

Henry, Carl F.H. *Confessions of a Theologian.* Waco, TX: Word, 1986.

―――. *God, Revelation, and Authority.* 6 vols. Waco, TX: Word, 1976–83.

―――. *The Uneasy Conscience of Modern Fundamentalism.* Grand Rapids: Eerdmans, 1947.

Herberg, Will. "The Jewish Labor Movement in the United States." *American Jewish Year Book* 53 (1952): 3–74.

―――. *Protestant, Catholic, Jew: An Essay in American Religious Sociology.* Garden City, NY: Doubleday, 1955; rev. ed., Garden City, NY: Doubleday, 1960.

"Heresy Charged Dismissed." *Christian Century* 113, no. 18 (May 1996): 566.

Herkovitz, Melville J. *The Myth of the Negro Past.* 1941; Reprint with new introduction, Boston: Beacon, 1990

Heschel, Abraham J. *God in Search of Man: A Philosophy of Judaism.* New York: Farrar, Strauss, and Cudahy, 1955.

————. *Man Is Not Alone: A Philosophy of Religion*. New York: Farrar, Strauss, and Young, 1951.

————. *The Prophets*. New York: Harper, 1962.

————. *The Sabbath: Its Meaning for Modern Man*. New York: Farrar, Strauss, and Young, 1951.

————. *Who Is Man?* Stanford: Stanford University Press, 1965.

Hewitt, Emily, and Suzanne R. Hiatt. *Women Priests: Yes or No?* New York: Seabury, 1973.

Heyward, Carter. *Our Passion for Justice: Images of Power, Sexuality, and Liberation*. New York: Pilgrim, 1984.

————. *A Priest Forever*. New York: Harper, 1976.

————. *Staying Power: Reflections on Gender, Justice, and Compassion*. Cleveland: Pilgrim, 1995.

————. *Touching Our Strength: The Erotic as Power and the Love of God*. San Francisco: Harper, 1989.

Higgins, Randall. "South's Sundays Far from Old Days." *Chattanooga Times*, March 21, 1998, A1, A5.

Hill, George H. *Airwaves to the Soul: The Influence and Growth of Religious Broadcasting in America*. Saratoga, CA: R and E Publishers, 1983.

Hill, Robert A., and Barbara Bair, eds. *Marcus Garvey: Life and Lessons*. Berkeley: University of California Press, 1987.

Hill, Samuel S., Jr., and Dennis E. Owen. *The New Religious Political Right in America*. Nashville: Abingdon, 1982.

Hillquit, Morris. *Loose Leaves from a Busy Life*. New York: Macmillan, 1934. Reprint, New York: DaCapo, 1971.

Hirsh, Harold L., and Howard Phifer. "The Interface of Medicine, Religion, and the Law: Religious Objections to Medical Treatment." *Medicine and Law* 4, no. 2 (1985): 121–39.

Hiskett, M. *The Course of Islam in Africa*. Edinburgh, UK: Edinburgh University Press, 1994.

Hodge, Archibald Alexander, and Benjamin B. Warfield. "Inspiration." *Presbyterian Review* 2 (April 1881): 225–60.

Hoffecker, W. Andrew. *The Princeton Piety*. Nutley, NJ: Presbyterian Reformed, 1981.

Hoffman, Edward. *Despite All Odds: The Story of Lubavitch*. New York: Simon & Schuster, 1991.

Hoffmeier, James K., ed. *Abortion: A Christian Understanding*. Grand Rapids: Baker Book House, 1987.

Hoge, Dean R. *The Future of Catholic Leadership: Responses to the Priest Shortage*. Kansas City, MO: Sheed and Ward, 1987.

Hollenweger, Walter J. *Pentecostalism: Origins and Development Worldwide*. Peabody, MA: Hendrickson, 1997.

————. *The Pentecostals: The Charismatic Movement in the Churches*. Minneapolis: Augsburg, 1969.

Holler, Clyde. *Black Elk's Religion: The Sun Dance and Lakota Catholicism*. Syracuse: Syracuse University Press, 1995.

Hopkins, C. Howard. *History of the Y.M.C.A. in North America*. New York: Association Press, 1951.

————. *The Rise of the Social Gospel in American Protestantism, 1865–1915*. New Haven: Yale University Press, 1940.

Hordern, William. *The Case for a New Reformation Theology*. Philadelphia: Westminster, 1959.

Horner, Bob, Ron Ralston, and David Sunde. *Applying the Seven Promises*. Nashville: Word, 1999.

Howe, Irving. *The World of Our Fathers: The Journey of the Eastern European Jews to America and the Life They Found and Made*. New York: Harcourt, 1976.

Howe, Irving, and Kenneth Libo, eds. *How We Lived: A Documentary History of Immigrant Jews in America, 1880–1930*. New York: R. Marek, 1979.

Hubbard, L. Ron. *Dianetics: The Modern Science of Mental Health*. 1950. Reprint, Los Angeles: Bridge Publications, 1986.

Hudnut-Beumler, James. *Looking for God in the Suburbs: The Religion of the American Dream and Its Critics, 1945–1965*. New Brunswick, NJ: Rutgers University Press, 1994.

Hughes, George. *Fragrant Memories of the Tuesday Meeting and the Guide to Holiness*. Reprint, Metuchen, NJ: Scarecrow, 1980.

Hughes, Thomas. *The Believer as Citizen: John Courtney Murray in a New Context*. Mahwah, NJ: Paulist Press, 1993.

Hultkrantz, Ake. *Belief and Worship in Native North America*, ed. Christopher Vecsey. Syracuse: Syracuse University Press, 1982.

———. *The Study of American Indian Religions*, ed. Christopher Vecsey. New York: Crossroad, 1983.

The Humanist 1, no. 1– .

Humanist Manifestos I and II. Buffalo: Prometheus Books, 1973.

Hunt, Mary E. "Despite Silencing, Holy Spirit Prevails." *National Catholic Reporter* 35 no, 36 (August 13, 1999): 21.

Hurley, Mark J. *Anti-Catholicism in the American Experience*. Huntingdon, IN: Our Sunday Visitor, 1992.

Hutchison, John Alexander. *We Are Not Divided: A Critical and Historical Study of the Federal Council of Churches of Christ in America*. New York: Roundtable, 1941.

Hutchison, William R. *Errand to the World: American Protestant Thought and Foreign Missions*. Chicago: University of Chicago Press, 1987.

Hybels, Lynne, and Bill Hybels. *Rediscovering Church: The Story and Vision of Willow Creek Community Church*, Grand Rapids: Zondervan, 1993.

Hynes, William J. *Shirley Jackson Case and the Chicago School: The Socio-Historical Method*. Chico, CA: Scholars Press, 1981.

Ice, Jackson Lee, and John J. Carey. *The Death of God Debate*. Philadelphia: Westminster, 1967.

Inge, M. Thomas, ed. *Handbook of American Popular Culture*. 2 vols. Westport, CT: Greenwood, 1980.

Irwin, James Lithgow. *The Birth of the Anti-Saloon League*. Washington, DC: n.p., 1913.

Islam in Africa Conference. *Islam in Africa*. Ibadan, Nigeria: Spectrum Books, 1993.

Ismael, Jacqueline S., and Tareq Ismael. "The Arab Americans and the Middle East." *Middle East Journal* 30 (1976): 390–405.

"It's Official: Ordaining Gays Is Not Heresy." *U.S. News and World Report* 120, no. 21 (May 1996): 16.

Ives, Gregg. *To Build a Wall: American Jews and the Separation of Church and State*. Charlottesville: University Press of Virginia, 1995.

Ives, Joseph Moss. *The Ark and the Dove: The Beginning of Civil and Religious Liberties in America*. New York: Longmans, Green, 1936.

Jackson, Carl T. "The Counterculture Looks East: Beat Writers and Asian Religion." *American Studies* 29 (Spring 1989): 51–70.

———. *The Oriental Religions and American Thought: Nineteenth-Century Explorations*. Westport, CT: Greenwood, 1981.

———. *Vedanta for the West: The Ramakrishna Movement in the United States*. Bloomington: Indiana University Press, 1994.

Jackson, Kenneth T. *The Ku Klux Klan in the City, 1915–1930*. New York: Oxford University Press, 1967.

Jackson, M.B. *Transcendental Meditation as Taught by Maharishi Mahesh Yogi.* Los Angeles: Spiritual Regeneration Movement Foundation of America, 1967.

Jacoby, Russell. *The Last Intellectuals: American Culture in the Age of Aquarius.* New York: Basic Books, 1987.

Janowsky, Oscar I., ed. *The American Jew: A Reappraisal.* Philadelphia: Jewish Publication Society of America, 1964.

Jefferson, William. *The Story of the Maharishi.* New York: Pocket Books, 1976.

Jehovah's Witnesses and the Question of Blood. Brooklyn, NY: Watchtower Bible and Tract Society, 1977.

Jenkins, Philip. *Pedophiles and Priests: Anatomy of a Contemporary Crisis.* New York: Oxford University Press, 1995.

Jewish Influences in America. Dearborn, MI: Dearborn Independent Publishing, 1921. Reprint, New York: Gordon, 1981.

John Paul II. *The Gospel of Life (Evangelium Vitae).* New York: Times Books, 1995.

Johnson, Benton, Donald A. Luidens, and Dean R. Hoge. *Vanishing Boundaries: The Religion of Mainline Protestant Baby Boomers.* Louisville: Westminster/JohnKnox, 1994.

Johnson, Charles P. "Southern Baptists and the Social Gospel Movement." Th.D. diss., Southwestern Baptist Theological Seminary, 1948.

Johnson, Morris R. *Archbishop Daniel William Alexander and the African Orthodox Church.* San Francisco: International Scholars, 1999.

Johnson, Weldon T. "The Religious Crusade: Revival or Ritual?" *American Journal of Sociology* 76 (1971): 873–95.

Jones, Jacqueline. *"To Get Out of This Land of Sufring": Black Migrant Women, Work and Family in Northern Cities, 1900–1930.* Working Paper No 91. Wellesley, MA: Wellesley College Center for Research for Women, 1982.

Jones, Marcus E. *Black Migration in the United States with Emphasis on Selected Central Cities.* Saratoga, CA: Century Twenty-One Publishing, 1980.

Jorstad, Erling. *The Politics of Moralism: The New Christian Right in American Life.* Minneapolis: Augsburg, 1981.

Joshi, Vasant. *The Awakened One.* San Francisco: Harper, 1982.

Journal of the Central Jurisdictional Conference of The Methodist Church, 1944. New York: Abingdon-Cokesbury, 1944.

Journal of Church and State 1, no. 1– (November 1959)– .

Judah, J. Stillson. *Hare Krishna and the Counterculture.* New York: Wiley, 1974.

Kallen, Horace M. *Culture and Democracy in the United States.* New York: Boni and Liveright, 1924. Reprint, New York: Arno, 1970.

———. *Secularism Is the Will of God: An Essay in the Social Philosophy of Democracy and Religion.* New York: Twayne, 1954.

Kaminer, Wendy. "The Latest Fashion in Irrationality." *Atlantic Monthly* 278, no. 1 (July 1996): 103–6.

———. "Saving Therapy: Exploring the Religious Self-Help Literature." *Theology Today* 48 (Fall 1991): 301–25.

Kane, John J. "The Social Structure of American Catholics." *American Catholic Sociological Review* 16 (March 1955): 23–40.

Kaplan, Mordecai M. *Judaism as a Civilization.* New York: Macmillan, 1934.

———. *The Religion of Ethical Nationhood: Judaism's Contribution to World Peace.* New York: Macmillan, 1970.

Kapleau, Philip. *The Three Pillars of Zen.* Boston: Beacon, 1967.

Karenga, Maulana. *Kwanzaa: A Celebration of Family, Community, and Culture.* Los Angeles: University of Sankore Press, 1998.

Karp, Abraham, ed. *The Jewish Experience in America.* vol. 2: *In the Early Republic.* Waltham, MA: American Jewish Historical Society, 1968.

Kaufman, Peter Iver. *Redeeming Politics. Studies in Church and State.* Princeton: Princeton University Press, 1990.

Kaufman, Philip S. *Why You Can Disagree and Remain a Faithful Catholic.* New York: Crossroad, 1995.

Kegley, Charles W., and Robert W. Bretall, eds. *The Theology of Paul Tillich.* New York: Macmillan, 1952.

Kennedy, David M., ed. *Progressivism: The Critical Issues.* Boston: Little, Brown, 1971.

Kephart, William M., and W.W. Zellner. *Extraordinary Groups.* 4th ed. New York: St. Martin's, 1991.

Kerouac, Jack. *The Dharma Bums.* New York: Viking, 1958.

Kerr, K. Austin. *Organized for Prohibition: A New History of the Anti-Saloon League.* New Haven: Yale University Press, 1985.

Kilner, John F. *Life on the Line: Ethics, Aging, Ending Patients' Lives and Allocating Resources.* Grand Rapids: Eerdmans, 1992.

King, Noel O. *Religions of Africa.* New York: Harper, 1970.

King, William P., ed. *Humanism: Another Battle Line.* Nashville: Cokesbury, 1931.

King, Willis J. "The Negro Membership of the (Former) Methodist Church in the (New) United Methodist Church." *Methodist History* 7 (April 1969): 32–43.

Kirimura, Yasuji. *Fundamentals of Buddhism.* Tokyo: Nichiren Shoshu Center, 1977.

Klein, Christa Ressmeyer. "Literature for America's Roman Catholic Children (1865–1895): An Annotated Bibliography." *American Literary Realism, 1870–1910* 6 (1973): 137–52.

Klejment, Anne, and Alice Klejment. *Dorothy Day and the Catholic Worker: A Bibliography and Index.* New York: Garland, 1988.

Klicka, Christopher J. *The Right to Home School: A Guide to the Law on Parents' Rights in Education.* 2d ed. Durham: Carolina Academic Press, 1998.

Kluger, Richard. *Simple Justice: The History of Brown v. Board of Education and Black America's Struggle for Equality.* New York: Knopf, 1976.

Knudson, Albert C. *The Doctrine of God.* Nashville: Cokesbury, 1930.

———. *The Doctrine of Redemption.* Nashville: Cokesbury, 1937.

———. *The Philosophy of Personalism.* Boston: Boston University Press, 1927.

Knudten, Richard D. *The Systematic Thought of Washington Gladden.* New York: Humanities Press, 1968.

Kohl, Marvin, ed. *Beneficent Euthanasia.* Buffalo: Prometheus Books, 1975.

Koller, John. *Ardent Spirits: The Rise and Fall of Prohibition.* New York: DaCapo, 1993.

Kolsky, Thomas A. *Jews Against Zionism: The American Council for Judaism, 1942–1948.* Philadelphia: Temple University Press, 1990.

Konolige, Kit, and Frederica Konolige. *The Power of Their Glory: America's Ruling Class, the Episcopalians.* New York: Wyden Books, 1978.

Kontorovich, E.V. "... And at Yale." *National Review* 49, no. 25 (December 1997): 43.

Kranzler, George. "The Jewish Community of Williamsburg, Brooklyn." Ph.D. diss., Columbia University, 1954.

Krapohl, Robert H., and Charles H. Lippy. *The Evangelicals: A Historical, Thematic, and Biographical Guide.* Westport, CT: Greenwood, 1999.

Kraut, Benny. *From Reform Judaism to Ethical Culture.* Cincinnati: Hebrew Union College Press, 1979.

Krout, John A. *The Origins of Prohibition.* New York: Russell, 1967.

Kurland, Philip B., ed. *Church and State: The Supreme Court and The First Amendment.* Chicago: University of Chicago Press, 1975.

Kurtz, Paul, ed. *The Humanist Alternative.* Buffalo, NY: Prometheus Books, 1973.

Kyvig, David E. *Repealing National Prohibition.* Chicago: University of Chicago Press, 1979.

LaBarre, Weston. *The Peyote Cult.* New York: Schocken Books, 1969.

Lambelli, Robert P. "Catholic Identity After Vatican II." *Commonweal* 121 (March 11, 1994): 12–16.

————. "Vatican II—Twenty Years Later." *Commonweal* 109 (October 8, 1982): 522–26.

Langmuir, Gavin. *History, Religion, and Antisemitism*. Berkeley: University of California Press, 1990.

Larson, Edward J. *Summer for the Gods: The Scopes Trial and America's Continuing Debate over Science and Religion*. New York: Basic Books, 1997.

Larson, Edward J., and Darrell W. Amundsen. *A Different Death: Euthanasia and the Christian Tradition*. Downers Grove, IL: InterVarsity, 1998.

Laurentin, Rene. *Catholic Pentecostalism*. Translated by Matthew J. O'Connell. New York: Doubleday, 1977.

LaVey, Anton Szandor. *The Compleat Witch*. New York: Lancer Books, 1971.

————. *The Satanic Bible*. New York: Avon, 1969.

————. *The Satanic Rituals*. Secaucus, NJ: University Books, 1972.

Lawler, Philip F. *Operation Rescue: A Challenge to the Nation's Conscience*. Huntington, IN: Our Sunday Visitor, 1992.

Layman, Emma McCloy. *Buddhism in America*. Chicago: Nelson-Hall, 1976.

Lemann, Nicholas. *The Promised Land: The Great Migration and How It Changed America*. New York: Knopf, 1991.

Leonard, Bill J., ed. *Christianity in Appalachia: Profiles in Regional Pluralism*. Knoxville: University of Tennessee Press, 1999.

Levine, Carol, ed. *Taking Sides: Bioethical Issues*. 8th ed. Guilford, CT: Dushkin/McGraw-Hill, 1999.

Levine, Lawrence. *Black Culture and Black Consciousness: Afro-American Folk Thought from Slavery to Freedom*. New York: Oxford University Press, 1977.

Levine, Louis (pseud. of Lewis Levitzki Lorwin). *The Women's Garment Workers*. New York: B.W. Huebsch, 1924. Reprint, New York: Arno, 1969.

Levy, Beryl Harold. *Reform Judaism in America: A Study in Religious Adaptation*. New York: n.p., 1933.

Levy, Leonard W. *The Establishment Clause: Religion and the First Amendment*. 2d ed., rev. Chapel Hill: University of North Carolina Press, 1994.

Lewis, James R., and J. Gordon Melton, eds. *Perspectives on the New Age*. Albany: State University of New York Press, 1992.

Liberman, Paul. *The Fig Tree Blossoms: Messianic Judaism Emerges*. Indianola, IA: Fountain Press, 1976.

Libowitz, Richard. *Mordecai M. Kaplan and the Development of Reconstructionism*. New York: Edwin Mellen, 1983.

Liebman, Charles S. "Jewish Liberalism Revisited." *Commentary* 102, no. 5 (November 1996): 51.

Liebman, Joshua. *Peace of Mind*. New York: Simon & Schuster, 1946. Reprint, New York: Citadel Press Books, 1994.

Liebman, Robert C., and Robert Wuthnow, eds. *The New Christian Right: Mobilization and Legitimization*. New York: Aldine, 1983.

Lincoln, C. Eric. *The Black Muslims in America*. 3d ed. Grand Rapids: Eerdmans, 1994.

Lincoln, C. Eric, and Lawrence H. Mamiya. *The Black Church in the African American Experience*. Durham: Duke University Press, 1992.

Link, Arthur S., and William B. Cotton. *American Epoch: A History of the United States Since 1900*. 5th ed. 2 vols. New York: Knopf, 1980.

Lippy, Charles H. *Being Religious, American Style: A History of Popular Religiosity in the United States*. Westport, CT: Greenwood Press, 1994.

————. "The Camp Meeting in Transition: The Legacy of the Late Nineteenth Century." *Methodist History* 34, no. 1 (October 1995): 3–17.

——————. "Miles to Go: Promise Keepers in Historical and Cultural Context." *Soundings* 80, nos. 2–3 (Summer/Fall 1997): 289–304.

——————. *Modern American Popular Religion: A Critical Assessment and Annotated Bibliography*. Westport, CT: Greenwood, 1996.

——————. "Towards an Inclusive Church: South Carolina Methodism and Race, 1972–1982." In *Rethinking Methodist History: A Bicentennial Historical Consultation*, eds. Russell E. Richey and Kenneth E. Rowe, 220–27. Nashville: Kingswood, 1985.

——————, ed. *Religious Periodicals of the United States: Academic and Scholarly Journals*. Westport, CT: Greenwood, 1986.

——————, ed. *Twentieth-Century Shapers of American Popular Religion*. Westport, CT: Greenwood, 1989.

Lippy, Charles H., Robert Choquette, and Stafford Poole. *Christianity Comes to the Americas, 1492–1776*. New York: Paragon House, 1992.

Lippy, Charles H., and Peter W. Williams, eds. *Encyclopedia of the American Religious Experience*. 3 vols. New York: Scribners, 1988.

Lipson, Julienne G. *Jews for Jesus: An Ethnographic Study*. New York: AMS Press, 1990.

——————. "Jews for Jesus: An Illustration of Syncretism," *Anthropological Quarterly* 53 (April 1980): 101–110.

Little, Malcolm. *The Autobiography of Malcolm X*. New York: Grove, 1965.

Longfield, Bradley J. *The Presbyterian Controversy: Fundamentalists, Modernists, and Moderates*. New York: Oxford University Press, 1991.

Lovin, Robin. *Reinhold Niebuhr and Christian Realism*. Cambridge, UK: Cambridge University Press, 1995.

Lowell, C. Stanley. *Embattled Wall: Americans United, an Idea and a Man*. Washington, DC: Protestants and Other Americans United for Separation of Church and State, 1966.

Lucas, George R., Jr. *The Genesis of Modern Process Thought: A Historical Outline with Bibliography*. Metuchen, NJ: Scarecrow, 1983.

Luckmann, Thomas. *The Invisible Religion*. New York: Macmillan, 1967.

Luecke, Donald S. "Is Willow Creek the Wave of the Future?" *Christian Century* 114, no. 16 (May 1997): 479ff.

Lughod, Ibrahim Abu, and Baha Abu-Laban, eds. *Settler Regimes in Africa and the Arab World*. Wilmette, IL: Medina University Press International, 1974.

Luker, Kristen. *Abortion and the Politics of Motherhood*. Berkeley: University of California Press, 1984.

Luker, Ralph E. *The Social Gospel in Black and White: American Racial Reform, 1885–1912*. Chapel Hill: University of North Carolina Press, 1991.

Lynch, Christopher Owen. *Selling Catholicism: Bishop Sheen and the Power of Television*. Lexington: University Press of Kentucky, 1998.

Lyons, Arthur. *The Second Coming: Satanism in America*. New York: Dodd, Mead, 1970.

McAvoy, Thomas T. *The Great Crisis in American Catholic History, 1865–1900*. Chicago: Henry Regnery, 1957.

McCarthy, Mary. *Memories of a Catholic Girlhood*. San Diego: Harcourt, 1972.

McCartney, Bill, Greg Laurie, and Jack Hayford, comps. *Seven Promises of a Promise Keeper*. rev. ed. Nashville: Word, 1999.

McClester, Cedric. *Kwanzaa: Everything You Wanted to Know but Didn't Know Where to Ask*. New York: Gumbs and Thomas, 1994.

McClory, Robert J. *Turning Point*. New York: Crossroad, 1995.

McCloud, Aminah Berry. *African American Islam*. New York: Routledge, 1995.

McCluskey, Sally. "Black Elk Speaks and So Does John G. Neihardt." *Western American Literature* 6 (1972): 231–42.

McConnell, Francis J. *Borden Parker Bowne: His Life and His Philosophy*. New York: Abingdon, 1929.

McDannell, Colleen. *The Christian Home in Victorian America, 1840–1900*. Bloomington: Indiana University Press, 1986.

———. *Material Christianity: Religion and Popular Culture in America*. New Haven: Yale University Press, 1996.

McDowell, John P. *The Social Gospel in the South: The Women's Home Mission Movement in the Methodist Episcopal Church, South, 1886–1939*. Baton Rouge: Louisiana State University Press, 1982.

McElroy, Robert W. *The Search for an American Public Theology: The Contribution of John Courtney Murray*. New York: Paulist Press, 1989.

McInerny, Dennis Q. *Thomas Merton: The Man and His Work*. Washington, DC: Consortium Press for Cistercian Publications, 1974.

McKelway, Alexander J. *The Systematic Theology of Paul Tillich: A Review and Analysis*. Richmond: John Knox, 1964.

McKeown, Elizabeth K. *War and Welfare: American Catholics and World War I*. New York: Garland, 1988.

McKhann, Charles F. *A Time to Die: The Place for Physician Assistance*. New Haven: Yale University Press, 1999.

McKinley, Edward H. *Marching to Glory: The History of the Salvation Army in the United States, 1880–1992*. 2d ed., rev. Grand Rapids: Eerdmans, 1995.

McLarney, James John. *The Theism of Edgar Sheffield Brightman*. Washington, DC: Catholic University of America, 1936.

McNeill, John J., S.J. *The Church and the Homosexual*. 1976. Reprint, New York: Pocket Books, 1978.

MacDonald, Fergus. *The Catholic Church and the Secret Societies in the United States*, ed. Thomas H. McMahon. (*United States Catholic Historical Society Monograph Series* 22.) New York: U.S. Catholic Historical Society, 1946.

Macfarland, Charles Stedman. *Christian Unity in the Making: The First Twenty-Five Years of the Federal Council of Churches of Christ in America, 1905–1930*. New York: Federal Council of Churches, 1948.

Machen, J. Gresham. *Christianity and Liberalism*. New York: Macmillan, 1923.

———. *The Origin of Paul's Religion*. New York: Macmillan, 1921.

Mackin, Theodore, S.J. *Divorce and Remarriage*. New York: Paulist Press, 1984.

MacRobert, Iain. *The Black Roots and White Racism of Early Pentecostalism in the USA*. New York: St. Martin's Press, 1988.

Magnuson, Norris. *Salvation in the Slums: Evangelical Social Work, 1865–1920*. Metuchen, NJ: Scarecrow, 1977.

Magonet, Jonathan, ed. *Jewish Explorations of Sexuality*. Providence: Berghahn Books, 1995.

Maharaj Ji, Guru. *The Living Master*. Denver: Divine Light Mission, 1978.

Mahesh Yogi, Maharishi. *Love and God*. New York: Age of Enlightenment Press, 1973.

———. *The Science of Being and Art of Living*. London: International SRM Publications, 1966.

Malcolm, Teresa. "Pair Dealt a Lifetime Ban on Ministry to Homosexuals." *National Catholic Reporter* 35, no. 3 (July 30, 1999): 3.

Manning, Michael. *Euthanasia and Physician Assisted Suicide: Killing or Caring?* New York: Paulist Press: 1998.

Marcus, Jacob R. *Early American Jewry*. 2 vols. Philadelphia: Jewish Publication Society of America, 1951, 1953. Reprint, 2 vols. in 1, New York: KTAV, 1975.

———, ed. *The American Jewish Woman: A Documentary History*. New York: KTAV, 1981.

Marcus, Sheldon. *Father Coughlin: The Tumultuous Life of the Priest of the Little Flower.* Syracuse: Syracuse University Press, 1965.

Marriott, Alice, and Carol K. Rachlin. *Peyote.* New York: New American Library, 1971.

————, eds. *American Indian Mythology.* New York: New American Library, 1968.

Marsden, George M. *Reforming Fundamentalism: Fuller Seminary and the New Evangelicalism.* Grand Rapids: Eerdmans, 1987.

Marsh, Charles. *God's Long Summer: Stories of Faith and Civil Rights.* Princeton: Princeton University Press, 1997.

Marshall, Catherine. *A Man Called Peter.* New York: McGraw Hill, 1951.

Marshall, Charles C. "An Open Letter to the Honorable Alfred E. Smith." *Atlantic Monthly,* April 1927, 540–49.

Martin, Calvin, ed. *The American Indian and the Problem of History.* New York: Oxford University Press, 1987.

Martin, Tony. *Race First.* Westport, CT: Greenwood, 1976.

Martin, William C. *A Prophet with Honor: The Billy Graham Story.* New York: Morrow, 1991.

————. *With God on Our Side: The Rise of the Religious Right in America.* New York: Bantam Books, 1996.

Marty, Martin E. *The New Shape of American Religion.* New York: Harper, 1959.

————. *The Noise of Conflict, 1919–41. Modern American Religion* 2. Chicago: University of Chicago Press, 1991.

Marty, Martin E., and R. Scott Appleby, eds. *Fundamentalisms Observed.* Chicago: University of Chicago Press, 1991.

Mathews, Shailer. *The Atonement and the Social Process.* New York: Macmillan, 1930.

————. *Christianity and Social Process.* New York: Harper, 1934.

————. *The Faith of Modernism.* New York: Macmillan, 1924.

————. *The Growth of the Idea of God.* New York: Macmillan, 1931.

————. *The Social Gospel.* Philadelphia: Griffith and Rowland, 1910.

May, Henry F. *Protestant Churches and Industrial America.* New York: Harper, 1949.

May, William F. *Active Euthanasia and Health Care Reform: Testing the Medical Covenant.* Grand Rapids: Eerdmans, 1996.

Mbiti, J.S. *African Religions and Philosophy.* New York: Praeger, 1969.

Mead, Edwin D. *The Roman Catholic Church and the School Question.* N.p., 1880.

Mead, Sidney E. *The Lively Experiment: The Shaping of Christianity in America.* New York: Harper, 1963.

Mecklin, John Moffatt. *The Ku Klux Klan: A Study of the American Mind.* New York: Harcourt, 1924.

Meir, August. *Racial Ideologies in the Age of Booker T. Washington.* Ann Arbor: University of Michigan Press, 1963.

Melton, J. Gordon, ed. *Religious Leaders of America.* Detroit: Gale Research, 1991.

Menendez, Albert J. *Evangelicals at the Ballot Box.* Buffalo: Prometheus Books, 1996.

Merton, Thomas. *No Man Is an Island.* New York: Harcourt, 1955.

————. *The Seven Storey Mountain.* 1948; Reprint, New York: Harcourt, 1998.

————. *Thomas Merton, Spiritual Master: The Essential Writings,* ed. Lawrence S. Cunningham. Mahwah, NJ: Paulist Press, 1992.

————. *Zen and the Birds of Appetite.* New York: New Directions, 1968.

Meyendorff, John. *Byzantine Theology: Historical Trends and Doctrinal Themes.* 2d ed. New York: Fordham University Press, 1979.

————. *Christ in Eastern Christian Thought.* 2d Eng. ed. Crestwood, NY: St. Vladimir's Seminary Press, 1975.

————. *Living Tradition.* Crestwood, NY: St. Vladimir's Seminary Press, 1978.

Meyer, Donald B. *The Positive Thinkers: Popular Religious Psychology from Mary Baker Eddy to Norman Vincent Peale and Ronald Reagan.* Middletown, CT: Wesleyan University Press, 1988.

―――. *The Protestant Search for Political Realism, 1919–1941.* Berkeley: University of California Press, 1960.

Meyer, Michael A. *Response to Modernity: A History of the Reform Movement in Judaism.* New York: Oxford University Press, 1988.

Michaelsen, Robert S. "American Indian Religious Freedom Litigation: Promise and Perils." *Journal of Law and Religion* 3:47 (1985).

―――. *Piety in the Public School: Trends and Issues in the Relation Between Religion and the Public School in the United States.* New York: Macmillan, 1970.

Mickler, Michael L. *The Unification Church in America: A Bibliography.* New York: Garland, 1986.

Miller, J. Keith. *Hunger for Healing: The Twelve Steps as a Classic Model for Christian Spiritual Growth.* San Francisco: Harper-Collins, 1991.

Miller, Judith. "The Challenge of Radical Islam." *Foreign Affairs* 72, no. 2 (Spring 1993): 42–56.

Miller, Perry, and Thomas H. Johnson, eds. *The Puritans: A Sourcebook of Their Writings.* 2 vols. rev. ed. New York: Harper, 1963.

Miller, Randall M., and Thomas D. Marzik, eds. *Immigrants and Religion in Urban Culture.* Philadelphia: Temple University Press, 1977.

Miller, Robert Moats. *American Protestantism and Social Issues, 1919–1939.* Chapel Hill: University of North Carolina Press, 1958.

―――. *Harry Emerson Fosdick: Preacher, Pastor, Prophet.* New York: Oxford University Press, 1985.

Miller, Robert T., and Ronald B. Flowers. *Toward Benevolent Neutrality: Church, State, and the Supreme Court.* 3d ed. Waco, TX: Baylor University Press, 1987.

Miller, William D. *Dorothy Day: A Biography.* San Francisco: Harper, 1982.

―――. *A Harsh and Dreadful Love: Dorothy Day and the Catholic Worker Movement.* New York: Liveright, 1972.

Miller, William McElwee. *The Baha'i Faith.* South Pasadena, CA: William Carey Library, 1974.

Milne, Hugh. *Bhagwan: The God that Failed.* New York: St. Martin's Press, 1986.

Minor, William S. *Creativity in Henry Nelson Wieman.* Metuchen, NJ: Scarecrow, 1977.

Minus, Paul M. *Walter Rauschenbusch: American Reformer.* New York: Macmillan, 1988.

Mitchell, Henry H. *Black Preaching.* Philadelphia: Lippincott, 1970.

Monahan, Matthew G. "The Christian Coalition's New 'Catholic Alliance' Crass and Unnecessary (View from a Pew)." *America* 174, no. 1 (January 1996): 7.

Monk, Maria. *Awful Disclosures of the Hotel Dieu Nunnery of Montreal.* New York: Howe and Bates, 1836.

Moore, Edmund Arthur. *A Catholic Runs for President: The Campaign of 1928.* New York: Ronald Press, 1956. Reprint, Gloucester, MA: Peter Smith, 1968.

Moore, John M. *The Long Road to Methodist Union.* Nashville: Abingdon-Cokesbury, 1943.

Moore, R. Laurence. *Selling God: American Religion in the Marketplace of Culture.* New York: Oxford University Press, 1994.

Moran, Victoria. *Love Yourself Thin: The Revolutionary Spiritual Approach to Weight Loss.* Emmaus, PA: Rodale, 1998.

Morgan, Timothy C. "Biblical Feminists Press for Gender-Inclusive NIV." *Christianity Today* 41, no. 10 (September 1997): 78ff.

Morreale, Don. *Buddhist America: Centers, Retreats, Practices.* Santa Fe: John Muir, 1988.

Morris, Charles R. *American Catholic: The Saints and Sinners Who Built America's Most Powerful Church.* New York: Random House, 1997.

Morris, Henry M. *History of Modern Creationism.* San Diego: Master Book Publisher, 1984.

Mott, Michael. *The Seven Mountains of Thomas Merton.* 1984; Reprint, Chicago: University of Chicago Press, 1996.

Muelder, Walter G. *Methodism and Society in the Twentieth Century.* New York: Abingdon, 1961.

Mueller, Roger Chester. "The Orient in American Transcendental Periodicals, 1835–1886." Ph.D. diss., University of Minnesota, 1968.

Muller, Dorothea R. "The Social Philosophy of Josiah Strong: Social Christianity and American Progressivism." *Church History* 28 (June 1959): 183–201.

Murnion, Philip J. *New Parish Ministers: Laity and Religious on Parish Staffs.* New York: National Pastoral Life Center, 1992.

Murphy, Joseph M. *Santeria: African Spirits in America.* 2d ed. Boston: Beacon, 1992.

Murray, John Courtney. *Bridging the Sacred and the Secular: Selected Writings of John Courtney Murray, S.J.,* ed. J. Leon Hooper. Washington, DC: Georgetown University Press, 1995.

―――. *The Problem of God: Yesterday and Today.* New Haven: Yale University Press, 1964.

―――. *Religious Liberty: Catholic Struggles with Pluralism,* ed. J. Leon Hooper. Louisville: Westminster/John Knox, 1993.

―――. *We Hold These Truths.* New York: Sheed and Ward, 1960.

Murray, Robert K. *Red Scare: A Study in National Hysteria, 1919–1920.* Minneapolis: University of Minnesota Press, 1955.

Muslim World 1, no. 1– (January 1911–).

Nason, Michael, and Donna Nason. *Robert Schuller: An Inside Story.* Waco, TX: Word, 1983.

Nasr, Seyyed Hossein. *Ideals and Realities of Islam.* New York: Praeger, 1967.

―――. *Islam and the Plight of Modern Man.* London: Longman, 1975.

―――. *Traditional Islam in the Modern World.* London: Routledge and Kegan Paul, 1981.

National Association of Jewish Center Workers. *Aspects of the Jewish Community Center: Benjamin Rabinowitz Memorial Volume.* New York: National Jewish Welfare Board, 1954.

Needleman, Jacob. *The New Religions.* rev. ed. New York: Pocket Books, 1972.

Neihardt, John G. *When the Tree Flowered.* New York: Macmillan, 1951.

―――, ed. *Black Elk Speaks.* 1932. Reprint, Lincoln: University of Nebraska Press, 1972.

Nelson, Douglas J. "For Such a Time as This: The Story of William J. Seymour and the Azusa Street Revival." Ph.D. diss., University of Birmingham, 1981.

Nelson, Jack, and Ronald J. Ostrow. *The FBI and the Berrigans: The Making of a Conspiracy.* New York: Coward, McCann and Geoghegan, 1972.

Nelson, Rudolph. *The Making and Unmaking of an Evangelical Mind: The Case of Edward Carnell.* Cambridge, UK: Cambridge University Press, 1987.

Neuhaus, Richard John, ed. *Jews in Unsecular America.* Grand Rapids: Eerdmans, 1987; New York: Center for the Study of the American Jewish Experience, 1987.

Neusner, Jacob. *American Judaism: Adventure in Modernity.* Englewood Cliffs, NJ: Prentice-Hall, 1972.

―――, ed. *World Religions in America: An Introduction.* Louisville: Westminster/John Knox, 1994.

Niebuhr, Gustav. "Pastor's Trial Attests to Divisiveness of Gay Issue." *The New York Times,* February 15, 1998, 1.

―――. "Trial Opens for Methodist Minister Who United Two Women." *The New York Times,* March 13, 1998, A11.

Niebuhr, H. Richard. *Christ and Culture.* New York: Harper, 1951.

————. *The Kingdom of God in America*. Chicago: Willett, Clark, 1937.

————. *The Meaning of Revelation*. New York: Macmillan, 1941.

————. *Radical Monotheism and Western Culture*. New York: Harper, 1960.

————. *The Responsible Self: An Essay in Christian Moral Philosophy*. New York: Harper, 1963.

————. *The Social Sources of Denominationalism*. New York: Henry Holt, 1929.

Niebuhr, Reinhold. *The Children of Light and the Children of Darkness*. 1944; Reprint, New York: Scribners, 1972.

————. *Christian Realism and Political Problems*. New York: Scribners, 1953.

————. *An Interpretation of Christian Ethics*. New York: Harper, 1935.

————. *The Irony of American History*. New York: Scribners, 1952.

————. *Moral Man and Immoral Society*. 1932. Reprint, New York: Scribners, 1960.

————. *The Nature and Destiny of Man*. 2 vols. 1941–43. Reprint, New York: Scribners, 1964.

Noll, Mark A. *Between Faith and Criticism: Evangelicals, Scholarship, and the Bible in America*. 2d ed. Grand Rapids: Baker, 1991.

————. *A History of Christianity in the United States and Canada*. Grand Rapids: Eerdmans, 1992.

————. *The Princeton Theology, 1812–1921*. Grand Rapids: Baker, 1983.

Noonan, D.P. *The Passion of Fulton Sheen*. New York: Dodd, Mead, 1972.

Noonan, John T., Jr. *The Believer and the Powers that Are: Cases, History, and Other Data Bearing on the Relation of Religion to Government*. New York: Macmillan, 1987.

————. *Contraception: A History of Its Treatment by the Catholic Theologians and Canonists*. enl. ed. Cambridge: Harvard University Press, 1986.

————. *A Private Choice*. New York: Free Press, 1979.

————, ed. *The Morality of Abortion: Legal and Historical Perspectives*. Cambridge: Harvard University Press, 1970.

Norris, Kathleen. *Amazing Grace*. New York: Riverhead Books, 1998.

————. *The Cloister Walk*. New York: Riverhead Books, 1996.

————. *Dakota*. New York: Ticknor and Fields, 1993.

Norwood, Frederick A. *The Story of American Methodism*. Nashville: Abingdon, 1974.

Numbers, Ron L. "Creationism in Twentieth-Century America." *Science* 218 (1982): 534–44.

Obelkevich, Jim, Lyndal Roper, and Raphael Samuel, eds. *Disciplines of Faith: Studies in Religion, Politics, and Patriarchy*. New York: Routledge, 1987.

Obolensky, Dimitri. "John Meyendorff (1926–92)." *Sobornost* 15 (1993): 44–51.

O'Connor, John Cardinal. *The Essential Catholic Handbook*. Liguori, MO: Liguori Publications, 1997.

————. *A Moment of Grace: On the Catechism of the Catholic Church*. San Francisco: Ignatius Press, 1995.

O'Connor, John Cardinal, and Edward I. Koch. *His Eminence and Hizzoner: A Candid Exchange*. New York: Avon Books, 1989.

Odegard, Peter H. *Pressure Politics: The Story of the Anti-Saloon League*. 1928. New York: Octagon, 1966.

Ogden, Schubert M. *On Theology*. 1986. Reprint, Dallas: Southern Methodist University Press, 1992.

————. *The Point of Christology*. San Francisco: Harper, 1982.

————. *The Reality of God and Other Essays*. 1966. Reprint, Dallas: Southern Methodist University Press, 1992.

Ogletree, Thomas W. *The Death of God Controversy*. Nashville: Abingdon, 1966.

O'Hair, Madelyn Murray. *Bill Murray, the Bible, and the Baltimore Board of Education*. Austin, TX: American Atheist Press, 1970.

———. *What on Earth Is an Atheist?* Austin, TX: American Atheist Press, 1969.

Oko, Adolph S. *Solomon Schechter, M.A., LITT.D., a Bibliography.* Cambridge, UK: Cambridge University Press, 1938.

Oldfield, Duane M. *The Right and the Righteous: The Christian Right Confronts the Republican Party.* Lanham, MD: Rowman and Littlefield, 1996.

Olneck, Michael R., and Marvin Lazeron. "The School Achievement of Immigrant Children: 1900–1930." *History of Education Quarterly* 14 (Winter 1974): 453–82.

Olyan, Saul M., and Martha C. Nussbaum, eds. *Sexual Orientation and Human Rights in American Religious Discourse.* New York: Oxford University Press, 1998.

———. *Taking a Chance on God: Liberating Theology for Gays, Lesbians, and Their Lovers, Families, and Friends.* Boston: Beacon, 1988.

O'Neill, William L. *The Progressive Years: America Comes of Age.* New York: Dodd, Mead, 1975.

O'Rourke, William. *The Harrisburg 7 and the New Catholic Left.* New York: Thomas Y. Crowell, 1972.

Orsi, Robert A. *The Madonna of 115th Street: Faith and Community in Italian Harlem, 1880–1950.* New Haven: Yale University Press, 1985.

———. *Thank You, St. Jude: Women's Devotion to the Patron Saint of Hopeless Causes.* New Haven: Yale University Press, 1996.

Ostling, Richard N. "When God Was a Woman: Worshipers of Mother Earth Are Part of a Goddess Resurgence." *Time*, May 6, 1991, 73.

Pacific World 1, no. 1– (1925–). Suspended 1929–1982. New series, 1995–1996. Third series, no. 1 (Fall 1999–).

Palmer, Benjamin Morgan. "The Church, a Spiritual Kingdom." *Presbyterian of the South* 3 (February 15, 1911): 1–3; 3 (March 1, 1911): 2–3.

Pareles, Jon. "Music Moved by the Spirit Thrives." *The New York Times*, June 21, 1998, Sec. 2:1, 27.

Parham, Sarah. *The Life of Charles Fox Parham.* 3d ed. Birmingham: Commercial Printing, 1977.

Paris, Arthur. *Black Pentecostalism: A Southern Religion in a Northern Urban World.* Amherst: University of Massachusetts Press, 1982.

Parker, Alison M. *Purifying America: Women, Cultural Reform, and Pro-Censorship Activisim, 1973–1933.* Urbana: University of Illinois Press, 1997.

Parkhurst, Louis, Jr. *Francis Schaeffer: The Man and His Message.* Wheaton, IL: Tyndale, 1986.

Parrinder, Geoffrey. *West African Religion.* London: Epworth, 1969.

Parsons, Paul F. *Inside America's Christian Schools.* Macon, GA: Mercer University Press, 1987.

"Pastor Found Innocent in Lesbian Ceremony." *The New York Times*, March 14, 1998, A7.

Patai, Raphael, Francis Lee Utley, and Dov Noy, eds. *Studies in Biblical and Jewish Folklore.* Bloomington: Indiana University Press, 1960.

Patterson, Bob E. *Carl F.H. Henry.* Waco, TX: Word, 1983.

Pavlischek, Keith J. *John Courtney Murray and the Dilemma of Religious Toleration.* Kirksville, MO: Thomas Jefferson University Press, 1994.

Peale, Norman Vincent. *The Amazing Results of Positive Thinking.* Englewood Cliffs, NJ: Prentice-Hall, 1959.

———. *Positive Thinking for a Time Like This.* Pawling, NY: Foundation for Christian Living, 1975.

———. *The Power of Positive Thinking.* New York: Prentice-Hall, 1952.

———. *You Can If You Think You Can.* Greenwich, CT: Fawcett, 1974.

Pearlman, Selig. "Jewish-American Unionism: Its Birth Pangs and Contributions to the

General American Labor Movement." *Publications of the American Jewish Historical Society* 41 (June 1952): 297–337.

Peden, W. Creighton, and Jerome A. Stone, eds. *The Chicago School: Pioneers in Religious Inquiry.* 2 vols. Lewiston, NY: Edwin Mellen, 1996.

Pelotte, Donald E. *John Courtney Murray: Theologian in Conflict.* New York: Paulist Press, 1976.

Perkins, Mary, and Philip Hainsworth. *The Baha'i Faith.* London: Ward Lock International, 1980.

Perry, Troy D. *The Lord Is My Shepherd and He Knows I'm Gay.* Los Angeles: Nash, 1972.

Persons, Stow. *Free Religion: An American Faith.* New Haven: Yale University Press, 1947.

Peshkin, Alan. *God's Choice: The Total World of a Fundamentalist Christian School.* Chicago: University of Chicago Press, 1986.

Peters, Ted. *The Cosmic Self: A Penetrating Look at Today's New Age Movements.* San Francisco: Harper, 1991.

Philips, Clifton J. *Protestant America and the Pagan World: The First Half Century of the American Board of Commissioners for Foreign Missions, 1810–1860.* Cambridge: Harvard University Press, 1969.

Philipson, David. *The Reform Movement in Judaism.* New York: Macmillan, 1933.

Pinn, Anthony B. *Varieties of African American Religious Experience.* Minneapolis: Fortress, 1998.

Piper, John F., Jr. *The American Churches in World War I.* Athens: Ohio University Press, 1985.

Pointer, Richard W. *Protestant Pluralism and the New York Experience: A Study in Eighteenth-Century Diversity.* Bloomington: Indiana University Press, 1988.

Polner, Murray, and Jim O'Grady. *Disarmed and Dangerous: The Radical Lives and Times of Daniel and Philip Berrigan.* New York: Basic Books, 1997.

Porter, Philip. *Better Men: On the Path to Purity.* Grand Rapids: Zondervan, 1998.

Prabhupada, A.C. Bhaktivedanta. *Bhagavad-Gita As It Is.* New York: Bhaktivedanta Book Trust, 1972.

Praemonitus Praemunitus: The Protocols of the Wise Men of Zion. New York: Beckwith, 1920.

Prasad, Ram Chandra. *Rajneesh: The Mystic of Feeling.* Delhi: Motilal Banarsidass, 1978.

Prebish, Charles. *American Buddhism.* North Scituate, MA: Duxbury, 1979.

Price-Mars, Jean. *So Spoke the Uncle.* Translated by Magdalino W. Shannon. 1928. Reprint, Washington, DC: Three Continents Press, 1983.

Pritchard, Gregory Allen. "The Strategy of Willow Creek Community Church: A Study in the Sociology of Religion." Ph.D. diss., Northwestern University, 1994.

Prothero, Stephen. "On the Holy Road: The Beat Movement as Spiritual Protest." *Harvard Theological Review* 84 (1991): 205–22.

Pruter, Karl. *The Strange Partnership of George Alexander McGuire and Marcus Garvey.* San Bernardino, CA: Borgo, 1986.

Pyle, Charles B. *The Philosophy of Borden Parker Bowne.* Columbus: S.E. Harriman, 1910.

Quigley, Thomas E., ed. *American Catholics and Vietnam.* Grand Rapids: Eerdmans, 1968.

Raboteau, Albert J. *African-American Religion.* New York: Oxford University Press, 1999.

Rachlin, Carol K. *The Native American Church. Chronicles of Oklahoma* 52, no. 3 (Autumn 1964).

Rahman, Fazlur. *Islam and Modernity: Transformation of an Intellectual Tradition.* Chicago: University of Chicago Press, 1982.

———. *Major Themes in the Qur'an.* Minneapolis and Chicago: Bibliotheca Islamica, 1980.

———. *Prophecy in Islam: Philosophy and Orthodoxy.* London: Allen and Unwin, 1958.

Rajneesh, Bhagwan Shree. *The Great Challenge: A Rajneesh Reader*. New York: Grove, 1982.

Rajneeshism. Rajneeshpuram, OR: Rajneesh Foundation International, 1983.

Ranck, Shirley A. *Cakes for the Queen of Heaven: A Ten-Session Adult Seminar in Feminist Theology*. Boston: Unitarian Universalist Department of Religious Education, 1986.

————, ed. *Cakes for the Queen of Heaven: Readings, Songs, and Other Resources to Accompany the Seminar in Feminist Theology*. Boston: Unitarian Universalist Department of Religious Education, 1986.

Raphael, Marc Lee. *Profiles in American Judaism: The Reform, Conservative, Orthodox, and Reconstructionist Traditions in Historical Perspective*. New York: Harper, 1984.

Rausch, David A. "Chosen People: Christian Views of Judaism Are Changing." *Christianity Today* 32, no. 14 (1988): 53–58.

————. *Messianic Judaism: Its History, Theology, and Polity*. New York: Edwin Mellen, 1983.

Rauschenbusch, Walter. *Christianity and the Social Crisis*. New York: Macmillan, 1912.

————. *Christianizing the Social Order*, ed. Robert D. Cross. New York: Harper, 1964. First published, 1907.

————. *A Theology for the Social Gospel*. New York: Macmillan, 1917.

Redfield, James. *The Celestine Prophecy*. New York: Warner Books, 1995.

Reed, Ralph. *Active Faith: How Christians Are Changing the Soul of American Politics*. New York: Free Press, 1996.

Reese, Curtis W., ed. *Humanist Sermons*. Chicago: Open Court, 1927.

Reeves, Thomas C. *The Empty Church: The Suicide of Liberal Christianity*. New York: Free Press, 1996.

Reichley, A. James. *Religion in American Public Life*. Washington, DC: Brookings Institution, 1985.

Reilly, Daniel F., O.P. *The School Controversy, 1891–1893*. 1943. Reprint, New York: Arno, 1969.

Religion and Public Education 1, no. 1– (1906–).

Reynolds, Frank E., and Theodore M. Ludwig, eds. *Transitions and Transformations in the History of Religions*. Leiden: E.J. Brill, 1980.

Richardson, Harry V. *Dark Glory: A Picture of the Church Among Negroes in the Rural South*. New York: Friendship, 1947.

Richey, Russell E., and Donald G. Jones, eds. *American Civil Religion*. New York: Harper, 1974.

Richey, Russell E., and Kenneth E. Rowe, eds. *Rethinking Methodist History: A Bicentennial Consultation*. Nashville: Kingswood Books, 1985.

Riesman, Frank. "The New Self-Help Backlash." *Social Policy* 21 (Summer 1990): 42–48.

Rischin, Moses. *The Promised City: New York's Jews, 1870–1914*. Cambridge: Harvard University Press, 1962. Reprint, Cambridge: Harvard University Press, 1977.

Robbins, Thomas, and Dick Anthony, eds. *In Gods We Trust: New Patterns of Religious Pluralism in America*. New Brunswick, NJ: Transaction Publications, 1991.

Roberson, Houston B. "Fighting the Good Fight: A History of Dexter Avenue King Memorial Baptist Church, 1865–1977." Ph.D. diss., University of North Carolina at Chapel Hill, 1997.

Roberts, Jon H. *Darwinism and the Divine in America: Protestant Intellectuals and Organic Evolution, 1859–1900*. Madison: University of Wisconsin Press, 1988.

Roberts, Keith A. *Religion in Sociological Perspective*. 3d ed. Belmont, CA: Wadsworth, 1995.

Roberts, Nancy. *Dorothy Day and the Catholic Worker*. Albany: State University of New York Press, 1984.

Rochford, E. Burke, Jr. *Hare Krishna in America*. New Brunswick, NJ: Rutgers University Press, 1985.

Rockefeller, Steven C. *John Dewey: Religious Faith and Democratic Humanism*. New York: Columbia University Press, 1991.

Rogow, Faith. *Gone to Another Meeting: The National Council of Jewish Women, 1893–1993*. Tuscaloosa: University of Alabama Press, 1993.

Roof, Wade Clark. *A Generation of Seekers: The Spiritual Journeys of the Baby Boom Generation*. San Francisco: Harper, 1994.

———, ed. *Religion in the Nineties*. (*Annals of the American Academy of Political and Social Science* 527.) Newbury Park, CA: Sage, 1993.

Roof, Wade Clark, and William McKinney. *American Mainline Religion: Its Changing Shape and Future*. New Brunswick, NJ: Rutgers University Press, 1987.

Rorabaugh, W.J. *The Alcoholic Republic: An American Tradition*. New York: Oxford University Press, 1979.

Rose, Susan D. *Keeping Them Out of the Hands of Satan: Evangelical Schooling in America*. New York: Routledge, 1988.

Rosen, Moishe, with William Proctor. *Jews for Jesus*. Old Tappan, NJ: Revell, 1974.

Roth, Gabrielle. *Maps to Ecstasy: The Healing Power of Movement*. Novato, CA: New World, 1998.

———. *Sweat Your Prayers: Movement as Spiritual Practice*. New York: Putnam, 1998.

Rousseau, Jean Jacques. *The Social Contract, and Discourses*. Translated by G.D.H. Cole. *Everyman's Library—Philosophy and Theology*. vol. 660a. New York: Dutton, 1950.

Roy, Ralph Lord. *Communism and the Churches*. New York: Harcourt, 1960.

Rudwick, Elliott. *Race Riot at East St. Louis, July 2, 1917*. 1964. Reprint, Urbana: University of Illinois Press, 1982.

Ruether, Rosemary Radford. *Sexism and God-Talk: Toward a Feminist Theology*. Boston: Beacon, 1983.

———. *Women-Church: Theology and Practice of Feminist Liturgical Communities*. San Francisco: Harper, 1985.

Ruether, Rosemary Radford, and Rosemary Skinner Keller, eds. *In Our Own Voices: Four Centuries of American Women's Religious Writing*. San Francisco: Harper, 1995.

Rumbarger, John J. *Profits, Power, and Prohibition: Alcohol Reform and the Industrialization of America, 1800–1930*. Albany: State University of New York Press, 1989.

Rupp, Rebecca. *Getting Started on Home Learning: How and Why to Teach Your Kids at Home*. New York: Three Rivers Press, 1999.

Ryan, John A. *Economic Justice: Selections from Distributive Justice and A Living Wage*, ed. Harlan R. Beckley. Louisville: Westminster/John Knox, 1996.

———. "The Laborer's Right to a Living Wage." *Catholic University Bulletin* 8 (April 1902): 156–74.

———. *A Living Wage: Its Ethical and Economic Aspects*. 1906. Reprint, New York: Arno, 1971.

———. *Social Doctrine in Action: A Personal History*. New York: Harper, 1941.

Ryan, John A., and Joseph Husslein. *The Church and Labor*. New York: Macmillan, 1920.

Ryan, Penelope J. *Practicing Catholic: The Search for a Livable Catholicism*. New York: Henry Holt, 1998.

Sachs, William L. "Testing Church Doctrine: At the Righter Trial." *Christian Century* 113 (March 1996): 284ff.

Said, Edward W. *Covering Islam: How the Media and the Experts Determine How We See the Rest of the World*. New York: Pantheon Books, 1981.

Sanders, Elizabeth. *Roots of Reform*. Chicago: University of Chicago Press, 1999.

Sanford, Elias B. *The Federal Council of the Churches of Christ in America: Report of the First Meeting*. New York: Revell, 1909.

Sargeant, Kimon Howland. "Faith and Fulfillment: Willow Creek and the Future of Evangelicalism." Ph.D. diss., University of Virginia, 1996.

Sasaki, Ruth Fuller. *Zen: A Method for Religious Awakening.* Kyoto, Japan: First Zen Institute of America in Japan, 1959.

Scanzoni, Letha Dawson, and Nancy A. Hardesty. *All We're Meant to Be: Biblical Feminism for Today.* 3d ed. Grand Rapids: Eerdmans, 1992.

Scanzoni, Letha Dawson, and Virginia Ramey Mollenkott. *Is the Homosexual My Neighbor? A Positive Christian Response.* rev. ed. San Francisco: Harper, 1994.

Schaeffer, Francis A. *The Complete Works of Francis A. Schaeffer.* 5 vols. Wheaton, IL: Crossway, 1982.

Schechter, Solomon. *Aspects of Rabbinic Theology: Major Concepts of the Talmud.* 1909; New York: Schocken Books, 1961.

———. *Studies in Judaism.* 1st ser., 2d ser., 3d ser. Philadelphia: Jewish Publication Society of America, 1911–24. First series originally published, 1896.

Schilling, Harold K. *The University and the Church.* Philadelphia: United Church of Christ Department of Campus Christian Life, 1955.

Schlumpf, Heidi. "How Catholic Is the Catholic Alliance?" *Christianity Today* 40, no. 6 (May 1996): 76.

Schmidt, Jean Miller. *Souls or the Social Order: The Two-Party System in American Protestantism.* New York: Garland, 1991.

Schoenherr, Richard A., and Lawrence A. Young. *Full Pews and Empty Altars: Demographics of the Priest Shortage in the United States Catholic Dioceses.* Madison: University of Wisconsin Press, 1993.

Schuller, Robert. *Be Happy You Are Loved.* Nashville: Thomas Nelson, 1987.

———. *The Greatest Possibility Thinker that Ever Lived.* Old Tappan, NJ: Revell, 1973.

———. *Move Ahead with Possibility Thinking.* Old Tappan, NJ: Spire Books, 1967.

———. *Peace of Mind Through Possibility Thinking.* Garden City, NY: Doubleday, 1977.

———. *Pearls of Power.* Waco, TX: Word, 1997.

———. *Self-Esteem: The New Reformation.* Waco, TX: Word, 1982.

———. *Turning Hurts into Halos.* Nashville: Thomas Nelson, 1999.

Scott, Emmett J. *Negro Migration During the War.* 1920. Reprint, New York: AMS Press, 1969.

Scult, Mel. *Judaism Faces the Twentieth Century: A Biography of Mordecai M. Kaplan.* Detroit: Wayne State University Press, 1993.

Seager, Richard Hughes. *The World's Parliament of Religions: The East/West Encounter, Chicago, 1893.* Bloomington: Indiana University Press, 1995.

———, ed. *The Dawn of Religious Pluralism: Voices from the World's Parliament of Religions, 1893.* LaSalle, IL: Open Court, 1993.

Self-Realization Fellowship Manual of Services. Los Angeles: Self-Realization Fellowship, 1965.

Sernett, Milton C. *Bound for the Promised Land: African American Religion and the Great Migration.* Durham: Duke University Press, 1997.

Sevre, Leif. *The Story of the Upper Room.* Nashville: Parthenon, 1965.

Shad, 'Abdur Rahman. *Duties of an Imam.* Revised by 'Abdul Hameed Siddiqui. Chicago: Kazi, 1978.

Shapley, Harlow, ed. *Science Ponders Religion.* New York: Appleton-Century-Crofts, 1960.

Sharpe, Dores R. *Walter Rauschenbusch.* New York: Macmillan, 1942.

Shaw, Marvin. *Nature's Grace: Essays in Henry Nelson Wieman's Finite Theism.* New York: Peter Lang, 1995.

Sheen, Fulton. *Treasure in Clay.* Garden City, NY: Doubleday, 1980.

Sheldon, Charles M. *In His Steps: What Would Jesus Do?* Chicago: Advance, 1897. Published in serial form, 1896. Reprint, New Kensington, PA: Whitaker House, 1997.

Sheldon, Mark. "Ethical Issues in the Forced Transfusion of Jehovah's Witness Children." *Journal of Emergency Medicine* 14, no. 2 (1996): 251–57.

Shin Buddhist Handbook. Honolulu: Honpa Hongwanji Mission in Hawaii, 1972.

Shinn, Larry D. *The Dark Lord*. Philadelphia: Westminster, 1986.

Shokeid, Moshe. *A Gay Synagogue in New York*. New York: Columbia University Press, 1995.

Sibley, Mulford Q., and Philip E. Jacob. *Conscription of Conscience: The American State and the Conscientious Objector, 1940–1947*. Ithaca: Cornell University Press, 1952.

Silko, Leslie Marmon. *Almanac of the Dead*. New York: Penguin Group, 1992.

———. *Ceremony*. New York: Viking Penguin, 1977.

———. *Gardens in the Dunes*. New York: Simon & Schuster, 1999.

———. *Sacred Water: Narrative and Pictures*. Tucson: Flood Plain Press, 1993.

———. *Storyteller*. New York: Seaver Books, 1981.

———. *Yellow Woman and a Beauty of the Spirit: Essays on Native American Life Today*. New York: Simon & Schuster, 1997.

Simpson, Frank T. "The Moorish Science Temple and Its 'Koran.'" *Muslim World* 37 (1947): 56–61.

Simpson, George E. *Black Religion in the New World*. New York: Columbia University Press, 1978.

Simpson, Ida Harper. *Fifty Years of the Southern Sociological Society*. Athens: University of Georgia Press, 1988.

Sims, Mary S. *The Y.W.C.A.: An Unfolding Purpose*. New York: Women's Press, 1950.

Singer, Milton B., ed. *Krishna: Myth, Rites, and Attitudes*. Honolulu: East-West Center Press, 1966.

Sittser, Gerald L. *A Cautious Patriotism: The American Churches and the Second World War*. Chapel Hill: University of North Carolina Press, 1997.

Sklare, Marshall. *America's Jews*. New York: Random House, 1971.

———. *Conservative Judaism: An American Movement*. rev. ed. Lanham, MD: University Press of America, 1985.

———, ed. *The Jews: Social Patterns of an American Group*. New York: Free Press, 1958.

Sleeper, James A., and Alan L. Mintz, eds. *The New Jews*. New York: Vintage Books, 1971.

Slotkin, J.S. *The Peyote Religion: A Study in Indian-White Relations*. Glencoe, IL: Free Press, 1956.

Smidt, Corwin E. *Contemporary Evangelical Political Involvement: An Analysis and Assessment*. Lanham, MD: University Press of America, 1985.

Smith, Alfred E. "Catholic and Patriot: Governor Smith Replies." *Atlantic Monthly*, May 1927, 721–28.

Smith, David H. *The Achievement of John Coleman Bennett*. New York: Herder and Herder, 1970.

Smith, Edward D. *Climbing Jacob's Ladder: The Rise of Black Churches in Eastern Cities, 1740–1877*. Washington, DC: Smithsonian Institution, 1988.

Smith, Elwyn A., ed. *The Religion of the Republic*. Philadelphia: Fortress, 1971.

Smith, Gary Scott. "The Men and Religion Forward Movement of 1911–1912: New Perspectives on Evangelical Social Concerns and the Relationship Between Christianity and Progressivism." *Westminster Theological Journal* 49, no. 1 (Spring 1987): 91–118.

Smith, H. Shelton. "The Church and the Social Order as Interpreted by James Henley Thornwell." *Church History* 7 (1938): 115–24.

Smith, Huston, and Reuben Snake, eds. *One Nation Under God: The Triumph of the Native American Church*. Santa Fe: Clear Light Press, 1996.

Smith, Jane I. *Islam in America*. New York: Columbia University Press, 1999.

Smith, Janet E. *Humanae Vitae: A Generation Later*. Washington, DC: Catholic University of America Press, 1991.

Smith, Rodney K. *Public Prayer and the Constitution: A Case Study in Constitutional Interpretation*. Wilmington: Scholarly Resources, 1987.

Smith, Russell E., ed. *Trust the Truth: A Symposium on Humanae Vitae*. Boston: Pope John Center, 1991.

Snyder, Jill Donnie, and Eric K. Goodman. *Friend of the Court, 1947–1982: The Anti-Defamation League of B'nai B'rith: To Secure Justice and Fair Treatment for All*. New York: Anti-Defamation League, 1983.

Soden, Dale E. "The Social Gospel in Tennessee: Mark Allison Matthews." *Tennessee Historical Quarterly* 41 (1982): 159–70.

Soka Gakkai. Tokyo: Sokka Gakkai, 1983.

Sontag, Frederick. *Sun Myung Moon and the Unification Church*. Nashville: Abingdon, 1977.

Sosa, Juan. "Popular Religiosity and Religious Syncretism: Santeria and Spiritism." *Documentaciones sureste* 4 (March 1983): 14–26.

Spencer, Aida Besancon. "Power Play." *Christian Century* 114, no. 20 (July 1997): 618ff.

Spong, John Shelby. *Born of a Woman: A Bishop Rethinks the Birth of Jesus*. San Francisco: Harper, 1992.

———. *Rescuing the Bible from Fundamentalism: A Bishop Rethinks the Meaning of Scripture*. San Francisco: Harper, 1991.

———. *Why Christianity Must Change or Die: A Bishop Speaks to Believers*. San Francisco: Harper, 1998.

Sprinzak, Ehud. *The Ascendance of Israel's Radical Right*. New York: Oxford University Press, 1991.

Stafford, Tim. "The Hidden Gospel of the 12 Steps." *Christianity Today*, July 22, 1991, 14–19.

Stark, Rodney, ed. *Religious Movements: Genesis, Exodus, and Numbers*. New York: Paragon House, 1991.

Starhawk. *The Spiral Dance*. San Francisco: Harper, 1979.

Starker, Steven. *Oracle at the Supermarket: The American Preoccupation with Self-Help Books*. New Brunswick, NJ: Transaction Books, 1989.

Starkloff, Carl F. *The People of the Center: American Indian Religion and Christianity*. New York: Seabury, 1974.

Stein, Herman D. "Jewish Social Work in the United States, 1654–1954." In *American Jewish Year Book* 57, 3–98. Philadelphia: Jewish Publication Society of America, 1956.

Steinberg, Stephen. *The Academic Melting Pot*. New York: McGraw-Hill, 1973.

Steinmetz, Paul B. *Pipe, Bible, and Peyote Among the Oglala Lakota: A Study in Religious Identity*. Knoxville: University of Tennessee Press, 1989.

Stember, Charles Herbert, et al., eds. *Jews in the Mind of America*. New York: Basic Books, 1966.

Stewart, Omer C. *Peyote Religion*. Norman: University of Oklahoma Press, 1987.

———. *Peyotism in the West: A Historical and Cultural Perspective*. Salt Lake City: University of Utah Press, 1984.

Stokes, Anson Phelps, and Leo Pfeffer. *Church and State in the United States*. 1964; Reprint, Westport, CT: Greenwood, 1975.

Stone, Ronald H. *Reinhold Niebuhr: Prophet to Politicians*. Nashville: Abingdon, 1972.

Storey, John W. "Thomas Buford Maston and the Growth of Social Christianity Among Texas Baptists." *East Texas Historical Journal* 19 (1981): 27–42.

Strong, Josiah. *The New Era; or, The Coming Kingdom*. New York: Baker and Taylor, 1893.

———. *Our Country*, ed. Jurgen Herbst. 1986; Reprint, Cambridge: Belknap Press of Harvard University, 1963.

———. *Religious Movements for Social Betterment*. New York: Baker and Taylor, 1900.

Suzuki, Daisetz T. *The Awakening of Zen*. Boston: Shambhala, 1987.

———. *Buddha of Infinite Light*. Boston: Shambhala, 1997.

————. *The Chain of Compassion*. Cambridge, MA: Cambridge Buddhist Association, 1966.

————. *An Introduction to Zen Buddhism*. New York: Grove Weidenfeld, 1991.

————. *Japanese Spirituality*. New York: Greenwood, 1988.

————. *Living by Zen*. York Beach, ME: Samuel Weiser, 1972.

————. *Mysticism, Christian and Buddhist*. Boston: Unwin Paperbacks, 1979.

————. *The Training of the Zen Buddhist Monk*. New York: Globe Press Books, 1991.

————. *Zen and Japanese Culture*. Princeton: Princeton University Press, 1970.

————. *Zen Buddhism*. Garden City, NY: Doubleday Anchor, 1956.

————. *The Zen Doctrine of No-Mind*. York Beach, ME: Samuel Weiser, 1993.

Suzuki, Shunryu. *Zen Mind, Beginner's Mind*. New York: Weatherhill, 1970.

Sweet, William Warren. *Religion on the American Frontier*. 1: *The Baptists*. New York: Henry Holt, 1931. 2: *The Presbyterians*. New York: Harper, 1936. 3: *The Congregation-alists*. Chicago: University of Chicago Press, 1939. 4: *The Methodists*. Chicago: University of Chicago Press, 1946.

————. *The Story of Religion in America*. New York: Harper, 1950.

Swinson, Daniel L. "American Methodism and Temperance in the Antebellum Period." Ph.D. diss., University of Chicago, 1992.

Swomley, John M. "Catholics and the Religious Right (Watch on the Right)." *The Humanist* 56, no. 2 (March–April 1996): 36–37.

"Symposium on the Relation Between the Synagogue and the Center." *Conservative Judaism* 14 (Winter–Spring 1962): 1–50.

Synan, Vinson. *The Holiness-Pentecostal Tradition: Charismatic Movements in the Twentieth-Century*. 2d ed. Grand Rapids: Eerdmans, 1997.

Taves, Ann. *The Household of Faith: Roman Catholic Devotions in Mid-Nineteenth Century America*. Notre Dame: University of Notre Dame Press, 1986.

Terry-Thompson, Arthur Cornelius. *History of the African Orthodox Church*. N.p., 1956.

Thompson, Ernest Trice. *The Spirituality of the Church: A Distinctive Doctrine of the Presbyterian Church, U.S.* Richmond: John Knox, 1961.

Thomsen, Harry. *The New Religions of Japan*. Rutland, VT: C.E. Tuttle, 1963.

Tileston, Mary W. *Daily Strength for Daily Needs*. 1884; Boston: Roberts Bros., 1886. Reprint, Boston: Little, Brown, 1994.

Tillich, Paul. *The Eternal Now*. New York: Scribners, 1963.

————. *The New Being*. New York: Scribners, 1955.

————. *The Shaking of the Foundations*. New York: Scribners, 1948.

————. *Systematic Theology*. 3 vols. Chicago: University of Chicago Press, 1951–63.

Time Almanac 1999 with Information Please. Boston: Information Please, 1998.

Tinney, James. "William J. Seymour: Father of Modern-day Pentecostalism." *Journal of the Interdenominational Theological Center* 4 (Fall 1979): 34–44.

Toll, William. *The Resurgence of Race: Black Social Theory from Reconstruction to the Pan-African Conference*. Philadelphia: Temple University Press, 1979.

Tomasi, Silvano M. *Piety and Power: The Role of the Italian American Parishes in the New York Metropolitan Area, 1880–1930*. Staten Island, NY: Center for Migration Studies, 1975.

Toulouse, Mark G., and James O. Duke, eds. *Makers of Christian Theology in America*. Nashville: Abingdon, 1997.

Trachtenberg, Joshua. *Jewish Magic and Superstition: A Study in Folk Religion*. New York: Atheneum, 1974.

Tracy, David. *Blessed Rage for Order: The New Pluralism in Theology*. New York: Seabury Press, 1975.

Traditions of Jodoshinshu Hongwanji-Ha. [Los Angeles]: Shenshin Buddhist Temple, 1982.

Trent, John, with Charles Colson and others. *Go the Distance: The Making of a Promise Keeper*. Colorado Springs: Focus on the Family, 1996.

Trine, Ralph Waldo. *In Tune with the Infinite.* New York: Thomas Y. Crowell, 1897.

Trotter, Joe William, Jr., ed. *The Great Migration in Historical Perspective: New Dimensions of Race, Class and Gender.* Bloomington: Indiana University Press, 1991.

Tsai, Shin-Shan. *The Chinese Experience in America.* Bloomington: Indiana University Press, 1986.

Tull, Charles J. *Father Coughlin and the New Deal.* Syracuse: Syracuse University Press, 1965.

Turner, Richard Brent. *Islam in the African American Experience.* Bloomington: Indiana University Press, 1997.

Turner, William C. "The Musicality of Black Preaching: A Phenomenology." *Journal of Black Sacred Music* 2 (Spring 1988): 21–34.

Tuttle, William M., Jr. "Labor Conflict and Racial Violence: The Black Worker in Chicago, 1894–1919." *Labor History* 10 (Summer 1969): 408–432.

———. *Race Riot: Chicago in the Red Summer of 1919.* New York: Atheneum, 1970.

Tweed, Thomas A. *The American Encounter with Buddhism, 1844–1912.* Bloomington: Indiana University Press, 1992.

———. *Our Lady of the Exile: Diaspora Religion at a Cuban Catholic Shrine in Miami.* New York: Oxford University Press, 1997.

Tyrrell, Ian R. *Sobering Up: From Temperance to Prohibition in Antebellum America.* Westport, CT: Greenwood, 1979.

———. *Women's World/Women's Empire: The Women's Christian Temperance Union in International Perspective, 1880–1930.* Chapel Hill: University of North Carolina Press, 1991.

Umansky, Ellen M., and Dianne Ashton, eds. *Four Centuries of Jewish Women's Spirituality: A Sourcebook.* Boston: Beacon, 1992.

Unger, Roberto Mangabeira, and Cornel West. *The Future of American Progressivism: An Initiative for Political and Economic Reform.* Boston: Beacon, 1992.

Urofsky, Melvin I. *American Zionism from Herzl to the Holocaust.* Garden City, NY: Doubleday Anchor, 1975.

Vahanian, Gabriel. *The Death of God.* New York: G. Braziller, 1961.

Van Buren, Paul. *The Edges of Language: An Essay in the Logic of Religion.* New York: Macmillan, 1972.

Van Leeuwen, Mary Stewart. "Servanthood or Soft Patriarchy? A Christian Feminist Looks at the Promise Keepers Movement." *Journal of Men's Studies* 5, no. 3 (February 1997): 233–61.

Vance, James Scott. *Proof of Rome's Political Meddling in America.* Washington, DC: Fellowship Forum, 1927.

"Vatican Ban Ends Years of Investigation." *National Catholic Reporter* 35, no. 35 (July 30, 1999): 5.

Vecoli, Rudolph J. "Prelates and Peasants: Italian Immigrants and the Catholic Church." *Journal of Social History* 2 (Spring 1969): 217–68.

Vecsey, Christopher. *Imagine Ourselves Richly: Mythic Narratives of North American Indians.* San Francisco: Harper, 1988.

———. *On the Padres' Trail. American Indian Catholics*, 1. Notre Dame: University of Notre Dame Press, 1996.

———. *The Paths of Katari's Kin. American Indian Catholics*, 2. Notre Dame: University of Notre Dame Press, 1997.

———. *Where the Two Roads Meet. American Indian Catholics*, 3. Notre Dame: University of Notre Dame Press, 1999.

———, ed. *Religion in Native North America.* Moscow: University of Idaho Press, 1990.

Versluis, Arthur. *American Transcendentalism and Asian Religions.* New York: Oxford University Press, 1993.

Vincent, Leon H. *John Heyl Vincent: A Biographical Sketch.* 1925. Reprint, Freeport, NY: Books for Libraries, 1970.

Vincent, Theodore G. *Black Power and the Garvey Movement.* Berkeley: Ramparts, 1971.

Vinz, Warren L. *Pulpit Politics: Faces of American Protestant Nationalism in the Twentieth Century.* Albany: State University of New York Press, 1997.

Vivekananda, Swami. *The Complete Works of Swami Vivekananda.* 8 vols. Calcutta: Advaita Ashrama, 1970–73.

Voskuil, Dennis N. "America Encounters Karl Barth, 1919–1939." *Fides et Historia* 12 (1980): 61–74.

———. "American Protestant Neo-Orthodoxy and Its Search for Realism (1925–1939)." *Ultimate Reality and Meaning* 8 (1985): 277–87.

———. *Mountains into Goldmines: Robert Schuller and the Gospel of Success.* Grand Rapids: Eerdmans, 1983.

Wagner, Melinda Bollar. "Generic Conservative Christianity: The Demise of Denominationalism in Christian Schools." *Journal for the Scientific Study of Religion* 36, no. 1 (March 1997): 13–24.

———. *God's Schools: Choice and Compromise in American Society.* New Brunswick, NJ: Rutgers University Press, 1990.

Waldron, Samuel E. *We Must Obey God: The Biblical Doctrine of Conscientious Disobedience to Human Authority with Special Reference to Operation Rescue.* Avinger, TX: Simpson, 1992.

Wallis, Roy, ed. *Sectarianism: Analysis of Religious and Non-Religious Sects.* New York: Wiley, 1975.

Walsh, James, John Mayer, James Castelli, Eugene Hemrick, Melvin Blanquette, and Paul Theroux. *Grace Under Pressure: What Gives Life to American Priests.* Washington, DC: National Catholic Education Association, 1995.

Walton, Darwin McBeth. *Kwanzaa.* Austin, TX: Raintree Steck-Vaughn, 1999.

Ward, A. Dudley. *The Social Creed of the Methodist Church: A Living Document.* New York: Abingdon, 1961.

Warfield, Benjamin B. *The Works of Benjamin Breckinridge Warfield.* 10 vols. 1927–32; Grand Rapids: Baker, 1991.

Washington, George. *The Writings of George Washington from the Original Manuscript Sources, 1745–1799,* ed. John C. Fitzpatrick. 39 vols. Washington, DC: U.S. Government Printing Office, 1931–44.

Washington, Joseph R., Jr. *Black Religion: The Negro and Christianity in the United States.* Boston: Beacon, 1964.

———. *Black Sects and Cults: The Power Axis in an Ethnic Ethic.* Garden City, NY: Doubleday, 1972.

———. *The Politics of God: The Future of the Black Church.* Boston: Beacon, 1967.

Watson, Julian Austin. "Challenging Black College Students to Explore the Ordained Ministry in the United Methodist Church as a Profession." D.Min. diss., Candler School of Theology, Emory University, 1980.

Watts, Alan. *The Art of Contemplation.* New York: Schocken, 1989.

———. *Beat Zen, Square Zen, and Zen.* San Francisco: City Light Books, 1959.

———. *Buddhism: The Religion of No Religion.* Boston: Tuttle, 1996.

———. *In My Own Way: An Autobiography, 1915–1965.* New York: Vintage, 1973.

———. *Myth and Religion.* Boston: Tuttle, 1996.

———. *The Philosophies of Asia.* Boston: Tuttle, 1995.

———. *The Spirit of Zen.* Rutland, VT: Tuttle, 1992.

———. *Talking Zen.* New York: Weatherhill, 1994.

———. *The Way of Zen.* New York: Vintage, 1989.

———. *Zen and the Beat Way.* Boston: Tuttle, 1997.

Watts, Jill. *God, Harlem U.S.A.* Berkeley: University of California Press, 1992.

Waugh, Earle, Baha Abu-Laban, and Regula B. Qureshi, eds. *The Muslim Community in North America.* Edmonton: University of Alberta Press, 1983.

Webber, Robert. *Signs of Wonder: The Phenomenon of Convergence in Modern Liturgical and Charismatic Churches.* Nashville: Abbot Martyn, 1992.

Weigel, Gustave, S.J. *A Catholic Primer on the Ecumenical Movement.* Westminster, MD: Newman Press, 1957.

————. *The Modern God: Faith in a Secular Culture.* New York: Macmillan, 1963.

————. *A Survey of Protestant Theology in Our Times.* Westminster, MD: Newman Press, 1954.

Weigle, Marta. *Brothers of Light, Brothers of Blood: The Penitentes of the Southwest.* Santa Fe: University of New Mexico Press, 1976.

Weisberger, Jon. "American Jews and Israeli Policy." *New Politics* 4, no. 1 (Summer 1992): 14ff.

Wells, David F., ed. *Reformed Theology in America.* Grand Rapids: Baker, 1989.

Welter, Barbara. "The Cult of True Womanhood, 1820–1860." *American Quarterly* 18 (Summer 1966): 151–74.

Wertheimer, Jack, ed. *The American Synagogue: A Sanctuary Transformed.* New York: Cambridge University Press, 1987.

Wessinger, Catherine, ed. *Religious Institutions and Women's Leadership: New Roles Inside the Mainstream.* Columbia: University of South Carolina Press, 1996.

West, Charles L. *Communism and the Theologians: Study of an Encounter.* Philadelphia: Westminster, 1958.

Wheel of Dharma 1, no. 1– (1973–).

White, James W. *The Sokagakkai and Mass Society.* Stanford: Stanford University Press, 1970.

White, O. Kendall, and Daryl White, eds. *Religion in the Contemporary South.* Athens: University of Georgia Press, 1995.

White, Ronald C., Jr. "Beyond the Sacred: Edgar Gardner Mullins and a Ministry of Social Reform." *Historical Magazine of the Protestant Episcopal Church* 49 (1980): 51–69.

————. *Liberty and Justice for All: Racial Reform and the Social Gospel (1877–1925).* San Francisco: Harper, 1990.

White, Ronald C., Jr., and C. Howard Hopkins. *The Social Gospel: Religion and Reform in Changing America.* Philadelphia: Temple University Press, 1976.

Whitney, Blair. *John G. Neihardt.* Boston: Twayne, 1976.

Whyte, William H. *The Organization Man.* New York: Simon & Schuster, 1956.

Wieman, Henry Nelson. *The Intellectual Foundation of Faith.* New York: Philosophical Library, 1961.

————. *Religious Experience and the Scientific Method.* New York: Macmillan, 1926.

————. *The Wrestle of Religion with Truth.* New York: Macmillan, 1927.

Wilcox, Clyde. *Onward, Christian Soldiers: The Religious Right in American Politics.* Boulder, CO: Westview, 1996.

Williams, Daniel Day. *Essays in Process Theology.* Edited by Perry LeFevre. Chicago: Exploration Press, 1985.

————. *God's Grace and Man's Hope.* New York: Harper, 1949.

————. *The Spirit and the Forms of Love.* 1968; Reprint, Washington, DC: University Press of America, 1981.

Williams, George M. *Freedom and Influence.* Santa Monica: World Tribune Press, 1985.

Williams, Michael. *American Catholics in the War: The National Catholic War Council, 1917–1921.* New York: Macmillan, 1921.

Williams, Peter W. *America's Religions: Traditions and Culture.* New York: Macmillan, 1990.

————. *Popular Religion in America: Symbolic Change and the Modernization Process in Historical Perspective*. Englewood Cliffs, NJ: Prentice-Hall, 1980.

————, ed. *Perspectives on American Religion and Culture*. Oxford, UK: Blackwell, 1999.

Williams, Raymond Brady. *Religions of Immigrants from India and Pakistan: New Threads in the American Tapestry*. New York: Cambridge University Press, 1988.

Wills, Garry. *Bare, Ruined Choirs: Doubt, Prophecy, and Radical Religion*. Garden City, NY: Doubleday, 1972.

————. *Reagan's America: Innocents at Home*. Garden City, NY: Doubleday, 1987.

Wilmore, Gayraud S. *Black Religion and Black Radicalism: An Examination of the Black Experience in Religion*. Garden City, NY: Doubleday, 1972.

Wilson, Bryan, ed. *The Social Impact of New Religious Movements*. Conference Series 9. Barrytown, NY: Unification Theological Seminary, 1981.

Wilson, John F., ed. *Church and State in America: A Bibliographical Guide*. 2 vols. New York: Greenwood, 1986–87.

Wilson, John F., and Donald L. Drakeman, eds. *Church and State in American History: The Burden of Religious Pluralism*. 2d ed. Boston: Beacon, 1987.

Wilson, Marvin R. "An Evangelical View of the Current State of Evangelical-Jewish Relations." *Journal of the Evangelical Theological Society* 25 (1983): 139–60.

Wilson, Sule Greg. *Kwanzaa: Africa Lives in a New World Festival*. New York: Rosen Publishing Group, 1999.

Wind Bell 1, no. 1– (December 1961–).

Winter, Gibson. *The Suburban Captivity of the Churches: An Analysis of Protestant Responsibility in the Expanding Metropolis*. Garden City, NY: Doubleday, 1961.

Winters, Clyde Ahmad. "African American Muslims from Slavery to Freedom." *Islamic Studies* 17, no. 4 (1978): 187–205.

————. "Origins of Muslim Slaves in the U.S." *al-Ittihad* 21 (Spring 1986): 49–51.

Wisbey, Herbert A., Jr. *Soldiers Without Swords: A History of the Salvation Army in the United States*. New York: Macmillan, 1955.

Wogaman, Philip J. "Focus on the Central Jurisdiction." *Christian Century*, October 23, 1963, 1296.

Wood, Joe, ed. *Malcolm X: In Our Own Image*. New York: St. Martin's Press, 1973.

Woodward, C. Vann. *The Strange Career of Jim Crow*. 3d ed. New York: Oxford University Press, 1974.

Woodward, Kenneth, and Anne Underwood. "A Bishop in the Dock: A Heresy Trial for Ordaining a Noncelibate Gay." *Newsweek* 127, no. 9 (February 26, 1996): 62.

Woofter, Thomas J. *Negro Migration*. 1920. Reprint, New York: AMS Press, 1971.

Worship Leader 1, no. 1– (1992–). Nashville: CCM Publications.

Wrobel, Paul. *Our Way: Family, Parish, and Neighborhood in a Polish American Community*. Notre Dame: University of Notre Dame Press, 1979.

Wuthnow, Robert. *The Restructuring of American Religion: Society and Faith Since World War II*. Studies in Church and State. Princeton: Princeton University Press, 1988.

Wyszkowski, Charles. *A Community in Conflict: American Jewry During the Great European Immigration*. Lanham, MD: University Press of America, 1991.

Yancey, Philip. "Angel Envy." *Christianity Today* 39, no. 8 (July 1995): 72.

Yogananda, Paramahansa. *Autobiography of a Yogi*. Los Angeles: Self-Realization Fellowship, 1971.

————. *Descriptive Outlines of Yogoda*. Los Angeles: Yogoda Satsang Society, 1928.

Ziolkowski, Eric, ed. *A Museum of Faiths: Histories and Legacies of the 1893 World's Parliament of Religions*. Atlanta: Scholars Press, 1993.

Zygon: A Journal of Religion and Science 1, no. 1 (March 1966–).

Index

Radio, religious, 22–23, 28, 47, 155
Radio Bible Class, 100
Rahner, Karl, 148
Rajneesh, Bhagwan Shree, 114
Rajneesh International Foundation, 114
Rajneeshpuram (OR), 114
Ramakrishna, 109
Ramakrishna Mission, 109
Rastafarians, 75
Rationalism, Enlightenment, 149
Rauschenbusch, Walter, 127, 137–38
Reagan, Ronald, 61
Realism, Christian, 144
Reality, alternate, 87
Reconciliation, racial, 74
Reconstructionism
    See Jews, Reconstructionist
Reconstructionist Rabbinical College, 54
Red Scare, 58, 128
Redfield, James, 98
Reed, Ralph, 136
Reformed Church in America, 101
Religion
    academic study of, 133
    civil, 16, 141–42
    culture, 16, 27
    domestication of, 98–99
    ecstatic, 102–4
    feminization of, 14
    fertility, 94, 104
    folk, 47
    lived, 92
    and nationalism, 16
    popular, 92–106
    privatization of, 14, 23, 28, 93, 103–4,
        106, 159–60
    revitalization of, 80, 159
    tribal, 65, 69, 79, 89–91, 122, 159
    universal, 121
Religions, Asian, interest in, 108–17
Religiosity, 91–106
    eclectic, 32, 47
    male, 15
    personal, 14
    See Spirituality

Religious right, 135–36, 145
Religious thought, 137–52, 161
    Eastern Orthodox, 148–50
    evangelical, 144–45
    formal, 144
    informal, 145
    Jewish, 148–49, 150–51
    patristic, 149
    Protestant, 137–46
    Roman Catholic, 146, 148
    See Theology
Removal, Native American, to
        reservations, 79
Republican Party, 135, 162
Rescue missions, 127
Reservations, Native American tribal,
        79, 80
Resorts, 60
Revelation, biblical, 150
Revitalization, Native American
        religious, 89–91
Rights, minority, 134
    minority religious, 132–33, 161
Ritual, peyote, 86
Rituals, women's, 104
Riverside Church (New York City), 22
Road Men, Native American, 86
Roberts, Oral, 28
Robertson, Pat, 135–36, 162
Roe v. Wade, 42, 131
Roman Catholicism
    characteristics of, 34–35
    missionary status of, 36
Roman Catholics, 6, 8, 10, 11, 15, 18,
        34–49, 83–84, 92–93, 103, 122,
        125, 131–32, 133, 134, 136, 142,
        153, 156, 157, 158, 159, 162
    Americanization of, 146–47
    charismatic, 46
    English, 5
    Hispanic, 47, 107–8, 122, 158
    Irish, 3
    Italian, 3, 47
    Latino, 122
Roof, Wade Clark, 103–4

About the Author

Charles H. Lippy is the LeRoy A. Martin Distinguished Professor at the University of Tennessee at Chattanooga. He holds degrees from Dickinson College, Union Theological Seminary, and Princeton University. He previously taught at Clemson University, West Virginia Wesleyan College, and Oberlin College, and was a visiting professor at both Emory University and Miami University. A specialist in the history of religion in the United States, he is the author or editor of more than a dozen volumes dealing with religion in American culture. The most recent include *The Evangelicals* (written with Robert H. Krapohl), *Popular Religious Magazines of the United States* (edited with P. Mark Fackler), and *Being Religious, American Style*.